The Insistence of the Letter

Pittsburgh Series in Composition, Literacy, and Culture
David Bartholomae and Jean Ferguson Carr, Editors

Academic Discourse and Critical Consciousness
Patricia Bizzell

Eating on the Street:
Teaching Literacy in a Multicultural Society
David Schaafsma

Fragments of Rationality:
Postmodernity and the Subject of Composition
Lester Faigley

The Insistence of the Letter:
Literacy Studies and Curriculum Theorizing
Bill Green, Editor

Knowledge, Culture and Power:
International Perspectives on Literacy as Policy and Practice
Peter Freebody and Anthony R. Welch, Editors

Literacy Online:
The Promise (and Peril) of Reading and Writing with Computers
Myron C. Tuman, Editor

Word Perfect:
Literacy in the Computer Age
Myron C. Tuman

The Insistence of the Letter:
Literacy Studies and Curriculum Theorizing

Edited by
Bill Green

University of Pittsburgh Press

UK   The Falmer Press, 4 John St., London WC1N 2ET
USA   University of Pittsburgh Press, 127 North Bellefield Avenue, Pittsburgh,
          Pa. 15260

First published 1993 by The Falmer Press

Published in the United States by the University of Pittsburgh Press, Pittsburgh, Pa. 15260

A catalogue record for this book is available from the British Library

Library of Congress Cataloging in Publication Data are available on request

ISBN 0-8229-1176-0
ISBN 0-8229-6101-6 (pbk)

Jacket design by Benedict Evans
Typeset in 9.5/11pt Bembo
by Graphicraft Typesetters Ltd., Hong Kong

Printed in Great Britain by Burgess Science Press, Basingstoke on paper which has a specified pH value on final paper manufacture of not less than 7.5 and is therefore 'acid free'.

Contents

Foreword   vii

Introduction   1

Chapter 1
Literacy, Orality, and the Functions of Curriculum   13
William A. Reid

Chapter 2
Technologies of Learning and Alphabetic Culture: The History of
Writing as the History of Education   27
Keith Hoskin

Chapter 3
Texts, Literacy and Schooling   46
David Hamilton

Chapter 4
Lessons from the Literacy Before Schooling 1800–1850   58
John Willinsky

Chapter 5
The 'Received Tradition' of English Teaching: The Decline of Rhetoric
and the Corruption of Grammar   75
Frances Christie

Chapter 6
Returning History: Literacy, Difference, and English Teaching in the
Post-War Period   107
Tony Burgess

Chapter 7
Literacy and the Limits of Democracy   120
James Donald

Chapter 8
Stories of Social Regulation: The Micropolitics of Classroom Narrative   137
Allan Luke

Contents

Chapter 9
Curriculum as Literacy: Reading and Writing in 'New Times'   154
Colin Lankshear

Chapter 10
Television Curriculum and Popular Literacy: Feminine Identity Politics
and Family Discourse   175
Carmen Luke

Chapter 11
Literacy Studies and Curriculum Theorizing; or, The Insistence of the Letter 195
Bill Green

Notes on Contributors   226

Index   228

Foreword

Teachers today in Australia, Canada, New Zealand, the United States and Britain are contending with the effects of late twentieth-century cultural configurations and economic conditions: They encounter powerful signifiers of popular and community cultures in students' writing and talk. The increased presence of multilingual and multicultural student clienteles has forced many schools to reappraise curricular policy and practice, in spite of the attempts of some jurisdictions to act as if such students aren't there. Schooling for gender equity and gender-inclusive curricula remain controversial practices. There is increasing instability in the occupational paths of graduates and uncertainty about the value of many school credentials. And, in many sites, schools and curricula barely have begun to address the power and potential of new technologies in classrooms and workplaces.

These are not historical aberrations, likely to go away on their own accord as part of a 'pendulum swing' back to the alleged normalcy of post-World War II institutional life. Nor does one have to be a particularly astute student of social change to recognize major shifts underway across nation states and multinational economies, shifts with visible effects on families and communities, schooling and work. Several articles in this volume caution of the dangers in generalizations about the attributes and effects of postmodernity and postindustrialism. But what remains at issue, David Hamilton reminds us, is a simple curriculum question: What kinds of literacy are appropriate for life and work in the twenty-first century?

The recurrent economic 'crises' in the West have placed literacy and education on governmental and industry agendas. Yet in many communities public debates over 'cultural literacy', 'high tech skills', 'job training' and so forth have contributed to an erosion of support for English teaching. These debates play on the well-established move of blaming socioeconomic uncertainties of all sorts — from changing demographies to national debts — on schools and teachers. In spite of International Literacy Year rhetoric about the challenges for literacy education in the next century, morale among many educators is low; many schools are embattled and defensive. Teachers face the implementation of top-down agendas for 'reform' which offer little hope of addressing the afore-mentioned changes and problems, including: returns to a varied menu of 'basics' from phonics to traditional school grammar; official state monolingualism laws in the United States; the press for national core curricula in the Britain, Australia,

New Zealand and Canada; increased use of standardized tests; and the call for a return to an Anglo-European literacy curriculum.

But did we ever depart? The irony of such reforms is that they are premised on the belief that English language and literacy teaching has been undergoing an inexorable drift and decay over the last two or so decades. Rereading the historical studies in this volume, I am struck not by a tenor of innovation but by the persistence of particular approaches to literacy and curriculum — in some cases, quite literally across centuries. The tenacity of what Colin Lankshear here calls 'forms of literacy' in schools and curricula, usually in the face of cultural and social change, is remarkable. A US teacher-educator who has been instrumental in thirty years of language in education reform recently commented that it is quite possible to walk into a primary classroom in any state and encounter a spelling or basal reader, skill-and-drill lesson much as it was performed sixty years ago. Similarly, she added, one could visit secondary classrooms and find students mass producing three point expository essays on the 'greats' of literature, as American students have for most of this century.

This isn't to devalue innovations in many classrooms and districts, or to underestimate the significance of the theoretical shifts and ideological movements documented here by Christie, Burgess, Willinsky and others, but rather to underline what Bill Green aptly describes as the 'insistence of the letter'. The sociocultural contexts and clienteles of schooling across English-speaking countries, and the ways with written and spoken languages in many communities have indeed reconfigured and diversified. Yet so much about mainstream curriculum and instruction remains the same, driven by a continuity of convention, orthodoxies old and new, and the generational folk wisdom and simple idiosyncrasies of the teaching of 'school literacy'.

The questions of which literacies to teach, Green insists, can only be addressed through social analyses of education. Unfortunately, literacy education in its practical syllabus forms — language arts, reading, children's literature, secondary composition, English as a Second Language, and so forth — typically fails to connect with critical histories and sociologies of curriculum. By default as much as by design, decisions about practice in curriculum planning agencies, editorial offices and staffrooms are more likely to be based upon, for example, student needs hierarchies, ability grouping and standardized tests, organic growth and process models, learning styles, cognitive hierarchies and skill taxonomies, and other commonplace approaches to curriculum, than they are to be based upon articulated understandings of how languages and literacies work in communities and institutions. These are the political legacies of modernist literacy curriculum which continue to exert a powerful influence over schooling, even as it turns to address postmodern economic, social and political conditions.

The Insistence of the Letter is about reframing and redrawing the boundaries between literacy and curriculum studies, between sociocultural theories and classroom practices, in ways which take into account the movement from industrial to postindustrial, from monopoly to multinational, from modern to postmodern cultures. Green reminds us that what counts as school literacy, what is authorized as reading and writing practice and convention, is written in the 'message systems' of curriculum, instruction and assessment. Yet not all constructions of literacy are equally powerful, are distributed equitably, have equivalent benefits as accredited forms of cultural capital or as functional competences for doing things with text in the world. English language and literacy courses thus stand as the significant gatekeepers for regulating membership and access to dominant discourses and traditions, relations of knowledge, power and authority.

There are no quick fixes for remaking curriculum in the interests of an increasingly diverse student populace, in a popular culture constructed in image and text, and a volatile multinational labor market. The diverse curricular agendas proposed by the authors in this volume share a concern with the kinds of cultural and economic participation the discourses and practices of school literacy enable. They include calls for more explicit attention to knowledge about how language works, critical approaches to genre teaching, cultural studies models of curriculum, and approaches to 'thematizing' literacy in economically marginal situations.

Taken together, these strategies question the value of what has come to count as school literacy. Many texts, genres and literacy events are indigenous only to the school, based on the tacit assurance that they generate moral, cognitive and political effects which allegedly transfer to other community, work and educational sites. Changing conditions and relations of work and community culture can provide the criteria for us to reevaluate longstanding classroom practices and procedures, school texts and assignments, some of which serve no apparent purpose other than the maintenance of school authority relations. At the same time, Donald, Christie, Lankshear and I here emphasize the necessity for students to develop competence with extant discourses and texts, while engaging critical analyses and innovative reconstruction of those same discourses and texts.

It would be convenient to claim that these and other issues are brought together into a univocal curricular agenda for literacy in postmodern conditions. But *The Insistence of the Letter* is a multivoiced anthology, one that consistently emphasizes the need for plurality, difference and standpoint in literacy education. Many of the studies here indicate that the effects of the social technology of literacy are not natural and universal, but are contingent on historic and culture-specific institutional practices and contexts, discourses and ideologies. If indeed this is the case, we need to be wary of claims and guarantees of universal effectiveness which accompany modern instructional approaches to literacy.

There is no golden age of literacy teaching, no going back to a singular curricular content and instructional method that will deal with the 'problem' of student reading and writing once and for all. The remaking of literacy education requires a reconsideration and renegotiation of how languages and literacies are used to construct tradition and authority, agency and identity. The rebuilding of curriculum requires a normative 'reading of the world': an analysis of which textual practices are possible and viable in diverse communities and locales, which textual practices have cultural efficacy and economic power, to what ends, and in whose interests.

Allan Luke
Townsville, Australia
October 20, 1991

Introduction

Bill Green

> Of course, as it is said, the letter killeth while the spirit giveth life. We can't help but agree, having had to play homage elsewhere to a noble victim of the error of seeking the spirit in the letter; but we should also like to know how the spirit could live without the letter (Jacques Lacan).

Recently there has been an enormous upsurge of educational research and public interest in literacy studies and literacy issues. This ranges from work in school-based curriculum, with specific regard to reading and writing pedagogies, through critical-revisionist historical, ethnographic and sociological work, to various forms of popular and public debate, all of which draw in contributions across the full range of the political spectrum. Several points can be made about these developments.

First, it is clear that a major revision is required in our traditional assumptions and beliefs about literacy, as both a distinctive human accomplishment and a social phenomenon. This will require, in turn, significant reconceptualization of the relationship between literacy and schooling, with particular and urgent reference to questions and problems of social structure, self-production and cultural mobilization, and also — increasingly — ecological politics. Second, it can be argued that we now have available to us, and increasingly so, an extraordinarily rich pool of 'really useful knowledge' about literacy education, in the form both of text *about* pedagogy and text *for* pedagogy (Giroux, 1983). Third, however, what may well be unprecedented public and professional interest in literacy issues does not mean that the prospects for enlightened, socially-critical literacy education in the latter part of the twentieth century, and beyond, look as positive as might be expected, given these apparently otherwise favourable conditions. This suggests that the notion 'literacy' is a particularly complex social, cultural and political issue, and one which requires therefore a correspondingly complex and sophisticated theoretical investigation.

The principal thesis of this book is that we can productively refer to *the insistence of the letter* in curriculum and schooling. This is to be understood not only as a matter of language (and the symbolic order, more generally), conceived as absolutely crucial to considerations of curriculum and schooling, but also more particularly of *written* language and its associated cultural politics, social relations and epistemological effects. Hence, 'literacy' becomes a curriculum issue *par*

1

excellence and a particularly significant 'topic' in and for curriculum history and theory, particularly with regard to the semiotic possibilities and curriculum politics associated with the all-important 'oral'/'literate', 'speech'/'writing' relationships and dichotomies.

There are several matters worth considering here. One is Reid's account of the significance of 'external publics' in shaping and determining educational practices and policies, including those associated with literacy. In recent times, there has been increasing intervention on the part of the state into the arenas of curriculum and schooling, with particular attention given to matters of literacy and educational 'standards', and relatedly, the role and significance of subject English and the English subjects more generally (Ball, Kenny and Gardiner, 1990). As Reid (1984: 68) observes:

> while it may appear that the professionals have power to determine what is taught (at school, district or national levels, depending on the country in question), their scope is limited by the fact that only those forms and activities which have significance for external publics can, in the long run survive.

This is a strong assertion of the contextualist thesis in curriculum studies, albeit one which is surprisingly reticent when it comes to assessing the political and ideological framework informing curricular and policy decisions.

What is interesting, however, is how literacy — as a curriculum topic linked decisively to the history of schooling as a state-sponsored cultural apparatus, and particularly significant in the twentieth-century development of a rationalized schooling system organized around school-subjects and textbooks, examinations and testing regimes — has been relatively neglected. This is so even in the case of English teaching, long seen as the proper domain of literacy education as a distinctive educational concern in itself, and in Reid's (1984: 69) terms, a striking instance of what he describes as 'the critical role that certain topics may play in the organization of school subjects'. Given this, the great upsurge in public and political anxiety in the 1980s over English teaching, literacy pedagogy and assessment, and the quality of schooling in changing socio-economic conditions — relatedly, the increasing rhetorical nexus between 'productive schooling' and 'enterprise culture' — becomes of particular interest from the viewpoint of curriculum studies, especially that associated with a critical-democratic educational reform agenda (Ball, Kenny and Gardiner, 1990). How is it that the original emphasis on 'literacy' in the early establishment of mass compulsory schooling systems — literacy understood in a particular way, it must be said; as Donald (1985: 218) puts it, '[w]hat children were taught was limited to the most basic instruction in literacy, computation and morality' — first became transmuted into the 'disciplines' and later realized as a distinct array of school-subjects, albeit one which has undergone various changes and re-orderings over that time? What does this mean with regard to literacy, however understood, being at once the *means* of schooling and the *goal* of schooling?

Referring back to the phrase 'the insistence of the letter', which is to be seen as an overarching concept-metaphor for the book as a whole: What is at issue here is not simply this crucial relationship to be observed between curriculum and literacy, historically and institutionally, but also, importantly, the relevance of what is broadly termed 'poststructuralism' for literacy studies and curriculum theorizing, with perhaps particular regard for the work of figures such Michel Foucault, Jacques Lacan and Jacques Derrida, among various others, including feminist work such as that of Julia Kristeva. Derrida's work is especially important, I would suggest, albeit much disregarded and misunderstood, and hence little utilized, especially in Anglo-Australian educational research — unlike Foucault's work, in recent times at least (Ball, 1990). Here it is specifically Derrida's discussion of the concepts of 'Writing' and the 'letter', in *Of Grammatology* (1976) and elsewhere, which is of concern. A further reference-point, of particular relevance, is Jacques Lacan's (1977) work on the priority of the signifier over the signified, and also the relationship between language and the unconscious. More generally, what is addressed here is what might be called the *significant materiality* of language and literacy, something which arguably has been overlooked if not actively repressed in the logocentric project of modern(ist) schooling. Among other things, such a focus serves to highlight the significance of notions of 'textuality' and 'rhetoric' in the production of school knowledge, right across the curriculum.

This book is addressed to the curriculum-theoretical implications of recent developments in literacy studies. More specifically, it explores the relationship between literacy studies and curriculum theorizing. Within this, a major proposition is that the concepts 'literacy' and 'curriculum', and the relationship between them, are usefully examined from the point of view of recent debates over the relationship between 'modernism' and 'postmodernism', as terms of increasing significance in educational enquiry and curriculum research. The principal aim of the book is, therefore, to provide a forum for scholarship from what are often two quite distinct enterprises: that is, literacy scholarship and curriculum scholarship. All too often there has been little serious attention given to the links that might very profitably be made between work in these different realms of research and praxis — differences largely predicated on longstanding disciplinary, institutional and careerist distinctions, which actively work against the rich kinds of interdisciplinary and cross-disciplinary enquiry which are now urgently needed at every level of educational endeavour, so as draw into a new relationship the often distinct emphases of research and pedagogy, teacher education and educational enquiry more generally. Accordingly, the aim here has been to bring together literacy scholars seeking to reflect more specifically on the curriculum implications of their work, and curriculum scholars seeing in recent developments in literacy research and pedagogy significant insights into the nature and meaning of curriculum more generally. The task, therefore, has been to bring together these two concerns — on the one hand, about 'literacy', and on the other, about 'curriculum' — in moving towards a new conceptual-theoretical synthesis, in the context of what are increasingly described as 'postmodern conditions'.

With specific reference to the concept of *literacy*: what may be seen as emerging in recent research and scholarship in the area, as well as in popular debate, is a structured sense of the possibilities for 'thinking' about literacy. This can be described as a matter of there being certain available discourses, as contexts for the 'thinkable' as regards to literacy and related matters. Of the currently available discourses on literacy, three in particular may be distinguished: these are those statements organized by the concept of '*functional* literacy'; those organized by the concept of *'cultural* literacy'; and those organized by the concept of *'critical* literacy'. As Lankshear (1991: 223–4) writes:

> Three political discourses on literacy dominate current debate. One is the powerful functional literacy and human capital discourse. A second is the increasingly influential cultural literacy discourse, represented by figures as various as E.D. Hirsch Jr., Allan Bloom ... and John Searle ... The third is the highly marginalized discourse of critical literacy.

These represent distinctive discourses and serve and are characterized by distinctive social and knowledge-constitutive interests; as such, they each offer a specific vision of curriculum and schooling, and have quite different implications and consequences in this regard. That is, at the level of general educational debate, these discourses circulate and contend with each other in the public sphere, as distinct and separate ideological-discursive ensembles which are ultimately incompatible and incommensurate with each other, at least in their present formulations. Each constructs the category 'literacy' differently, and this means by extension not only different constructions of education and society, as well as the relationship between them, but also — more specifically — the category 'curriculum' itself. That is to say, each of these discourses implies different forms of curriculum. Research is urgently needed to examine these implications, and to explore the links between these developments and debates in literacy studies and curriculum theorizing.

Some general research questions: What forms of curriculum development and classroom practice, and what kinds of pedagogy, are implied by Hirsch's (1987) notion of 'cultural literacy'? How does it differ from, for instance, other such formulations (e.g. Bowers, 1984)? How does the notion of 'critical literacy' map onto recent calls for a 'critical pedagogy' (e.g. Simon, 1988)? In this regard, to what extent have these increasingly fashionable notions moved beyond ideological critique and cultural criticism — and the confines of the academy — to speak more directly to teacher educators and teachers in general, thus entering into their daily practices in classrooms and becoming therefore an integral feature of mainstream educational praxis? As Reid (1984: 68) observes: 'When curricular practice strays too far and too visibly from the category as understood by interested publics the result is loss of support, student alienation and failure and the collapse of efforts to sustain the legitimacy of the activity'. This is particularly pertinent to the project of 'critical literacy', I suggest, since that project clearly questions some of the basic assumptions driving and informing normative mainstream schooling and its associated educational ideologies, and thereby challenges the expectations and investments of those 'external publics' which, as Reid (1984: 74) notes, comprise 'the carriers of categorical identities, parents, employers, scholars, politicians, administrators and others'.

We can further ask: What curriculum changes forms of educational restructuring are attendant on the notions of 'cultural literacy' and 'critical literacy'? What institutional and political changes? Also: there is clearly a need to understand further and more systematically the implications and consequences of the discourse of 'functional literacy'? What restrictions on curriculum possibility are evident in this regard? What is the social meaning of the 'Back-to-Basics' argument and the 'literacy debate', and how is this registered in curriculum? Can the notion of 'functional literacy' be reclaimed, via counter-hegemonic work, from its current, largely conservative contexts? This is something requiring particularly urgent attention at this present historical juncture, when it is becoming more and more evident that, certainly in Australia but arguably elsewhere as well, across Western educational systems, the discourse of 'functional literacy' is being drawn into new technocratic and technological agendas, in accordance with the emergence of a postmodern educational culture. Finally: What *social* visions are to be observed in each of these different discourses on literacy, schooling and society?

Further questions: How might we better understand the notion of *disciplinary literacies*, and what is the relationship between this notion and theoretical work on school-subjects (Popkewitz, 1987; Green, 1988), including the proposition — somewhat scandalous, for some at least — that this cannot be dissociated from the politics of what might be called 'subjection/subjectification', or the politics of subjectivity more generally? Indeed, it is at least conceivable that so-called 'successful' schooling, predicated upon and incorporating as it does certain kinds of literate behaviours and sensibilities (and the systematic exclusion of others), might well be seen as constituting and contributing to an 'improper literacy' (Lankshear, 1987), given that much schooling practice can be understood not simply as *constructing* social differences by differentiating among populations and cohorts, on the basis of the 'difference-dynamics' of class, gender, ethnicity and race, religion and generation, but as working actively against the development of political and social forms of imagination, including but not limited to those associated with literacy itself.

Further matters to consider: Can a significant principle for curriculum theorizing emerge out of recent attempts to think through the relations among gender, literacy and curriculum? What connection exists between dominant-hegemonic notions of *rationality*, linked as that is with particular versions of masculinism, and the literacy/curriculum nexus? To what extent might currently available theories of the so-called 'hidden curriculum' be advanced by recasting them specifically in terms of language, literacy and the symbolic order? And finally: what is the likely impact of new technologies of culture and communication on curriculum and literacy, and on schooling more generally? What are the educational implications, for instance, of the convergence of the broadcasting, publishing and computing industries, and both the global extension of information culture and the increasing penetration of computer-based technologies into what was previously understood as the private sphere? (Brand, 1988; Poster, 1990).

Clearly, then, there is much to be done in these and other related respects, and much that follows, given the organizing proposition that a particularly significant relationship is to be observed not simply between curriculum and literacy as forms of praxis but also between the research that focuses on these matters. Bringing together these two fields of research and praxis, and engaging questions and consideration of these kinds, is precisely what this collection aims to do. The chapters all focus on the relationship between curriculum and literacy, and hence between literacy studies and curriculum theorizing, within an overarching conceptual framework whose informing thesis is that language, 'Writing' and the symbolic order are crucial considerations for understanding curriculum and schooling. This thesis is variously explored via renderings of the modernism/postmodernism debate and specific studies in curriculum politics and history, rhetoric, language and literacy education, English teaching, and media and cultural studies. The book therefore constitutes a timely forum for the integration of what are often quite distinct and disparate enterprises, bringing together researchers and scholars from Australia, New Zealand, the United Kingdom and Canada, and a range of interests and projects organized by a common concern: the critical reassessment of the nexus between curriculum and literacy, in a time of considerable turmoil in the educational scene generally.

There are, in one way or another, several common themes informing the chapters that follow, and indeed the overall project of the collection. One is the explicit significance of notions of *language* and *representation* in and for educational practice, including but not limited to that which is organized in the form of schooling. This I refer to, in the concluding chapter, in terms of what has been called 'the linguistic turn', by which I mean not just a new linguistic sensibility in educational and cultural research — that is, a new heightened awareness of language, information and the symbolic order, something which has emerged and burgeoned in the postwar period, right across the cultural and intellectual field — but also the growing recognition that we must review history itself in these terms and through such a lens. This applies as much to the larger history of the human race (*Homo sapiens*, or perhaps more appropriately still: *Homo symbolicus*) as it does to the more specific history of the West, which is the primary frame for this present focus on curriculum and literacy.

Within this frame, a crucial consideration is the complex question of speech and writing, conceived as different but related and indeed complementary — despite also being at times and in certain respects conflicting — modes of 'practical consciousness' and human expression. For Derrida, the history of the West is inextricable from the problem of the Logos, of logocentrism as the play of ambivalence in the relations between speech and writing, voice and text, presence and absence — the Letter that killeth and the Spirit that giveth Life, to evoke the ontotheological rhetoric which often characterizes such discussions, extending well beyond their more mundane and common-sense frames of understanding. Life and Death: the great themes that drive culture and civilization, now as much as in antiquity. Derrida's perhaps most fundamental concern is with the relationship between speech and writing as what he presents as a politico-metaphysical problem *par excellence*, one which bears directly on the notion of rationality and meaning as an always open question, that is, open to history and difference, within the changing orders of knowledge, power and desire. His emphasis, it must be stressed, is on what he presents as a superordinate concept, which he names variously as 'Writing', the 'trace', and 'differance', which for him constitutes the very condition of possibility for language, meaning, and the institution (Derrida, 1976: 9). Within such a perspective, it becomes possible to draw in such seemingly diverse considerations as Foucault's work on discourse, subjectivity and disciplinary power, Bakhtin's view of the inescapable social tensions in language between what he describes as counterposing 'centripetal' and 'centrifugal' forces and tendencies, Freire's political readings of the wor(l)d in terms of 'voice' and 'silence', as well as Gramsci's arguments concerning common sense, grammar and politics — all as, in certain significant ways, coming together within a reconceptualized view of the speech/writing relationship.

Halliday's work in this regard is of particular importance, notwithstanding the major differences that must be acknowledged between his project and

Derrida's, with respect specifically to understanding 'speech' and 'writing' as distinctive forms of human semiosis and principles of knowledge. As Halliday writes:

> Writing and speech, in [the] technical sense of written language and spoken language are different grammars which therefore constitute different ways of knowing, such that any theory of knowledge, and of learning, must encompass both. Our understanding of the social and natural order depends on both, and on the complementarity between the two as interpretations of experience (1987: 150).

Yet, as he also observes, writing 'puts language in chains; it freezes it, so that it becomes a thing to be reflected on', and hence 'it changes the way that language is used for meaning with'. He continues in this fashion: 'Writing deprives language of the power to intuit, to make indefinitely many connections in different directions at once, to explore (by tolerating them) contradictions, to represent experience as fluid and indeterminate'. Consequently he describes writing as 'destructive of one fundamental human potential: to think on your feet, as we put it'. Yet such is the rich, complex, contradictory nature of language that this '*destructiveness*', this '*reductiveness*', goes hand-in-hand with a significant '*constructiveness*', a radical expansion in the possibilities of human sensibility: 'in destroying [one] potential, it creates another: that of structuring, categorizing, disciplining. It creates a new kind of knowledge: scientific knowledge; and a new way of learning, called education' (Halliday, 1987: 148–9). Although extremely generative, there is arguably a striking ambivalence in Halliday's position here: on the one hand, he explicitly privileges speech, stressing its dynamic, open-ended, evolutionary nature, but on the other, he emphasizes the positivity and special significance of written language in the formalization and institutionalization of science and knowledge and the achievement of modernity.

Such views and such ambivalence broadly inform a number of the chapters in this book, either implicitly or explicitly. Reid's chapter for instance, although influenced more directly by the work of Walter Ong, focuses specifically on the relationship between 'literacy' and 'orality' with regard to what he describes as the 'functions' of curriculum, as well as the tensions generated in actual curriculum practice. His account of these tensions, and the changing nature of curriculum and literacy, becomes immediately understandable as a matter of the interaction of quite different and even opposing worldviews. This is something, furthermore, recapitulated in the 'socialization' process whereby children become schooled into literate culture and accordingly, as it were, 'modernized' (that is to say: 'civilized'). Reid presents curriculum as specifically 'a literate concept', involving the rationalization of language, knowledge, teaching and learning, and the promotion of certain experiences and sensibilities rather than others, and indeed more often than not at their expense. The different effects and implications of speech and writing, literacy and orality, are evident also in the chapters by Hamilton, Willinsky and Christie, in varying ways. Hamilton traces the development of the curriculum concept itself and, relatedly, the invention of the 'textbook' and the formal syllabus document, while Christie and Willinsky from different perspectives indicate the significance of the codification of language practices in the production of manuals and dictionaries and the controls exerted over popular literacy initiatives, as well as the formal establishment of legislation relating to a mass schooling system subsidized and managed by the state. Each of these chapters in the first part of the book turns significantly on the shift from 'speech' to 'writing', both literally and symbolically, in the active suppression of linguistic and other differences and an assertion of pedagogic authority which links up directly with an insistent ideo-logic of exclusion and identity. This latter point is one that Donald also makes later in the book, in referring to those schooling practices and ideologies predicated by the relationship between language and power and the (re)production of inequalities. Similarly, his account of Hirsch's 'cultural literacy' arguments and those associated with contemporary 'progressive' literacy pedagogies is usefully read with reference to their respective orientations towards 'written' and 'oral' forms of language, culture and curriculum.

In varying ways, all the chapters assembled here can be similarly seen as engaging a further common theme, albeit one which is clearly related to the speech/writing nexus: that is, the problem of *modernity*, and hence within this, the relationship between literacy and modern(ist) schooling. Addressing in particular current reformulations and repositionings in science and theology, one commentator has observed: 'Modernity, rather than being regarded as the norm for human societies towards which all history has been aiming and into which all societies should be ushered — forcibly, if necessary — is instead increasingly seen as an aberration'. As he notes, in recent years there has been 'a growing dissatisfaction with modernity and ... an increasing sense that the modern age not only has a beginning but can have an end as well'. Hence:

> Whereas the word *modern* was almost always used until recently as a word of praise and as a synonym for *contemporary*, a growing sense is now evidenced that we can and should leave modernity behind — in fact, that we *must* if we are to avoid destroying ourselves and most of the life on our planet (Griffin, 1988: ix).

Part of what is at issue here is the problem of *rationality*, understood specifically in terms of the convergence of notions of 'rationalization' and 'modernization', and hence the historically specific articulation of ideologies of Reason and Progress, within what is basically a capitalist framework. This groundswell of reaction and resistance across a wide range of fields needs to be understood as registering a growing recognition on the part of many, inside and outside the academy and the school, of what might well be described as the pathologies of modernism, and is a movement increasingly subsumed within the notion of 'postmodernism'. This is currently a heavily contested term, and indeed there is much confusion as to its precise field of reference and considerable concern expressed by many about its political and epistemological implications. Nonetheless, it seems that it can be appropriately argued that we are currently living through what has been described as 'the post-age' (Ulmer, 1981). This is indicated recently for instance in the speculative formulations of such notions as 'post-curriculum' and 'post-literacy'. Regardless of how these controversies and confusions are resolved, it seems undeniable that we are indeed living through a time of unsettling change and upheaval, both conceptually and culturally, something which warrants due consideration of what it is that comes 'after modernism', and accordingly how to understand this rather ambivalent prefix ('post-'). In the context of new initiatives in psychiatry and psychotherapy, Levin writes the following:

> [P]ostmodern thinking ... begins with a strong sense — articulated, however, only with difficulty — that we are living in a time of trans- ition, a moment between two worlds: the known and the unknown. Postmodern thinking begins with a sense that the foundations of the world we inherited are crumbling, and that we are being called upon, being challenged in a historically unique way, to build a very different world for the future. Postmodern thinking problematizes what was once unquestionable: the paradigm of knowledge, truth, and reality that has dominated the whole of modern history (1987: 2).

This present collection, focused on curriculum research and literacy studies, is simi- larly characterized, I submit, by what is described here as 'postmodern thinking'. Several of the chapters directly question various consequences of the modern(ist) tradition in curriculum and schooling, while others explore the possibilities for a radical revitalization and revising of certain features of modernity, features argu- ably worth preserving and renewing in and for these unsettling new times. For instance, Donald reviews Alisdair MacIntyre's account of the Scottish Enlighten- ment and proposes accordingly a reassessment of the democratic possibilities of literacy and schooling (including the limits of democracy itself), by way of sustained cultural-political work on 'the conditions of existence of an ... educated public' in what he calls 'our post-Enlightenment times'. Other chapters — those in the first half of the collection, in particular — are premised on a felt need to overcome or counter what are increasingly perceived as the failings of the modernist project in curriculum and schooling, and either explicitly argue for or seek to demonstrate the value of restoring *historical imagination* in research and pedagogy alike. This goes hand in hand, of course, with what Lankshear, following C. Wright Mills, has described in various contexts as 'sociological imagination'.

What these chapters indicate, overall, is an insistent sense of the absolute centrality of considerations of history and society in and for a critical reimagining of curriculum and schooling, with reference specifically to literacy pedagogy and literacy studies. Hence Hoskin and Hamilton provide historical accounts ranging from Greek antiquity through the Reformation and beyond, while Willinsky and Christie focus on the more immediate 'prehistory' of state-subsidized schooling. Burgess provides, similarly, a historical account of English teaching in Britain in the post-1945 period, an account which is also to a significant degree a personal history as much as an (auto-)biography of the English teaching profession more generally, across the international community. Like Willinsky, he suggests that current literacy pedagogy would be greatly enhanced by introducing greater socio-cultural sensitivity and historical awareness, a point also made by Christie with regard to the curriculum history of English teaching and literacy pedagogy — although part of her concern here is to critique what she sees as the in- adequacies of recent forms of English teaching, with specific regard to its liter- acy project and what she presents as its pervasive 'romanticism'. Donald's chapter, as I have indicated, addresses more particularly the immediate historical moment in British curriculum politics, but is clearly informed by a similarly critical sense of historical developments in the emergence of mass education systems and universal literacy programmes. All in all, there is across these chapters a shared sense of what it means educationally to be living in 'a time of transition', necessitating among other things the need to 'take a critical stand in relation to modernity as a whole', and thus bearing out Levin's observations on the emergence of what he calls 'postmodern thinking'.

That this new sensibility also involves *new* perspectives and projects is similarly evidenced in the collection as a whole, although it is something more specifically addressed in the second half of the book, including my own chapter. As Levin (1987: 3) notes: 'Being on the edge of modernity, postmodern thinking faces into the future. So there is also, in such thinking, a sense of new historical possibilities ...' Furthermore, this is most emphatically not a matter of nostalgia, a yearning for the sureties and simplicities of some imaginary past, since it crucially 'includes the sense that modernity can be successfully overcome only by going beyond it, not by attempting to return to a premodern form of existence' (Griffin, 1988: ix–x). Here, the chapters by Allan Luke, Colin Lankshear and Carmen Luke provide intriguing guidelines for such enquiry. Lankshear outlines what may well be seen as a controversial reconceptualization of literacy and historical agency, in accordance with the emergent context of 'post-industrial' culture, within what might be called a 'post-progressivist' pedagogy, while both chapters by the Lukes draw directly, although not at all uncritically, on postmodernist social and cultural theory as an important resource for contemporary work in literacy studies and curriculum theorizing. Allan Luke's account of what he describes as the binary organization of curricular knowledge within modernist framings of curriculum and literacy suggests that, while maintaining a critical-sociological sense of the social regulations effected through normative schooling, we might also look to challenging the dominant-hegemonic rationality inscribed in literacy lessons and classroom learning, via a 'postmodern' reassessment of the relationship between expository and narrative genres in school knowledge. Drawing on contemporary work in cultural studies, feminism and postmodernist theory, Carmen Luke takes us out of the contextualization of curriculum and literacy within schooling as traditionally conceived, focusing instead on television culture, family discourse, and the informal pedagogies associated with what she describes as 'popular literacy'. The collection thus draws towards its conclusion with a provocative movement beyond what, for some, are the very limits of 'curriculum' and 'literacy' as specific concepts, at least in their current traditional forms. In the final chapter, I seek to provide both a further retrospective survey of the conceptual territory of the book as a whole and to explore certain postmodern(ist) proposals in literacy pedagogy, as an invitation to further speculations and deliberations as to the changing nature of curriculum and literacy.

Taking such considerations into account alongside the other proposals and critiques assembled here, the question then becomes, inevitably: Where to now, with regard to further work in the areas of curriculum research and literacy studies, in the context of the 'post-age'? It is my sincere hope that this collection will help to provoke such work, at the same time as it contributes to it.

This project, originally conceived in the early part of 1989, has involved much time and effort in coming to its fruition. As always in such matters, what has finally emerged is both more and less than my original imaginings — in one sense, a shadow of sorts, with regard to what I thought was possible or desirable in those early, now somewhat blurry days, which was in essence to bring together the often seemingly disparate threads of my own rather eclectic reading and learning, in what I experienced as these so strangely and frustratingly separate domains of research and praxis; but on the other, something exceeding and indeed quite different from what I initially thought was at issue here, in seeking to forge links between the fields of curriculum studies and literacy pedagogy.

I want to thank, first, all the contributors; some have been extremely patient and supportive over what must have seemed an exceedingly long period of gestation for a project such as this, while others more recently drawn into its folds have honoured me greatly with both their enthusiasm and their commitment, in what have often been trying and stressful circumstances. I want to acknowledge also the support and extremely helpful advice of several of my Deakin colleagues, in particular Marie Brennan and Fazal Rizvi. Lindsay Fitzclarence provided useful comments on the early drafts of several of the chapters, which was much appreciated. Allan Luke, my Series Editor, has similarly provided me with advice and encouragement, and has demonstrated throughout a respect for my judgment with regard to the scope and direction of a project which at times must have seemed nebulous indeed. Jacinta Evans, from Falmer Press, has also been most patient and helpful throughout. Last but certainly not least, I want to register here my particular appreciation to Renate Moles, both for her secretarial assistance — at times, especially in the final stages of readying the manuscript for publication, well beyond the call of duty — and for her unstinting support more generally. All in all, this has been from the outset a truly collective enterprise, and there is no doubt in my mind that it has emerged all the richer and more worthwhile as a consequence.

References

BALL, S.J. (Ed.) (1990) *Foucault and Education: Disciplines and Knowledge*, London, Routledge.

BALL, S., KENNY, A. and GARDINER, D. (1990) 'Literacy, Politics, and the Teaching of English', in GOODSON, I. and MEDWAY, P. (Eds) *Bringing English to Order: The History and Politics of a School Subject*, London, Falmer Press, pp. 47–86.

BOWERS, C.A. (1984) *The Promise of Theory*, New York, Teachers College Press.

BRAND, S. (1988) *The Media Lab: Inventing the Future at MIT*, Harmondsworth, Penguin.

DERRIDA, J. (1976) *Of Grammatology*, translated by G.C. SPIVACK, Baltimore, The Johns Hopkins University Press.

DONALD, J. (1985) 'Beacons of the Future: Schooling, Subjection, and Subjectification', in BEECHEY, V. and DONALD, J. (Eds) *Subjectivity and Social Relations*, Milton Keynes, Open University Press, pp. 214–49.

GIROUX, H.A. (1983) *Theory and Resistance in Education: A Pedagogy for the Opposition*, Cambridge, MA, Bergin and Garvey.

GREEN, B. (1988) 'Subject-Specific Literacy and School Learning: A Focus on Writing', *Australian Journal of Education*, **32**, 2, August, pp. 156–79.

GRIFFIN, D.R. (Ed.) (1988) *The Reenchantment of Science: Postmodern Proposals*, Albany, NY, State University of New York Press.

HALLIDAY, M.A.K. (1987) 'Language and the Order of Nature', in FABB, N., ATTRIDGE, D., DURANT, A. and MACCABE, C. (Eds) *The Linguistics of Writing;*

Arguments between Language and Literature, Manchester, Manchester University Press, pp. 135–54.

HIRSCH, E.D. JR. (1987) *Cultural Literacy: What Every American Needs to Know*, Boston, Houghton Mifflin.

LACAN, J. (1977) *Ecrits: A Selection*, translated by A. Sheridan, London, Tavistock Publications.

LANKSHEAR, C. with LAWLER, M. (1987) *Literacy, Schooling and Revolution*, New York, Falmer Press.

LANKSHEAR, C. (1991) 'Getting It Right is Hard: Redressing the Politics of Literacy in the 1990s', in CORMACK, P. (Ed.) *Literacy: Making It Explicit, Making It Possible — Selected Papers from the 16th Australian Reading Association Conference, Adelaide, South Australia, 7–11 July, 1991*, Carlton South, Victoria, Australian Reading Association, pp. 209–28.

LEVIN, D.M. (Ed.) (1987) *Pathologies of the Modern Self: Postmodern Studies in Narcissism, Schizophrenia, and Depression*, New York, New York University Press.

POPKEWITZ, T.S. (Ed.) (1987) *The Formation of the School Subjects: The Struggle for Creating an American Institution*, New York, Falmer Press.

POSTER, M. (1990) *The Mode of Information: Poststructuralism and Social Context*, Cambridge, Polity Press.

REID, W. (1984) Curriculum Topics as Institutional Categories: Implications for Theory and Research in the History and Sociology of School Subjects', in GOODSON, I. and BALL, S.J. (Eds) *Defining the Curriculum*, London, Falmer Press, pp. 67–76.

SIMON, B. (1988) 'For a Pedagogy of Possibility', *Critical Pedagogy Networker*, **1**, 1, pp. 1–4.

ULMER, G. (1981) 'The Post-Age', *Diacritics*, **11**, pp. 39–56.

Chapter 1

Literacy, Orality, and the Functions of Curriculum

William A. Reid

Many writers, from Plato onwards, have drawn attention to the problems of reconciling literacy — mastery of the written word — with orality — mastery of the spoken word. Curriculum, which addresses itself to skills of both kinds, offers a particularly fertile ground for manifestations of this conflict, ranging from the purely technical to the deeply cultural. My present concern is with the cultural end of this spectrum. I shall be treating literacy and orality not simply as matters of skill acquisition, but as contrasting and conflicting ways of understanding the world and of acting in it and on it.[1] The view of literacy/orality which I shall adopt is well illustrated by the findings of the Soviet psychologist Luria who carried out testing programs on 'unschooled' populations in remote areas of the USSR in the 1930s:

> Luria and his associates gathered data in the course of long conversations with subjects in the relaxed atmosphere of a tea house, introducing the questions for the survey itself informally, as something like riddles, with which the subjects were familiar. Thus every effort was made to adapt the questions to the subjects in their own milieu. The subjects were not leaders in their societies, but there is every reason to suppose that they had a normal range of intelligence and were quite representative of the culture. Among Luria's findings the following may be noted as of special interest here.
>
> (1) Illiterate (oral) subjects identified geometrical figures by assigning them the names of objects, never abstractly as circles, squares, etc. A circle would be called a plate, sieve, bucket, watch, or moon; a square would be called a mirror, door, house, apricot drying-board. Luria's subjects identified the designs as representations of real things they knew. They never dealt with abstract circles or squares but rather with concrete objects. Teachers' school students, on the other hand, moderately literate, identified geometrical figures by categorical geometric names: circles, squares, triangles, and so on.... They had been trained to give school-room answers, not real-life responses.
>
> (2) Subjects were presented with drawings of four objects, three belonging to one category and the fourth to another, and were asked to

group together those that were similar or could be placed in one group
or designated by one word. One series consisted of drawings of the
objects *hammer, saw, log, hatchet*. Illiterate subjects consistently thought
of the group not in categorical terms (three tools, the log not a tool)
but in terms of practical situations — 'situational thinking' — without
adverting at all to the classification 'tool' as applying to all but the log. If
you are a workman with tools and see a log, you think of applying the
tool to it, not of keeping the tool away from what it was made for — in
some weird intellectual game. A 25-year-old illiterate peasant: 'They're
all alike. The saw will saw the log and the hatchet will chop it into small
pieces. If one of these has to go, I'd throw out the hatchet. It doesn't do
as a good a job as a saw'.... Told that the hammer, saw, and hatchet are
all tools, he discounts the categorical class and persists in situational
thinking: 'Yes, but even if we have tools, we still need wood — otherwise we can't build anything'.... By contrast an 18-year-old who had
studied at a village school for only two years, not only classified a similar
series in categorical terms, but insisted on the correctness of the classification under attack ... (Ong, 1982: 50–52).

This example conveys the essence of the kind of distinction between literacy and
orality that I want to work with in this paper; it also points to the intrinsic link
between 'literate' behaviour and the curriculum — subjects with even a little
schooling saw Luria's questions in a different light from those who had had no
experience of it at all: they shared, at least to some extent, a view of the world
that we would recognize as 'modern'. The ability and inclination to behave
according to canons of modernity is symbiotically linked with skills in the
practices of literacy, and the prime cultural agency for establishing this relationship is the school curriculum.[2]

The world seen through the lens of modernity has, according to Meyer
(1980), the following leading characteristics:

1   It is *ordered*: it is understood as 'a dense network of causal flows: events
    have origins and explanations and problems have answers'.
2   It is *rational*: this order can be deciphered and problems solved by calcu-
    lation.
3   It is *objective and impersonal*: it is 'external to social life and human mean-
    ing. Answers to problems are both objectively correct and the same for
    everyone'.
4   It is to be confronted on the basis of *authoritative individualism*: 'Individual
    persons have the collectively defined right and obligation to approach the
    world and its problems. They do not act as agents of larger corporate
    entities, whose rules and traditions define correct approaches to the
    world, and they do not need to consult such authorities. Each individual
    is directly linked to the rational, orderly, objectified cosmos' (Meyer,
    1980: 36–37).

Such a world, Meyer remarks, would have seemed alien to most people in
human history — including, of course, Luria's Uzbekistanis and Kirghiz. It was
not a world they could inhabit because they lacked the essential key which

enables objects and events to be construed as ordered, rational, and impersonal. That key is literacy. At the heart of the skills and practice of literacy is the notion that meaning can be objectified, and, from that central notion, flow all the characteristics of modernity as defined by Meyer. Thus, whether or not it was so intended, the function of the curriculum has always been not only to make people *literate* but to make them *modern*. Indeed, it can be claimed that the modernizing function of the curriculum has always been more effective than its function as a means of bringing about high levels of literacy. As we saw from Luria's example, even people who have only limited skills in the use of written language may nevertheless have internalized the knack of responding in a thoroughly modern way to questions set by psychologists. Therefore, when I claim that to move people from a 'traditional' to a 'modern' view of the world is a central function of the school curriculum — if not *the* central function — I am not on that account making an extravagant assessment of its ability to bring about a high degree of literacy as measured by achievement in reading and writing. The modernizing function can, and often does, go hand in hand with only moderate success in raising levels of attainment. The potency of the curriculum, in terms of its promotion of a literate view of the world, lies first of all in the very substantial undermining of the oral perspective which even a brief acquaintance with text-based learning can bring about, and second, in the connection it establishes between levels of attainment in literacy and access to positions of authority. Even if the many do not make notable progress, the few who succeed in mastering literacy at a high level obtain thereby the freedom to define the modernized world as the only 'real' one, and to characterize as 'illiterate' anyone who is not equipped to participate in it on their terms.

But, to return again to Luria's peasants, they were not simply lacking in an ability to adopt a modern world view; they applied to his questions a positive world view of their own — one associated with an oral culture which was, until recently, the one within which most people lived. The work of the curriculum, then, is not to introduce to modernity those who would otherwise lack the ability to make sense of their world, but actively to destroy, or at least severely modify, the cultural and intellectual resources they already possess. However, in doing this, it operates in curiously ambiguous ways: while devoted to goals of literacy and modernity, the school curriculum, in some of its manifestations such as the classroom recitation (Hoetker and Ahlbrand, 1969), nevertheless has strong oral characteristics. Moreover, the relationship between oral and literate activities, curricular goals, and student groups can be problematic, as I shall try to show later in this chapter. In order to understand how curricular ideas and practices are connected with oral and literate cultures and with the modernizing process, it is necessary first of all to examine their historical development.

Curriculum as a Literate Concept

Walter Ong (1982: 9) points out that 'people in primary oral cultures do not study'. For them, learning is part of the general experience of living. The notion of 'study' as something self-contained and apart from the activities of everyday life only becomes possible with the availability of written texts. In making this point, I am arguing, with Hamilton (1989) and others, that we should avoid making historical and conceptual confusions between 'learning' and 'curriculum'. Much learning has to go on in an oral culture, but to make a list of the knowledge which is acquired and call it a 'curriculum' is to miss the point that the nature of this learning is intrinsically different from that which takes place in geographical and historical circumstances where use of the word 'curriculum' is appropriate. Oral cultures lack fixed written records where knowledge can be retrieved or verified. Therefore, the vast amount of information which has to be reliably remembered must be inculcated by frequent repetition. Havelock (1963: 36ff.) in his *Preface to Plato* points out that in an oral culture 'the educational mechanisms ... cannot be narrowly identified with schools ... or with teachers, as though these represented a unique source of indoctrination, as they do in a literate society.' The only verbal technology available to guarantee fixity of transmission is 'that of the rhythmic word organized cunningly in verbal and metric patterns ... All memorisation of the poetized tradition depends on constant and reiterated recitation ... the pupil will grow and perhaps forget. His living memory must be at every turn reinforced by social pressure.' For Greek society, this is the state of affairs described by Plato in *The Republic*. His description is of a 'total technology of the preserved word which has since his day in Europe ceased to exist'.

There are a number of ways in which the style of learning described by Havelock is fundamentally different from that associated with curricular learning, the forms of which emerge from, and are supportive of, a culture in an advanced stage of literacy:

1 *Curriculum* depends on the employment of analytical procedures, both in its specification and its delivery. Especially, it disassociates aspects of activities and objects such as appearance, properties, and practical or aesthetic worth: *oral learning* depends on the use of narrative and dramatic techniques and treats qualities and applications of activities and objects as intrinsic.

2 *Curriculum* presents objectified knowledge which can be critically discussed: *oral learning* deals in contextualized facts to the truth of which teacher and learner have an emotional commitment.

3 *Curriculum* is sequential and capable of completion: *oral learning* is episodic and continuously available.

4 Mastery of *curriculum* is assessed internally to the teaching process: mastery of *oral learning* is a matter for societal judgment.

5 Mastery of *curriculum* can be judged on a scale of competence and can work with a concept of failure: mastery of *oral learning* demands total recall and does not incorporate the concept of failure.[3]

These are, of course, gross generalizations. But they provide us with ideas for understanding how, within Western cultures, curriculum, as a tool of literate learning, became a necessary social institution. At a certain point, as the character of society changed, oral learning began to appear dysfunctional. It was not a case of an inferior technology being superseded by a superior one; indeed, some of the characteristics of oral learning which I have listed, such as the non-separation of the practical and the theoretic, or the contextualization of information, still claim widespread support as characteristics of school learning. But it stood in the way of attempts to bring about social and economic change *according to prespecified plans*. Those, such as Plato, who wanted to be rid of oral learning, claimed that it promoted 'resistance to change'. For him, it was the oral state of mind which

> constituted the chief obstacle to scientific rationalism, to the use of analysis, to the classification of experience, to its rearrangement in sequence of cause and effect ... He [asked] of men that ... they should become the 'subject' who stands apart from the 'object' and reconsiders it and analyzes it, instead of just 'imitating' it (Havelock, 1963: 47).

But, of course, Plato, like so many other 'literate' reformers, already had a plan for what should be done. The purpose of detaching subject from object was less that analysis should take place (since that might lead people to conclusions different from the ones he thought they should adopt) than that the capacity of practical oral wisdom for standing against his schemes should be diminished. The conventional view that 'illiterate' populations are deeply conservative and cannot adapt to change is manifestly false. Given an alternative to the traditional way of doing things, so-called 'illiterates' are capable of embracing new ways of living with amazing speed, as examples from the Inuit of the Arctic to the Bushmen of the Kalahari testify. But they adapt on their own terms and not in accordance with the preconceived plans of literate 'experts'.

It is this obstacle which literate forms of learning are intended to overcome, and, by the time of Plato, Greek civilization already had some of the tools needed for de-emphasizing oral learning and promoting literacy and modernity. It had an alphabet, and skills of reading and writing flourished in scholarly circles. It possessed written texts and had developed geometrical symbolism. But the new tradition had to grow from the old. Though the encouragement of students to become subjects who stand apart from the content and materials of learning was now a realistic project, the practical means for achieving it were still largely drawn from the old 'total technology of the preserved word'. Teaching, even of literacy, still depended on listening, memorizing, repetition, recitation, and imitation. Moreover, in the absence of technologies for the widespread copying and distribution of texts, the core literate experiences could be available only to the minority. For most students, contact with the ideas of Plato and Aristotle, or the propositions of Euclid, could occur only through hearing the texts read by others, or through listening to commentaries on the texts presented by lectures.[4] Thus, proto-literate teaching and learning were, to a considerable extent, still dependent on the old traditional oral skills. However, while in one way this put a brake on the development and spread of literate learning, in another way it made literacy friendly and approachable for the whole populace. As Clanchy (1979: 219) remarks: 'Reading aloud and dictating permit the nonliterate to participate in the use of documents, whereas reading and writing silently exclude the illiterate'.[5]

Clanchy explains how the next stage in the progressive movement from oral learning to curriculum came about. The most significant event in this was the invention of printing which led to the ready availability of texts, and to a further and more divisive objectification of the written word. But Clanchy claims that the shift towards a more recognizably modern style of literate learning actually preceded and provided a stimulus for the invention of printing. In the case of

England, the needs of post-Conquest government, coupled with the respect accorded to liturgical books, produced a new emphasis on the importance of texts, and this was accompanied by significant changes in the way in which those who were exposed to texts understood the world. For example, in the early part of the period which Clanchy describes, more legal respect was likely to be given to people who testified that they had seen someone seal a document than would be given to the existence of the document itself. Later, however, and before the invention of printing, a stage was reached where authenticity of the written text became the key issue, and conditions existed for the appearance of the modern concept of forgery; people of the early Middle Ages did not, according to Clanchy, share our concern about whether charters, as texts, were 'genuine' or not.

When printed books did become widely available, new dimensions were added to this important development. Since many people — in principle, every-one — could have access to texts, reading no longer had to be thought of as an extension of speaking. Moreover, texts multiplied beyond the number needed to serve the small numbers of an educated group whose lingua franca was Latin. English, like other European languages, became the language of a literate culture, paving the way for the act of composition to be linked with writing rather than dictation.

This further development of the pedagogic capabilities of literate culture brings us to the point where learning could, for many people, be described in terms of 'following a curriculum'. The socio-technical resources now existed to enable realization of the key features of 'curriculum' which we have identified: plans and methods for learning which are objective and analytic; the represen-tation of courses of learning as sequential and capable of completion; and means for specifying and measuring success and failure. It is, in fact, at this point, as Hamilton (1989: 45) has claimed, that the word 'curriculum' enters into usage in its modern meaning. From simply denoting elapse of time in the most basic sense, it now stands for elapse of structured time filled with specific, sequenced learning.[6] Not only is study possible, but those who engage in it can be said 'to have completed the curriculum of their studies' and so deserve the status recog-nition that comes with the granting of degrees and diplomas.

Central to the accomplishment of this transition was the invention of the textbook. Learning based on original texts is literate without being particularly curricular. Who is to say whether one should read Plato rather than Euripides? Or, if both, in what order they should be read? And how much reading of Plato or Euripides is 'enough'? These were not important questions for scholars of the Middle Ages. What one read was first of all determined by the availability of a scarce resource: maybe there were no texts of Plato to be had. It was also influenced by the preferences of teachers who themselves had limited access to texts. The object of the exercise was to learn what could be learned, and what could be learned was a function of the hazards of opportunity. The textbook had the potential for changing all of that. The philosophy of Plato, or the dramatic art of Euripides, could now be distilled in the vernacular language, in the form of discrete, learnable facts, in a sequence, and in uniformly printed books which were available to large numbers of students. Or, at another level, textbooks could be produced to aid in the teaching of the basic skills of reading and writing. Liter-ate learning, which had for long preserved much of the episodic quality of oral learning — Hamilton (1989: 38) speaks of the 'loose-textured organizational form' of the medieval university — could now become methodic. Peter Ramus, in the introduction to the 1569 edition of his dialectic, could write: 'Method is the disposition by which that enunciation is placed first which is first in the absolute order of knowledge, the next which is next, and so on: and thus there is an unbroken progression' (Hamilton, 1989: 46). One feels that Ramus would have done well on Luria's tests.

Literate Ends and Oral Means

If the sixteenth century saw the advent of the sociotechnologies which were to make possible the planning and teaching of curricula, realization of their potentialities was to chart a slow and uncertain course. In the first place, the structuring and regulation of learning for large populations is an expensive matter. In the second place, established and time-honoured methods of teaching are resistant to the implantation of new materials and procedures. What we still see in most education systems is an uneasy coexistence of literate ends and oral means. Like other oral cultures, teaching embraced the new technology on its own terms. Its centrepiece, the textbook, has gained the status of an indispensable artefact, but it functions, to a large extent, as a tool of the old protoliterate method of instruction. A standard type of lesson, or lesson segment, in American classrooms of the 1990s takes the form of the medieval 'lecture': the teacher reads from the textbook. Another standard form consists of the 'recitation' at whose durability Hoetker and Ahlbrand marvelled: the naming of key words and phrases from the textbook is rehearsed through question and answer. What, as a rule, does not happen is that students are taught how to use textbooks as a means for 'studying' on their own. And, at a deeper level, implicit theories of teaching associated with oral and proto-literate cultures still abound. Homer believed that much important teaching took place through learners entering into the personality of someone who acted as an exemplar, in terms of the skills, belief, or habits that were to be acquired. This process was known as *mimesis* and was central to the oral style of teaching of which Plato was so fiercely critical. But, over two thousand years later, mimetic theories are still alive and well in our schools and universities. The other side to the coin of mimesis was agonistic learning: the pupil's knowledge depended on an adversary contest with the teacher, marked by baiting on the one side and punishment on the other. Teachers were conventionally depicted cane in hand. The cane has, in most places gone, but its demise is recent and attitudes that accompanied its use are still with us.[7]

What is curious about this partial and uneven adoption of the modern, literature curriculum is the kind of relationship that exists between the degree of observed modernity of the curriculum and the type of student at which it is aimed. Which groups would we expect to be experiencing a curriculum having many of the marks of the proto-literate model ... and which a curriculum of a thoroughly modern character? In considering this question, we might first of all look at the extent to which children are, or are not, attuned to a *modern, literate* view of the world before they enter school. The newborn child in a Western society is, in many ways, in the same situation as a child born into an oral culture.

Almost certainly, the adults who are associated with its early learning will behave in a literate way, but the only means the child has for communicating with them will be oral. Spoken language is the prime means by which the first understandings of the world are acquired, and reliance on spoken language induces many of the traits of character which belong to oral cultures. As the Opies observed in the introduction to their classic study *The Lore and Language of Schoolchildren*, 'the world-wide fraternity of children is the greatest of savage tribes, and the only one which shows no sign of dying out' (Opie and Opie, 1959: 2). However, children will display greater or lesser levels of orality and, along with Bernstein (1975) and others who have studied questions of this kind, we would expect that, generally speaking, children of lower socio-economic status will tend towards greater orality and children of higher status towards greater literacy, both in the sense of specific skills (can they read before they enter school?) and in the sense of attitude towards learning (do they, along with Luria's peasants, see much school learning as 'some weird intellectual game'?). On these grounds, we might predict that, in those classrooms where we find children who lack specific skills and who have difficulty in adapting to the demands of school, we will also find a friendly, proto-literate culture which stresses narrative and contextualization, de-emphasizes strict evaluation, and allows learning to be 'on demand' rather than rigidly sequential. This would be with the aim of gradually introducing children to a literate mode of learning without exposing them to the risk of experiencing failure and alienation at an early stage in their school careers.

If, on the other hand, we went in search of the thoroughly modernized curriculum, we might expect to find it in classes with large numbers of children who already possess some skills of literacy and are well attuned to objective, analytical, sequential thinking. Were we to check out our hypothesis, however, we would almost certainly conclude that we were wrong. Practice is, of course, very varied, but we would stand a very good chance of observing 'low achieving' elementary school children being exposed to highly analytical schemes for the teaching of reading and mathematics which atomize what is to be learned into decontextualized, Ramist-like lists of sequential facts and skills. These, we will be told, are designed to make learning simple and easy. But whose version of ease and simplicity is this? Not that of the inhabitant of the primary oral world, whose memory is likely to be stuffed with complex formulae which stick because of their association with activity, narrative, and shared emotion. Of course, we might also find a similar elementary classroom run by a teacher in the old mould, her/himself only imperfectly inducted into a modern, literate frame of mind, who understands all of this and ensures that her/his classroom is full of formulaic, narrative discourse, with plenty of emphasis on purposing in common. But such people are becoming rare as they are hunted down by accountability schemes in the USA, or the National Curriculum in England. If we were seriously concerned to find a truly proto-literate classroom, there is a very good chance that when we succeeded we would encounter in it a group of high-achieving, school-oriented children whose parents have opted for private education.

Another consideration which might occur to us as we ponder the connection between classroom cultures and student populations is that a process of education for the modern world should ensure that those who have expectations of high status in society should experience the most thoroughly literate curriculum, while those likely to occupy lower status positions might follow courses retaining a greater residue of the 'technology of the preserved word'. Again our expectations will most likely be unfulfilled. In the highest classes of English secondary schools, we could observe students reading texts — not textbooks — listed in a 'syllabus' having few of the marks of a Ramist curriculum, and reliant on discussions with their teacher to discover exactly what one should know about Milton, Goethe, or Voltaire, how much reading of texts or commentaries on texts is 'enough', and how what one knows about the texts can be cast into rhetorical forms which would have been thoroughly familiar to Quintilian (all of this, and more, was no doubt in Ong's [1982: 158] mind as he was moved to speak of the 'highly effective residual orality in British public schools'). But were we to seek out students following less successful educational careers, we should stand a very good chance of finding them enrolled in modular curricula built around closely specified skills and knowledge and involving frequent evaluation of progress through profile checklists and multiple-choice testing. In the secondary schools, just as in the elementary school, it is, as often as not, the 'lower achieving' student who is exposed to the full force of the curriculum of modernity.[8]

Of course, these paradoxes are, to some degree, resolved if we resist the fundamental rhetorical claims of modernity. What we expected to find is what rationality and objectivity suggested; but the modern world, like all the worlds that have ever existed, is not rational and objective. At a practical level it is contingent and personal. Those who are to make decisions have to understand this: too much objectivity can be a handicap. On the other hand, those who are 'followers' rather than 'leaders' have to be persuaded that the rhetoric of modernity is real. On these grounds, it is only to be expected that this rhetoric will be strongest in classrooms occupied by those who will enter the lower levels of the labour force (one might go even further and argue that those most in need of a belief in the 'rational, objective' nature of the world are those to whom it will offer no employment at all). History seems to bear out this view of the nature of the curriculum of the classroom. Nineteenth-century efforts to bring about universal elementary education were often supported by references to the need to produce an obedient workforce, and it was in connection with the expansion of elementary education that the most thoroughgoing experiments in the rationalization of the curriculum of the classroom were carried out. The monitorial system of the early nineteenth century went far beyond any modern method of curricular organization in its efforts to realize Ramist principles at the point of instruction, while attempts to move the elementary school away from modernity — as, for example, in the endorsement of the oral culture offered by the Plowden Report of 1968 — have been short-lived in their effects.

However, the monitorial system too failed to become institutionalized and it does seem to be the case that, so far, the modernizing effect of the literate curriculum has always been moderated at the classroom level because the practice of teaching, as it is currently understood, necessarily entails the employment of oral or proto-literate means in pursuit of literate ends. This attachment to traditionally oral methods of delivering the curriculum at the classroom level seems to apply to all schools. We should therefore expect that oral traits will be stronger where students are drawn from groups with more power to resist political and administrative pressures to 'modernize' the curriculum, and weaker in settings where the more disadvantaged groups are enrolled. But, in the face of these countervailing forces, how is the curriculum able to exert such a powerful modernizing effect?

The Modernizing Impact of the Curriculum

A number of aspects of the curriculum have been reviewed: its analytic thrust, its concern with objective knowledge, its sequential nature, and its evaluative stance towards the student. What all of these aspects depend on for their practical effect is the idea of *generalization*: that schemes of analysis, items of knowledge, sequences of learning, or tools for evaluation can derive their authority from their universal nature, their capability for being in all places and at all times equally valid. The curriculum both projects and presumes the characateristics of the modern world as described by Meyer: its order, rationality, and objectivity, its refusal to recognize any other authority than that implied by its own inherent capability for applying a logical calculus to the explanation of events and to the discovery of solutions to problems. At the theoretical level, this is a potentially sustainable position. Theory deals in universals. It treats problems of a universal nature, depends on universal subject matter, uses methods based on universally applicable principles, and arrives at universally valid explanations. Thus, for example, the project of organizing knowledge within the framework of an encyclopedia can be successful on a theoretic level. Knowledge can be selected, organized, and presented according to universal principles. It then becomes acceptable for curricular purposes where the miscellanies of the era before the introduction of printing would be rejected with derision (one feels, for example, that Guy de Beauchamp's *Little Red Book* of 1306 which 'reflected the interests of the ... owner' and was made up of 'diverse contents [which] had unity in his own experience and needs, rather than in any external scheme of things' [Clanchy, 1979: 62] would not have won a seal of approval from Peter Ramus).

Similarly, somewhat credible schemes for the overall organization of the curriculum, such as the Swedish 'Monsterplan' or Bloom's *Taxonomy of Educational Objectives*, can be derived from principles of universalism. In these ways, involving applications of theoretic reasoning, curriculum exerts a powerful modernizing effect. Consumers of curriculum, by which I mean not only students, but also wider publics of parents and employers, are persuaded of the reality of the rational, universally ordered world of the bureaucrat and the planner. They 'believe' — in spite of much common-sense evidence to the contrary — that the third grade is the third grade everywhere, that IQ tests measure intelligence, and that a high school diploma is always a high school diploma. 'Believe' here needs to have quotation marks to accommodate those occasions, which are not infrequent, when people complain that their child is getting poor teaching in the third grade, that IQ tests discriminate against certain groups, or that some diplomas are not worth the paper they are printed on. The point is that these complaints usually stem from a modern 'literate' belief that it is perfectly feasible to homogenize third grade teaching, devise fair IQ tests, and apply common standards to the award of diplomas; if these things are not happening, then the system is at fault. They rarely arise from the conclusions that orally enculturated people would draw from the evidence of their senses: that there is no third grade, only a lot of unique collections of teachers and students who assume that label; that IQ testing really *is* a 'weird intellectual game', the results of which tell us nothing worth knowing; and that the idea of universal accreditation is just as nugatory as the idea of the universal third grade. Literate culture, which believes in the objectivity of the word, accepts the reality of the label; oral culture, which pays careful attention to circumstance, rejects it. As circumstance is the reflection not of theory but of practice — this student in that school, on the South side of Columbus, with Principal Jones during the present mayoralty of Ed Tweed and in view of the probability of his reelection', as Schwab (1978: 289) put it — the view espoused by the oral culture has something to be said for it. But once the members of that culture are coopted into the modern school system, the labels begin to exert their power. The macro-level capacity of curriculum to further the project of the universalization of meaning blankets out the idiosyncracy of individual situations. Students, as Meyer (1980: 54) points out, soon learn to look beyond the accidents of the classroom in which they find themselves and focus instead on the universal category — the third grade — which gives meaning to their enrolment in it.[9] In this way, the modernizing effects of the curriculum overcome obstacles posed by the residual orality of the process of instruction.

Curriculum, Literacy, and the New Technology

The account I have given of oral and literate aspects of curriculum and their relationship to processes of modernization stops at a point in the late twentieth century, when education systems are still powered by the impact of key developments in the history of literacy dating back to the sixteenth century. But now we are beginning to see the first effects of the next stage in the 'technologizing of the word' (Ong, 1982). How this will modify the situation is, as yet, unclear. On the one hand, enhanced powers of data gathering, analysis, and transmission are being harnessed to a strengthening of the capacity of the curriculum to universalize categories of knowledge, role, and organization. The computer can become a major force for homogenizing the content of the curriculum, regulating its management, and evaluating its outcomes, thus adding to its already strong modernizing impact at the macro-level. The possibility also has to be entertained that similar effects could be produced at the micro-level of instruction, and this is clearly the ambition of some efforts to introduce modern technology into the classroom. However, to this point, research shows that, once again, the proclivities of the predominantly oral culture of teaching are tending to overcome the modernizing impact of technical innovation. Olson (1988: 33), in one of his studies of computer use in classrooms, describes how

> Mr Heiburg has integrated the computer into familiar teaching routines — he has not risked dramatic changes in his way of teaching which might undermine his ability to effectively cover the curriculum in an acceptable way — he has protected the core of the work.

Indeed, the possibility exists that the power of the written word to act as a reinforcer of notions of impersonality and objectivity will actually be diminished as students learn, through use of computers, that words are readily manipulable. Might we then see a resurgence of some features of the oral world? Will miscellanies outflank the encyclopedia and gain a new lease of life on computer bulletin boards? Will databases give renewed access to texts rather than textbooks? Will talk take priority over literate composition as channels of electronic mail are opened up, and as machines take over the artisan work of writing, once the province of the medieval scribe? These are important questions affecting the investment of large resources, the future nature of society, and the careers of many millions of students. History, of the kind we have discussed, provides us with one resource for understanding what is involved in providing answers to them. Another resource is offered by the oral tradition itself. The story of curricular evolution has been one of subversion by the oral tradition, at the level of instruction, of the modernizing influence exerted at the societal level. The arrival of the new technologies might mark the beginning of an era when this process needs to be reversed, so that the oral tradition can assume a more positive role and weaken the literate assumptions which have guided curriculum activity at the macro-level. As I have suggested elsewhere (Reid, 1988), arguments drawn from the facts of the information revolution can be linked to two totally opposed kinds of conclusion about educational practice. Seen within a 'logistic' perspective, they lead to the proposition that what is needed is more of what I would call 'traditional modernity', that is, a firmer and wider application of policies based on Meyer's criteria. But we might have to consider that modern technologies are only modern in the sense that they belong to the present day. In terms of how they ought to influence our thinking, they could be seen as marking the end of 'traditional modernity', the origins of which are to be found in technical, governmental, and intellectual developments of the sixteenth and seventeenth centuries. They might be more appropriately conceived of in what I have termed a 'problematic' perspective which

> ... embraces a historically rooted rather than future-oriented conception of how society works. It does not see the possibility of an 'end of ideology' through technical, political, or any other means and regards adaptation to change as something in which the whole society should play a part and not simply political leaders or professional experts. Whatever is new takes its place as part of the problem to be deliberated on (Reid, 1988: 119).

Notions of inclusiveness, of taking account of the particulars of problems, and of scepticism about proposals based on technical arguments are intimately linked to the oral view of the world. They are marks of the orality which lingers at the level of instruction. Teachers are more likely than planners or politicians to be worried about nurturing the identity of the class, even at the expense of 'standards', to act in terms of specific situations rather than general principles, and to view proposals for the modernization of the curriculum with suspicion. But they are not members of an oral society; their practice springs from, and depends on, literacy. Similarly, it is possible at the level of the overall planning of the curriculum for the conception of the work to be done to be grounded in a proto-literate tradition of deliberation, as advocated by Schwab (1978) and others. Deliberation, like other practical arts, can only exist within a context of literacy (Ong, 1982: 109).

However, through its emphasis on the spoken word, it preserves many of the virtues of the oral world, the benefits of which are now being advocated not only in curriculum but in many other areas of macro-level planning.[10] We should consider that it may not, after all, be necessary for oral and literate traditions to be thought of as conflicting. Certainly, the perception of conflict has been almost universal, but I suspect that this is due less to the intrinsic nature of oral and literate world views, and more to the ways in which the resources of literacy have been allowed to become an engine of modernization, using that word in what, I suggest, may be its historic sense.

The advance of modern technologies focuses attention on problems of co-existence, and on problems of what might be irretrievably lost if their destructive propensities goes unchecked. One of our cultural resources that we should be concerned to preserve is that represented by the oral tradition. The history of the interaction of literacy and orality has been one of constant evolution. The next stage in that evolution could be one in which the virtues of orality are resurrected to halt the advance of the 'pedagogical juggernaut' which was launched upon the world through the project of subsuming learning within the universally directive idea of curriculum.[11]

Notes

1 In choosing to argue in this way, I reveal the consequences of my own proto-literate education. In Aristotelian fashion, I set up a binary rhetorical device for considering some curriculum problems and issues. Of course, 'literacy' and 'orality' could as well be examined for what they have in common as what holds them apart. In the end, they are abstractions, not realities. For a discussion of these subtleties, in a curricular context, which is far better than any I could offer, see Egan (1987).

2 But school is not the only one. Other institutions such as factories have been cited as agents of enculturation into modern 'literate' behaviour (see, for example, Inkeles and Smith, 1974).

3 Oral cultures make sure that what everyone knows is what they need to know, and that they do not forget it. Curricular learning involves not only failure to learn, which can go uncorrected because most curricular knowledge is not in any universal sense essential, but also widespread forgetting on the part of 'successful' students. I consider that studies of 'forgetting', which are non-existent, might tell us more about education than the studies of 'remembering' with which books and journals are crammed. Note, however, that even in literate societies things that have to be (almost) universally known, like how to drive a car, are successfully taught to (almost) everyone, and are not forgotten.

4 Lecturer is a title which persists in the present day English university. In the Middle Ages there was much dispute about whether hearers should or should not write down what lecturers read out.

5 As long as texts were intended to be read aloud, written knowledge was a public property. Printing turned acquaintance with texts into a private experience which is easily avoided (see Goody and Watt, 1968: 63).

6 See Reid (1990: 206), also (1990: 216 [Note 5]).

7 As Ong (1974) points out, agonism in learning did not relate solely to relations between teachers and pupils. Subject matter was also treated in an agonistic way, as, for example, in the disputation. 'Until the age of romanticism ... academic teaching of all subjects had been more or less polemic' (Ong, 1977: 76).

8 In this connection it is noteworthy that the English 'National' Curriculum is binding only on maintained (state) schools and not on public (private) schools.

9 For a discussion of the universal categories of schooling, see Reid (1990).

10 For a discussion of deliberative planning and comparisons with other areas of planning activity, see Holt (1987).

11 The term 'pedagogical juggernaut' was coined by Walter Ong. See also Hamilton (1987).

References

BERNSTEIN, B. (1975) *Class, Codes and Control Vol. 3*, London, Routledge.

CLANCHY, M.T. (1979) *From Memory to Written Record: England 1066–1307*, London, Arnold.

EGAN, K. (1987) 'Literacy and the Oral Foundations of Education', *Harvard Educational Review*, **57**, pp. 445–72.

GOODY, J. and WATT, I. (1968) 'The Consequences of Literacy', in GOODY, J. (Ed.) *Literacy in Traditional Societies*, Cambridge, Cambridge University Press.

HAMILTON, D. (1987) 'The Pedagogical Juggernaut', *British Journal of Educational Studies*, **35**, 1, pp. 18–29.

HAMILTON, D. (1989) *Towards a Theory of Schooling*, London, Falmer Press.

HAVELOCK, E.A. (1963) *Preface to Plato*, Oxford, Blackwell.

HOETKER, J. and AHLBRAND, W.P. (1969) 'The Persistence of the Recitation', *American Educational Research Journal*, **6**, pp. 145–67.

HOLT, M.J. (1987) *Judgment, Planning and Educational Change*, London, Harper and Row.

INKELES, A. and SMITH, D. (1974) *Becoming Modern: Individual Change in Six Developing Countries*, Cambridge, MA, Harvard University Press.

MEYER, J.W. (1980) 'Levels of the Educational System and Schooling Effects', in BIDWELL, C.E. and WINDHAM, D.M. (Eds) *The Analysis of Educational Productivity*, **2**, *Issues in Macroanalysis*, Cambridge, MA, Ballinger.

OLSON, J. (1988) *Schoolworlds/Microworlds: Computers and the Culture of the Classroom*, Oxford, Pergamon Press.

ONG, W.J. (1974) 'Agonistic Structures', *Interchange*, **5**, pp. 1–12.

ONG, W.J. (1977) *Interfaces of the Word: Studies in the Evolution of Consciousness and Culture*, Ithaca, NY, Cornell University Press.

ONG, W.J. (1982) *Orality and Literacy: The Technologizing of the Word*, London, Methuen.

OPIE, I. and OPIE, J. (1959) *The Lore and Language of Schoolchildren*, London, Oxford University Press.

REID, W.A. (1988) 'The Technological Society and the Concept of General Education', in WESTBURY, I. and PURVES, A.C. (Eds) *Cultural Literacy and the Concept of General Education*, 87th Yearbook of the National Society for the Study of Education, Part 2, Chicago, University of Chicago Press, pp. 115–31.

REID, W.A. (1990) 'Strange Curricula: Origins and Development of the Institutional Categories of Schooling', *Journal of Curriculum Studies*, **22**, 3, pp. 203–16.

SCHWAB, J.J. (1978) 'The Practical: A Language for Curriculum', in WESTBURY, I. and WILKOF, N. (Eds) *Science, Curriculum and Liberal Education*, Chicago, University of Chicago Press.

Chapter 2

Technologies of Learning and Alphabetic Culture: The History of Writing as the History of Education

Keith Hoskin

Introduction

'The history of education is the history of writing'. Thus I began, a decade ago, an earlier reflection upon the power of writing and the extent to which educational practices — that is, technologies of teaching and learning — have been involved throughout writing's history in generating writing's power.[1] My concern then was this. We have in recent decades come to understand how the invention of the technology of writing is perhaps the most significant single invention in human history: at a stroke (literally), it enabled a new kind of (i) storage of information, (ii) communication, and (iii) cognitive ordering of thinking. On the last point in particular it is now widely understood, as Walter Ong has put it:

> what functionally literate human beings really are: beings whose thought processes do not grow out of simply natural powers but out of these powers as structured, directly or indirectly, by the technology of writing. Without writing, the literate mind would not and could not think as it does, not only when engaged in writing but normally even when it is composing its thoughts in oral form. More than any other single invention, writing has transformed human consciousness (Ong, 1982: 78).

We have consequently begun to acknowledge a previously-overlooked cultural blindspot of Western thought, seeing how deeply, culturally and within the self, we are the products or the extensions of those technologies which we once thought we simply 'used'.

My concern was that in all this new insight the focus had been too exclusively on the *visible* technology of writing in itself. So for instance there were (and still are, as we shall see) arguments concerning which is the most significant moment in writing's history: was it the initial invention of writing (*c.* 3200 BC), or the invention of the alphabet (*c.* 1500 BC, or alternatively *c.* 750 BC)? Or further on, what of the medium shift when script gave way to print (*c.* 1500 AD), or when finally the modern electronic media emerged? But despite their differences, all these arguments seemed to accept that the focus of attention should be the visible technology in itself and its own 'inherent' power. All in effect acceded to the dictum of Marshall McLuhan (1964: 7): 'the medium is the message'.

Here was my concern: that in exposing our cultural blindspot, this new understanding of writing's power was developing a blindspot of its own. What was getting overlooked was the constitutive role in developing writing's power played by the *invisible* technologies of learning. The problem is perhaps best expressed in the chicken-and-egg paradox: namely, which comes first, writing or reading? Like the chicken-and-egg question it is both maddening but, ultimately, unavoidable. For, as we know from our own learning, no medium is ever just there as a given; instead, it has always to be *learned*. And what applies to each individual also applies culturally. Indeed, a case can be made that the way in which, in any given generation, the medium of writing is learned will become fundamental to how that generation more generally learns *to* learn (see, for example, Bateson, 1973).[2] More generally, the learning of a medium will shape the way in which that medium is internalized and deployed to the point where it becomes a constitutive part of what the medium itself is.

A decade ago, my concern led me to write an unpublishable treatise on how changes in the form of writing (such as the shift to the alphabetic culture of 'the Logos' in ancient Greece) were associated with changes in the power of knowledge, and how both were somehow linked to changes in educational practice. But that paper, 'The History of Education and the History of Writing', was at once too long and as yet unable to theorize the precise way in which educational practices constructed ways of knowing and forms of power within the history of 'the Logos'.[3]

As a result I moved, at the surface, away from a concern with writing-in-itself and towards a tighter focus on the more recent relations between power, knowledge and education. In particular, in a reformulation of Michel Foucault's ideas about the relations between forms of knowledge and technologies of power (Foucault, 1977), I began to show how transformations in what he described as 'power-knowledge' relations are the result of prior changes in how humans learn. Taking up Foucault's idea that 'micro-technologies' such as examination play an overlooked role in transforming the way we think and act, being technologies which combine 'the deployment of force with the establishment of truth' (Foucault, 1977: 184), I pursued the theme that major transformations in the nature and scope of knowledge and its power begin from *prior* changes in educational practice.[4]

Recently, I have concentrated mostly on the shift in the late eighteenth century to three new educational practices: (i) constant rigorous examination (ii) numerical grading of the results of these examinations, and (iii) an insistent process of writing by students, about students, and organizationally around students. I have been able to show how from such tiny micro-technological beginnings students do learn to learn in new ways. Learning under conditions of grading and examination, they become Foucault's 'calculable persons', persons who accept the presupposition that human qualities (from good looks to such new constructs as 'intelligence' and 'leadership potential') can be quantified (Hoskin, 1990: 33). But as they learn also under the constant pressure to produce written work for grades (in such new forms as critical essays and lab reports, as well as actual examination scripts), and also within a system which keeps constant records and reports upon them, they become centred upon writing as the real heart of learning. They become, in a term I have coined, 'grammatocentric'.

My conclusion now is that the first generation which learned to learn under these new practices, around 1800, went on to invent the modern 'disciplinary' society, where we all become rendered both calculable and educable. For following the introduction of these new micro-technologies, the modern academic disciplines get invented (Hoskin, forthcoming); but also the modern professions, modern mass education, and even modern business and the modern power of accounting (Hoskin, 1986; Hoskin and Macve, 1986, 1988). And in each case, the key pioneers of modernity come from the first generation of those who 'learn to learn' under these three new little practices.[5]

From these micro-technological beginnings in small elite educational settings, humans have now world-wide come to learn and live under the practices of writing, grading and examination, to the point where such learning appears natural and inevitable. Thus it is not only the case, as Foucault pointed out, that our behaviour becomes shaped by disciplinary micro-technologies; but also at the same time our ways of knowing become discipline-based. As we now learn to learn under these ubiquitous practices, we become disciplinary persons in the double sense. In the grammatocentric era, everyone needs to learn not just to read but also to *write*; and all are to be disciplined by the learning of the disciplines. Meanwhile, the historical strangeness of this way of learning is lost in the overwhelming mundanity of the 'invisible' practices through which it is transmitted.

Thus while at the surface I have moved away from my earlier concern, I have really not moved at all. Instead, I now have a more general but also more tightly argued thesis than I had a decade ago, concerning how the invisible technologies of learning construct a new power of and for writing. I see our 'grammatocentric' world as the ultimate form, so far, of 'logocentric' culture. And I see this latest phase in logocentrism being invented only when humans began to learn through and under constant writing, grading and examination. On this basis, I have suggested that more generally

> what we may well need to consider is how 'the educational' may in different epochs, in different ways, function as the hyphen in the power-knowledge relation. We may come to regard hitherto unregarded shifts in 'learning how to learn' as the principle by which we can interpret fundamental shifts both in social organization and in the construction of the individual human subject (Hoskin, 1990: 51).

It is with this in mind that, returning finally to my departure point of a decade ago, I now reiterate that 'the history of education is the history of writing'. Reversing the usual direction of explanation, I wish to show how far educational practices have been the fulcrum producing new power when modes of writing get invented or transformed. Indeed, concerning the first invention of writing I would now suggest that, unlike the case of the chicken and the egg, there is a definitive answer to the conundrum I posed. Counter-intuitively, before writing there is reading: for the first writing emerges when humans learn to read already-existing non-linguistic signs *as* 'writing'.[6] Furthermore, the subsequent genesis of 'logocentric' culture (which I place within the post-alphabetic era) begins not when a certain visible form of alphabetic writing gets invented, but when humans begin to learn how to read it *systematically*: specifically, with the invention of the alphabetic method of teaching reading in Greece in the fifth century BC.

Thus in general the invisible technologies, not the visible, hold the key to understanding how the power of writing, and more specifically the culture of the Logos, get disseminated both within selves and across societies. For too long in considering the history of writing, education has been the invisible afterthought, the supplement to the central focus of concern. But now the supplement becomes the centre ...

Towards a New Reading of History of Writing

'Alphabetic script is in itself and for itself the most intelligent' Hegel, *Enzyklopadie* (Derrida, 1976: 3).

Any reading of writing's history has to confront the predisposition to concentrate on the technology-in-itself. Indeed, perhaps the greatest problem confronting a new reading of writing's history like this is the difficulty in unlearning such deeply-engrained presuppositions: particularly since there is an important truth in the 'medium is the message' position. For writing certainly did restructure the human life-world. It is, as Ong remarks, the most 'drastic' technological invention, for 'it initiated what print and computers only continue, the reduction of dynamic sound to quiescent space, the separation of the word from the living present' (Ong, 1982: 80–82).

Furthermore, within the history of logocentric writing there has been, as Hegel's remark confirms, a predisposition to see the alphabet as somehow special. Indeed, from Plato to Hegel to Derrida and beyond, the special power and status of the alphabet haunts us. Thus Derrida, in the introduction to *Of Grammatology* cited here, quotes Hegel as the great if unthinking example of an 'ethnocentrism which everywhere and always had controlled the concept of writing', for this praise of alphabetic writing promotes that 'logocentrism' which is 'nothing but the most original and powerful ethnocentrism' (Derrida, 1976: 3).

The great problem then is, while now acknowledging the ethnocentrism inspired by alphabetic writing, to move beyond the level where debate still focuses on the technology-in-itself. And to date, there has been little movement. Debate still continues over whether the alphabet is the most 'intelligent' script, either in the Greek past or in some Derridean 'grammatological' future; or whether other earlier forms of writing already manifested its supposed qualities of 'intelligence', as for instance Jack Goody has argued in recent years (Goody, 1986, 1987). Within this debate, Derrida has produced the most memorable philosophical reflection of our time concerning writing's problematic power and status. However, and ironically, even as he opens up a path to a new reading of writing and its history, he still fails to look systematically beyond the visible technology in itself.

Derrida's views remain nonetheless crucial to any new reading. Both in *Of Grammatology* (1976) and 'Plato's Pharmacy' (1981), he reflects on writing's status as the dissimulating and dangerous 'supplement'. It is a three-fold reflection, as follows. Writing first dissimulates because it presents itself throughout Western philosophy as just a secondary technology, a pale shadow of the spoken word which alone is the 'hot line' to meaning and thus guarantee of truth: this privileging of the spoken word over writing in Western philosophy Derrida describes as the 'metaphysics of presence'. Second, writing is dangerous because this dissimulation precisely inverts its relation to speech; for once there is writing, writing comes to re-shape our speaking and thinking, as Ong above points out. Third, however, writing *is* the supplement, since it emerges, both historically and in our individual experience, as the supplement to speech.

This is where Derrida produces his great insight. For the paradox of human history — expressed by Derrida as the 'logic of the supplement' — is that the supplement continually tends to become the centre, while always remaining 'just' the supplement. Thus the history of writing reveals how writing has moved from marginal afterthought to central dominating feature of social and individual life; but even as it does so, writing remains always the dissimulating dangerous supplement, leading us to distrust it even as it works its power upon us.

This, as Derrida argues in 'Plato's Pharmacy', has been so from the first writing of the Logos, that of Plato. Plato, as is well-known, frequently attacks writing as the dangerous supplement to speech; most famously in the *Phaedrus*, (ll. 274–7) where it is attacked for freezing meaning and stopping the flow of dialogue, replacing 'living' thought with 'dead' ideas. Writing, Socrates says, is the *pharmakon*, a two-edged Greek term meaning both poison and salve: for writing poisons and weakens memory, replacing it with the salve of the external visible resource, the *aide-memoire*.

At the same time this attack carries its own deconstruction. For as soon as there is writing, there is no possibility of expressing this fear of writing except through writing. Plato's argument depends for its very articulation on that which it attacks. Indeed, as we now see, his whole philosophical, analytical way of knowing was only being made possible because of the way writing was restructuring human thinking. Thus the logic of the supplement is revealed: for what Plato would define as the supplement to speech has already displaced it at the centre of his thought. The full measure of the paradox swiftly becomes explicit inasmuch as Plato goes straight on in the *Phaedrus*, (l. 276A–B) to argue that what he rejects is the trust that people put in *visible* texts; meanwhile, he re-inscribes writing — a purified invisible writing — as the basis of truth: for the genuine Logos is 'that which is written with understanding in the soul of the learner'.

On the other hand, Derrida's grammatological move is not quite such a radical break as it takes itself to be. For Derrida still, like Plato, leaves us focused on the visible technology, even as he deepens our appreciation of its ambivalent power. This, perhaps, was bound to happen as soon as he fastened on the 'metaphysics of presence' as the distinguishing feature in Western philosophy, as if it were enough to argue that all philosophy since Plato, and including Plato, simply privileges 'voice'. In so doing, he like others (indeed back to Plato) concentrates too much on the power of writing-in-itself, thus ironically paying a form of tribute to Hegel. Derrida inevitably concedes that there remains an 'intelligence' residing *within* the technology, for his central argument is that there is now underway a new logos not of voice but of writing, being 'the science of writing

— *grammatology* ...' (Derrida, 1976: 4). Ong (1982: 167) is unfortunately absolutely right when he says: 'Derrida is performing a welcome service, in the same territory that Marshall McLuhan swept through with his famous dictum, "The medium is the message"'.

It is an unfortunate irony that Derrida fails to pursue the logic of the supplement that he here articulates. For it is ironic to go so far in seeing how writing is the deceptive supplement, and then to be deceived into overlooking the significance of *its* supplement. But, even more, it is unfortunate since it means that Derrida is left unable to recognize that there is a crucial gap in the usual explanations offered of writing's 'intelligence', whether that is identified with the alphabet itself or whether writing is deemed 'intelligent' before the alphabet's invention. It is a gap that can be closed only by recognizing the central role played by the invisible supplement, the technologies of learning.

The Visible Technologies of Writing: The Failure of Self-Explanation

The gap in explanation only becomes apparent once we acknowledge the weight of evidence showing how 'intelligent' writing is. First, let me take the dominant Hegelian view of the alphabet's special status. In its most sophisticated modern forms, this stresses how the Greek alphabet reverses the principle of all previous linguistic sign systems. Where they all attempted either to represent with pictographs and ideographs the thing-units and idea-units of a language, or else, as in the syllabaries, to represent in syllable form its sound-units, the Greek system radically separates writing from speech by going below the level of such units altogether. By decomposing sound units into two complementary letter-types, vowels and consonants, the so-called 'vocalic' (that is, vowel-based) alphabet introduces the zero-point of language. For the consonant (what is literally 'sounded with' a vowel) has no existence *except* as writing. It cannot be spoken: try saying 't' without the 'ee'.

This new writing had two advantages over the earlier Canaanite and Semitic syllabaries from which it borrows its letters. Such syllabaries all faced the same dilemma: either they attempted to cover all or most of the possible sound-units of their language, which might require up to 100 or more separate signs (a parallel might be the generation of separate signs for the main English consonant-vowel combinations from BA to ZY); or they ended up as 'consonantal alphabets', restricting the number of signs to a manageable few by omitting any indication of vowel differences; however, that made signs highly ambiguous (the English parallel again: would CT stand for CAT, COT, CUT, COAT, COOT, CUTE, or even KATE, KIT or KITE?) and writing therefore had to be highly context-dependent, often ritualistic, to reduce ambiguity.[7] The alphabet, by going below the sound-unit level, solved both problems; it reduced the number of signifiers to an easily learnable number, between twenty and thirty, and at the same time was able with that small number to translate the range of phonemes spoken in the language into written syllable form with low residual ambiguity.

Here is a most important implication: the alphabet as a system differs from its predecessors because it does not attempt to *represent* sound; it traces it closely, thus proving itself sound's most effective supplement. For this reason it is arguably not, as is frequently stated, the invention of the vowel which is so significant (for the vowel is still a means of representing sound). It is the invention of the consonant, the antithesis of sound's representation, which matters. If writing, as Ong says, differs from speech 'in the reduction of dynamic sound to quiescent space', then the consonant is the ultimate sign of that reduction. It is that clever paradox: absence made presence. The consonant is the zero-point which makes possible what de Kerckhove (1988: 156) has called 'the principle of *syllabic synthesis*, by which I mean the combination of discrete and usually unpronounceable elements to form the representation of a pronounceable sound.[8]

Thanks to the consonant, the alphabet turns language from an event into a thing, which 'can be cut into little pieces' below the level of sound (Ong, 1982: 91). There is a supple and extensive new power embodied here. As a script, the alphabet proves to be 'democratizing' in the sense that its twenty-five-odd letters can be learned (relatively) easily, and thus literacy cannot remain an elite priestly craft; it is also 'internationalizing', since it can transliterate the phonemes of other languages as well as translating meanings. Subsequently it will become, as Havelock (1975: 72) remarks, the basis for the world's first copying culture, when the Romans translate into their Latin alphabet whole texts and genres from the Greek, along with the idea that translation can be 'word-for-word' (Hoskin, 1985). And finally (but not until the medieval Western era) that secondary Latin form will be adopted by an increasing number of vernacular languages as the shared transparent medium of their written expression.

Where in all this is the gap in explanation? It lies beneath the one great anomaly in the alphabet's early history, long since pointed out by Havelock, but still not sufficiently reflected upon. The anomaly is that the triumph of the supple new alphabetic sign-system does not happen when it should. For if the medium were indeed the message, it should happen swiftly, within a generation or so of its invention. Yet, instead, the early use of the technology (from say 750 to 600 BC) is strangely restricted, being mainly for information storage, and used almost exclusively in the low-status world of artisans and merchants. The elite of Greece remain resistant to the alphabet's charms. They were not uncultured: far from it. But their system of culture, education and literature was orally-focused and poetic, reflecting the continuing status of the old Homeric world. What Ong calls the 'noetic economy' remains 'phonocentric', focused on speaking and singing well, not on writing, for at least three centuries. That gap needs explaining.

An almost inverted anomaly infects the alternative position, that is, that the supposedly special attributes of alphabetic writing are already to be found in other earlier scripts. On this side, the great exponent is Jack Goody (e.g. Goody, 1977, 1986, 1987). He has long since abandoned the view set out in his pathbreaking article with Ian Watt, 'The Consequences of Literacy' (1963), which accepted that the alphabet had a special status. He has instead pointed out (Goody, 1977: 17–18) how many of the 'figures of the written word ... tables, lists, formulae, recipes' are to be found in earlier writing systems. Writing begins in the pre-alphabetic cultures of Mesopotamia, Assyria and Egypt as a bureaucratic and governmental technique. Inventories, tax-lists, tribute-lists, and forms of book-keeping and archiving are developed in all such cultures before writing is appropriated for literary discourse. In all such systems (not just in the alphabet), there is a decontextualization of information promoted by writing (which, as he notes, is also a *re*contextualization), which then begins to operate reflexively back onto the sign-systems themselves.

Writing therefore from its outset begins to function as a technology for the three great purposes: storage, communication, and the repatterning of human thinking. A new listing mentality takes shape. Lists of the signs in the system are developed, as are various other kinds of lexical lists: lists of signs beginning with the sound 'i' (Goody, 1977: 89), or of signs which represent classes of objects (trees, animals, etc.) Time is to an extent linearized, the past by event lists, annals and archives, the future by prospective lists of things to be done. The world becomes divided abstractly into categories of objects; it also tends to be divided *exhaustively* into such categories, which as he says suggests how the written list operates not just in one linear dimension but in two, along both a vertical and a horizontal axis, like a graph or a table, creating a whole *field* in which to re-present the world. (The classic modern example, as he points out elsewhere [Goody, 1987: 272–3], is the crossword puzzle. But even ancient Egypt has its tabular acrostics, and such tables apparently abhor an empty box: 'Anyone composing a matrix is almost forced to fill all the gaps' [Goody, 1987: 276]).

In a related variant of attack, the special 'intelligence' claimed for the Greek alphabet has been pushed back in time by the argument that certain earlier scripts are already alphabetic or quasi-alphabetic. Thus for instance Morpurgo Davies (1986) shows how in certain crucial respects supposed alphabetic characteristics are found in earlier logographic or syllabic scripts; for example, the desire to trust a written text rather than the spoken word (Morpurgo Davies, 1986: 64) is found in a cuneiform Hittite text; and the use of 'word' division techniques such as empty spaces or special signs or dots marking a division is fairly widespread before the Greek era.[9] Meanwhile other scholars (e.g. Cross, 1980; Naveh, 1988) follow a slightly different tack, concentrating on the fact that the correlations are closer between the Greek letters and Canaanite script before 1000 BC than they are between the Greek alphabet and its usual cited source, the Phoenician script of the eighth century BC. This suggests that even Greek alphabetic writing pre-dates the usual date of its invention, *c.* 750 BC, by some two or three centuries. This emphasis on the range of alphabetic or near-alphabetic scripts in the ancient Near East helps, as Goody (1987: 40–41) argues, to counteract the 'over-emphasis, by classicists and others, on the addition of specific vowel sounds' as being the distinguishing characteristic of a true alphabet. In this approach, the discovery of parallels of all the Greek letter forms in much earlier Canaanite script, as has now been done in a Canaanite text dating to before 1000 BC (Goody, 1987: 47), offers a corrective to what is seen as an uncritical obsession with the glory of the Greek genius.

That, by reason of the ethnocentrism which logocentrism promotes, is a laudable goal. Yet on the one hand, this kind of counter-argument runs the risk of reinforcing the presupposition that there is a special virtue in the alphabet in itself, which is why that virtue is sought for these other scripts. Goody comes close to conceding this, for instance, when he notes that both in North Africa and the Near East, the Greek alphabet once invented 'quickly replaced earlier systems of logo-syllabic writing in a way that emphasizes its greater efficiency for many tasks' (Goody, 1987: 52). And on the other, it draws attention away from the great anomaly posed by assuming that pre-alphabetic writing was already itself 'intelligent': namely, that writing does not come into existence in the first place 'in itself and for itself'. Instead, its invention in Mesopotamia (*c.* 3200 BC) proves to be an afterthought and unintended consequence. For writing is the outcome of a prior practice of *accounting*.

The Medium is not the Message (1): The Invisible Genesis of Writing

We need now to dwell on these two anomalies. For only thus can we hope to overcome our cultural blindspot where the invisible technologies of learning are concerned. In so doing, we shall pursue Derrida's 'logic of the supplement' to the conclusion which he only adumbrates. Let me begin with the earlier problem, the manner of writing's initial invention.

Its derivation from accounting was first brought to public attention in the research of Denise Schmandt-Besserat (Schmandt-Besserat, 1978). She started from two apparently separate problems. First, why were there, in many sites from Egypt to Mesopotamia and extending over a time-period from around 9000 to 3000 BC, artefacts variously described by archaeologists as amulets, religious tokens, children's toys, etc., but generally conforming to a regular range of forms (spheres, disks, cones, ovoids, cylinders)? Second, why was the first known script, Sumerian cuneiform, written in the first instance on cylindrical 'clay tablets' (which is hardly, as she notes, the most obvious or convenient medium for writing)? Schmandt-Besserat saw a particular significance in the fact that the tokens were sometimes found in association with clay 'envelopes' in which they had apparently been enclosed, plus the fact that in some cases the envelopes bore marks where the tokens had been impressed in the soft clay before being sealed within them.

She proposed first that the 'tokens' were not amulets but had begun life (before the invention of writing) as a form of accounting. Second, the first clay 'tablets' are an evolved form of the earlier clay envelopes, which had begun as a means of encasing the tokens as a supplementary check on the accounting record (the envelopes being either carried with goods in transit or kept at the point of despatch as proof of the consignment). Thus thousands of years before writing, there was already, in a very simple form, accounting. But then a critical moment of transition comes (perhaps *c.* 3500 BC) when the tokens began to be pressed into the outside of the still-soft envelope. With this second supplementary check on the accuracy of the inventory, we have what we might call the genesis of the *accounting* sign. But still we do not as yet have writing.

The implication of Schmandt-Besserat's insight is clear. Already before writing we must in a certain sense have reading: the reading of the accounting signs impressed in the envelopes. Hence my apparently paradoxical claim that before there is writing there is reading. But the claim is not paradoxical at all. For from this new perspective, the 'invention' of writing becomes quite straight-forward, occurring when, in a discontinuous irreversible leap precisely like that made by every person ever since who has learned to read, the accounting signs suddenly become read in a new way, as equivalents or substitutes for what is said. The sense of paradox is illusory. The claim remains discomfiting only because we are so unused to acknowledging the hidden power of educational practice. Hence writing, but not as a leap of genius: instead, as a translation, unremarked and perhaps even unconscious, of simple pre-existing mundane practices. Far from being 'intelligent' in and of itself, writing comes in with a whimper, as the old accounting technology is simply adapted to a new purpose whose initial significance was secondary. The hidden catalyst? The overlooked invisible technology of reading. Thus the supplement to the supplement proves to be central, as the indispensible precondition to the supplement — that is, writing's invention.

Thus even here in the earliest moment of writing's history, we discover that the history of writing is also the history of education. But education's role here is a small thing compared with the central and determining part it plays in resolving the second of the great anomalies: the strangely-deferred invention of the culture of the Logos.

The Medium is not the Message (2): The Invention of Logocentrism

Logocentric culture, as Havelock has now quite definitely shown, does not begin with the invention of the visible technology of the alphabet. For it came about only when the power — a power which modern scholarship sees as always implicit in the alphabet — became explicit. It happened only when the Greeks interiorized a bias towards writing, and thus abandoned the 'phonocentric' thought-world of earlier elite Greek culture. That change, so Havelock's *Preface to Plato* first argued, took place only in the last third of the fifth century BC, with the first great exponent of the new literate, logocentric way of thinking being Plato himself.[10] But the intriguing question is why and how it happened then. What displaced the old oral bias of Greek culture? The answer to that question seems to be that it happened when and only when elite Greeks unlearned their attachment to the old oral 'noetic economy' by learning to learn under the invisible but pervasive power of the alphabetic method.

This conclusion, let me stress, is not mine but Havelock's, reached in a late reflection upon his whole life-work (Havelock, 1982). In this reflection, he sums up the whole series of his conclusions, reached as he says 'only slowly and reluctantly by the investigator himself' (Havelock, 1982: 185).

These conclusions are as follows: first, that the alphabet constitutes a special event in history 'the importance of which has not yet been fully grasped', because of the way that

> it became possible for the first time to document all possible forms of linguistic statement with fluency and to achieve fluent recognition, that is fluent reading ... on the part of a majority of any population. On this facility were built the foundations of those twin forms of knowledge: literature in the post-Greek sense and science, also in the post-Greek sense (Havelock, 1982: 185).

Second, however, 'the classical culture of the Greeks was already in existence', but on a nonliterate basis. This is what causes such problems: that culture remained dominant because down late into the fifth century the education of the elite remained phonocentric (as evidenced by its ancient name, *mousike*):

It consisted in the memorization of poetry, the improvisation of verse, the oral delivery of verse, the oral delivery of a prose rhetoric based on verse principles, performance on instruments ... and singing and dancing. For a long time after the invention of the alphabet letters were not included, and when they were first introduced they were treated as ancillary to memorisation (Havelock, 1982: 187).

Thus down to the late fifth century, Greek literature remains 'predominantly poetic' (even the philosophers Parmenides and Heraclitus and the law-giver Solon write in verse). As a result, the main users of the early alphabet are craftsmen and traders. But that poses problems for our subsequent logocentric way of thinking where 'the maximum of education is identified with the maximum of literacy' (Havelock, 1982: 189). For even though the vast majority of early inscriptions are the work of craftsmen, the significance of this fact tends to be ignored, as

> it is assumed *a fortiori* that the upper classes must have previously mastered this skill which had now filtered down to the artisan or conversely, that the artisan was not really an artisan but a very educated type (Havelock, 1982: 189).

Havelock, by resisting this cultural imperialism, has shown that the old oral education remains dominant until very late, thus keeping the elite from a systematic engagement with writing. He pays attention to what he calls the 'nuts and bolts of Greek education' (Havelock, 1982: 205 [n.4]) and shows how far earlier scholars, like their ancient counterparts who lived after the change in learning, have presumed that the practices they learned under must go back to or near the invention of the visible technology.

Yet the evidence of writing before *c.* 430 BC shows that overwhelmingly it remains a preserve of artisans (Havelock, 1982: 191–200). Within the literary sphere writing is only an *aide-memoire*, a genuine supplement enabling the preservation of the word of the author-poet, which is (a) orally composed and then (b) read aloud. Literary evidence concerning an interest in reading as a cultural activity (Havelock, 1982: 203–4) only appears after 430 BC, with the first references appearing in the plays of Euripides and Aristophanes. (He further notes that the Douros cup, dated to round 480 BC and usually taken to show young children at a reading and writing school, actually shows teenagers playing the lyre and reciting; the only reading is done by the teacher who recites from the text for the pupils to echo. Thus what has been taken as evidence of early 'literacy' is just more evidence for the longevity of the old education in *mousike* [Havelock, 1982: 201–3]).

So, how, according to Havelock, does the great shift into logocentrism take place? At the level of educational practice: 'A functioning literacy depends upon an elementary school curriculum designed to drill the small child in reading', he concludes (Havelock, 1982: 201). And the earliest date that can be reasonably assigned to this?

> Organized instruction in reading at the primary level, that is before the age of ten, cannot have been introduced into the Athenian schools much earlier than about 430 BC. It is described in Plato's *Protagoras*, written

in the early part of the next century, as by then standard practice, as it indeed had become by the time Plato grew up (Havelock, 1982: 187).

Why should this be such a dramatic and powerful change? We need only consider the 'nuts and bolts' of the ancient alphabetic method to see how it would re-shape patterns of thinking. It was the ultimate meaningless but analytically rigorous technique, and as such a total break with the whole structure of elite learning before this. It began by teaching the letters in alphabetic order, both forwards and backwards, then proceeded to demand that the learner theoretically learn every conceivable two-letter and three-letter syllabic combination in the language (in English, from BA to ZY and BAB to ZYZ). Only when there was perfect recognition of every syllabic combination did one move on to the level of the individual word. And lack of meaning continued to be a virtue. Thus learners were given long tongue-twisting combinations of nonsense-syllables known as 'bridles' (*chalinoi*), plus esoteric rare words to decipher. Then, finally, learners progressed to reading words in context as phrases and sentences.

The assumption was that 'perfect' deciphering of letters and syllables led inevitably to 'perfect' reading. But at the same time it promoted a new power of knowledge (and pedagogy). The learner was thrown totally into the control of the teacher who was the sole path to the rational and desired outcome, of being able to read the Logos. The new invisible technology of learning thus ruptured the old oral bias. For once it had become systematized and employed on the very young, it structured the way they learned from before they were able to resist, simultaneously offering the path to the new power of writing. Thus at this moment and not before, we enter the era of logocentrism.

In saying this, all that I am adding to Havelock's exemplary analysis is a heightened awareness of the power of educational practice: that just as the grammatocentric phase in logocentric culture begins with the introduction of written examinations and grading, so the first constitution of logocentrism begins with a similar but even more humble educational change, this new method of teaching reading. Here most decisively the history of education proves to be the history of writing.

We may see this in various coincidences. First, this is the time when the writing of the alphabet becomes regularized, with the establishment of the practice of writing it left to right, ending the earlier variations, with some writing it right to left or *boustrophedon* (first to the left and then to the right). This, as de Kerckhove (1988: 155–7) notes, is in itself an event of great cultural and psycho-physiological significance. For virtually all known syllabaries (including all Semitic scripts) are written right to left. Only the vocalic Greek alphabet reverses the direction of writing, and therefore, as is now hypothesized, the pattern of psycho-physiological processing of information. For right-to-left scripts are (Skoyles, 1988: 370–2) processed in the left visual field of both eyes which is more closely connected to right cortical hemisphere processing, usually taken to be the more holistic integrative side of the brain; while the alphabet read left-to-right is processed in the opposite way in the left so-called 'rational analytic' hemisphere.[11] But the crucial point, as de Kerckhove himself concedes, is that this regularization only happens in this late fifth century period. (The hold of this new standard is formally recognized in the legal adoption in Athens in 403/2 BC of the Ionian form of alphabet as the one official state alphabet, thus standardizing the Greek form which remains in use down to this day.) Thus again it is not due to the medium in itself.

But the ultimate and most significant proof of the central power of education lies in the focus of Havelock's work, Plato. For in Plato's logocentric philosophy, the whole alphabetic way of seeing is replicated. Like the alphabet, Plato's logocentrism builds things up from supposedly basic elements into meaningful wholes, passing from analysis to synthesis. And like the alphabet, this logocentric philosophy proves to be both powerful and (relatively) easily learned. It discovers a power to pass, on the wings of the alphabet, out from its Greek beginning until it too (along with its Aristotelian supplement) apparently colonizes the whole world.

But the connection is more intimate than that. For the Platonic ideas, it now becomes clear, are only a translation of the alphabet's power. For like the letters, as Ong (1982: 80) puts it:

> The Platonic ideas are voiceless, immobile, devoid of all warmth, not interactive but isolated, not part of the human lifeworld at all but utterly above and beyond it.

This is not the place to engage in a full rereading of all the passages where Plato has recourse to the letters of the alphabet in order to explain the nature of the world of Ideas. However, what we saw above in the *Phaedrus*, that Plato rejects writing only to reinstate it at the heart of his thinking, is a consistent theme in the dialogues. He frequently uses the letters as an example of the elementary constituents (the *stoicheia*) of a given unity: an art such as music, mathematics or art. But the letters prove to be more than just any example. As Derrida shows at great length in 'Plato's Pharmacy', they are a founding metaphor of Western philosophy, and perhaps even more than a metaphor. For Plato both loves and hates the *pharmakon* of writing. To distance its power, he frames it in mythic contexts, given to man by some demiurge (Thoth in *Phaedrus*, 1. 274 and *Philebus*, 1. 18, Prometheus or Palamedes elsewhere). He rejects it, as in the *Phaedrus*, but only to re-embrace it in a purified form, where he posits beyond the fallible physical letters the invisible true writing of the Logos which only the properly learned can grasp. Similarly, in the *Sophist*, (1. 253ff.) the problem of how unity and infinity can coexist is resolved through the example of the letters which take the infinity of voice and through their limited finite number reconcile that infinity with the unity of Logos. Again in the *Philebus*, (1. 15ff.) and *Politicus* (1. 278ff.), the letters are the 'example' explaining how the soul recognizes the elements (*stoicheia*) of everything. But by this time, Plato's punning ruse begins to become evident, for the letters themselves are also called by him the *stoicheia*. In other words, the example of the letters is not just any example: it is the *exemplar*, which hides the secret to the invisible structuring of the world which is the Logos.

'Perhaps Plato's "ideas" were the first "grammatology"'. Thus Ong (1982: 168) exposes the truth about the Platonic project. Nowhere is this clearer than in the great dialogue concerning the nature of the physical world, the *Timaeus*. Here we get the first modern approach to doing science, in the sense of looking beneath the surface of things for their underlying regularities. But the way it is done is wholly alphabetic. Thus Plato denies Earth, Air, Fire and Water, the four elements of earlier philosophy, any *elemental* status as *stoicheia* (*Timaeus*, 1. 48c). Indeed, 'they cannot even be reasonably compared to the syllables of nature', he says. Instead, beneath this phenomenal surface, the syllables of nature exist as regular solid figures, and in his ultimate reduction, the letters out of which the solids are formed are two kinds of right-angled triangle, the scalene and the isosceles. Here it is important to underline: Plato is not saying that the elements have triangular shapes; he is saying quite explicitly that they are triangular shapes, of just two kinds. Here in translated geometrical form, we have the vowels and consonants of nature. The homology is quite exact and deliberate.[12]

At the level of content this science is of course fanciful; yet in its presumption that the cosmos is ordered and that this order is discoverable, but always only beneath the visible surface and only by those who know how to read the invisible regularities aright, this Platonic approach is within a tradition that continues to today. And, as in the *Phaedrus*, Plato has discovered a grammatology — a *logos* of purified *grammata* — as the underlying principle of coherence in the world.

Thus indeed it is not Derrida who launches grammatology. It had existed from the beginning, and at the heart, of logocentric culture. This is where Derrida is wrong to treat Plato as a defender of the pure presence of voice. For Plato in all his philosophy never abandons writing to return to the pure world of speech. He is, instead, raising writing's power. For him, the whole world is grammatologically structured, from the cosmos to the human soul, where the true logos waits to be grammatologically written, though only in the soul of one who has learned to see beneath the false surface of things. Ironically, then, Derrida's attempt to see Plato as defender of speech over writing ultimately deconstructs itself in the most ignominious way, with the most basic form of mis-reading. For Derrida argues that 'in all these *comparisons* with writing, we are not supposed to take the letters *literally*'. But in proof of this strange conclusion he cites the passage from the *Timaeus* just mentioned, saying that Plato here warns us:

> The *stoikheia tou pantos*, the elements (or letters) of the whole are not assembled like syllables (48c). 'They cannot reasonably be compared by a man of sense even to syllables' (Derrida, 1981: 159).

But it is the four *visible* elements that are not even syllables in Plato's cosmology. Nothing deters Plato from discovering the true invisible letters and syllables of the cosmos beneath the surface.

That leaves one last question. Why, though, should this obsession with the letters, totally absent in earlier Greek thinking, be so marked in Plato? Havelock's analysis holds the key. Plato was born around 425 BC into an aristocratic Athenian family. He therefore was in the first generation of those who learned to learn under the new alphabetic method of teaching reading. Plato thus, through his learning as a child, grew up to become, in a quite specific sense, the first philosopher. Again before pure knowledge, there is power-knowledge. And the key to the great transition into logocentrism is educational practice.

The proof is there, under our noses, in the dialogues. For Plato bears the scars of the struggle and its humiliations. For instance, he recalls the problem of being a child, recognizing the letters in the easy syllables but then getting them wrong in harder ones (*Politicus*, l. 278A). The same memory of grinding struggle is there in the *Theaetetus* when Socrates tells Theaetetus to remember how he learned to read: how 'you went on and on learning nothing other than the letters' (*Theaetetus*, l. 206A); and the passage then continues (l. 207E) with Socrates saying: 'Do you forget what you yourself and all the others did in learning to read?' 'You mean how we thought first one letter then another belonged to a particular syllable and how we would put one particular letter first into the right syllable, then the wrong one?' 'That's what I mean.' 'Oh by Zeus I don't forget!'

But at the same time Plato had come through the trial. Ending up as the great Teacher of Philosophy, he then turned the power under which he had suffered to new greater purpose. The message in Platonic philosophy is quite clear: however painful is the acquisition of learning, there is only this one straight and narrow path to Truth, as this final passage (*Republic*, l. 402ff.) makes clear:

> Just as in learning to read, we were satisfied when we knew the letters of the alphabet ... in all their recurring sizes and combinations ... not thinking ourselves perfect in the art of reading until we recognize them wherever they are found ... so neither we nor our guardians can ever become 'musical' until we know the essential Forms of temperance, courage, and their kindred, as well as their opposites, in all their combinations and can recognize them and their images wherever they are found, whether in small form or large.

Conclusion: The Still-Invisible Technologies of Learning

Plato is thus the first grammatologist. But his 'logos of purified grammata' is not some pure expression of the power of writing-in-itself; instead, it underlines the supplementary power of educational practice. Indeed, his constant search for the invisible Logos suggests how central and strong was the hold over him of the invisible supplement to writing. At the heart of his philosophy is not pure writing, but the pure alphabetic method of deciphering the world.

The problem for all us literate citizens of the logocentric world who come after Plato is that none of us escape that self-same hold. For all the subsequent methods of teaching reading, however improved, humanized and psychologically aware, still derive from that ancient alphabetic method. Thus we all learn to learn under the same principles.

That suggests one final reflection. Perhaps it will prove too difficult to incorporate some such reflexive awareness of how we are structured by the power of educational practices into our understandings of writing's power. We have as yet little experience in how it might be done. But at the same time there are signs that we need in some way to attempt it, for we may be approaching the limits of the competence of older theories of literacy and learning. I offer just one example: the work of Scribner and Cole (1981), perhaps the most significant empirical study of the psychological effects of literacy in the past two decades. Here we have a study undertaken among a people, the Vai, who had three different scripts each with its own set of learning conditions: Vai writing learned informally, Arabic learned in the Koranic school, and English writing learned in Western-style schools. The outcome is well known: the acquisition of literacy as such did not create a great divide in modes of thinking amongst the Vai. Extended testing found that, on the contrary, it was the educational practices — that is, how people learned to learn — that made the significant difference.

To date, for most literacy researchers this result has been seen more as a problem than an opportunity. I suggest, on the contrary, that it is the most profound contemporary evidence for the continuing power of educational practice.

Notes

1 That reflection (Hoskin, 1981) began life as a review essay on Michael Clanchy's *From Memory to Written Record*, but then rapidly ran away with itself, turning into a general reflection on how from before the invention of the alphabet (i) forms of writing and (ii) the relations between power and knowledge are constantly shaped and occasionally transformed by the way in which humans learn, specifically focusing on the practices through which we learn *to* learn.

2 See in particular Bateson's chapter 'Social Planning and the Concept of Deutero-Learning'. Although he was not thinking along the precise lines followed here, he discusses 'learning to learn' as 'the sort of habit which is a by-product of the learning process' (Bateson, 1973: 138). He differentiates 'proto-learning' (typically the object of concern, in orthodox psychological experiment) from 'deutero-learning', drawing on the observation that 'the experimental subject — whether animal or man — becomes a better subject after repeated experiments. He not only learns to salivate at the appropriate moments, or to recite the appropriate nonsense syllables; he also, in some way, *learns to learn*' (Bateson, 1973: 140). In this analysis, he clearly has a more general concern along the lines developed here, i.e. that we need to turn towards understanding the power that our own modes of learning exercise over us. Thus he advances the possibility 'that "learning to learn" is a synonym for the acquisition of that class of abstract habits of thought ... which we call "free will", instrumental thinking, dominance, passivity, etc.' (Bateson, 1973: 140).

3 The Logos being seen as the guiding principle of Western Reason, embodied in such forms as philosophy, logic, science, technology and hermeneutics, but always referring back to its Greek root, where the term signifies, variously: the Word: Meaning: Sense: underlying Structure. In our logocentric culture, the Logos is what underlies our understanding of the world and our selves, preceding logic, science and the rest, as the guarantee of their being-thinkable.

4 Indeed I have argued (Hoskin, 1990) that Foucault himself should be seen as a 'crypto-educationist'. For he kept naming 'examination' as the technology which transforms the world and the self, from the early *Birth of the Clinic* through *Discipline and Punish* to the last works on the care of the Self, such as *Le Souci de Soi* (Hoskin, 1990: 34–40).

5 Concerning the academic disciplines, the introduction of the new micro-technologies is accompanied by the invention of new pedagogical arenas (the Seminar in Germany, the teaching Laboratory in France) where before 1800 a new way of knowing based on examining problems and writing up one's results is imposed on students: the results respectively are the invention of the hermeneutic study of philology and the lab-based experimental study of chemistry, biology, etc. (Hoskin, forthcoming). Concerning the professionalization of work, these students not only become expert under the new practices, they simultaneously gain a new form of academic credential and found the first modern professional

organizations (Hoskin, 1986: 8–14). Finally, it transpires that the two pioneers of modern managerialism in the US, which is where the modern business enterprise was invented (Chandler, 1977), were both graduates in 1819 of the US Military Academy at West Point. In 1817, Sylvanus Thayer as Academy Superintendent had introduced the educational practices of writing, grading and examination. The subsequent managerial innovations of the West Point graduates prove to be translations of these practices. The first known system of work accountability (developed following a time-and-motion study at the Springfield Armory in 1832) is based on examining, grading, and normalizing work performance; and the first line-and-staff management system, introduced on the Western Railroad in 1839, is based on Thayer's 'grammatocentric' management system for the Academy (Hoskin and Macve, 1988: 45–60).

6   This poses the question of what is writing. I follow Ong's view that writing is not just any semiotic mark, e.g. a notch on a stick, a score in a tree, a deposit of urine (as used by many species to mark territory); writing would then become co-terminous with all signing behaviour. Writing began 'when a coded system of visible marks was invented' such that 'encoded visible markings engage words fully so that ... structures and references evolved in sound can be visibly recorded' (Ong, 1982: 84–85).

7   There is a definitional problem haunting all discussions of the alphabet and its predecessors. For a term such as 'consonant' only makes sense under the assumption that the vowel has already been invented. So there is a certain anachronistic impossibility about referring to a 'consonantal alphabet' presumed to exist before the invention of the vocalic alphabet.

8   I reiterate again that what de Kerckhove describes as 'representation' is *a trace*; however, like the 'representation' produced by perspectival art, it is a accurate trace made possible only because of the introduction of the zero point: the consonant for the alphabet, the vanishing point for geometrical perspective.

9   'Word' itself is a problematic concept in this context: what is being marked off is a perceived 'sense' division, which may be a meaning or sound, i.e. at the level of the syllable or of several 'words'.

10   For those who wish to push the invention of the alphabet back from around 750 BC to around 1100 BC or earlier, this poses a particularly acute version of the problem caused by fixating on the visible technology. Why this extraordinarily lengthy lag?

11   This is not the place to enter the left-right hemisphere debate except to note that the analysis here suggests that if there is a relation between left-hemisphere processing and rational analytic thinking, this is not necessarily *physiologically* determined. We must again factor into our modern psychological understandings the influence of systems of learning to learn, in particular the overlooked role of the alphabetic methods of teaching reading still adopted world-wide.

12   In this system, earth is the cube, water the icosahedron, air the octahedron, and fire the tetrahedron. And these 'letters' are written on the 'paper' of the world, the invisible receptacle or womb (*hypodochen*) within which the physical forms of the Logos are inscribed (*Timaeus*, 1.48–53). Also, the transmutation of elements to form specific bodies takes place only on the alphabetic principle, by the recombination of combinations of triangles (ll.56c–57c).

References

BATESON, G. (1973) *Steps to an Ecology of Mind*, London, Paladin.

CHANDLER, A. (1977) *The Visible Hand: The Managerial Revolution in American Business*, Cambridge, MA, Harvard University Press.

CLANCHY, M. (1979) *From Memory to Written Record*, London, Arnold.

CROSS, F. (1980) 'Newly Found Inscriptions in Old Canaanite and Early Phoenician Script', *Bulletin of the American Schools of Oriental Research*, **238**, pp. 1–20.

DE KERCKHOVE, D. (1988) 'Logical Principles Underlying the Layout of Greek Orthography', in DE KERCKHOVE, D. and LUMSDEN, C. (Eds) *The Alphabet and the Brain: The Lateralization of Writing*, Berlin, Springer-Verlag, pp. 153–72.

DERRIDA, J. (1976) *Of Grammatology*, translated by G. Spivak, Baltimore, Johns Hopkins.

DERRIDA, J. (1981) 'Plato's Pharmacy', *Dissemination*, translated by B. Johnson, Chicago, University of Chicago Press.

FOUCAULT, M. (1977) *Discipline and Punish*, London, Allen Lane.

GOODY, J. (1977) *The Domestication of the Savage Mind*, Cambridge, Cambridge University Press.

GOODY, J. (1986) *The Logic of Writing and the Organization of Society*, Cambridge, Cambridge University Press.

GOODY, J. (1987) *The Interface between the Oral and the Written*, Cambridge, Cambridge University Press.

GOODY, J. and WATT, I. (1963) 'The Consequences of Literacy', *Comparative Studies in Society and History*, **5**, pp. 304–45.

HAVELOCK, E. (1963) *Preface to Plato*, Cambridge, MA, Belknap Press.

HAVELOCK, E. (1975) *Origins of Western Literacy*, Toronto, OISE.

HAVELOCK, E. (1982) 'The Preliteracy of the Greeks', in HAVELOCK, E. *The Literate Revolution in Greece and its Cultural Consequences*, Princeton, Princeton University Press, pp. 185–207.

HOSKIN, K. (1979) 'The Examination, Disciplinary Power and Rational Schooling', *History of Education*, **8**, 2, pp. 135–46.

HOSKIN, K. (1981) 'The History of Education and the History of Writing', unpublished Paper, University of Warwick, Coventry, England.

HOSKIN, K. (1985) '*Verbum de Verbo*: The Perennial Changing Paradox of Translation', in HERMANS, T. (Ed.) *Second Hand: Papers on the Theory and Historical Study of Translation*, Antwerp, ALW Cahiers, No. 3, pp. 10–45.

HOSKIN, K. (1986) 'The Professional in Educational History', in WILKES, J. (Ed.) *The Professional Teacher*, London, History of Education Society, pp. 19–28.

HOSKIN, K. (1990) 'Foucault under Examination: The Crypto-Educationist Unmasked', in BALL, S. (Ed.) *Foucault and Education*, London, Routledge, pp. 29–53.

HOSKIN, K. (forthcoming) 'Education and the Genesis of Disciplinarity: The Unexpected Reversal', in MESSER-DAVIDOW, E. *et al.* (Eds) *Knowledges: Historical and Critical Studies in Disciplinarity*, Charlottesville, VA, University of Virginia Press.

HOSKIN, K. and MACVE, R. (1986) 'Accounting and the Examination: A Genealogy of Disciplinary Power', *Accounting, Organizations and Society*, **11**, 2, pp. 105–36.

HOSKIN, K. and MACVE, R. (1988) 'The Genesis of Accountability: The West Point Connections', *Accounting, Organizations and Society*, **13**, 1, pp. 37–73.

MCLUHAN, M. (1964) *Understanding Media: The Extensions of Man*, London, Routledge and Kegan Paul.

MORPURGO DAVIES, A. (1986) 'Forms of Writing in the Ancient Mediterranean World', in BAUMANN, G. (Ed.) *The Written Word: Literacy in Transition*, Oxford, Clarendon Press, pp. 51–77.

NAVEH, J. (1988) 'The Origin of the Greek Alphabet', in DE KERCKHOVE, D. and LUMSDEN, C. (Eds) *The Alphabet and the Brain: The Lateralization of Writing*, Berlin, Springer-Verlag, pp. 84–91.

OLSON, D. (1988) 'The Origin of the Greek Alphabet', in DE KERCKHOVE, D. and LUMSDEN, C. (Eds) *The Alphabet and the Brain: The Lateralization of Writing*, Berlin, Springer-Verlag, pp. 422–41.

ONG, W. (1982) *Orality and Literacy*, London, Methuen.

SCHMANDT-BESSERAT, D. (1978) 'The Earliest Precursors of Writing', *Scientific American*, **238**, pp. 38–47.

SCRIBNER, S. and COLE, M. (1981) *The Psychology of Literacy*, Princeton, Princeton University Press.

SKOYLES, J. (1988) 'Right Hemisphere Literacy in the Ancient World', in DE KERCKHOVE, O. and LUMSDEN, C. (Eds) *The Alphabet and the Brain: The Lateralization of Writing*, Berlin, Springer-Verlag, pp. 362–80.

Chapter 3

Texts, Literacy and Schooling

David Hamilton

Near the University of Liverpool there is a small public library that was built in the nineteenth century. Above its entrance — clearly visible from the road — is the claim that 'reading maketh the full man, conference a ready man, and writing an exact man'. These are the words of Francis Bacon (1561–1627), one of the pioneers of the Scientific Revolution.

Bacon's writings and eloquence were remembered for many years. In Liverpool, for instance, their impact can be discerned in a variety of educational institutions. Besides influencing the municipal library committee, Baconian references to the 'advancement of learning' and 'knowledge is power' were used, respectively, in the University's mission statement of 1892, and in the foundation of another local citadel of adult and higher learning: the Liverpool Mechanics Institute (opened 1825).

If these quotations and institutions are representative, nineteenth-century celebration of Bacon's writings focused upon two notions: the informed, em-powered citizen and the learning, progressing society. In turn, these visions of popular literacy underwrote a political agenda for the 'relief of man's estate' — a phrase from Bacon's *Novum Organum* (1620). Further, these Baconian ideas about literacy and emancipation were also caught up with debates about the reform of schooling (see, for instance, Simon, 1960, *passim*).

Two hundred years earlier, however, Bacon's ideas had surfaced in a differ-ent ideological context, one that was more theological than political. To his con-temporaries, Bacon projected a protestant, even millenial, view of learning and literacy (see, for instance, Webster, 1975). The advancement of learning would rescue humankind from the biblical Fall and take it to another spiritual home, a 'New Jerusalem' (Cohn, 1970: 24) just beyond the historical horizon. In the seven-teenth century, therefore, the dissemination of literacy was a harbinger of human salvation, not a lever of human progress.

The seventeenth-century links between salvation, progress and the advance-ment of learning are also evident in John Bunyan's adventure story *The Pilgrim's Progress* (1678). Called by God, Christian (the eponymous pilgrim) leaves his home in the 'City of Destruction' and survives a series of challenging encounters while passing through the 'Slough of Despond', the 'Valley of Humiliation' and the distractions of 'Vanity Fair'. Morally re-educated by his adventures, Christian eventually reaches the 'Celestial City'.

As suggested, Bunyan and Bacon espoused comparable views. Yet, Bunyan's allegory is also historically significant insofar as it conflates two senses of progress. Not only did Christian progress (compare proceed) on his worldly journey, he simultaneously progressed to a better world (namely the 'other side'). Indeed, the juxtaposition of these contrasting models of progress has been described by Christopher Hill as 'rather unusual in the seventeenth century'. Progress did not usually denote spatial or linear displacement. Instead, it related to circular journeys — as when royal households progressed around a kingdom, collecting hospitality and taxes.

Hill also identifies another anomalous feature of Christian's progress. Succeeding episodes in *The Pilgrim's Progress* are 'not necessarily sequential, nor is there a steady advance across country'. To accommodate this 'mystical' feature of Bunyan's book, Hill suggests that Christian's peregrinations were 'psychological, not geographical'. The landscape of *The Pilgrim's Progress* reflected, that is, the 'inner state' of its hero (Hill, 1989: 222).

From the seventeenth to the nineteenth centuries, large numbers of human beings embarked upon a series of post-Baconian pilgrimages. Armed with new tools (for example, literacy), motivated by new faiths (or inner states) and guided by new pathways (for example, schooling), they drove themselves towards spiritual salvation in the seventeenth century and/or secular progress in the nineteenth century. In these terms, then, the sixteenth-century Reformation, the Scientific Revolution, and the Industrial Revolution can be regarded in the same light. They were successive landmarks on the same millenial highway.

Post-Reformation attitudes to literacy, religion and progress were widely translated into social practices. These practices did not just happen. Typically, they were structured, channelled and regulated along church- or state-prescribed pathways (see, for instance, Tawney, 1942 and Oestreich, 1982). In fact, sixteenth-century literacy is remembered simply because it took place alongside a seemingly contradictory development: the 'revolution in ... self instruction' (J. Simon, 1966: 56) facilitated by the post-Gutenberg multiplication of printed books. It is no accident, for instance, that the *Index Librorum Prohibitorum* was first issued by Pope Paul IV in 1557, and that from 1538 all printed works in England had to be approved by the Privy Council of the Crown (Davies, 1973: 108; see also Morgan, 1986, chs. 3 and 4). Thus, the channelling associated with socially-approved texts took placed within a much wider arena — a readership of non-approved texts, itself conjoined with adherents to non-approved interpretations of approved texts (see, for instance, Dickens, 1976).

The remainder of this chapter examines schooling and the structuring and channelling of literacy. Using evidence drawn from the twelfth to the seventeenth centuries, it focuses upon three developments: (1) the emergence of 'instruction' as a key activity in educational practice; (2) the emergence of 'textbooks' as instruments of teaching and learning; and (3) the emergence of curriculum thinking as an instrument for steering teaching and learning (i.e. the idea of 'curriculum' itself).

The Historical Record: A Cautionary Interjection

The historical record of educational ideas, institutions and practices has a complexity that renders it both under-used and ill-used. Two established historians,

Anthony Grafton and Lisa Jardine, have observed that 'until quite recently' the historical literature on education was 'composed by antiquaries, purchased by retired historians, and read by almost nobody'. Such work, they conclude, was tackled at 'too primitive a level' to capture the interests of professional historians (Grafton and Jardine, 1986: xi). Like a range of similar commentators (e.g. Bailyn, 1960; Silver, 1977; B. Simon, 1966; Withrington, 1970), Grafton and Jardine imply that educationists have misread and misconstrued the educational record, often for similar reasons.

One recurrent difficulty, for instance, arises whenever the historical record is scrutinized from the standpoint of present-day logic. Reformation manifestos may, indeed, have proposed that all children should attend school, but it does not necessarily follow that all children attended the same type of school. Likewise, 'presentism' may lead to the conflation of two logically and historically-distinct phenomena: school enrolment and school attendance. And, twentieth-century assumptions may misdirect attention whenever it is assumed that children always attended school throughout the calendar years. In fact, enrolment and attendance may have been organized around different units of time (e.g. quarters).

A second chronic problem arises if educationists rely unilaterally on second-ary sources. This problem is further exacerbated whenever secondary sources take the form of translations. With respect to sixteenth- and seventeenth-century educational history, for instance, relevant primary and secondary sources may be written in French, German, Italian or Latin (see, for example, the first eight pages of Grafton and Jardine 1986). All translations, therefore, should be handled with due — and, as important, duly-acknowledged — caution. And it should also be recognized that even seemingly 'original' sources may have suffered at the hands of subsequent editors and typesetters, as I indicate later in this chapter.

A third historiographic problem arises whenever educationists address the historical record with their arguments already intact. In such cases, historical evidence is used to illustrate rather than to test theoretical propositions. Sources are plundered merely for supportive evidence. The resultant analyses are not so much woven, as warped.

A final historiographic difficulty is that secondary accounts often mask the complexity — or messiness — of the historical record. They project an unwar-ranted neatness and cleanliness that, in fact, undervalues the cultural diversity, political uncertainty and social turbulence that suffuse the historical record. It must always be remembered — when reading this chapter or any other — that an educationist's desire to construct a persuasive argument may rest uneasily with an historian's commitment to communicate a plausible argument.

Teaching, Learning, Instruction and Didactics

In 'Toward a Place for Study in the World of Instruction', Robert McLintock (1971) focused attention on the educational concept of 'study'. His thesis was that, before the sixteenth century, educational thought was driven more by assumptions about 'study' than by assumptions about 'teaching'. He suggests, for instance, that the task of classical teachers was merely to excite the learning desires of their charges:

[T]he Socrates of historic influence, the hero of early dialogues, depicted himself explicitly as the spiritual midwife, the teacher who could not teach but who could help another give birth to his soul; Plato immortalized this Socrates as the Delphic martyr, the inspiring questioner who provoked others to know that they did not know and thus to join the thoughtful search for self (McLintock, 1971: 169).

McLintock also suggests that important medieval theorists advanced a similar view of learning. Thus, the disciplines of the Liberal Arts were held to be liberating insofar as they served as a preparation for subsequent self-(i.e. teacher-free)study. McLintock notes, for instance, that John of Salisbury (*c.* 1115–1180) — eventually Bishop of Chartres — commented that:

Those to whom the system of the Trivium has disclosed the significance of all words, or the rules of the Quadrivium have unveiled the secrets of all nature, do not need the help of a teacher in order to understand the meaning of books and to find the solutions of questions (quoted in McLintock, 1971: 174).

Further, McLintock includes Erasmus and the Jesuits within the same framework. Desiderius Erasmus (1466–1536), he suggests, wrote such works as the *Colloquies, Adages*, and *De Copia* speaking directly to the learner. The 1524 edition of the *Colloquies*, for instance, was dedicated to John Erasmius Froben, a 'boy of excellent promise' who, with its assistance, might become a 'better latin scholar' and a 'better man' (Erasmus, 1900: xi). Thus, early educational texts typically projected states of intellectual and moral virtue that, presumably, learners were intended to emulate and internalize.

For McLintock, too, the *Ratio Studiorum* (1599) of the Jesuits included 'almost nothing' about instruction, merely incorporating assessment procedures (e.g. verbal disputations) that enabled teachers to monitor the self-instruction of their charges. 'In the Jesuit system, and most systems of education well into the Enlightenment', McLintock concludes, 'the moving force was the student, and the teacher's function was not to instruct, but to initiate, discipline and moderate that youthful energy' (McLintock, 1971: 176–7).

McLintock's selection of evidence undoubtedly reflects his admiration for Platonic and Socratic educational practice. At the same time, however, he acknowledges his predilections. He is careful to admit, for instance, that 'instruction and study at all times co-exist' (McLintock, 1971: 170). He still concludes, however, that:

[T]o a remarkable degree the trivial teachers of the Middle Ages and the Renaissance agreed with Plato that their job was not 'to put knowledge into a soul which does not possess it'; rather, they simply directed, disciplined, and exercised the inborn organ of learning possessed by every man (sic) (McLintock, 1971: 174).

By the seventeenth century, however, change was under way. According to McLintock (1971: 177) 'religious, political, social, economic, [and] humanitarian pressures' began to mount upon the schools. A 'new tendency' (McLintock, 1971:

178) arose. Schools became sites of instruction, not learning. And the leading proponent of this tendency was Jan Amos Comenius (1592–1670). According to McLintock (1971: 178), 'Comenius cared nought for study'. His alternative educational credo, blazoned on the title page of *The Great Didactic* (1632), was that 'all things' could be taught to 'all men' (see also Hamilton, 1987a). In short, McLintock (1971: 179) laments that from Comenius onwards, 'teaching ... won precedence from study'.

The empirical validity (or generalizability) of McLintock's provocative claim rests upon an important assumption: that Platonic notions dominated educational theory and practice until the seventeenth century. This proposition is difficult to evaluate. Nevertheless, McLintock's thesis resonates with claims about the emergence of modern forms of schooling (see, for instance, Hamilton, 1989, 1990a and Maynes, 1985). Accordingly, the emergence of 'instruction' (McLintock's term) or 'didactics' (its mainland European equivalent) was closely associated with pedagogic reforms that, in effect, created modern schooling.

Combining these propositions about pedagogy and schooling, two further claims can be made about educational practice before the seventeenth century. First, that it focused upon circumstances to promote *learning* rather than upon structures to enact *teaching*. And second, that children were shaped by *texts* — written or spoken — rather than by school-based didactic instruction. In an important sense, therefore, the shaping of texts preceded the shaping of children.

Schoolbooks and Textbooks

Arguments about the shaping and reshaping of texts are included in McLintock's analysis of teaching and learning. He characterizes Erasmus, for instance, as the 'first tycoon of the text' and the 'exemplary editor of all time' (McLintock, 1971: 162–3). Erasmus, therefore, was a transposer as much as a transmitter of texts. 'Little of Erasmus' work was original', McLintock adds:

> It turned the seeds of others into fruit: he transformed the oral medieval tradition, the newly dynamic classical literature, and even the consecrated work of the Church; he adapted all for publication, each as befit the type, revising, translating, reorganizing, elucidating, collating, emending, correcting, perfecting — in sum, preparing the texts for profitable study by a growing reading public (McLintock, 1971: 163).

Much editorial tinkering by Renaissance authors like Erasmus is unacknowledged and, as a result, relatively invisible. Its extent was probably far greater than is popularly imagined. Such editorial discretion, however, has operated for centuries, which is why, for instance, translations of Aristotle are currently characterized as 'inexact' (Barnes, 1976: 14). Indeed, many of Aristotle's works reached European universities already extensively edited, having passed through intermediate translations in Syrian, Persian, Hebrew and Arabic (see Pieper, 1964: 104–6).

By the end of the sixteenth century, however, the invisible hand of editors like Erasmus was joined by editorial styles of the 'new tendency'. Texts were gradually reorganized — particularly with regard to layout and typography — to conform with the exigencies of instruction rather than study (see, for instance, Hebrard, 1983).

Yet even these post-Gutenberg editorial developments had been fore-shadowed in earlier reorganizations of manuscript books. A key source on medieval textual organization is *Preachers, Florilegia and Sermons* (1978) by Richard and Mary Rouse. Volumes of reading materials ('florilegia') are the focus of their study. According to the Rouses, the *Manipulus Florum* (i.e. florilegium) of Thomas of Ireland was one of the earliest 'alphabetically-arranged' and 'search-able' texts. Florilegia of this sophistication, they claim, were 'unknown in clas-sical Antiquity' but appeared in a 'veritable flood' between 1220 and 1306 and became 'commonplace' after the 1280s (Rouse and Rouse, 1978: 3–4).

What, then, were the early circumstances that evoked such bibliographic in-novation? The Rouses suggest that the new florilegia appeared because they met a 'pressing need', itself associated with a new 'institutional framework' adopted by the Church (Rouse and Rouse, 1978: 5). The Church, that is, began to divert its attention away from monastic forms of life towards new practices of pastoral work and preaching (see also Hamilton, 1989: 13–15; Knowles, 1962, chapters 13–15; and Stock, 1983, *passim*).

Most of the textual tools prominent by the twelfth century echoed monastic practice, supporting private study. *Concordances* and *Distinctions*, for instance, enabled students to identify, respectively, the textual locations and figurative meanings of biblical terms. *Indexes* also existed in the twelfth century; but topics were often arranged non-alphabetically and clustered according to their subject matter. Alphabetic indexes, however, began to appear in the middle of the thirteenth century, many derived from the reorganization of *Concordances*.

But why were such texts rendered searchable? As noted, religious texts had originally been designed for spiritual reading. They contained words and phrases 'to turn over frequently in one's heart' (quoted in Rouse and Rouse, 1978: 41). Yet, by the thirteenth century, books also began to be designed for preaching (instruction). For the clergy, then, study was to be combined with preaching — a juxtaposition also reflected in Hugh of St Cher's aphorism 'first the bow is bent in study, then the arrow is released in preaching' (quoted in Rouse and Rouse, 1978: 41). Bolstered with the fruits of text-searching, preaching was intended to capture — or recapture — the faithful for God. Political investment in preaching, there-fore, encouraged the recasting of texts to serve new instrumental goals. Florilegia were not so much storehouses of spiritual ideas as armouries of the theological ammunition.

From at least the thirteenth century, then, the invisible editing of texts was widely influenced by social and political considerations. Such purposive editing, for instance, shaped the medieval trivium and quadrivium (the 'seven liberal arts'). By studying the liberal arts through designated texts — discussed, vari-ously, in Knowles (1962), Piltz (1981) and Wagner (1983) — students reshaped them-selves and, in the process, accumulated further social, political and civic capital.

The liberal arts, that is, were explicitly skill-based — the Latin word for 'art' is equivalent to the Greek word for 'technique'. Indeed, as the social valuation of these skills changed, so did the texts. The liberal arts, therefore, were competence-driven rather than text-driven. The labels attached to the arts may have remained constant over the centuries, but the choice of texts and the varia-bility of associated commentaries were considerable. By the beginning of the sixteenth century, then, such textual diversity was a long way from the coherence and uniformity of church- or state-prescribed pathways.

Indeed, Ong has observed that 'there was almost as many [sixteenth-century] explanations of what dialectic was ... as there were masters at Paris, (Ong, 1958: 63). And Grafton and Jardine make an equivalent point. Early humanists, they suggest, often focused their attention upon specific commentators and their commentaries, leading to an 'individualism' that verged on 'hero-worship' (Grafton and Jardine, 1986: 123). Within decades, however, the conspectus of these names was broadened. They became attached to 'entire sets of pedagogic and ideological commitments', and were labelled as the 'Erasmian method' or the 'Agricolan dialectic' (Grafton and Jardine, 1986: 122).

In these early decades of the sixteenth century, however, Grafton and Jardine suggest that the 'reverence' enjoyed by these key figures, together with the associated 'urge to organize humanistic teaching', encountered a major difficulty. The creation of a 'generalized humanist curriculum' was, they claim, vitiated by a 'clear understanding that the problem [was] the absence of a structured programme' (Grafton and Jardine, 1986: 123–4).

Grafton and Jardine's interest in structured programmes is acknowledged in the title of their book: *From Humanism to the Humanities*. They seek to demonstrate that between 1450 and 1650 individualistic humanism was recast in the organizational and normative structures of the humanities curriculum. Early humanism, that is, gave way to 'Christian' humanism (Grafton and Jardine, 1986: 122), itself based on 'an ideology of routine, order and, above all, "method"' (Grafton and Jardine, 1986: 123). According to the subtitle of their sixth chapter, the fundamental shift was 'from teachers to textbooks'.

The transformation of humanism into the humanities, and the associated attention to order and method were also, I suggest, linked to two other related developments: (1) the reorganization of texts to conform with the 'natural order' of things; and (2) the emergence of the term 'curriculum'.

Curriculum and the Natural Order

The harmonization of texts with the natural order of things was a major new development in the history of knowledge. Whereas the Rouses report the adumbration, indexing and cataloguing of knowledge in the twelfth century, Grafton and Jardine prefigure a new intellectual activity: the mapping of knowledge.

Cartographic conceptions of the natural order were central, for instance, to the creation of encyclopedia in the latter half of the sixteenth century (Fischer, 1966: 278–9). One of the 'most popular' encyclopedic ('encircling') works was Sebastian Munster's *Cosmography*, first published in 1544 (Strauss, 1966: 145). Early editions of the *Cosmography* were originally organized, in Munster's words, around 'a tour from country to country and across the oceans', with each account duly embroidered with 'cities, mountains, rivers, deserts ... and customs and ways and activities of strange peoples' (quoted in Strauss, 1966: 152).

Gradually, however, the editors of cosmographic compendia — including Munster's — abandoned geographic organizational principles. Instead, they began to follow logical, rational or natural principles. Through these new projections of knowledge, the clustering rules of compendia became the topographic principles of encyclopedia. According to Strauss:

Clarity and logic of organization, the disposition of matter on the printed page, became, in fact, a preoccupation of editors, almost an end in itself. It is a phenomenon familiar to a student of encyclopedic books of the late sixteenth century, related to the increased fascination with the technical possibilities of typesetting and the great influence exerted by the methodology of Peter Ramus on the accumulation and distribution of knowledge (Strauss, 1966: 152).

In the sixteenth century, too, notions about the natural order (or disposition) of knowledge seemed to have become linked to the concept of 'curriculum'. Indeed, the curriculum concept served as a conceptual bridge between the ordering or methodizing movement described by Grafton and Jardine, and the instructional basis of schooling identified by McLintock. Moreover, indeed, Grafton and Jardine also point directly to a connection between the ordering of teaching and the paraphernalia of schooling:

> 'Method' was the catchword of promoters of humanist education from the 1510s onwards. The practical emphasis on procedure signals a shift in intellectual focus on the part of pedagogic reformers, from the ideal end product of a classical education (the perfect orator ...) to the classroom aids (textbooks, manuals and teaching drills) which would compartmentalize the *bonae litterae* and reduce them to system (Grafton and Jardine, 1986: 124).

Despite the central argument of *From Humanism to the Humanities*, Grafton and Jardine fail to connect 'structured programme' with 'curriculum'. Nevertheless, the hypothesis that sixteenth-century changes in the conception of method and order served as the forcing house of the curriculum idea also receives support in Walter Ong's (1958) *Ramus, Method and the Decay of Dialogue*. For instance, three of Ong's translations seem to shadow the emergence of the curriculum idea. First, note the juxtaposition of 'collection of propositions' (a late medieval notion) and 'method' (a Renaissance idea) that occurs in the 1539 observation of John Sturm, founder of the Strasburg Gymnasium:

> An art is an abundant collection of propositions. But in setting up the various arts a certain, short and direct way, a kind of short cut, has to be used. This the Greeks call method and teaching procedure, such as may be used for teaching and communication (Ong, 1958: 232–3; quotation abridged).

Second, the founder of the Lutheran Gymnasium of Nuremburg, Philip Melanchthon, links methodizing and ordering in *Questions of Dialectic* (first edition 1547):

> Method is a habit, that is, a science or an art, which finds and opens a way through overgrown and impenetrable places and pulls out and ranges in order the things pertaining to the matter proposed (Ong, 1958: 237; quotation abridged)

Finally, the relationship between method and the natural ordering of knowledge is celebrated by Peter Ramus (1515?–1567), a Paris professor and former student of John Sturm. 'Method', Ramus proposes in the 1569 edition of his *Dialectic*:

> is deposition by which that enunciation is placed first which is first in the absolute order of knowledge, that next which is next, and so on: and thus there is an unbroken progression from universals to singulars (Ong, 1958: 249; quotation abridged).

Despite these data, Ong's analysis is as anomalous as Grafton and Jardine's. None of these authors notes the emergence of the word 'curriculum'. And recent analyses by Patricia Rief and Sheldon Wolin are similarly silent, despite their equivalent views on method and pedagogy:

> If one were to select a single epithet to describe the educational atmosphere of the early seventeenth century, it would be 'methodical'. In this period the intense interest in method which prevailed throughout the sixteenth century seems to have reached its peak. There are numerous treatises on method in general, books of all sorts frequently contained the word 'method' in their titles, and textbook authors advertised their wares as 'methodically presented' or *'arranged in methodological order'* ... But the method on which they insist has little, if any, connection with scientific method as we understand it. It is fundamentally a pedagogical method, the method by which all curricular disciplines are taught (Reif, 1969: 28; emphasis added).

And:

> One way to get at the idea of method is to recognise that it has a history reaching back to ancient Greek philosophy. Like *philosophia, methodus* was often used in association with the notion of a 'way' (aporie) to truth. Before long, *methodus* and *philosophia* began to diverge. Generally speaking, while *philosophia* and its sister, *theoria*, tended to stress the arduous difficulties awaiting those who sought truth, the devotees of *methodus* began to emphasize the economy of being methodical, that is of faithfully following a prescribed sequence of mental steps, a 'straight road' in Descartes' phrase. The old metaphor of the 'way' was subtly altered and became associated with the advantages of adhering to a beaten path rather than 'blazing' a trail. A premonition of this change appeared in the Middle Ages when *methodus* tended to acquire the connotation of a 'shortcut'. It found popular expression in numerous attempts to compose *compendia* on various subjects (Wolin, 1973: 32–3).

Overall, then, there is strong circumstantial evidence that the curriculum concept emerged and took root in a fertile and supportive environment. But why the silence of such noted neo-Latin scholars as Ong, Grafton and Jardine? Was the term absent before that time? Or is it absent because no one has looked for it?

The earliest reported use of the term 'curriculum' (see Hamilton, 1989) appears in the *Professio Regia* (1576), a compilation of Ramist 'arts', usually attributed to Peter Ramus but produced after Ramus' death by a Protestant printer/publisher, Thomas Fregius of Basel. In pedagogic terms, the Ramist method comprised the clustering of related commonplaces along the lines, quite literally, of a branching taxonomy. Pedagogically, these taxonomies provided teachers with a series of procedural templates (or route maps) to steer their teaching from topic to topic, that is, from 'universals to singulars'. In the late sixteenth century, therefore, Ramus and his followers filled the lacuna — the missing 'structured programme' — identified by Grafton and Jardine. In short, Ramist notions brought a new order to teacher-led instruction and schooling.

Indeed, Ramus' contribution to schooling was probably no less significant than Comenius'. Echoing McLintock, for instance, McLean has observed that the Ramist corpus of writings was 'principally to do with schools, and much less to do with scholars'. Further, McLean also identifies a possible direct connection between Ramism, schooling and textbooks:

> It seems also legitimate to inquire whether editions [of Ramus] ... represent timeless scholarship or ephemeral textbooks, and whether the constant revisions they underwent are less the trace of a generation of indefatigable scholars in pursuit of truth than the sign of a teaching profession justifying its existence and fostering the economic machine of publishing at the same time (McLean, 1990: 262; see also Sharratt, 1987).

Whither Curriculum?

This chapter is an essay on the material and historical context of literacy, curriculum and schooling. It begins with the premise that the literature of schooling is functionally related to the schooling of literacy — even if the full extent and force of this functional relationship is not fully understood.

During the sixteenth and seventeenth centuries, assumptions that the world was an ordered place, and that the elements of the world of knowledge were topologically invariant, brought an absolutism to schooling that, in varying degrees, has survived for more than 300 years (e.g. the survival of subject-based curricula). And, at the centre of this cosmology stood a normative notion of curriculum, fashioned by Ramists and disseminated by Comenius and his followers. In turn, such curriculum thinking and its hegemonic symbolic order of, among other things, 'subjects' and 'sequences' has shaped the common sense of schooling.

Yet, in the twentieth century, the curriculum worldview has come under critical scrutiny. Most notably, absolutism has been questioned (e.g. Hamilton, 1987b, 1990b). Does such scrutiny foreshadow a 'post-structuralist', 'post-curriculum' epoch — an educational era with neither universally-accepted maps of knowledge nor univariant, sequential models of learners and learning?

'What shall we teach them?' and 'How shall we teach them?' are no less problematic for us than they were when Herbert Spencer asked his classical curriculum question, 'What knowledge is of most worth?', in 1859. Spencer, however, answered his own question, to the extent that popular literacy should be strengthened through the schoolteaching of 'science'. But what kind of science and what kind of literacy are appropriate to schooling in the twenty-first century?

References

BAILYN, B. (1960) *Education in the Forming of American Society: Needs and Opportunities for Study* (1972 reprint), New York, Norton.

BARNES, J. (1976) 'Introduction', *The Ethics of Aristotle*, Harmondsworth, Penguin.

COHN, N. (1970) *The Pursuit of the Millenium: Revolutionary Millenarians and Mystical Anarchists of the Middle Ages*, New York, Oxford University Press.

COMENIUS (1632) *The Great Didactic*, (1896 reprint), London, Adam and Charles Black.

DAVIES, F. (1973) *Teaching Reading in Early England*, London, Pitman.

DICKENS, A.G. (1976) *The German Nation and Martin Luther*, London, Fontana.

ERASMUS, D. (1900) *Colloquies Concerning Men, Manners and Things*, translated by N. Bailey, London, Gibbings.

FISCHER, H. (1966) 'Conrad Gessner (1516–1565) as Bibliographer and Encyclopedist', *The Library*, **21**, pp. 269–81.

GRAFTON, A. and JARDINE, L. (1986) *From Humanism to the Humanities: Education and the Liberal Arts in Fifteenth- and Sixteenth-Century Europe*, London, Duckworth.

HAMILTON, D. (1987a) 'The Pedagogical Juggernaut', *British Journal of Educational Studies*, **35**, 1, pp. 18–29.

HAMILTON, D. (1987b) 'Curriculum Design: Historical Perspectives on the Art of the State', paper presented at the Annual Convention of the American Educational Research Association, Washington DC.

HAMILTON, D. (1989) *Towards a Theory of Schooling*, London, Falmer Press.

HAMILTON, D. (1990a) *Curriculum History*, Geelong, Deakin University Press.

HAMILTON, D. (1990b) 'The Uncommon Sense of Curriculum Studies', paper presented at a *Journal of Curriculum Studies* Seminar, Sheffield University, England.

HEBRARD, J. (1983) 'L'Evolution de l'Espace Graphique d'un Manuel Scolaire: le "Despautere" de 1512 a 1759', *Langue Francaise*, **59**, pp. 68–87.

HILL, C. (1989) *A Turbulent, Seditious and Factious People: John Bunyan and his Church*, Oxford, Oxford University Press.

KNOWLES, D. (1962) *The Evolution of Medieval Thought*, New York, Vintage Books.

MAYNES, M.J. (1985) *Schooling in Western Europe*, Albany, NY, State University of New York Press.

McLEAN, I. (1990) 'Philosophical Books in European Markets, 1660–1630: The Case of Ramus', in HENRY, J. and HUTTON, S. (Eds) *New Perspectives on Renaissance Thought: Essays in the History of Science, Education and Philosophy*, London, Duckworth, pp. 253–63.

McLINTOCK, R. (1971) 'Toward a Place for Study in a World of Instruction', *Teachers College Record*, **73**, pp. 161–205.

MORGAN, J. (1986) *Godly Learning: Puritan Attitudes towards Reason, Learning and Education*, Cambridge, Cambridge University Press.

OESTREICH, G. (1982) *Neostoicism and the Early Modern State*, Cambridge, Cambridge University Press.

ONG, W. (1958) *Ramus, Method, and the Decay of Dialogue*, Cambridge, MA, Harvard University Press.

PIEPER, J. (1964) *Scholasticism: Personalities and Problems of Medieval Philosophy*, New York, McGraw-Hill.

PILTZ, A. (1981) *The World of Medieval Learning*, Totowa, NJ, Barnes and Noble.

RIEF, P. (1969) 'The Textbook Tradition in Natural Philosophy, 1600–1650', *Journal of the History of Ideas*, **44**, pp. 17–32.

ROUSE, R.H. and ROUSE, M.A. (1979) *Preachers, Florilegia and Sermons: Studies in the Manipulus Florum of Thomas of Ireland*, Toronto, Pontifical Institute of Medieval Studies.

SHARRATT, P. (1987) 'Recent Works on Peter Ramus (1970–1986)' *Rhetorica*, **5**, pp. 7–58.

SILVER, H. (1977) 'Aspects of Neglect: The Strange Case of Victorian Popular Education', *Oxford Review of Education*, **3**, pp. 57–69.

SIMON, B. (1960) *Studies in the History of Education 1780–1870*, London, Lawrence and Wishart.

SIMON, B. (1966) 'The History of Education', in TIBBLE, J.W. (Ed.) *The Study of Education*, London, Routledge, pp. 91–131.

SIMON, J. (1966) *Education and Society in Tudor England*, Cambridge, Cambridge University Press.

STOCK, B. (1983) *The Implications of Literacy: Written Language and Models of Interpretation in the Eleventh and Twelfth Centuries*, Princeton, Princeton University Press.

STRAUSS, G. (1966) 'A Sixteenth-Century Encyclopedia: Sebestion Munster's *Cosmography* and its Editions', in CARTER, C.H. (Ed.) *From the Renaissance to the Counter-Reformation: Essays in Honour of Garrett Mattingly*, London, Cape, pp. 145–63.

TAWNEY, R.H. (1942) *Religion and the Rise of Capitalism*, Harmondsworth, Penguin.

WAGNER, D.L. (Ed.) (1983) *The Seven Liberal Arts in the Middle Ages*, Bloomington, Indiana University Press.

WEBSTER, C. (1975) *The Great Instauration: Science, Medicine and Reform 1626–1660*, London, Duckworth.

WITHRINGTON, D. (1970) 'What Is and What Might Be: Some Reflections on the Writing of Scottish Educational History', *Scottish Educational Studies*, **2**, pp. 110–18.

WOLIN, S. (1973) 'Political Thought as Vocation', in FLEISCHER, M. (Ed.) *Machiavelli and the Nature of Political Thought*, London, Croom Helm, pp. 23–75.

Chapter 4

Lessons from the Literacy Before Schooling 1800–1850

John Willinsky

In August 1832, during the celebrations for the passing of the first Reform Act, a hand press was drawn on a cart by four horses through the streets of Manchester and Salford. Before it marched a pageant representing printing in the times of Caxton and of Elizabeth I, under banners bearing the slogans 'PRESS' and 'TERROR OF BAD GOVERNMENT'. The press itself was covered by a large canopy, festooned with more phrases such as 'THE LIBERTY OF THE PRESS' and 'ENLIGHTENER OF MANKIND'. It was working. There were men busy printing elaborate pamphlets celebrating ' "the PRESS", so eminently distinguished as a means of expanding knowledge and most essential to the best interests of society, and wonderfully effective in giving utterance to the irresistible power of the public voice'. Still wet, the leaflets were passed down to the watching crowd (James, 1976: 17).

This celebration of print, with wet leaflets streaming off a parading press, forms a prelude to the institution of public schooling half a century later. It speaks to a faith in print during a time when broadsides and ballads papered all the available spaces along the streets of London, Manchester, and Birmingham; vendors worked the crowds, hawking newspapers and pamphlets; handbills and penny dreadfuls littered the tables in coffee houses and pubs. It was a period of 'spontaneous composition', to use A.E. Dobbs' (1969: 202) felicitous term, and often enough the writing had just such an inflammatory effect, especially among a working class otherwise disenfranchised. By 1816, every manufacturing town of any size had been infected by what the proper press quickly identified as 'seditious' journals, which is to say, working-class papers that dared to represent workers' interests (Dobbs, 1969: 199). With only a smattering of learning to their names, these people soon found themselves caught up in what was, in many ways, a heroic dedication to print as humanity's great enlightener.

In portraying the nature of literacy prior to the establishment of state schooling, this chapter forms a backdrop of Dickensian proportions. It has ragged men hawking illegal newspapers and a *Bad Alphabet for the Use of Children of Female Reformers*. Yet in this, the chapter holds to a minor critical tradition, as it employs the historical study of education to review how the schools deterred what they first promised to ensure (Johnson, 1976; Graff, 1979; Lankshear, 1987). This particular return to the museum, without admittedly offering much by way of original scholarship, finds its justification in three parts: the first is to remind educators again of the engaged and vital literacy which the schools sought to replace; the second is to encourage this very way of talking about literacy, shifting attention from assessing the capability of individuals to examining the material practices of people reading and writing, to recall the pleasure and power it evokes; the final reason is to suggest the sort of excitement that might arise in teaching this dramatic social history of literacy to students of the subject. In the postmodern spirit of appropriation, those with an interest in a literacy that goes beyond 'personal growth' and the like must find, with some insistency, the social situation of a reading and writing that also makes a difference in people's public lives.

These Unruly Scenes ...

The drama and history of those earlier days, when literacy was at the forefront of the battle for democracy, are a lesson about literacy that often goes missing in schools today. These scenes from the nineteenth century throw considerations of current literature-based English programs into relief, as if to meet the inevitable question, 'the teaching of literature compared to what?' After all, what else could an English class be if not the study of the best that has been thought and said? In order to appreciate what we have made of English teaching over the course of the last hundred years, we need to realize what an education in literacy and literature was like prior to the rise of public schooling and the triumph of literature. It had been promised, after all, that state-sponsored education in Great Britain, which finally became law in 1870, would discipline, among other things, the unruly ways of this earlier interest in reading and writing.[1]

Long after the Reform Act of 1832 proved a great disappointment to workers as it pushed the vote farther out of reach, the working-class hopes for reform remained pinned on 'the liberty of the press'. 'The art of Printing is a multiplication of the mind,' explained Richard Carlile, one of the period's often persecuted writers and publishers, adding that 'pamphlet vendors are the most important springs in the machinery of reform' (cited by Thompson, 1963: 805). Perhaps the most heroic aspect of this earnest trade in print was the part of it intent on representing an otherwise unwritten working class. It was this segment of printers and writers which created an immense appetite for print, for useful knowledge, radical politics, sensational fiction that swept up the entire community of readers and nonreaders. It was no literate garden of Eden. It did not produce universal literacy among the working class, even if it did establish the value of a newspaper that could be trusted. Providing educational opportunities of even the most basic sort tested the resources and initiative of working-class parents and resulted in a variety of innovative programs and stop-gap measures. Yet the working-class struggle to establish its place in print led to a highly sociable literacy closely linking adult and child in life-long, if sporadic, learning among a class that constituted roughly two-thirds of the United Kingdom's 17 million citizens, to use estimates from 1817 (Altick, 1957: 82). In terms of the literate accomplishment of the people, between 1780 and 1830, the number of readers in England increased by a factor of five, to between 7 and 8 million people, in a population that had only doubled to 14 million people during those five decades. By 1840, about two-thirds of all men and one-half of the women were signing their name in the local church marriage registry, a measure commonly used by historians to ascertain literacy levels (Stone, 1969). But, always, we must appreciate that more than mastering one's letters and signing a marriage certificate was at stake.

These scenes from the social history of literacy — contested, engaging, probing, sensational — are often overlooked when educators speak about the importance of reading and writing. More's the pity, for this manner of addressing literacy seems to me capable of stirring a little excitement in the young over the pleasures and powers of print; an introduction to these times could set them on their way as students of literacy, ready to practise it as trade and craft, as a form of democratic participation in the state and a ticket to one of the longest running shows on earth. If England were occupied at this time by two nations, rich and poor, as Disraeli and others noted at the time, then they met on literacy's playing fields as conservative and radical forces fought for the minds and the future of British society. Philanthropic interests attempted to divert radical aspirations for political reform to more wholesome topics by gaining control of working-class educational organizations. Writers and speakers hotly debated the fate of the nation and the causes of injustice, with those taking up working-class interests often facing jail for their choice. Within this contested national arena, the working class managed to fashion a culture of literacy in their Halls of Science and Sunday Schools, their newspapers and pamphlets.

The formation of the English working class during this period, E.P. Thompson has argued in his great work on the period, was based on the principles which have traditionally linked literacy to democracy: 'The working class ideology which matured in the 1830s (and which has endured, through various translations, ever since) put an exceptionally high value upon the rights of the press, of speech, of meeting and of personal liberty' (Thompson, 1963: 805). These people, by no means all of whom could read and write, contributed to a politically aware, class-conscious literacy that drank deeply of the high moral tone of the age; they developed a thirst for the news and politics, as well as for serialized fiction, accounts of hangings and plagiarized Dickens.

The arrival of the nineteenth century found England in the midst of a long war abroad against republicanism, while at home it was busily and crudely transforming itself into an industrial nation. Neither event boded well for the development of literacy among the common people. Still, members of the working class had increasingly begun to band together into various forms of association, pooling by subscription what limited resources they had for purchasing and publishing texts that spoke to their condition. The most notable of these early associations were the Corresponding Societies which modeled the democratic governance they called for, as workers gathered to share and debate works of social import, as well as to extend the organizing of worker associations across the land, before they were banned by a series of parliamentary acts in 1799 (Lankshear, 1987: 84–93). However, among the English Parliament's more anxious responses to revolutionary events in France had been to pass the Seditious Meetings Act of 1795 which was used on many occasions to close the numerous reading rooms and lecture halls which workers had established (Dobbs, 1969:

122–123). Fortunately, the resulting court appearances for those charged proved an opportunity to make working-class concerns part of the public record. Here, for example, a Sheffield Society member gives a succinct statement about the aims of working-class literacy during one of the numerous 'treason' trials from the period: 'To enlighten the people, to show the people the reason, the ground of all complaints and suffering; when a man works hard for fourteen hours of the day, the week through, and is not able to maintain his family; that is what I understood of it; to show the ground of this' (cited by Simon, 1974: 180). By claiming the right to know the reason for this injustice, this fellow demands what might be taken as an expanded notion of *functional* literacy in which we all might be thought to have a considerable stake. 'To show the ground of this' bespeaks a Miltonic project for explaining, if not God's ways to man, then those of his seemingly appointed and anointed — as if to explain why 'the LORD giveth and the LORDS taketh away', to use a bit of biblical play from the time. Indeed, the governing classes had something to fear in the dissemination of such knowledge; it took little imagination to realize that this working-class interest in enlightenment sought more than the consolation of philosophy (Johnson, 1976).

Among the literate expressions of this active inquiry during this period was the Chartist movement. It united workers from across Great Britain in an effort to petition for political change, principally universal male suffrage. The initial unifying theme for Chartism was the people's disappointment and sense of betrayal over the Reform Act of 1833. The Act further limited working-class enfranchisement with its property restrictions on the vote, while considerably increasing middle-class representation through the redistribution of seats. Yet working-class organizations had lent whatever support they could to the difficult passage of the Act, thinking that any expansion of democracy was bound to benefit them. Once the Act had become law, it became clear that the middle class was intent on deploying its newly won enfranchisement to further its own economic and industrial concerns at the workers' expense.

Chartism fought back against this denial of the rights of the majority, using petition and print, numerous local periodicals, and dozens of Chartist newspapers. The first Charter, in the form of a petition demanding parliamentary reform, took shape in 1838 and within a decade the movement had dissipated. Yet during that period, workers from across the nation rallied around the People's Charter in one of the most articulate assertions, before or since, of a common cause.[2] The People's Charter, as a declaration of rights, proved a remarkably massive vehicle for mobilizing the people. Across the nation, people marched with placards declaring a 'Strike for the Charter!', although the movement fell short of the general strike that many called for (Thompson, 1984: 298). After decades of local and individual acts of radicalism, this united stand behind the People's Charter led to a network of 400 sister societies. Chartism's *Northern Star* could claim to be the nation's newspaper with its circulation of 50,000 in 1838–39. Pointed works of drama, political ballads, and satirical poetry freely circulated among local societies. But in essence, the movement was underwritten by the signature of the people as they petitioned for parliamentary reform. Here was the apparently simple use of literacy, to sign one's name, as the expression of an inalienable right to be heard, to be a part of the state. Petitions supporting the Charter were presented to Parliament three times over the course of a decade, with the first in 1839 and the last in 1848, with perhaps a million and a half genuine and, unfortunately, more than a few spurious signatures. The final Charter still failed to move the government, although those who were young at the time lived long enough to see most of the Charter's 'radical' points become the law of the land.

Among the educational accomplishments of the Chartists was the inauguration of a People's College at Sheffield in 1842. The College was controlled by a committee of students and was financed solely on the basis of the modest fees charged for the program of study. It deliberately steered away from vocational concerns — it was not in the business of training better workers — and offered courses in such areas as English language and literature. This was the beginning of post-secondary education of the working class. Not many years later, the People's College was followed by the establishment of the Working Men's College in London which grew out of night classes offered by faculty at King's College. These were, in a sense, demonstration projects. Not only did they offer a greater hope for the educational interests of the working class, but they made plain the determination of working-class educational aspirations and the potential contribution of what was, after all, the majority of the citizenry.

Accompanying the working-class struggle to achieve universal suffrage for men was a redefinition of women's place in the social order enacted in print and assembly halls. In her history of the movement, Dorothy Thompson provides a record of women's unflinching attempt to advance the Chartist cause, whether by speaking at meetings, going to jail, setting up defence funds, or simply taking over when their husbands were imprisoned. She concludes that their presence added a strong sense of community to the movement and by virtue of their contribution convinced others of their right to suffrage and improved education (Thompson, 1984: 120–51). But if support for female suffrage was accepted in principle by male Chartists, it was ultimately rejected by the movement as unrealistic and set aside from its demands. That is to say, women made modest gains during the period, and yet were able to discover and demonstrate to others the strength of their contribution to the political forum. In open defiance of the Victorian model of separate spheres for the sexes, they formed political unions which embraced a wide range of issues, including the subjection of women. In 1839, the Female Political Union of Newcastle published its open letter to fellow countrywomen in the *Northern Star*, calling for them to 'help our fathers, husbands and brothers, to free themselves and us from political, physical and mental bondage'. They understood that by virtue of taking this stance, they were rewriting their place in the order of things: 'We have been told that the province of woman is her home, and that the field of politics should be left to men; this we deny' (cited in Hampton, 1984: 472).

This was a literacy of affirmation, which both declared that the current order was wrong and by that very outspokenness initiated a change within it. Yet, as Catherine Hall (1986) warns, in spite of numerous instances of women taking up where their imprisoned menfolk left off in the fight for free press, facing trial and jail themselves, there remained considerable pressures from within and from above the working class for women to find their proper sphere by the hearth-fire, to support but not to lead. Nonetheless, a process of rewriting history had begun, by signing petitions, forming political unions, and attending to radical culture of print. Literacy, although not easily come by, was at the forefront of this struggle as the Chartists were not long in recognizing.

An Education without System: Literacy, Politics and Popular Pedagogy

Although literacy rates improved considerably over the first half of the nineteenth century, it was not a steady progress. Where the industrial revolution made greatest headway, in the decades around the close of the eighteenth century, the number of literate people actually declined in factory centres (Sanderson, 1972). During those dark, desperate days for mill and factory hands, a generation of the young saw the opportunity to learn their letters evaporate for a series of linked reasons: reduced or frozen wage rates diminished their parents' ability to pay school fees, while forcing them to spend fourteen to sixteen hours a day at the mill or in the mines, before returning home to join seven or eight other members of the family sharing a dank room in the industrial slums. In the textile mills, the new machinery reduced the need for brute force, and adult workers were replaced by agile, docile children who could easily slip among the gears and belts, piecing the broken spinning threads together, as well as scavenging, cleaning and reeling the cotton (Sanderson, 1972: 78–79). In Lancashire, to provide some idea of the numbers involved, there were 30,000 children in 1836 who, instead of heading to school each morning, trudged off to work at the local cotton mills (Walvin, 1982: 62).[3]

If there was now considerably less opportunity for these young people to gain even a few years of schooling in those years, literacy's job value also declined. Smokestack and steam mule ensured a certain 'disengagement of economic development and literacy', as economist Michael Sanderson (1972: 75) neatly describes it. The upshot of this disengagement was that it no longer paid workers to be literate as it had only decades before, and jobs in areas such as weaving were now carried out by successively less educated workers. The dour fact of the matter was that literacy among the newly industrialized working class was under economic assault. Yet if literacy was robbed of its economic advantages, its role in the fight for a better collective life through political agitation for the rights of the people took on even greater prominence. Reading and writing were part of an alternative political economy gradually established by the working class around the radical newspaper business, from writer to hawker, the public meeting, and other forms of public broadcasting.

I can, perhaps, best introduce the nature of this education without system by turning to the testimony of an anonymous advocate from the end of the period under consideration. He was speaking before the Committee on Public Libraries, one of the countless official inquiries that marked Victorian England and the rise of a sense of civil responsibility, and took the opportunity to explain what was at stake in the forms of incidental education available to the working class:

Q: In a large town the influences which educate a man against his will are incessant; there are so many public meetings … That forms the most valuable part of the education an Englishman receives?

A: Yes. It has put us beyond some of the nations of the Continent who have more school instruction.

Q: Do you hold that this *Education by Collision*, as it may be called is the best of all?

A: It makes them citizens (cited by Dobbs, 1969: 206).

The making and educating of citizens was indeed an constant process in large towns and small. It often began for working-class children as they played among the benches during those incessant public meetings the Committee member clearly had little time for (apart from, presumably, official Committee hearings). Of the more systematic efforts of the working-class effort to educate their young during this period, three forms prevailed: 'dame schools', Sunday schools, and independent institutions of learning.

The reports from the period often denounce the dame schools for the half-hearted instruction that went on in classes conducted, in Richard Altick's (1957: 146) estimate, 'by women or by men whose fortunes, if they had ever bloomed, were now in the last stages of decay'. But then these women served parents for whom questions of fortunes blooming did not really seem pertinent. Richard Johnson (1976: 44) is a little fairer with the dame schools, pointing out that they 'were really no more than a form of co-operation among women, improvised for the care of children under seven'. The dame schools figure prominently in the 142 working-class autobiographies that we have from the period, according to David Vincent's (1982) count (with only six of them by women). Among a class in which such acts of self-assertion on the page were out of the ordinary at best, these students of the written word proved ready to presume that their possession of literacy gave them licence to set a modest life to paper. Thomas Cooper, the Chartist poet, learned to read in the lower room of a two-story cottage kept by Old Gatty. He developed his reading with the help of a circulating library he was able to subscribe to at the stationers. In his own *Life of Thomas Cooper*, he records how 'the wondrous knowledge of the heart unfolded by Shakespeare, made me shrink into insignificance; while the sweetness, the marvellous power of expression and grandeur of his poetry seemed to transport me, at times, out of the vulgar world of circumstances in which I bodily lived' (Cooper, 1879: 64). As it was, Cooper did not shrink so much as blossom into a political poet and autobiographer willing to tell the tale of a life that was not otherwise regarded as worth the telling, although his life did serve as a colorful model for Charles Kingsley's (1893) popular *Alton Locke: Tailor and Poet*.

A second, more pervasive if less frequent source of working-class education arose out of the Sunday School movement, which itself took a number of forms. It could be as informal as teaching a neighbour's child the abc's on a Sunday afternoon. And it encompassed the organizational might of the interdenominational Stockport Sunday School, set among the factories in the north of England, which drew 5,000 children of a Sunday during the 1830s (Laqueur, 1976: 42). Taking advantage of one's sole day off was for many the only opportunity to learn their letters. Having had their start in the final years of the previous century, the organized Sunday schools were at least initially a philanthropic gesture by members of the respectable classes intended to assist the poor on the road to heaven. Although the working class was grateful enough for these acts of Christian charity, in more than a few cases, parents worked hard to relieve their patrons of their obligations by bringing the classes within their own network of educational devices (Johnson, 1976: 45). To gain a sense of the educational scope and significance of the Sunday school movement, one need only consider that by the middle of the nineteenth century close to two million children were attending for up to six hours a Sunday (Laqueur, 1976: 44).

The weekly classes were only one aspect of the movement's educational initiative. The Sunday School Union distributed ten million reading and spelling books in the first half of the century. Its highly successful *Youth Magazine and Evangelical Miscellany* virtually initiated an entire periodical market for the young, and its tracts, on historical as well as religious topics, ran to ten million copies a year by 1839 (Laqueur, 1976: 113–8). Both texts and magazines served child and adult as education was a continuing affair for the working class. Simon (1974: 188) reports that after their initial success with the young, many of the Sunday schools began to open in the evenings as adults stopped by to 'read the news or hear it read'. Another area of innovation for a number of the Sunday schools was the use of the same curriculum for both sexes in reading, writing, arithmetic and grammar. Yet, it should be added, the aim for even the most radical of schools remained for each student 'to promote by all just means in his power, a radical reform of parliament, by means of suffrage in all male persons of mature age and sane minds' (cited in Simon, 1974: 190).

As should be apparent, nineteenth-century Sunday Schools are not to be confused with the Sunday mornings spent in the Church basements in our own times. In his substantial study of the movement, Thomas Laqueur gives an emphatic sense of what was at stake: 'It was the product of the infinite in-ventiveness and ingenuity of men and women who, under the most adverse conditions, created a culture of discipline, self-respect and improvement within which to wage the battle for social justice and political equality' (Laqueur, 1976: 241). Although secular and radical interests did get involved in the movement, with Socialist Sunday Schools founded in a dozen communities, the majority retained their religious commitments for the most part, principally Methodism. They certainly fell well short of developing the 'revolutionary consciousness' that some would have hoped for and others feared. Yet the Bible still proved a source for radicalism, and Laqueur (1976: 245) quips that 'for every socialist created by *Das Kapital*, a thousand were created by the Bible'. Certainly the Bible offered a strong source of imagery and archetype for the radical press quick to play on a shared cultural literacy among the rich and poor.

A third and perhaps more promising, if not so widespread, source of education, in conjunction with the Sunday School movement and dame schools, were the independent educational organizations. They are especially worth con-sidering for the way in which they attempted to reform education as a model for reforming the society at large. In a number of communities, for example, Female Societies were formed to further educational goals and political idealism among women, or as the Blackburn Female Union declared its educational objectives: 'to use our utmost endeavor to instil into the minds of our children a deep and rooted hatred of our corrupt and tyrannical rulers'. To assist in the achievement of such educational goals, they developed *The Bad Alphabet for the Use of Children of Female Reformers* in which B was for Bible, Bishop, Bigotry and W for Whig, Weakness, Wavering, and Wicked (Thompson, 1963: 788).

Other organizations were less overt in their political and more specialized in their educational aspirations. The British Association for Promoting Co-operative Knowledge formed in 1829 and Schools of Industry were set up explicitly 'for the formation of superior physical, moral and intellectual character … at the least expense to parents' (cited by Simon, 1974: 213). In spite of their utilitarian titles, a number of these schools had remarkably progressive programs. To take one ster-ling example, the constitution from the 1830s of the Charlotte School, a Free

School for followers of Robert Owen's form of humanism, was marked by utopian values that have lost none of their viability or importance for current advocates of progressive education:

1 Every child shall be encouraged to express his or her opinion.
2 No creed or dogma shall be imposed on any.
3 Admitted facts alone shall be placed before the pupils, from which they shall be allowed to draw their own deductions.
4 No distinction shall exist, but all shall be treated with equal kindness.
5 Neither praise nor blame, merit nor de-merit, rewards nor punishments, shall be awarded of any kind; kindness and love to be the only ruling powers.
6 Both sexes shall have equal opportunities of acquiring useful knowledge (cited by Simon, 1974: 214).

Knowledge is Power

These sporadic forms of education, from dame school to progressive independent, were supplemented by large doses of shared and lone autodidactism. Altick (1957: 243), for example, tells of a small group of young women in a mill town who met at five o'clock in the morning to read Shakespeare for an hour before dragging themselves off to work. This was literacy in defiance of what was expected from them, art snatched from a life that was otherwise owned on an hourly basis by the mill bosses, as if these girls could steal away one great privilege that made them secretly worthy of more than the brutish day ahead of them. Stories also abound of books smuggled into the factories, as they still are today, if only to slip unnoticed through a few pages when the machines break down. And if my romantic instances of a love of literature seem quirky, consider Charles Dickens regaling the complacent dinner meeting of the Birmingham Society of Artists in 1853 with his barbed reminder that 'there are in Birmingham at this moment many working men infinitely better versed in Shakespeare and in Milton than the average of fine gentlemen in the days of bought and sold dedication and dear books' (Altick, 1957: 242).

Literary societies formed and other organizations held lecture series which almost always included mention of literature, along with science, the fine arts, theology, morals, social and political economy. In 1836, Frederick Hill's book, *National Education*, lent a special emphasis to the fact that *'popular lectures on Poetry and the Drama have been most of all attractive'* at the Mechanics' Institute in Birmingham with a special interest in Shakespeare common to Institutes throughout the land (cited in Altick, 1957: 203; original emphasis). In such halls, rooms were named after Shakespeare, and school classes after Milton and Marvel as well as working-class heroes. This interest in literature led to a profitable circuit for travelling lecturers who took their knowledge of Shakespeare and Milton on the road. It was also met by the publication of such collections as *The National: A Library for the People*, which the Chartists issued in 1839 to provide an affordable selection of the standard English authors from Spencer to Tennyson. Simon (1974: 251) reports that the radical newspaper, *Northern Star*, devoted an occasional page to poetry (with Byron a special favorite) on which the works of

Burns, Shelley, Whittier, Mackay and Clare (himself a working-class success story) were mixed with Chartist verse written by working-class poets. This healthy appetite for literature and its discussion among the people contributed to English literature's acceptance as a suitable course of study for more democratically minded schools and universities.

The thirst for print-knowledge had been awakened among the people and was soon met by the publication of various miscellanies that amounted to encyclopedias of 'useful knowledge', the best of which rivalled the *Britannica* in their thoroughness and attention to detail. One of the most successful of these publications, *Mechanics' Magazine*, a monthly that began in 1823, invited its readers to contribute in areas of their own expertise. Here artisans could read and write about the history, background, and innovation in their respective trades; they also maintained active correspondence columns to which readers regularly brought their own expertise. Trade magazines survive to this day, with more general magazines such as *Popular Science* and *Popular Mechanics* bearing traces of this earlier interest in the workings of the new industrial age.

Another manifestation of this cultural appetite was the informal society of the sort that, to draw on an account from the day, 'assembled nightly at Lunn's Coffee House, Clerkenwell, devoting two evenings to reading, two to discussion, and one for music' (cited by Simon, 1974: 154). One response among workers to the bourgeois encroachment on the Mechanics' Institutes was simply to leave the things to those bustling, bighearted patrons and the increasingly middle-class clientele, and wander back to the coffee houses where they had first begun to realize and then organize their interests in learning and inquiry. There were 1,600 coffee houses in London prior to the mid-century, and many of them seemed amenable to serving in whatever educational capacity might lead to a gathering of coffee drinkers. The largest of them served nearly two thousand customers a day, as they came in for a cup of coffee and a look at the day's papers (Altick, 1957: 342). Agnes Reach, in her account for the New Parley Library in 1845, described them as 'schools of instruction'; the outside of the coffee house was plastered in playbills — the 'language of the walls' — while within there was 'an air of stillness and repose, yet perhaps a hundred people are seated in different boxes, conning over books and newspapers, and sipping coffee at the same time. You can see at a glance that a majority of the guests are working men' (cited in James, 1963: 7).[4] Some coffee houses pursued a specifically political profile. When Doherty decided that he had enough of front-line union radicalism, he opened a coffee house which he stocked with no less than subscriptions to ninety-six newspapers and periodicals, charging his customers a reading fee equivalent to the price of an egg. A few organizations took a more organized approach to the pursuit of letters and current events. The Hampden Clubs and Political Unions developed Reading Societies which offered nightly reading of the London papers, often leading to charged discussions among literate and illiterate about the state of the world and the fate of England.

A Nineteenth-Century Literacy Crisis

For all of their promise, a good number of these educational literate undertakings were met by a considerable backlash from inside and outside of the working class. The school-promoters were soon accused by the radical press of abandoning the pressing political struggle for a limited working day and universal suffrage 'for the more profitable pursuit of literature and the arts,' as the Chartist *Northern Star* ironically put it in 1839. The *Star* insisted that education should follow, not lead, in the battle for human rights: 'Let the people have their rights, and those comforts to which they are so justly entitled, and they will instruct themselves.' It seemed obvious to the *Star*, for example, that first children had to be freed of factory work before time could be given to schooling.

While there was a lack of solidarity on issues of schooling withing the working class, a far more substantial attack on this concerted educational effort came from the ruling classes. Earlier, I described the economic forces which militated against the acquisition of literacy by the industrial classes. But more direct action was also taken as part of a long-standing fear that literacy was, indeed, a dangerous thing in the hands of those who had the most to gain by it.[5] In 1807, for example, Whig efforts to establish parish schools in 1807 were defeated in the House of Commons led by a Tory attack on the idea as flawed in principle and more than a little dangerous in practice:

> However specious in theory the project might be of giving education to the labouring classes of the poor, it would in effect, be found to be prejudicial to their morals and happiness ... instead of teaching them subordination, it would render them factious and refractory ... it would enable them to read seditious pamphlets, vicious books, and publications against Christianity; it would render them insolent to their superiors; and in a few years, the result would be that the legislature would find it necessary to direct the strong arm of power towards them (Cited by Simon, 1974: 132).

Other such anti-educational incidents include the actions of a committee representing the manufacturing and commercial class in Leeds to exclude the 'poor' children for whom the grammar school was originally endowed, taking specific aim at the teaching of writing where the poor 'should be wholly excluded'.[6] One of His Majesty's Justices of the Peace also focused on the particular dangers of writing in his remarks on the Poor Bill of 1807:

> It is doubtless desirable that the poor should be generally instructed in *reading*, if it were only the best of purposes — that they may read the scriptures. As to *writing* and *arithmetic*, it may be apprehended that such a degree of knowledge would produce in them a disrelish for the laborious occupations of life (cited by Dobbs, 1969: 148).

Equally so, the famous Sunday School missionary, Hannah Moore, put it plainly in defence of her contribution to the orderliness of society: 'I allow no writing of the poor,' for as she explained it: 'My Object is not to make fanatics, but to train up the lower classes in habits of industry and piety' (cited by Simon, 1974: 106, 133). Her *Cheap Repository Tracts* were well supported by philanthropic interests for their 'training up' features.

The Mechanics' Institutes, which had become a well-known symbol of the upright, self-taught artisan, also caught the attention of members of the middle class keen on investing their philanthropic energies carefully in sites which seemed to promise civilizing and disinterested learning among the working class. It was not long before the Institutes fell under philanthropic control, forsaking their independence and political edge in favor of respectability. Literacy was at the center of this battle for the mind, and working from within through patronage was considered fair game. With the transparent instance of middle-class patronage in the Society for the Diffusion of Useful Knowledge (SDUK) founded in 1826, the question of 'useful to whom' was almost immediately raised by the workers who joined. While many appreciated learning about the habits of boa constrictors and other bits of exotic information, this still left many of their questions unanswered: '*Useful* knowledge indeed,' declared a correspondent to the *Poor Man's Guardian*, 'would it be those who live idly on our skills and industry, who would cajole us into apathetic resignation to their iron sway' (James, 1976: 35). Concerned that labourers were missing the point of it all, the Society also issued such useful, if not intentionally entertaining, pamphlets as *An Address to the Labourers on the Subject of Destroying Machinery* (1830) and other works speaking to the advantages of increased mechanization of work. The Society did not fail to demonstrate its buoyant spirit of charming condescension in its best advice to the labourer: 'You have, in too many cases, nothing but your labour for support. We say to you, get something else; acquire something to fall back upon. When there is a glut of labour go at once out of the market; become yourselves capitalists' (cited by Simon, 1974: 161). Needless to say, such sagacious and practical advice did not pass without due comment.

Nowhere was the contest among forms of literacy between state and worker as evident as in the campaign mounted against the 'Taxes on Knowledge'. The government had become increasingly alarmed with the sort of literate activity taking place among the working class. The Committee of Secrecy in the House of Lords, the *Annual Register* of 1817 notes, met to examine the unprecedented 'publication of the most seditious and inflammatory nature, marked with a peculiar character of irreligion and blasphemy, and tending not only to overturn the existing form of government and order of society, but to root out those principles upon which any government or any society can be supported.' The government response was to profit by its oppression of this literate activity. Taxes had already been increased on windows, as they let in the light of day by which to read, among other things. But the taxes on knowledge — the duty on paper, advertising and newspapers — were intent on pushing the price of the news out of reach of many, even as new paper-making machinery and the introduction of the rotary steam press in the 1820s succeeded in driving down production costs for publishers (James, 1963: 10). In 1819, the government escalated the stakes with the first of the infamous 'Six Acts' which passed laws curtailing a free press and freedom of assembly. The fear was widespread. The poet and essayist Robert Southey, who had offered kind enough words on behalf of 'poor poets', felt compelled during this period to advise Lord Liverpool: 'You must crush the press or it will destroy the Constitution' (cited by Dobbs, 1969: 200).

The Stamp Act was aimed specifically at the radical papers. The tax was restricted to newspapers that sold for less than 6d. and contained news or *comment on the news* (while exempting works of 'devotion, piety and charity'). The *Poor Man's Guardian* had actually been started in 1831 as the first shot to be fired in the

'War of the Unstamped Press'; it was to be, its masthead declared, 'A Weekly Newspaper for the People Established Contrary to Law to Try the Power of Might against Right'. The newspaper, and dozens of others soon following suit, simply refused to pay the taxes due on the paper and the advertising. The radical printer who founded the paper served three prison terms, and 800 hawkers of the papers were arrested in what amounted to a harassment campaign to cut the paper off from those it would protect. As the trial transcripts of one hawker make apparent, these street vendors had no illusions about the paper's political role, or their own:

Bench:	What have you to say in your defence?
Defendant:	Well, sir, I have been out of employment for some time; neither can I obtain work; my family are all starving ... And for another reason, the weightiest of them all; I sell them for the good of my fellow countrymen; to let them see how they are misrepresented in parliament ... I wish to let the people know how they are being humbugged ...
Bench:	Hold your tongue a moment.
Defendant:	I shall not! for I wish every man to read these publications.
Bench:	You are very insolent, therefore you are committed to three months imprisonment in Knutsford House of Corrections, to hard labor.
Defendant:	I've nothing to thank you for; and whenever I come out I'll hawk them again. And mind you, the first that I hawk shall be to your house ... (Hampton, 1984: 454–5).

This able defendant was not issuing an isolated cry of defiance. By the year 1850, hawkers were selling 29 million copies of unstamped periodicals a year; it constituted an alternative economy for the otherwise unemployed, as well as an education for the readers. The newspaper sensitive to their interests had become a staple of working-class literacy and culture. Even among those papers that reluctantly paid the tax, estimates have it that the radical Sunday papers, with a total circulation of 100,000, outsold the conservative ones at a ratio of ten to one (Altick, 1957: 329). Added to that is Webb's estimation that a London paper might pass through thirty hands, with somewhat less in the provinces. Many a public house kept a reader under contract to provide a daily local 'newscast', complete with impromptu background pieces. Eventually, the government was forced to concede that the legislative strategy of its Six Acts, designed in various ways to suppress these literary interests, may have been counter-productive and, ultimately, unconscionable in a nation calling itself a democracy. The Stamp Act was repealed in 1855, after the *Times* and other respectable papers had joined in the fight against the 'taxes on knowledge'; the advertisement duty was removed in 1853, and the paper duty lifted in 1861 (Dobbs, 1969: 201n; Westmancoat, 1985: 24).

But what had also become apparent by mid-century was that the poor had, in many instances, taken education into their own hands, and this in spite of two church charity school systems with their highly touted monitorial schools. It was, indeed, seen as a potential source of discontent and danger. In 1851, the *Times* launched a front-page attack on self-education among the working class, asking that their schooling be taken in hand by their betters because of the licentious content:

> Systems the most destructive of the peace, the happiness, and the virtue of society, are boldly, perseveringly, and without let or hindrance, openly taught and recommended to the acceptance of the people with great zeal, if not great ability. Cheap publications containing the wildest and most anarchial doctrines are scattered broadcast over the land ... Let a prudent spirit of conciliation enable the wise and the good to offer to the people a beneficial education in place of this abominable teaching (cited by Simon, 1974: 346–7).

The remarkable perseverance noted by the *Times* is much to the point of these educational efforts. The solution, however, was not to compete on the open market of ideas, with cheap publications broadcast over the land. Rather, it was that of cutting off the problem at the root. After ignoring the education of the poor for so long, there arose a desperate call for wresting control of education from these 'instructors ... for evil'. The call was met in less than two decades by free and compulsory education in the hands of state and church. Matthew Arnold would play an instrumental role during that period in promoting the educational value of literature as the means of forming the souls of the young.

Conclusion

This account of literacy among the working class during this half-century is riven with pathos. I can appreciate how this suffuses it with its own form of Victorian sentimentality. But I found it hard to write it otherwise. This literacy emerged against the odds; it took on an assertive, aggressive shape as the working class lost ground in wages, in the fight for suffrage, in claims on freedom of expression and assembly, and in school positions for the young. But if there were political and economic setbacks for the labouring classes, especially in the early years of the century, it was a time in which their interests in literacy and self-education developed all the more urgently. This pursuit of print offered little economic advantage. People read out of an interest in the new sciences and for the stories that literature had to tell; they signed petitions and hawked papers in the name of universal suffrage, a ten-hour working day, and fair prices.

But make no mistake, the point of this chapter has not been to spearhead a movement for marching arm-in-arm back to the vanquished coal mines and textile mills of the nineteenth century. I want only to take the level of engagement and activism found in that print community as a strong example of what literacy can mean, of the forms that it can take in ways that extend, as I suggested above, the meaning of 'functional literacy'. The plan which the state eventually adopted for the teaching of English language and literature took too little from the literacy that it attempted to replace, too little of the oral and written traditions, the mix of street and lecture hall, coffee house and classroom, placard, and poetry. The problem was not simply that the new English curriculum had other goals, interests, and aspirations. It was all too convenient for state schooling to quietly bury this earlier, exuberant and outspoken form of literacy. As it turned out, however, this education in a civilizing literacy produced generations of students still keen to speak out on the part of the working class. The trade union movement and labour party have continued the tradition of championing the interests of those outside the governing classes.

In the history of public education, these elements of literate engagement with society continue to resurface, principally in progressive education programs. Today, we have signs of a 'new literacy' taking root in the schools, as the young are encouraged to write their own stories from the first grade onward, while they are encouraged to find in their response to the most sophisticated literature an opportunity to represent themselves and their interests (Willinsky, 1990). But as well as fostering responsive students of literature and reflective writers, it would seem worthwhile for English teachers to find ways to nurture students of literacy. Lessons from the social history of literacy and texts, although it has only begun to be written, might assist the young in understanding the social force which writing and reading can bring to bear on a situation; they might gain a greater sense of how an abstract force such as literacy works on the world, turning heads and minds.[7] The students might then turn their attention, in the insistence of the letter, to the determination of meaning in their participation in the word. It is as if they could explore, as that Sheffield worker so wanted, 'the grounds of all complaint and suffering', and could have, too, 'the wondrous knowledge of the heart' that Thomas Cooper found in Shakespeare.

Notes

1   I have focused on the rise of mass literacy in England, in part because of the wealth of materials available and because the larger project of which this is part (Willinsky, 1991) begins with Matthew Arnold, a figure of influence across the English-speaking world; excellent studies of nineteenth-century literacy, education, and culture in America include Levine (1988), Soltow and Stevens (1981), and Davidson's (1989) collection, and in Canada, Graham (1989), Houston and Prentice (1988), and Graff (1979).

2   The Charter itself was composed in conjunction with the Working-Men's Association and a few radical members of the House of Commons, and put forward six points for political reform: 1) annual parliaments, 2) universal (male) suffrage, 3) vote by ballot, 4) abolition of property qualifications for membership in House of Commons, 5) payment of members, 6) equal electoral districts.

3   Working-class radical, William Cobbett, pointed out to the House of Commons in 1833 that 'a startling discovery has been made, namely, that all greatness and prosperity, that our superiority over other nations, is owing to 300,000 little girls in Lancashire. We have made the discovery that, if these little girls worked two hours less in a day than they do now, it would occasion the ruin of the country; that it would enable other countries to compete with us; and thus make an end to our boasted wealth, and bring us to beggary!' (cited by Hampton, 1984: 460).

4   These working men were not all reading politics by any means, nor books of poetry or self-improvement, for this was also the age of cheap and popular fiction. In his book on the worker's taste for narrative, Louis James suggests that the popular reading ranged from Dickens' *Pickwick*, *Bentley's Miscellany*, and *The Mirror of Literature, Amusement and Instruction* to what he refers to as lower class fiction in the form of *Penny Storyteller* and *The Calendar of Horrors* (James, 1963: 7). A survey of reading habits made in 1840, one of the many in this incipient age

of surveys and statistical reasoning, found that there were eighty cheap periodicals (at less than twopence) available in London: nine of these were scientific in content, four were political, five were 'licentious', four featured drama, sixteen favoured biographies and memoirs, while twenty-two were filled with romances and stories (James, 1963: 27, 44). Fiction was the growth area for publishing during this period, and this appetite for fiction also betrays the winding down, especially toward mid-century, of the political urgency that literacy originally embodied.

5   Charlton (1989) provides an excellent analysis of the three-fold apprehensions over popular literacy felt by the state church during the Reformation: 'Armed with the skill of reading for itself, a laity would first of all be able to interpret what it read, and especially a vernacular Bible in a possibly heterodox fashion. Secondly, it would now be able to read nonapproved productions of the printing press and there were plenty of these. Thirdly and most importantly, it would be able to read such books and pass on such interpretations to the illiterate laity, the mass of people, who hitherto heard only received word handed down by the clergy' (Charlton, 1989: 449).

6   During this period, the working class faced a considerable loss of endowed school positions that had been set up for the poor in the grammar schools by benefactors over the centuries. Middle-class interests saw to it that these historic rights were abolished and the positions opened to a 'fair' competition that tended to exclude the poorly prepared young of the community (Simon, 1974: 315–16, 325).

7   While the subject known in France as *histoire du livre* has only begun to be written in for the English speaking world, there are fine beginnings to be found in Cathy Davidson's (1989) multi-disciplinary collection of essays which she claims to be the first history of the books in America. My own most practical classroom labours at bringing the history of the urge to publish to the young awaits development into a more substantial program (Willinsky, 1984).

References

ALTICK, R.D. (1957) *The English Common Reader: A Social History of the Mass Reading Public, 1800–1900*, Chicago, Chicago University Press.

CHARLTON, K. (1989) '"False Fonde Books, Ballades and Rimes": An Aspect of Informal Education in Early Modern England', *History of Education Quarterly*, **27**, pp. 449–71.

COOPER, T. (1879) *Life of Thomas Cooper*, London, Macmillan.

DAVIDSON, C. (Ed.) (1989) *Reading in America: Literature and Social History*, Baltimore, Johns Hopkins University Press.

DOBBS, A.E. (1919, 1969) *Educational and Social Movements, 1700–1850*, New York, Augustus Kelley, 1969.

GRAFF, H.J. (1979) *The Literacy Myth: Literacy and Social Structure in the Nineteenth Century City*, New York, Academic Press.

GRAHAM, R.J. (1989) 'The Irish Reader Revisited: The Power of the Text(book)', *Canadian Journal of Education*, **14**, 4, pp. 414–26.

HALL, C. (1986) 'The Tale of Samuel and Jemima: Gender and Working-Class Culture in Early Nineteenth-Century England', in BENNETT, T., MERCER, C. and WOLLACOTT, J. (Eds) *Popular Culture and Social Relations*, Milton Keynes, Open University Press, pp. 73–92.

HAMPTON, C. (Ed.) (1984) *A Radical Reader: The Struggle of Change in England, 1381–1914*, Harmondsworth, UK, Penguin.

HOUSTON, S.E. and PRENTICE, A. (1988) *Schooling and Scholars in Nineteenth Century Ontario*, Toronto, University of Toronto Press.

JAMES, L. (1963) *Fiction for the Working Man 1830–1850: A Study of the Literature Produced for the Working Classes in Early Victorian Urban England*, London, Oxford University Press.

JAMES, L. (Ed.) (1976) *English Popular Literature 1819–1851*, New York, Columbia University Press.

JOHNSON, R. (1976) 'Notes on the Schooling of the English Working Class 1780–1850', in DALE, R. *et al.* (Eds) *Schooling and Capitalism: A Sociological Reader*, London, Routledge and Kegan Paul.

KINGSLEY, C. (1893) *Alton Locke: Tailor and Poet, An Autobiography*, 2 vols, London, Macmillan.

LANKSHEAR, C. with LAWLER, M. (1987) *Literacy, Schooling and Revolution*, New York, Falmer Press.

LAQUEUR, T.W. (1976) *Religion and Respectability: Sunday Schools and Working Class Culture, 1780–1850*, New Haven, CT, Yale University Press.

LEVINE, L.W. (1988) *Highbrow/Lowbrow: The Emergence of Cultural Hierarchy in America*, Cambridge, MA, Harvard University Press.

SANDERSON, M. (1972) 'Literacy and Social Mobility in the Industrial Revolution in England', *Past and Present*, **56**, pp. 75–104.

SIMON, B. (1974) *The New Nations and the Educational Structure, 1780–1870*, London, Lawrence and Wishart.

SOLTOW, L. and STEVENS, E. (1981) *The Rise of Literacy and the Common School in the United States: A Socioeconomic Analysis to 1870*, Chicago, University of Chicago Press.

STONE, L. (1969) 'Literacy and Education in England, 1640–1900', *Past and Present*, **42**, pp. 69–139.

THOMPSON, D. (1984) *The Chartists: Popular Politics in the Industrial Revolution*, New York, Pantheon.

THOMPSON, E.P. (1963) *The Making of the English Working Class*, Harmondsworth, Penguin.

VINCENT, D. (1982) 'The Decline of the Oral Tradition in Popular Culture', in STORCH, R.D. (Ed.) *Popular Culture and Custom in Nineteenth-Century England*, London, Croom Helm, pp. 20–47.

WALVIN, J. (1982) *A Child's World: A Social History of English Childhood, 1800–1914*, Harmondsworth, Penguin.

WESTMANCOAT, J. (1985) *Newspapers*, London, British Library.

WILLINSKY, J. (1984) 'To Publish and Publish and Publish', *Language Arts*, **23**, 2, pp. 23–28.

WILLINSKY, J. (1990) *The New Literacy: Redefining Reading and Writing in the Schools*, New York, Routledge.

WILLINSKY, J. (1991) *The Triumph of Literature/The Fate of Literature*, New York, Teachers College Press.

Chapter 5

The 'Received Tradition' of English Teaching: The Decline of Rhetoric and the Corruption of Grammar[1]

Frances Christie

Introduction

When in 1755 Samuel Johnson published his *Dictionary of the English Language*, he included a brief examination of the history of the language and a very summary treatment of the English grammar. In the manner of scholars who dealt with the classical languages, Johnson distinguished the following as those areas of language study that concerned the grammarian: Grammar, defined as 'the art of using words properly'; Orthography, defined as 'the art of combining letters into syllables, and syllables into words'; Etymology, which 'teaches the deduction of one word from another, and the various modifications by which the sense of the same word is diversified'; and Syntax, which hardly merited serious attention at all. Johnson actually wrote:

> The established practice of grammarians requires that I should here treat of the syntax; but our language has so little inflexion, or variety of terminations, that its construction neither requires nor admits many rules (Johnson, 1755, Vol 1 [no page number]).

Alluding to the authority of John Wallis, whose *Grammatica Linguæ Anglicanæ* had appeared in 1653, Johnson noted that the latter had omitted any mention of English syntax at all, and he went on to say of himself:

> Johnson, whose desire of following the writers upon the learned languages made him think a syntax indispensably necessary, has published such petty observations as were better omitted.

The 'petty observations' were as follows:

> The verb, as in other languages, agrees with the nominative in number and person; as Thou fliest from good; he runs to death. Of two substantives the noun possessive is the genitive; as His father's glory; the sun's heat. Verbs transitive require an oblique case; as He loves me; You

fear him. All prepositions require an oblique case; He gave this to me; He took this from me; He says this of me; He came with me.

In Johnson's terms (but also in the traditional classical view of grammar on which he drew), grammatical studies were about 'words', whether those studies involved concern for using words 'properly'; for spelling them correctly; for examining their roots and origins; or for identifying the 'rules' by which words worked in the construction of the language. The latter practices for identifying the rules by which language was constructed led, incidentally, to various principles of parsing and sentence analysis, although these were not well developed by Johnson, as we have seen.

Grammar, it should be noted, was not concerned with meaning. Perhaps the latter observation should cause no surprise. Indeed, Johnson would probably have been the first to point out that meaning was not the province of the grammarian. On the contrary, it was the province of the rhetorician. The classical distinction between rhetoric and grammar had a long history by the time Johnson and his contemporaries used it in the eighteenth century. In fact, the distinction went back to the Greeks. On the one hand, grammar was conceived as about words, the rules that govern them, and their relationship to one another. On the other hand, rhetoric was conceived as about the construction of meaning in language, and it involved the study of ways to use language to inform, to explain, to argue or to persuade. The distinction between grammar and rhetoric, as Firth (1968), in a much later period of history was to note, led to what he termed the 'part philosophical, part logico-grammatical' tradition by which many linguists concentrated on words and also sentences, at the expense of a concern with the 'speech events' in which human beings engaged in 'the living processes of ... maintaining themselves in society' (Firth, 1968: 12–13). (I would add that many language teachers, as well as linguists, have also worked in such a tradition.)

Firth is but one of a number of linguists in the twentieth century who have challenged the distinction conventionally made in language studies between grammar and meaning. However, as I shall argue in this chapter, that distinction has survived, and while it has been seriously misleading in many areas of life, nowhere has it been more misleading or damaging in its consequences than in traditions of English teaching. In fact, by the mid-twentieth century, the distinction had led to the emergence of what I have elsewhere argued (Christie, 1981) was a 'received tradition' of English language teaching. Such a tradition, with its dissociation of grammar (or sometimes 'form' or 'structure') from meaning (or sometimes 'composition'), has lain at the heart of many of the debates generated about English teaching from the 1960s on.

Among those mother tongue specialists who sought to reform the practices for teaching the English language and who gathered at the Dartmouth Seminar in 1966, for example (see Dixon, 1967), the drive for reform was in particular born of a reaction against many sterile practices for teaching about language which were themselves a part of the 'received tradition'. These practices were sterile because they did dissociate 'language study' from meaning, whether the interest in meaning lay in the examination of literature or in the writing of a 'composition', as that term had developed particularly in the nineteenth century. Those who gathered at Dartmouth were concerned to find a more vital tradition of English teaching, one which acknowledged the functions that language served persons in making sense of their world. But the 'growth model' that emerged actually promised more than it could ever really deliver, in terms of an improved pedagogy for the teaching of English. There were, broadly, two reasons for this. First, the 'growth model' had an essentially romantic notion of the individual, conceived in some idealized sense as 'growing' while developing personally important meanings, and it failed to acknowledge the social nature of human existence. Second, and for related reasons, in that the model focused primarily on persons constructing their 'own' meanings in an idealized way, its effect was to deflect attention from the nature of language itself. The result was that it offered little of use to the teacher in terms of a model for teaching *about* language. Indeed, its effect, more often than not, was to cause teachers actively to resist teaching about language, on the grounds that this in some way interfered with the capacity of children to come to terms with building meaning in language in their 'own' way.

In that the 'growth model' was romantic in its origins, it derived from different traditions from the classical traditions in which Johnson and many others of the eighteenth century worked. Romantic notions of the individual, while having their origins in the sociopolitical developments of the late eighteenth century, became better established in the nineteenth century. Their effects were felt in various ways in English-speaking cultures, including some at least of the English literary traditions of the period. As I shall argue later, pedagogical theories to do with the teaching of English in the nineteenth century were more fully developed for the purposes of elementary, than for secondary, education. A good deal of the pedagogical theorizing of that century, at least with respect to the teaching of English literacy, perpetuated the dissociation of grammar and meaning. Indeed, grammar came to dominate at the expense of rhetoric, bringing about a steady decline in the quality of English language teaching generally as the century proceeded. Hence — and as I shall suggest later, not coincidentally — this led to the development of an enfeebled educational tradition for the children of the poor, in whose interests elementary education was primarily provided. A great deal of the pedagogical theorizing of the time showed little of the impact of romanticism, other than in a commitment to the view that poetry-reading was a civilizing or enlightening force. Romanticism would become a more fully established element of English-teaching theory, with the spread of English literary teaching both in universities and in secondary schools, which, while it had its origins in the nineteenth century, was in fact a development of the twentieth century.

As grammar came to dominate during the nineteenth century, the study of rhetoric gave way to that of 'composition', a very pale shadow of the older tradition. With the loss of a robust tradition for examining language as a resource used for the construction of meaning, a number of other time-consuming exercises came to absorb the energies of teachers and students alike: exercises in parsing and analysis, in correcting 'faulty sentences', in rehearsing the creation of simple sentences, in copying improving tales, in writing paraphrases of the writings of others — particularly excerpts from literature. It was a debilitating tradition of English teaching at best. Moreover, because it shut out systematic concern for the manner in which language worked to build meaning, the tradition both accompanied and helped make possible the eventual adoption of a view of literature as representing 'great works' which must be admired, even celebrated, but not analyzed in any systematic way to understand how they worked.

In short, the eventual decline of interest in rhetoric and all that this involved with its concern for meaning had the effect over time of rendering language 'invisible'. The effects of that invisibility were evident of the Dartmouth Seminar in 1966. The participants at that Seminar, paradoxically enough, were unable to see that in promoting a 'growth model' of language learning as they did, they actually left out of consideration the nature of language itself. In consequence, while they had much to say of use concerning the need to involve children in using language to learn, they had little to offer as a theory for teaching *about* language. Moreover, as already noted, because they also lacked a sense of a social theory that could motivate or explain the nature of human experience and the particular role of language in that experience, they could do no more than promote a view of the teacher as 'trusted' or 'sympathetic' adult, facilitating growth in students. That is to say, they not only had no agenda for direct intervention in the language development of students: they actually had a general philosophy that tended to discourage such intervention.

I would argue that a more robust theory of human experience, and of the nature of language as an aspect of that experience, will view language primarily as a tool or resource for making meaning, to use Halliday's (1974) term. Moreover, it will view language as a social phenomenon, powerfully involved in the many ways humans build and construct their experience, and systematically organized in order to build that experience. Such a language theory will thus not dissociate meaning from 'structure', and it will seek to render 'visible' or explicit a great deal of the ways in which language works to make meaning. Indeed, the theory will propose that unless language study is made *overtly* part of the curriculum, generations of students will be disempowered, and unable to use their language properly, especially in the literate mode. In addition, since such a theory of language is itself committed to the view that language is a social phenomenon and as such learned in use, it proposes a directly interventionist role on the part of the teacher to bring about improved opportunity for students to use it. Such a role is not 'facilitative' of growth; rather, it involves overt teaching and guidance of students as they learn language.

By way of developing the arguments here, I propose in this chapter first to discuss in some detail the development of the 'received tradition' of English teaching from the eighteenth century onwards, and to indicate something of the changing social and political contexts which fostered the development of that tradition. Among other matters, I shall consider the models of English rhetoric and grammar that became a part of the 'received tradition', and I shall show how the relationship between these two changed over time. I shall suggest that the tradition of English teaching that had emerged by the mid-twentieth century was a poor one, disadvantaging many in its refusal to take seriously the cause of language study as a necessary part of school learning. I shall also briefly consider what was said of the teaching of English literature and its values in the nineteenth century, noting that while it was not widely taught, claims were made quite early by some for the civilizing powers of literature. A romantic view of literature teaching had appeared, I shall argue, although it was not very influential for the purposes of educational practice until well into the twentieth century. Once into the twentieth century, in the light both of the changing nature of

English-speaking societies such as England and Australia, and in the light of changing pedagogical theories, a romantic view of the role of literature did become more influential. However, in that it eschewed systematic study of language, focusing instead upon the claimed moral benefits of reading great works of literature, such approaches to teaching literature as appeared served to perpetuate the by now well established tendency to trivialize the teaching of language. In discussing trends since the 1960s, as already indicated, I shall suggest that the 'new English' which the period ushered in was less revolutionary and relevant than was sometimes thought.

I shall conclude by arguing that appropriate models of the English language and its teaching for the future will: first, address the nature of the English language as a social phenomenon, centrally involved in the building of experience; and second, teach for an explicit knowledge about the language.

The Development of the 'Received Tradition' of English Language Studies

Despite Johnson's dismissal of the claims of English syntax to be taken seriously by authorities such as himself, much of the scholarly activity of his time was in fact devoted to its study, and before the eighteenth century was over, a great deal more would be written on the subject. It was a century in many ways remarkable for the scholarly preoccupations with the English language which it actually generated. In 1721, for example, Isaac Watts published an account of the English spelling and pronunciation systems of London speakers of his day in *The Art of Reading and Writing English*. Much later in the century, Thomas Sheridan, famous as a teacher of elocution, published his *A Complete Dictionary of the English Language* (1780), in which he sought to give an authoritative and complete account of the pronunciation system of English. It was also a century in which the study of rhetoric was important. Rhetorical studies, which had flourished in England in the sixteenth century, had continued to have importance right down to the eighteenth century. However, as I shall suggest later, rhetoric was beginning to alter under the impact of a changing society, so that its concerns shifted primarily from language in the oral mode to language in the written mode. Two of the most influential rhetoricians of the eighteenth century were Scots: George Campbell, who wrote *Philosophy of Rhetoric* in 1776, and Hugh Blair who wrote *Lectures on Rhetoric and Belles Lettres* in 1783. A third important rhetorician, an Englishman, Whately, was to publish his *Elements of Rhetoric* in 1828.

The eighteenth-century interest in the English language was itself a consequence of shifting political and economic priorities, for the nature of English society was changing. One source of change in the closing years of the previous century had been the advent of constitutional monarchy, with the reign of William and Mary (1689–94; William alone 1694–1702). During the reign of Queen Anne (1702–1714), English became the official language at Court. Anne's reign has sometimes been referred to as bringing in the 'Augustan Age' — a period known for its concerns with neoclassical notions of order and purity. Such concerns, among other areas of life, were turned to regularizing the English language, and to purging it of what were sometimes held to be excessive borrowings from other languages, including French.

Sheridan noted that, with the accession of the Hanoverians after Anne's time, English had been banished at Court in favour of French. In consequence, he regretted what he saw as the decline in the standard of English spoken in the cultivated classes (quoted in McKnight, 1928: 351–2). However, because of the advent of constitutional rule, Parliament had come to have a significant role in the life of the nation, and, such were the political realities of the early to mid-eighteenth century, parliamentarians had a great need to influence public opinion. They therefore continued to use English to reach the public, through electioneering, political ballads, political pamphlets, newspapers and journals. Thus, while the niceties of English pronunciation so dear to Sheridan might suffer, the language itself was alive and well, and the steady growth of relatively cheap print materials that was a feature of the eighteenth century did much to ensure the continuing role of the English language in the life of the nation.

The expansion of print materials was itself a symptom of a quiet revolution that had been some centuries in the making: the revolution by which English society was transformed from being primarily an oral culture to a literate one. That is to say, although it would be another two centuries at least before English society could claim to have conferred some kind of literacy on most of its citizens, the fact was that by the eighteenth century, literacy was available to significant numbers of people, and they had access to quite varied print materials.[2] Written language was increasingly becoming the primary resource in which knowledge, information, opinions, arguments and ideas were created, stored and passed on to others. The adoption of a written mode, available to a larger and larger number of people, brings about important differences in the manner in which language is used. As both Ong (1982) and Halliday (1985a) have demonstrated, arguing from very different methodologies, it also brings about differences in the consciousness of a people about their language. That is because, once the language is set down on the page, it is available for interpretation and analysis in new ways. In particular, it brings about a consciousness of the syntax of the language, and a curiosity about how this works.

To be sure, people who operate in primarily oral cultures also have a consciousness about their language, but this is of a different sort. Indeed, oral cultures as far back as the Greeks have fostered distinctive traditions of oratory. In such cultures, the skilled orator practises and develops facility in using language to inform, to persuade, to move, to argue, to entertain. Where a people passes on its important information and stories primarily through the arts of orators, the features of the language used by these orators show many devices needed both for the orator to retain and control what is to be said, and for the listeners to follow and retain what is to be heard. Thus, oral language for the oratorical tradition makes much use of various mnemonic devices, such as rhythm and rhyme, repetition and effectively paced pauses. But in addition oral language has different grammatical patternings from written language.

Thus, written language tends to be 'denser' than speech, for it carries more 'content' words per clause than does speech. Speech, on the other hand, makes greater use of grammatical items rather than 'content' items per clause than does writing; the effect is that the clause in speech is easier to follow to the human ear. In writing, we tend to produce one or more drafts, and to throw away the editings and the 'false starts'; in speech, on the other hand, the editings are necessarily present and quite audible to our listeners. Finally, the very patterns by which a series of clauses are strung together in speech are different from those in writing. In speech, we tolerate and can follow quite a complex series of inter-connecting clauses, but the patterns of clauses and their relationships in writing tend to be simpler.[3]

We can demonstrate these points in a number of ways, as I regularly ask my students to do. For example, they can take a transcript of talk, for example, and create a written version. Conversely, they can take a written text, and 'deconstruct' it, to create a version more characteristic of what would be said in the spoken mode. Consider the following sentence as an example, taken from a booklet on drug addiction in Australia:

> The full extent of the drug problem in Australia is difficult to gauge due to a lack of reliable comprehensive and uniform statistics.

Here, two nominal groups (Halliday, 1985a) are created, within which most of the 'content' is compressed: 'the full extent of the drug problem in Australia' and 'a lack of reliable comprehensive and uniform statistics'. Nominal groups, it will be noted, create 'things', about which we can write. In speech, the 'things' named in writing are more characteristically constructed as processes or 'doings', each built through a different verb choice, and each helping to create a different clause. Furthermore, explicit connections are built between the clauses, using several different linguistic items, all of which build steps in reasoning:

> No one *can gauge* how many people *take drugs* in Australia because nobody *keeps statistics* that we can *rely on* or that we *can comprehend* or that *are* uniform.

Each clause here carries a 'content', primarily realized in the processes, all of which are underlined. The reasoning involved is made explicitly available to the listener through a ('what is') question ('how many'), conjunctions ('because', 'or') or relatives ('that'). Reasoning is also present in the written version, of course, but it is constructed very differently, making use of 'due to' only to com-mence the phrase 'due to a lack of reliable comprehensive and uniform statistics'. The information built up over six clauses in talk is 'packed in', or compressed, in the written mode, into one clause, making use of the relational process, realized in the verb choice 'is', to bring its elements together.

Overall, we can say that the two texts say more or less 'the same thing', but the truth is that the grammatical resources of the language are deployed in very different ways for the two modes, creating the 'density' that is a feature of writing, and the 'grammatical complexity' that is a feature of speech.

Of course, many of the above matters to do with differences between speech and writing were not available to eighteenth-century scholars to understand. However, the emergence of significant numbers of middle-class people who enjoyed the benefits of an education and of frequent access to print materials of many kinds, created a group of folk who had the cultivation and the leisure to undertake systematic study of the language. Driven in many cases by what was felt to be the need to 'regularize' and tidy up the language, they turned, among other things, to investigating the syntax of English. What they actually addressed was the syntax of the written English sentence, rather than that of the utterance of speech, and that in itself said much for the power that written language had already assumed over the minds of eighteenth-century scholars. Indeed, the pre-occupation with the syntax of written English sentences was to become so pronounced by the twentieth century, that it is now quite difficult to disabuse teachers and others of the idea that transcripts of talk are not 'poorly expressed' or examples of 'bad grammar'. Speech truly is differently organized from writing, but on the whole teachers have not been educated to recognize or understand the differences. One of the most unfortunate of the educational consequences of the advent of the print age, in fact, has been the general loss of consciousness of, or interest in, speech. In general, to this day, it seems to me that talk is not much valued in schools, despite the important claims made by many educators since the 1960s concerning the role and power of oral language in learning. The reason I make such a claim is that, overwhelmingly, the assessment procedures that apply at all levels of schooling continue primarily to focus on students' ability to write.

I earlier noted that the advance of print materials had its impact upon the study of rhetoric, and I shall turn briefly to this now, by way of developing a sense of the changing nature of English society and of how language was perceived within it. The oratorical or rhetorical tradition, as already noted, arose in oral cultures such as Greece and Rome. Great orators studied and taught the skills of addressing audiences with a view to moving, persuading and informing them. In the English tradition, rhetoric was actively taught in the sixteenth century, and although it was an age in which many were also literate, this was still a time in which language in the oral mode was much prized. It can be no accident, historically, that one of Shakespeare's particular achievements was his capacity to write his plays with a strong sense of the cadences of speech. Like the greatest poets of his time, he wrote for a generation still very much attuned to the power of the language in the oral mode.

By the eighteenth century, the impact of writing was already such that language was perceived differently, at least for the purposes of teaching rhetoric. Campbell (1838 [1776]), Blair (1783) and Whately (1828) all argued that they were teaching of rhetoric both in speech and in writing, and they all suggested the same three contexts in which oratory still had a role: the bar, the pulpit and parliament. But writing was sufficiently important that it appears to have attracted increasing attention among rhetoricians as the years passed. Thus, it is notable that Whately (who published his study fifty-two years after Campbell's first appeared, and forty-five years after Blair's was published) observed that the invention of the popular press had caused a decline in the number of occasions in public life in which skilled oratory was needed. Argument about what constituted the proper province of rhetorical studies therefore led him to say that his concern was with 'argumentative composition', a point of view, he said, which trod a middle point between interests in speaking and in writing (Whately, 1828; quoted in Golden and Corbett, 1968: 281). By the time the mid-nineteenth-century rhetorician Bain was to produce his *English Composition and Rhetoric: A Manual* in 1866 (subsequently republished in 1887 in a much enlarged version), the preoccupation with written 'composition' was almost complete.

The three rhetoricians, Campbell, Blair and Whately, all sought to develop a perspective on language, its nature and significance, against which to explore its particular uses. While many of their observations were intended to hold with respect to writing as well as speech, it was clear that the rhetoricians' sense of the power and value of language was informed by an appreciation of it in the oral mode in particular. Thus, language was to be understood primarily in social terms, as an instrument that served important social needs and goals. The ultimate arbiter of what was acceptable in speech or writing was that of actual use. Since grammarians had sometimes suggested they had a higher claim in such matters, Campbell was quite forceful in making his point:

> Only let us rest in these as fixed principles that use or the custom of speaking, is the sole original standard as far as regards the expression, and the custom of writing is the sole standard of style: that the latter comprehends the former, and something more; that to the tribunal of use, as to the supreme authority, and consequently, in every grammatical controversy, the last resort, we are entitled to appeal from the laws and the decisions of grammarians; and that this order of subordination ought never, on any account, to be reversed (Campbell, 1838: 145).

In a manner which often bore a relation to twentieth century discussions of register theory (Ellis and Ure, 1976; Gregory and Carroll, 1978; Halliday and Hasan, 1985), rhetoricians such as Campbell and Blair discussed the factors which determined the particular features of discourse at any time. Campbell, adopting a position that Blair and Whately both shared, wrote that consideration of what constituted appropriate discourse for any situation involved examination of:

> the speaker, the hearer or persons addressed, the subject, the occasion, and the end in view, or the effect intended to be produced by the discourse (Campbell, 1838: 102).

The overall object of rhetorical studies was to uncover and master the principles by which language was adapted to serve the needs of particular discourse situations. Blair and Campbell provided somewhat different accounts of oratory, although there were close parallels. According to Campbell, some forms of oratory were intended to instruct or to teach. Depending upon the purposes, the orator might want to dispel ignorance by seeking to inform, or to eradicate error by seeking to convince. Other forms of oratory were used on those occasions where the object was to address the imagination, and the language built images in the minds of the listeners. In addition, other forms of oratory addressed the passions, and the purpose was to move the feelings of those who listened. The most complex of all forms of oratory was that which was intended to influence people, with a view to persuading them to take up a particular course of action (Campbell, 1838: 1–7). More detailed discussions provided accounts of the various 'parts' of the various discourse types.

All three rhetoricians — Campbell, Blair and Whately — sought to examine both oral and written discourses. Whately in particular focused on the qualities of argument and the conditions of proof if a discourse were to appeal to the understanding and the will. All rhetoricians devoted themselves to lengthy discussions of good 'style', about which Blair wrote that 'the foundation of all good style, is good sense, accompanied with a lively imagination' (Blair, 1783: 1). The pursuit of good 'style' should not become an empty exercise, however, according to Blair, for the 'ideas' dealt with were always of primary importance in talk or writing (Blair, 1783: 407). Collectively, the rhetoricians were committed to the view that the art of oratory or of 'composition' was a matter of craft to be learned by frequent practice and exposure to the example of others. In the contemporary world, we would no doubt question many of the principles they laid down concerning the good 'style' of particular sentences. However, the fact remains that the rhetoricians had a primary commitment to the character of the 'discourse' and to its construction or 'composition'. That is to say, in contemporary terms, theirs was a commitment to the overall organization of the text type or genre selected, and to its particular value as a vehicle for constructing socially valued meaning. This was overwhelmingly the greatest strength of the rhetoricians. Yet it was this very strength which waned as the nineteenth century wore on, and as the written mode came to dominate in the preoccupations of even those who wrote on 'composition', such as Bain, referred to above, but also Morell (1872).

The former was the best known authority on 'rhetoric' or 'composition', in the mid to latter part of the nineteenth century. However, a reading of Bain's most substantial and authoritative work, *English Composition and Rhetoric: A Manual* (1866), showed that considerations of oral language had virtually disappeared in his work. In addition, it showed that his attention was focused primarily on considerations of the propriety of particular sentence types, not on the unity that was the text itself. As a result, the concern for meaning and purpose in writing, so crucial in the writing of Campbell (who was, in my view, by far the finest of the rhetoricians discussed) was simply lost.

Morell, incidentally, the other authority on composition referred to, was one of Her Majesty's Inspectors in the nineteenth-century schools, and he produced grammars (e.g. Morell, 1881) and composition books (Morell, 1872). His composition books (to be referred to again later in this chapter) effectively stripped rhetorical studies of their concern for meaning. Both his compositions and grammar books were quite widely used in England and Australia (Christie, 1976).

To return to the eighteenth-century middle-class groups referred to earlier, the nonconformists in particular saw advantages in extending educational opportunity in the vernacular. They were, in many cases, involved in trade and commerce, and English was very much the language of trade, banking and business. According to Parker (1914), nonconformists were active in running their academies in England from 1600–1800, despite suffering periodic bouts of persecution, some of which caused them to settle in America. Certainly their academies were influential in the eighteenth century in England (including a number devoted to the education of girls) and they extolled the virtues of teaching 'modern subjects' rather than the classical ones, including English in particular. Nonconformist educational reformers, such as the Quaker, Penn, for example, lamented the trend to require children to pursue a classical education, with the particular prominence given to languages such as Latin (quoted by McKnight, 1928: 355). Since a number of the nonconformists were of a scholarly turn of mind, many did contribute to the systematic study of the English language, its grammar in particular. Their impact was to be felt in the provision of elementary education in the nineteenth century, although the curriculum of the grammar schools and the public schools would remain for the most part untouched. In the latter schools, in fact, throughout the nineteenth century and into the twentieth, English, like other 'modern subjects', had a minor and diminishing role as students progressed up the school.

The interest in examining, and in 'regularizing' English, which, as we have already noted, was a feature of the early years of the eighteenth century, had led to some attempts to develop accounts of the grammar of English even before Johnson wrote his Dictionary. However, the really authoritative English grammars emerged after Johnson's work appeared. By far the most authoritative of them all was that of Lindley Murray (1968 [1795]), an American Quaker who settled in England, and who wrote his *English Grammar* for a nonconformist academy for girls. At least two other English grammars of some authority had appeared earlier than Murray's, and these are worthy of comment here, for Murray did borrow from both, although it was his achievement that he wrote a much more complete and systematic account than did the earlier two writers. The first of these was the nonconformist, Joseph Priestley, whose *The Rudiments of English Grammar* appeared in 1761, while in 1762, he published *A Course of Lectures on the Theory of Language and Universal Grammar*. The other authority on English grammar was the Anglican Bishop, Robert Lowth, whose *English Grammar* was published in 1762.

Lowth, in an oblique reference, commented unfavourably on Johnson, who though he was the 'Person best qualified' to have given a complete account of English syntax, had dismissed it in a few lines. Lowth, like Priestley, wrote for the enlightenment of children, and both expressed concern at the 'abuses' to which the English language was often subject. A knowledge of the grammar of English, wrote Priestley (1969 [1761]: viii), was 'absolutely necessary to all persons of a liberal education'. Priestley included four sections in his book, devoted to orthography, etymology, syntax and prosody, while Lowth discussed letters, syllables, words and sentences. It was in their treatment of syntax that Priestley and Lowth differed most.

Here, Priestley took a line very like Johnson's. Indeed, Priestley considered the English language a reasonably simple one, and its simplicity he attributed to 'the long continued barbarism of the people from whom we received it' (Priestley, 1969 [1761]: iv). Lowth's was a more comprehensive and systematic treatment of syntax. He chose to deal with 'sentences' rather than to use the term 'syntax', and he identified three kinds of simple sentence: the explicative, the interrogative and the imperative. Compound sentences could be formed by the use of relatives and conjunctions joining simple sentences together.

Lowth's approach to syntax was more systematic than was Priestley's, and if nothing else, it made clear that considerably more could be said on the subject than Johnson had suggested. It remained, however, for Lindley Murray to develop the discussion of English syntax even further. Murray's volume was in every way more detailed and scholarly than were the works of Priestley and Lowth. Like the latter two, Murray recognized nine parts of speech, and went on to illustrate each by use of copious examples. Where Priestley and Lowth had offered relatively brief discussions of tense, Murray gave a detailed discussion, identifying a greater range of tenses than they did, and developing these at some length.

Murray's most original contribution, however, lay in his treatment of syntax, for he produced what he termed the twenty-two rules of syntax by which one might achieve the correct agreement and disposition of words in a sentence. It was these rules, with minor variations, which were to appear in all textbooks for the teaching of English grammar throughout the nineteenth century, and well into the twentieth. It will not be necessary here to outline all Murray's twenty-two rules. In fact, if I cite just two of them, they will be in any case familiar to most readers of this volume. Thus, the first rule stated: 'A verb must agree with its nominative case, in number and person.' The second stated: 'Two or more nouns in the singular number, joined together by one or more copulative conjunctions, have verbs, nouns, and pronouns agreeing with them in the plural.' Variants of these, as well as of the other twenty rules of syntax, were still being taught when I attended school in the 1950s, although their character and significance had changed over the intervening century and a half.

Indeed, as the nineteenth century proceeded, the quality of the grammar textbooks declined generally, as did the practices for teaching grammar overall. By the twentieth century the 'received tradition' of grammar teaching was well established, and the scholarly concern which Murray had brought to the articulation of his rules was largely gone. Murray sought to explain and give reasons for his account of features of syntax, and he was clear that grammatical studies were not to be understood as subsuming the concerns of those rhetoricians who addressed issues of 'perspicuity' in writing. But into the nineteenth century, generations of teachers were increasingly encouraged to have students commit the various rules to memory. In practice, the relationship of these rules to the activity of writing became ever more tenuous over time, although many, including Bain and Morell, referred to earlier, would have asserted a strong relationship.

Nowhere was the trend stronger to let studies of parts of speech and syntax dominate than in the many nineteenth-century elementary schools for the children of the poor. The very practices of educating children in large numbers, such as those developed using monitorial principles, required children to be drilled and rehearsed, to do much parsing of sentences, much copying and correction of 'faulty sentences'. Teaching in large numbers also required that children be kept in order and quiet. The many exercises in the identification of parts of speech and their parsing, as well as in sentence analysis for advanced students, provided activities through which children might be disciplined and silenced. In short, nineteenth-century elementary schools were not intended as places in which the spoken language would flourish (Brice Heath, 1986), and performance in writing increasingly became the measure by which students' progress was measured. Capacities in grammatical parsing and sentence analysis were seen as prerequisites to performance in writing, so much so that in the case of many students in schools the pursuit of these things came to take the place of writing itself. Moreover, in a century in which the standards of teacher education for elementary school teaching were often very low, the activities of drilling children in such things as recognizing the parts of speech and in parsing them were often the most that many teachers felt competent to teach.

In 1868 Charles Badham, Professor of Classics and Logic at Sydney University, criticized practices that prevailed at the time for the teaching of English in the then colony of New South Wales. The help of Morell, referred to above, was enlisted by those whom Badham had criticized, in developing their defence (Badham, 1890). Despite the arguments that Badham proposed and continued to propose for some years about practices for teaching English language, those very practices continued to apply well into the twentieth century (Christie, 1976, 1981).

How then are we to explain this? In part, some explanation has been offered above in the general suggestion about the gaining power of the written word over the minds of many, and the particular interest this appeared to engender in the nature of words and syntax. In part, too, some explanation has been given in terms of the traditional distinction made between grammar, on the one hand, and rhetoric or 'meaning' or 'composition', on the other. In that such a distinction exists, that in itself creates the possibility, even the likelihood, that the concern for meaning can be simply overturned, leaving in its stead the rather barren pursuit of the parts of speech, their parsing and sentence analysis. But these explanations in themselves are insufficient to tell us why the 'received tradition' of English teaching came to prevail, particularly in the elementary schools of the nineteenth century. Our final explanation, then, must address the nature of the education that the elementary school was intended to provide, and the particular role that language studies were intended to play in that school.

The Nineteenth-Century Elementary School Curriculum

The nineteenth-century elementary school, conceived primarily for the education of the poor, was intended to produce generations of sober, law-abiding and industrious workers. It did not aim to produce independent persons, capable of developing and sustaining arguments and opinions of their own. Hence, such practices as the teaching of rhetoric with its commitment to argument and the shaping of meaning, had no place in the educational theories proposed for the teaching of the children of nineteenth-century schools. Insofar as the schools were to teach literacy skills, these were of an extremely minimal kind, and not calculated to produce other than compliant workers. The ability to read religious tracts or a little 'general knowledge' of the kind found in a school reader, or the ability to write a letter or a short piece on an improving 'theme', the ability to identify parts of speech and parse sentences, were about the limit of the literacy skills most schools sought to confer. In practice, throughout the nineteenth century, many elementary schools conferred significantly less.

Reviewing the early efforts at providing elementary education by a variety of church or charitable institutions in England in the eighteenth and nineteenth centuries, one historian wrote that 'their ideal may with little exaggeration be summed up as training the poor to poverty' (Birchenough, 1938: 9). Where a school prepares for poverty, it cannot tolerate a pedagogical theory which seeks to develop capacity to argue, to challenge or to change. Later in the nineteenth century, when middle-class activity brought about the intervention of the state in the provision of education, there was a concern to confer literacy on those who would eventually be given the vote. Even then, however, the political and educational reformers were no radicals, nor did they seek to develop habits of radical independence in those whom they educated in schools. As the century wore on, it is true, many reformers sought to improve the quality of the education offered in schools. But the preoccupation with the trivial and the largely meaningless in the name of language studies too often served to keep those who came to school ignorant and unskilled, unable on the whole to challenge their political masters.

An examination of the various teachers' manuals (e.g. Currie, n.d.a, n.d.b; Dawes, n.d.; Dunn, 1837; Fitch, 1880; see Christie, 1976, 1981) that appeared in the nineteenth century for the preparation of teachers in the elementary school shows that the language activities of reading, spelling, grammar, sentence analysis, knowledge of the origins of words, as well as a little 'composition', were all addressed. Theorists like Currie (n.d.a: 74–85) for example, drew a broad distinction between knowledge that was 'instrumentary' and that which was 'general'. The former subjects included all the English language studies as well as arithmetic. Such studies were 'instrumentary' because they made possible access to general knowledge. Moreover, the instrumentary subjects had a function in promoting the various mental 'faculties'. Capacity in certain language areas could be assessed and used to grade students. In fact, following the advice of the various teacher manuals, the New South Wales authorities adopted the policy of grading children on the basis of attainments in reading, arithmetic and grammar (New South Wales Council of Education, 1867, Appendix A: 199).

The distinction between the 'instrumentary' and the 'general', it should be noted, had the effect of marginalizing language, rendering it merely a neutral phenomenon, serving the cause of 'expressing' or 'clothing' knowledge, ideas and information. Such a distinction creates a dichotomy, in other words, between language or 'form', on the one hand, and 'content' or meaning, on the other. This is but another manifestation of the dichotomy or distinction we have seen was already well established in the eighteenth century, when rhetoric contrasted with grammar. The tendency to dichotomize in this manner has been referred to by Reddy (1979) as an instance of what he termed the 'conduit metaphor'. He has argued that such dichotomizing tendencies are well established in western traditions, and realized constantly in the ways English speakers use language. Nowhere have they been more harmful, in my view, than in educational literature, and the traditions of English language teaching have done much to perpetuate such distinctions. I refer to such contemporary distinctions as those made between 'language' and 'thought', 'form' and 'function', 'process' and 'product', as well as those earlier alluded to in the rhetoric/grammar split to do with 'form' and 'meaning'.

The pedagogical theories of the nineteenth century, as outlined in the various teachers' manuals, did much to entrench such distinctions in the thinking of educators, with what have continued to be unfortunate consequences. Where language is seen as merely 'instrumentary', then meaning itself is simply overlooked. The 'received tradition' of English language teaching as that developed in the nineteenth century focused increasingly on language as words, parts of speech, or parts of sentences. Such a model of language permits no significant engagement with language as text, or language as meaning.

Insofar as writing was taught in the nineteenth-century elementary school, it was introduced after some instruction in spelling and the parts of speech, instruction in which often occupied the first two or three years of schooling, along with some instruction in reading. Writing then progressed to writing single sentences, often copied from other sources, while subsequent programs for teaching 'composition' writing tended also to involve copying from other sources. Morell (1872), for instance, the Inspector of Schools mentioned much earlier, recommended giving children fables and other stories to read with the teacher, after which they were to write out the outlines of these and their principal 'phraseology'. This done, they subsequently wrote the stories out themselves. This hardly constituted a basis for producing independent writers. Indeed, the tendency of

Morell's advice was to perpetuate the preoccupation with language as 'words' and 'sentences'. It did not tend towards a wider concern for the organization of the text being written, or its social purposes.

Morell was in distinguished company in outlining the study of 'composition' as he did, for the most widely known authority on rhetoric of his time was Bain, to whom reference was made earlier. Bain claimed a close relationship with Campbell, Blair and Whately, but the connection was in fact quite superficial. It is significant, moreover, that Bain also published several grammar books (e.g. Bain, 1863, 1872, 1874), for the evidence suggests that he was primarily preoccupied with syntax rather than with the nature of the larger thing that was the text. Whatever the merits of a concern for syntax — and as Murray at least had discussed the matter, this was in my view a defensible if limited achievement — it is not a sufficient basis for undertaking language study.

There are in fact three related limitations of a concern with syntax alone, and these are worth mentioning here because of their significance in the development of the 'received tradition' of English teaching. In the first place, as already noted, the concern for syntax was born primarily of an interest in the written language rather than the spoken language. The study of syntax as Murray proposed it does not illuminate the thing that is speech at all. On the contrary, as I earlier suggested, a preoccupation with syntax has actually done harm, in that over time it has helped produce generations of people unable to see that the grammar of speech is simply different from, not inferior to, that of writing.

In the second place, the study of syntax does not illuminate the study of meaning. That is because, as I also noted, the classical tradition of grammatical study in which Johnson, but also Murray, actually wrote, did divorce grammar from the study of rhetoric. Where once the two are torn asunder, as certainly did happen over the nineteenth century, the study of grammar itself becomes a mere shadow of its former self. Small wonder then, that traditional school grammar as that had emerged by the middle years years of this century, was the impoverished thing it had become.

The third limitation of the traditional study of syntax is that it can never enable the student to address the character or the organization of the text. I use the latter term here in its technical sense, as discussed by Halliday (in Halliday and Hasan, 1985: 10), as 'language that is functional ... language that is doing some job in some context'. A theory of text, as Halliday goes on to argue, can never be seen as 'an extension of grammatical theory' because a text is primarily a 'semantic unit'. Rhetorical studies in their older sense were always primarily concerned with texts — passages of language constructed to make meaning and hence to achieve important purposes. It was the concern for meaning that was lost with the particular models of composition that both Morell and Bain proposed.

The tendency to remove rhetorical concerns for the organization of meaning from the curriculum served to relegate such issues to the realm of the 'invisible', as I have previously suggested. Yet the expectation that texts be composed according to principles well established in an English-speaking culture certainly did remain. That is because it is of the nature of any culture that such expectations will apply, whether the matter is consciously understood this way or not. A language is a primary semiotic system with which meanings are made, and the various linguistic choices made in order to realize significant meanings are neither arbitrary nor random. On the contrary, such choices are made in systematic ways to create meanings relevant to the culture. The earlier rhetoricians at their best always acknowledged this (though they would not have put the matter in the terms adopted here), and in consequence they taught for some conscious reflection upon the ways in which language was used to shape meaning. Once such matters are rendered invisible, then some social groups will always be very much more advantaged than others, for the purposes of their educational opportunity, as such scholars as Bernstein among others have shown. Indeed, some years ago, Halliday (1969), citing Bernstein, argued that school failure is in a deep sense a language failure — a failure to recognize and use the linguistic patterns in which significant meanings are made.

Overall, the nineteenth century was the century of the slow growth and acceptance of elementary education, although, such were the attendance rates, it was not till after the First World War that most children were actually to attend elementary schools in either England or Australia. The written word came to dominate as the principal means by which information was stored and communicated, and an often misplaced attention was paid to practices of teaching features of the written English language in the elementary schools. The effect of these practices was to develop generations of students who had a degree of basic literacy, in that many achieved capacity to read or write simple texts. But they were not, on the whole, able to do more. Even among the more privileged students who attended the grammar schools or the selective state high schools that appeared in Australia in the late nineteenth and early twentieth centuries, rhetoric was not really taught. As the century proceeded, the practices of using language effectively were no doubt often difficult to see. They were not, for instance, a feature of my own education in a girls' high school in Sydney in the 1950s. Nonetheless, like other privileged students, life opportunity advantaged me in that I could relatively easily develop some facility for recognizing and using the text types valued in the culture. Such a development was not available to students less socially privileged than I, and so it remains to this day. Studies by Gray (1985), Walton (1986), Christie (1989), Martin and Rothery (1980, 1981), Kamler (1990) and Rothery and Macken (1991) all tend to demonstrate that what children do in their linguistic choices in writing is overwhelmingly a condition of what they have been enabled to learn to do. Where life opportunity exposes children to the patterns of language actually rewarded in an education, they come to school very much advantaged over those not so exposed. For so long as we continue to leave the linguistic choices necessary for school success a matter of the 'invisible' agenda of schooling, so too we perpetuate disadvantage.

Views of Literature Teaching and its Role in the 'Received Tradition'

I earlier alluded to the development of romanticism in the nineteenth century, and I noted that its impact on English teaching in that century was not extensive. It related mainly to the teaching of the older students in the upper grades of the elementary school. The most important of the educational theorists in nineteenth century Australia, Wilkins (1886: 38), referred to Morell, in arguing the values of reading poetry to develop 'sentiment' or feeling in youth. Arnold, Professor of

Poetry at Oxford from 1857–67, but also Inspector of Schools, noted in his General Report for 1872 that 'recitation' was the subject in the elementary schools which did the 'most good' (Arnold, 1908 [1872]: 147). In the 'forming' of pupils, he went on, 'familiarity with masterpieces' was of great importance. For the less able pupils, the number of masterpieces selected for learning should be relatively few, but for the more advanced, the works should be selected according to 'some well-planned order'. Commenting on what he saw as a regrettable absence in the schools of attempts to raise reading to the examination of literary study, he wrote, 'recitation must be relied upon for carrying the power of perception onward' (Arnold, 1908 [1872]: 148).

Elsewhere, both in his annual reports and in such works as *Culture and Anarchy* (1869), Arnold wrote of the evils of a culture rapidly being overtaken by industrialization and by what he saw as the destruction of older values. The teaching of literature — poetry in particular — he argued, was the best means of defending a people from moral decline. Mathieson (1975: 40) notes, following Raymond Williams, how much such a view drew upon romantic ideas, as these had been developed by poets such as Wordsworth and Shelley, earlier in the century. A view of the role of literature as a 'civilizing' force in a culture was to be very influential in theories of English teaching in the twentieth century, in particular in the work of Leavis.

Apart from learning to recite poetry, literary studies sometimes also involved the training of students to write paraphrases of literary extracts — a practice Arnold seemed to approve (see, for example, his *General Report for the Year 1874*: 157–9); in addition, literature of a sort was taught in dealing with histories of English literature. Morell, mentioned earlier, who wrote many books for schools, wrote a volume (Morell, n.d.) called *A Biographical History of English Literature. Being an Elementary Introduction to the Greater English Writers with Three Hundred Exercises.*

In general then, insofar as it had a role in the pedagogical theories of the nineteenth-century elementary school, literature had a function in forming character and in the development of finer feeling. Insofar as it featured in any secondary education, it consisted either in writing a paraphrase of a poem or an extract from Shakespeare, or in learning accounts of the lives of famous writers. In any case, at the secondary level, English studies, whether of language or of literature, played a minor role to the turn of the century at least. There were several factors responsible for this.

In the first place, the nonconformist academies which had done so much to foster the development of English studies declined in significance in the nineteenth century, as the policies of discrimination against dissenters also gradually disappeared. Secondary education — available for the most part to the more privileged classes — was thus primarily offered in the grammar schools and the public schools. Here, English did not enjoy much status, any more than it did in most universities. Arnold, as we have seen, held the role of Professor of Poetry at Oxford, although this was an honorary position. While some English courses were offered at Oxford, it was not till 1897 that the University opened a Department of English Philology and Old English. The latter title implied a very partial commitment to the values of studying English, and in particular it implied no strong commitment to contemporary English literature. London University had begun offering an English Literature course in its BA program in 1859, and most of the other provincial universities similarly introduced English courses (Shayer, 1972: 2). In 1887 the University of Sydney created a Chair of Modern Literature, embracing English, French and German, and a subsequent additional Chair of Modern Literature was created in the 1890s. At Cambridge University it would be well into the twentieth century before English studies became important, and this would owe much to the influence of Leavis, as we shall see later. Even after university departments devoted to teaching English had opened, they did not attract large numbers of students for some years. University entrance requirements emphasized performance in the classical languages well into the twentieth century.

It said much for the changed political and social significance attaching to the English language that, in the aftermath of the First World War, the British called for the first enquiry into *The Teaching of English in England* (The Newbolt Report, 1921). Among other matters, the Newbolt Commissioners regretted the preoccupation with teaching the rules of English grammar in the elementary schools at the expense of more imaginative activities. They were, in addition, very much committed to a belief in the values of teaching English to children. They made the following observations, redolent of Arnold's beliefs in the civilizing effects of literature:

> We claim that no personality can be complete, can see life steadily and see it whole, without that unifying influence, that purifying of the emotions which art and literature can alone bestow. It follows then from what we have said above that the bulk of our people, of whatever class, are unconsciously living starved existences, that one of the richest fields of our spiritual being is left uncultivated — if not indeed barren, for the weeds of literature have never been so prolific as in our day (The Newbolt Report, 1921: 257).

Ballard was one of the experts who testified before the Newbolt enquiry. His observations were addressed to reflections on the limitations of much traditional school grammar. In the same year that the Newbolt Report appeared, he published *Teaching the Mother Tongue*, in which he observed regretfully that while rhetoric had survived in both Scotland and America, in England it had become associated with rather shallow devices for using language (Ballard, 1921).

The Newbolt Report was influential. Even if it did not bring about immediate changes, according to Mathieson (1975: 69–82) its impact, like that of George Sampson's *English for the English* (1921), was to be felt powerfully among English specialists, in particular giving support to the growing significance attached to English literature teaching.

The times were changing. The growth of industry had transformed Great Britain over the previous century, while the extension of the franchise and the social changes brought about by the First World War had created a society in which the importance of the English language was increasingly recognized. As for the former colonies of Australia, now united as a self-governing dominion, they too felt something of the changes, and the numbers of children achieving an elementary education began to increase in the aftermath of the war. The extension of secondary education for all lay ahead. Partly in the light of the changed nature of English-speaking societies, partly in the light of changing significance attaching to schooling, English studies were to gain in significance in the secondary schools curriculum as the century proceeded. But the 'received tradition' of English teaching lay heavily on educational practices. In the 1950s and 1960s, moves would be made to bring about change and develop new paradigms for teaching English, although as I shall suggest, the new models offered less than was often claimed. In the next section, therefore, I intend to discuss briefly developments since the turn of the century. Before I do so, I shall attempt to bring together several threads in the argument to this point, the better to proceed with what is to be argued of developments this century.

In brief, then, I have suggested that in the eighteenth century there was a considerable upsurge of interest in the English language, and that this interest led to attempts to 'regularize' what was known of English grammar. In particular, it led to the writing of descriptions of the parts of speech and the syntax of the written English sentence. The scholarly effort devoted to this activity, at least as represented in Murray's work, had the modest but useful merit that it established principles controlling the syntax of what in another age would be referred to as 'standard written English'. Grammatical studies, however, were potentially always open to corruption or compromise, because they were conceived apart from broader questions of functions, purpose and meaning in using language. Rhetorical studies, traditionally those studies in which such matters were examined and taught, were still of significance in the eighteenth century. However, under the impact of the changing significance of literacy in English-speaking cultures, such studies were transformed in character, and they died out in the nineteenth century, their place taken by a rather enfeebled subject called 'composition'. A scholarly preoccupation with grammar, a declining value attaching to speech, and a corresponding value attaching to writing, had caused a shift in approaches to the study of the English language by the early years of the nineteenth century.

At the same time, and for historically related reasons, the development of elementary schooling brought with it various practices for teaching and disciplining children in large numbers. Exercises in drilling children in parts of speech, correction of 'faulty sentences' and — sometimes — writing 'compositions' to set themes, became a part of the basic English curriculum. Such activities were sterile because they had become dissociated from the wider rhetorical preoccupations with text and purpose. They were, however, consistent with the aims of an elementary education, conceived, as it was, primarily to teach a degree of minimal literacy, but not to develop generations of persons capable of developing and sustaining arguments, or expressing independent points of view.

Hence, what was taught in the name of the 'received tradition' about the English language was trivial indeed. In any rigorous or empowering sense, language had been rendered invisible. Moreover, another element in the 'received tradition' of English teaching had begun to emerge by the late nineteenth and early twentieth centuries. It concerned the values attaching to literature, and it partook of the romantic view that literature served to safeguard and preserve much that was best in the culture. Such a view of literature did not predispose people to a close study of a literary text. On the contrary, since it rested on claims about the capacity of the literary artist to forge great truths in some private way, this manner of thinking about literature discouraged close study of texts. In any case, the growth of romanticism in thinking about literature was in part responsible for the view that had emerged by the end of the nineteenth century, that rhetoric was a rather shabby study, exposing no more than a few shallow tricks in using language for the purposes of persuading others.

In short, the romantic view of literature actually came over time to endorse the notion that close study of texts in the rhetorical manner was inappropriate. Small wonder then, that into the twentieth century, all that remained of any commitment to language study were the activities of identifying parts of speech, correcting 'faulty sentences', analyzing sentences and so on, with some rather pallid work on 'composition' sometimes thrown in.

Dartmouth and After

The Dartmouth Seminar of 1966 is often spoken of among specialists in English teaching as marking a new shift in thinking — as ushering in a 'new English'. While there is some truth in this, many of the ideas that emerged and that were argued so persuasively in Dixon's book *Growth through English* (1967) had in fact been about for some time. Dixon reported that three 'models' of English teaching had been identified at the seminar as having been of significance. They were the 'skills model', which 'fitted an era when initial literacy was the prime demand'; the 'cultural heritage model', which stressed 'a civilizing and socially unifying content'; and the third and current model was that of 'personal growth', whose focus was 'on the need to re-examine the learning processes and the meaning to the individual of what he (sic) is doing in English lessons'. The skills model, Dixon noted, was unsatisfactory because it focused in a very limited way on the minimal steps of achieving basic literacy only. Dixon argued that the cultural heritage model, deriving from the influence of Matthew Arnold in particular, had the merit in that it did focus on broader matters than skills, including great litera-ture, and that great literature was enriching. The principal limitation of the cultural model, according to Dixon, was that it took culture as 'given', while often ignoring the experience of children in living the culture of family and neighbourhood.

The 'personal growth' model of learning the English language focused on the needs of students building their own experiences of life in their own language uses. Where personal growth programs applied, Dixon (1967: 5) wrote, the language and the meaning used were both owned by the student, 'not a product handed over by the teacher'. A little later, Dixon (1967: 13) wrote that the student operating in a 'personal growth' classroom would perhaps gain 'new insight into himself (as creator of his own world)'.

The first of Dixon's models belongs most clearly with the nineteenth-century elementary schools, some sense of which I have developed much earlier. The second of his models — that of the cultural heritage — did indeed derive from Arnold among others, but it had also been given particular life in the twen-tieth century both by the Newbolt Commissioners as we saw above, and by Leavis as well as several of his former students at Cambridge University. About Leavis and his former students I shall say a little more below. First, however, I shall say something of Dixon's 'growth model', as its influence was to be quite considerable following Dartmouth.[4]

This model — sometimes referred to as the 'new English' — attracted a great deal of favourable support in the 1970s and the 1980s, both in England and

Australia. In a review of Australian English language curriculum documents undertaken in 1978, Rothery and I (1979) found that 'personal growth' was an enduring theme in all the documents examined. Among other matters, we observed that:

> It is the growth of the child which is seen to be central to the teaching of English, and crucial to personal growth, in the terms of the various documents, is development in language (Christie and Rothery, 1979: 203).

A little later, we noted that:

> The child's own experience is seen as a major resource to be drawn on for language activities and in exploring literature, and there is strong emphasis on writing about personal and imaginative experience (Christie and Rothery, 1979: 203).

There were two related themes in all the discussions of 'personal growth', from Dartmouth on, that are worthy of comment. The one was the concern for the 'person' — idealized, unique and distinctive — who was to emerge in 'personal growth' classrooms. The other theme was that of 'ownership', where that referred to the manner in which, it was said, children should be encouraged to develop their 'own' experience, their 'own' language to deal with such experience, their 'own' sense of the world. The 'growth model' of English with its notions of individuality and personhood was both a phenomenon of the 1960s, and at the same time directly in the line of older traditions. There was, in fact, a significant relationship between the 'growth model' and the model of English literary studies that Leavis and others had done much to develop, as Green (1990) has argued.

Mathieson (1975: 123) observes that, as early as the 1930s, Leavis and his students had expressed concern at what they saw as an impoverished culture, and they had argued the importance of the English teacher taking on the task of educating for the development of a people with finer sensibilities. Literary studies in particular, it was held, would help correct the evils of a popular culture in which the media were coming to exercise a hold on the minds of people. Later, former students of Leavis such as Whitehead (1966) and Holbrook (1967), among others, were to develop further arguments for the personal development and enrichment of persons through English literary studies. A number of Leavis' former students were also active in the formation in 1963 of the National Association of Teachers of English (Mathieson, 1975: 123).

Writing of the ideal English School of a university, Leavis said that the 'essence' of its discipline was its 'literary-critical' nature. Such a discipline, he went on:

> trains, in a way no other discipline can, intelligence and sensibility together, cultivating a sensitiveness and precision of response and a delicate integrity of intelligence — intelligence that integrates as well as

analyzes and must have pertinacity and staying power as well as delicacy (Leavis, 1979a: 34).

While Leavis elsewhere stated that he did not intend to slight the sciences or other specialist studies (Leavis, 1979b: 3), a strong impression was often left of the particular and privileged claims of English studies to develop sensibility, promote moral development, and foster the maintenance of culturally significant traditions. Many of Leavis' students, in fact, did much to promulgate such views. Thus, one of his former students, Inglis (1969), wrote of Leavis that he offered 'perhaps the only attempt at totality in a theory of education which [had] had visible effect upon English schools', and he went on:

> it would seem no accident that almost alone among schoolteachers in this country the teachers of English attempt to talk out with their pupils a moral position for the individual and a critique of the society he (sic) lives in (Inglis, 1969: 2–3).

Among those who had worked with Leavis, the privileged role of the English teacher as guardian of the culture was a constant theme, as was the rather arrogant view that English literary studies, more than any others, offered opportunity for the development of moral positions.

I have observed that Dixon stated that the 'cultural heritage model' had the merit that it focused on great literature, for this was enriching. The limitation of such a model, he had suggested, was that it overlooked the culture of the child lived in family and community. The 'growth' exponents, however, had much in common with those who espoused the 'cultural heritage' position. They were, for instance, committed to a privileged view of the role of English studies as a context for promoting personal and moral development. Many would have seen themselves, like Inglis, as developing 'literary-critical' skills. In their concern to promote children able to use their 'own' language to forge their 'own' truths and their 'own' sense of their world, they did, however, resist teaching for detailed examination of language.

In fact, a notable feature of the 'personal growth' model of language learning which developed after the 1960s was a disinclination to address seriously questions of what to do in the name of teaching about English language, as Australian experience in the 1970s and 1980s was to demonstrate. In the 1970s a national Language Development Project was instituted in Australia by the then Curriculum Development Centre (CDC). Its object was to bring together task forces or teams from all Australian States and Territories to develop materials for language teaching in the upper primary-junior secondary interface. The model of language development used in the project was one proposed by Halliday (CDC, 1978), who had suggested that language development involves three interrelated elements: learning language, learning through language, and learning about language. The third element referred to overt teaching about language, where that might include such things as the writing system, the spelling system, features of spoken and written language, and the different registers.

I was responsible for the national coordination of the Project. The work of the LDP was never brought to a satisfactory conclusion because the Federal

Government chose to close down the CDC, so that we can never know with any certainty what might have happened had it run its intended life. However, I can say that while the Project did have some notable achievement, it failed to address the question of appropriate models for teaching *about* the English language. The prevailing models of the English language and its teaching stressed teacher facilitation of student growth through language, rather than overt teaching about language. Teaching about the English language was largely rejected because it was understood as synonymous with those aspects of teaching about language that had become the 'received tradition' discussed in detail earlier in this chapter: namely, teaching the nine parts of speech, as well as traditional parsing and some analysis of written sentences.

Furthermore, overt teaching about language was often rejected because it was held, potentially, at least, to intrude upon, or diminish, the capacity of the romantically-conceived individual child to come to terms with experience in his or her 'own' language. Powerful support for the primacy of the individual 'voice' of children was provided by a number of authorities on English teaching, influential in Australia in the 1970s and 1980s. Thus, in *Language and Learning*, Britton (1970: 271) had written of young people that: '[I]t is *themselves they have to become*, by the hard road of *their own choices, their own intuitions, their commitment to themselves*' (my emphasis). Sometimes, the arguments for the primacy of young people's own voices were closely linked to arguments for the values and importance of their reading literature, and coming to terms with this in independent ways, drawn from private experience. Here, the influence of Leavis was apparent. Barnes, for example, in a paper given at a conference in Australia in 1977, talked of the influence on him of Leavis while he was the latter's student at Cambridge. He noted that Leavis had directed him to read Eliot on *Tradition and the Individual Talent*. He then went on to say:

> I was much struck by Eliot's insistence that each generation has to *remake* the tradition; it isn't just a matter of taking it over passively. And in Leavis' emphasis on close reading there seemed to be the individual equivalent of this remaking. How could we attribute meaning to black marks on a white sheet without bringing our own experience to bear on it? In literature lessons *the child must make sense of the poems and stories for himself, or the whole thing is a sham* (Barnes, 1977: 85; my emphasis).

The concern for students using their 'own' language has even been argued by Medway (quoted in Torbe, 1986: 155) as a 'human rights issue'.

It is true that students need opportunity to talk freely while learning. It is also true that they should be able to write independently about the various kinds of knowledge with which they are concerned in schools. To that extent, there is value in the arguments about students' use of language. However, there is also a great deal of naivety about the ways the arguments for students use of their 'own' language have been advanced. Language is overwhelmingly a social phenomenon, its patterns and its conventions operating for the collective use of a people in shaping and making meanings. When students learn and use language, they are certainly learning, ideally, to operate with independence in various cultural contexts. Their success will be dependent upon the extent to which they master the language patterns needed for working in those contexts. Language learning is not a private and/or independent matter, nor is the language used by anybody uniquely his/her 'own'. On the contrary, the language one uses draws quite fundamentally upon the linguistic system, and that system is shared, precisely because it operates for the building of socially valued meanings of many kinds. About these matters, the proponents of the 'growth model' have been largely silent.

The 'growth model' had in fact come into being partly in reaction against what its proponents quite properly saw as a deadening tradition of teaching about language, and they sought to develop an approach which more properly respected and was responsive to the language children used themselves. 'Growth' proponents (who did not necessarily always agree, of course) such as Britton (1970), Barnes (1976, 1977), Rosen and Rosen (1973; also Barnes, Britton and Rosen, 1969) argued both for a better recognition of the central role of talk in learning, and for teachers to appreciate the value and importance of the language patterns children themselves used. In this, they were joined by others who drew more directly upon linguistic research such as Halliday, McIntosh and Strevens (1964), or indeed the whole team of people including Peter Doughty and Geoffrey Thornton who worked with Halliday in the Nuffield/Schools Council *Programme in Linguistics and English Teaching* (see Pearce, Thornton and Mackay, 1989, for a discussion of this). While the latter programme was influential in many places, incidentally, its work was in general not as influential as the 'growth' model became.

Paradoxically enough, like the 'cultural model' exponents in the tradition of Arnold and Leavis, the 'growth' exponents were not primarily interested in language at all. On the one hand, the 'cultural heritage' exponents saw themselves as guardians of important cultural traditions which they sought to share with their students, thereby enriching them; on the other hand, the 'growth model' exponents saw themselves as facilitating the growth of individuals as they developed their own values and truths, in their talk, in their reading of literature and in their writing.

Whether the focus of concern be moral development, self expression, or capacity to reflect upon personal experience, all of which in varying ways did interest both 'cultural heritage' and 'growth' exponents, all were discussed with only passing or incidental reference to language itself. In short, in both models, language was indeed 'invisible' — relegated to the 'instrumentary' role which I have previously noted it was given in nineteenth century pedagogical theories.

In fact, once a strong rhetorical commitment to the study of language was lost, the historical evidence suggests that two equally unsatisfactory and related alternatives emerged. On the one hand, there was the preoccupation with parts of speech and syntax, pursued in some sense apart from meaning. On the other hand, there was the preoccupation with great works of literature, respected, even celebrated, as repositories of truth and wisdom, but not closely studied. The 'growth model' sought to tread a path between these two alternatives. It failed, however, because, like the two models it sought to supplant, it did not adequately address questions of the nature of language itself. In consequence, the 'growth model' had little to offer teachers as positive advice for teaching about the English language.

One result of this was that it led more than one English specialist to the proposition that English was 'contentless', or that it embraced less than the whole of life itself. Thus, Shayer (1972: 19) referred to the 'fallacy' that English had 'content'. Britton and Squires, on the other hand, in writing a Preface to the revised edition of *Growth through English* (1975) said of the content of English that:

> it proves impossible to mark out an area less than the sum total of the planned and unplanned experiences through language by means of which a child gains control of himself (sic) and of his relations with the surrounding world (Britton and Squires, in Dixon, 1975: xviii).

It was a sad commentary on the state to which English had been reduced that its concerns should be described in such diffuse and vague terms, offering nothing of guidance to teachers about principled choices for planning English programmes. The content of English is the English language itself, where the primary commitment should be to develop knowledge about the language and about the manner in which it operates to build meaning. As a study, the concerns of English should be primarily with language as a social institution, or in Halliday's terms as a 'social semiotic' (Halliday and Hasan, 1985), fundamentally involved in the shaping of meaning and hence in the construction of a culture. Programmes of English should include systematic study of its genres and its registers, its grammatical system (in particular, the grammatical differences between speech and writing), its dialects, its sound system, its spelling system and its handwriting system. Given such a sweep of interest, the concerns of English over the course of years of schooling should necessarily include systematic examination of literature, but they should also include the many elements of popular culture whose influence is so pervasive, most notably film and television. English teachers will, no doubt, have a concern for the moral welfare of their students, but such a concern they will share with teachers of other subjects. In this respect, English studies enjoy no privileged status, and it is not helpful to suggest that they do.

The view of English as 'contentless' or, alternatively, as embracing all of life itself, which the 'growth' movement did much to foster, became well accepted in English teaching theory in Australia, following Dartmouth. In part, this was because it accorded with various 'progressive' theories of education, many of which had had their origins in developing educational theories of the early twentieth century, and which received a new significance in the 1960s and after. Such theories — sometimes referred to as 'child-centred' — focused upon children developing their own truths and understandings, and upon the processes in which they should be encouraged to engage in order to learn.[5] Indeed, as I have argued elsewhere (Christie, 1989) a great deal of the wider curriculum theory promoted from the 1960s to the 1980s, both in the UK and in Australia, was both 'child-centred' and 'process-oriented'. It led to the dubious proposition that the 'process' of learning is more important than the 'product'. It also gave particular significance to the 'process writing movement' which developed in Australia in the late 1970s and 1980s, following the influence of Graves (1983, 1984), among others.

Educational theories which focus on 'facilitating' (rather than 'teaching') and which propose distinctions between learning 'process' and 'product', have at their heart a notion of the idealized romantic individual creating 'his own world' in Dixon's words, or developing his own truths. Yet all such educational theories fail because they never address the essentially social nature of individuality, or of the manner in which individuals forge and develop their being in social processes. In short, what is needed if we are to see real change in English language education is a theory of language which is itself grounded in a social theory. Persons operate and have their being in social processes, and if one is to understand the nature of human communication (and I would add, of human identity), 'one begins in the community system and arrives at the individual; not the other way round' (Butt, 1985: 139).

Language is itself a social institution, as a number of scholars of somewhat different methodologies (e.g. Whorf, 1956; Berger and Luckmann, 1966; Bernstein, 1975; Halliday 1978; Halliday and Hasan, 1985) have argued this century, though some of them have often been seriously criticized and misrepresented for their pains. Halliday (1985b) in fact proposes that such criticism demonstrates how painful it often is to bring language to consciousness. That is because knowledge about language brings us forcibly to recognize that 'language reflects and reveals the inequalities that are enshrined in the social process'.

An appropriate model of language for school teaching practices in the future will begin by addressing the nature of language as social semiotic, a term used in particular by Halliday (1978, 1985b). Within such a model, language is seen as the primary resource with which humans build meaning. Alternatively, it may be thought of as a symbolic system with which people 'sign' (Halliday, 1985a: 4–9), though it is not to be understood in any idealized sense as operating independently of other signing systems. It is a resource which is systematically employed to build and transmit 'the essential patterns of the culture', where these include, among other things, 'systems of knowledge, value systems, [and] the social structure' (Halliday 1974: 99). Whenever one uses language, so Halliday argues, one exercises choices in the linguistic system in order to mean, and the functional grammar he therefore proposes (Halliday, 1985b) is not a syntactically-driven one but a semantically-driven one. No distinction, in other words, is made between grammar on the one hand, and meaning on the other. The dilemmas created by the classical distinction between grammar and rhetoric hence do not arise.

Two important consequences of such a theoretical position follow for educational practice. In the first place, the individual is seen as a social being, achieving a sense of identity through learning to enter with increasing confidence into the ways of working that are a feature of the culture, particularly where such ways of working are linguistic. In this view, unlike the romantically-conceived individual who is involved in some sort of journey of 'personal discovery', the individual is to be seen much more as an apprentice: one who is initiated into ways of operating and dealing with experience, through guidance, advice, and experimentation with the models of others.

The second consequence of the model of language as a social semiotic is that it brings us face to face with the ways in which social groups and classes actively participate in the building of social reality in language, in many of the senses that Bernstein intends (1975, 1986). Different ways of working on and in the world are encoded in the linguistic patterns used by different social groups. Where schools remain silent about these things, they merely serve to privilege some and to disadvantage others. The advice to let children use their 'own language' is in these circumstances cruelly unfair, for those not possessed of the language patterns schooling actually rewards are left to deduce them for themselves.

Conclusion

In this chapter, I have discussed English teaching from the eighteenth century to the late twentieth century. I started with the eighteenth because, as I argued, a new significance was given to the language in that century. At its start, there was disagreement about the significance or status of English as a language, and Johnson at least had suggested that it was inferior to the classical languages. As the century proceeded, however, there was considerable scholarly interest in the language, both in terms of grammar and in terms of rhetoric. Such an interest could be accounted for partly in terms of the changing political and economic priorities that made English of more importance to many middle-class groups than it had been hitherto. For related reasons, it could also be accounted for in terms of the growing significance attached to written English. Grammar, as in the classical tradition, was held to be the study of the syntax of the sentence. Rhetoric was the study of the larger unit that was the text, crafted in some way to persuade, to move, to argue or to explain.

One of the advantages of the eighteenth-century interest in the language was that it led to the development of a better appreciation of the syntax of the written English sentence, and it led to some regularization of what would eventually become known as 'standard written English'. However, it also led to a decline of interest in the larger unity of the text. This was to have unfortunate consequences for educational practices as the nineteenth and twentieth centuries proceeded, coinciding as it did with the steady emergence of formally institutionalized education, initially at the elementary level, and later at the secondary level.

Provision of educational opportunity for the poor was brought about primarily to confer a little basic literacy as well as some general knowledge on those who went to school. It did not aim to develop much independence in those whom it taught, and the rhetorical interests in argument and opinion found little if any place in the nineteenth-century elementary school. Even among the more privileged students who were given a secondary education, they received little instruction in English rhetoric, principally because English was not much taught in these schools. Most of what was taught in the name of English in the nineteenth century involved exhaustive work on the nine parts of speech and the parsing and analysis of sentences, and correction of 'faulty sentences'. A little composition was sometimes taught to older students, but rhetoric as a study fell into disrepute as involving merely shallow use of devices in language. Literary studies, while not considerable, involved the writing of paraphrases of selected passages, learning something of the lives of famous writers, or learning to recite passages. 'Great works' of literature were held to have some improving effect upon the minds of persons, but study of the manners in which they worked to make their impact tended to be discouraged.

The collective effect of all the above developments over the nineteenth century was the emergence of a 'received tradition' of English studies which marginalized any serious interest in language. Because the rhetorical concerns for meanings had been lost, grammar (conceived as about parts of speech and rules of syntax) came to dominate. Into the twentieth century, the received tradition persisted, even though the Newbolt Commissioners and others often regretted the limitations of a preoccupation with grammar. Literary studies came to have much greater significance in the educational theory of the twentieth century, partly because they achieved better status in the universities, and partly because of the spread of secondary schools, where English came to be a more important subject than it had been in earlier times. The most impassioned of the teachers of literature, however, resisted systematic study of literary pieces, focusing instead on a vision of literature as culture, to be cherished as part of the heritage, but not closely examined.

By the time the 1960s had emerged, there was indeed a dead tradition of English teaching, to which many had begun to react, and those who gathered at Dartmouth sought to develop a new English for a new generation of students. In that they asserted the importance of spoken language in learning, they did much that was valuable. Nonetheless, the 'growth model' they proposed failed in the end, for the same reasons that the two other traditions had failed. All three models, in fact, rendered language itself 'invisible'. That was because all that remained in the enfeebled patterns of language teaching that the 'received tradition' offered by the mid-years of the twentieth century was a tendency to teach the parts of speech and sentence parsing and analysis.

The new models of the English language for the late twentieth century will seek to do what all the earlier three have failed to do. They will make overt teaching and learning about language a prime focus of the English language program. They will, in addition, teach for an appreciation of the many ways in which language is involved in the building of meaning. Above all, they will do these things in the interests of equity and justice. There is an important responsibility ahead both for teacher education and for the school education system.

Notes

1 The title of this chapter is actually the same as that of an MA thesis I wrote in 1980, and for that reason, I had not intended to use it again. However, after a great deal of thought as well as consultation with the editor of this volume, I have determined to use it, since it most satisfactorily captures what I want to argue. It is therefore important to note that in developing the argument, I have used a great deal of material not available to me ten or eleven years ago. Hence, while this discussion draws in part on what I had argued hitherto, it also attempts to break new ground in a number of important ways.

2 See Christie (1990) for some discussion of these matters; also Ong (1982) and Halliday (1985a) for discussion of some of what follows. Coulmas (1989) has offered a recent scholarly study of the development of writing systems.

3 Perrera (1990) has offered a recent interesting discussion of the differences between speech and writing. She works in a different linguistic tradition from the systemic-functional linguistic tradition of Halliday. It is notable that her general conclusions support much of what is argued here, drawn from Halliday's theory.

4 Rothery (1989) has offered a recent discussion of developments in the 'new English', following Dartmouth.

5 The development of 'progressive' theories of education is discussed in detail in Connell (1980). Edwards and Mercer (1987) have provided a discussion of some of the problems of progressivism, as has Cope (1986).

References

ARNOLD, M. (1869) *Culture and Anarchy. An Essay in Political and Social Criticism*, London, Thomas Nelson and Sons.

ARNOLD, M. (1908) *Reports on Elementary Education 1852–1882*, London, His Majesty's Stationery Office (New edition, F.S. MARWIN (Ed.), from the Inspectorial Report of 1872).

BADHAM, C. (1890) *Speeches and Lectures Delivered in Australia by the Late Charles Badham*, D.D. Sydney, Dymock (NB public speech originally delivered 1871).

BAIN, A. (1863) *An English Grammar*, London, Longman, Green and Longman, Roberts and Green.

BAIN, A. (1866) *English Composition and Rhetoric: A Manual*, London, Longman, Green and Co.

BAIN, A. (1872) *A First English Grammar*, London, Longmans and Co.

BAIN, A. (1874) *A Companion to the Higher English Grammar*, London, Longmans, Green and Co.

BAIN, A. (1887) *English Composition and Rhetoric, Revised in Two Parts — Part I, Intellectual Elements of Style, and Part II, Emotional Qualities of Style*, London, Longman, Green and Co.

BALLARD, P. (1921) *Teaching the Mother Tongue*, London, Hodder and Stoughton.

BARNES, D. (1976) *From Communication to Curriculum*, London, Penguin Education.

BARNES, D. (1977) 'The Study of Classroom Communication in Teacher Education', a paper given at the National Conference on English in Teacher Education, held at the University of New England, September 1977; Published in GILL, M. and CROCKER, W.K. (Eds) *English in Teacher Education*, Armidale, NSW, University of New England Press, pp. 85–94.

BARNES, D., BRITTON, J. and ROSEN, H. (1969) *Language, the Learner and the School*, London, Penguin Books.

BERGER, P.L. and LUCKMAN, T. (1966) *The Social Construction of Reality: A Treatise in the Sociology of Knowledge*, London, Allen Lane, Penguin.

BERNSTEIN, B. (1975) *Class, Codes and Control Vol. 3. Towards a Theory of Educational Transmissions*, London, Routledge and Kegan Paul.

BERNSTEIN, B. (1986) 'On Pedagogic Discourse', in RICHARDSON, J. (Ed.) *Handbook of Theory and Research in the Sociology of Education*, New York, Greenwood Press, pp. 205–39.

BIRCHENOUGH, G. (1938) *History of Elementary Education in England and Wales from 1800 to the Present Day*, 3rd ed., London, University Tutorial Press.

BLAIR, H. (1783) *Lectures on Rhetoric and Belles Letters, Volumes 1 and 11*, London, W. Strahan and T. Cadell.

BRICE HEATH, S. (1986) 'Literacy and Language Change', in TANNEN, D. and ALATIS, J. (Eds) *Languages and Linguistics: The Interdependence of Theory, Data and Application*, Georgetown University Roundtable on Languages and Linguistics, 1985, Washington, DC, Georgetown University Press.

BRITTON, J. (1970) *Language and Learning*, London, Penguin Books.

BRITTON, J. and SQUIRES, J. (1975) 'Foreword', in DIXON, J., *Growth through English*, 3rd ed., London, National Association for the Teaching of English and Oxford University Press, pp. vii–xviii.

BUTT, D. (1985) 'The Problem of Solipsism and the Semiotician's Reply', in *The Cultivated Australian. Festschrift in Honour of Arthur Delbridge*, Beitrage Zur Phonetik Und Linguistik **48**, pp. 129–41.

CAMPBELL, G. (1776, 1838) *The Philosophy of Rhetoric*, London, T. Tegg and Son.

CHRISTIE, F. (1976) 'The Teaching of English in Elementary Schools in New South Wales 1848–1900: An Enquiry into Social Conditions and Pedagogical Theories

Determining the Teaching of English', unpublished MEd thesis, University of Sydney.

CHRISTIE, F. (1981) 'The "Received Tradition"' of English Language Study in Schools: The Decline of Rhetoric and the Corruption of Grammar', unpublished MA thesis, University of Sydney.

CHRISTIE, F. (1989) 'Curriculum Genres in Early Childhood Education: A Case Study in Writing Development', unpublished PhD thesis, University of Sydney.

CHRISTIE, F. (Ed.) (1990) *Literacy for a Changing World*, Melbourne: ACER.

CHRISTIE, F. and ROTHERY, J. (1979) 'An Interpretation of Recent Trends in English Curriculum', in MALING-KEEPES, J. and KEEPES, B.D. (Eds) *Language in Education. The LDP Phase 1*, Canberra, Curriculum Development Centre.

CONNELL, W.F. (1980) *A History of Education in the Twentieth Century World*, Canberra, Curriculum Development Centre.

COPE, B. (1986) 'Traditional Versus Progressivist Pedagogies', *Social Literacy Monograph 11*, Sydney.

COULMAS, F. (1989) *The Writing Systems of the World*, Oxford, Blackwell.

CURRICULUM DEVELOPMENT CENTRE (CDC) (1978) *Language Development Project Occasional Paper Number 1*, Canberra, Curriculum Development Centre.

CURRIE, J. (n.d.a) *The Principles and Practice of Common-School Education*, new ed. London, Stewart.

CURRIE, J. (n.d.b) *The Principles and Practice of Early and Infant School Education*, new ed. London, Stewart.

DAWES, R. (n.d.) *Suggestive Hints towards Improved Instruction, Making it Bear upon Practical Life, Intended for the Use of Schoolmasters and Teachers in our Elementary Schools and for Others Taking an Interest in National Education*, 3rd ed. London, Greenbridge.

DIXON, J. (1967) *Growth through English*, London, National Association for the Teaching of English and Oxford University Press.

DIXON, J. (1975) *Growth through English*, 3rd ed. London, National Association for the Teaching of English and Oxford University Press.

DUNN, H. (1837) *Popular Education or, the Normal School Manual: Containing Practical Suggestions for Daily and Sunday School Teachers*, London, Sunday School Union.

EDWARDS, D. and MERCER, N. (1987) *Common Knowledge. The Development of Understanding in the Classroom*, London, Methuen.

ELLIS, J. and URE, J.N. (1976) 'Registers', in BUTLER, C.S. and HARTMANN, R.R.K. (Eds) *A Reader on Language Variety*, Volume 1, Exeter Linguistic Studies, University of Exeter, pp. 251–5.

FIRTH, J.R. (1968) *Selected Papers of J.R. Firth 1952–59*, edited by F.R. PALMER, London, Longmans.

FITCH, J. (1880) *Lectures on Teaching*, Cambridge, Cambridge University Press.

GILL, J. (1833) *Introductory Text Book to School Education, Method and School Management — A Treatise on the Principles, Aims and Instruments of Elementary Education*, new ed., London, Longmans Green.

GOLDEN, J.L. and CORBETT, E.P.J. (1968) *The Rhetoric of Blair, Campbell and Whately*. New York, Holt Rinehart and Winston.

GRAVES, D.H. (1983) *Writing: Teachers and Children at Work*, Exeter, Heinemann.

GRAVES, D.H. (1984) *A Researcher Learns to Write: Selected Articles and Monographs*, Exeter, Heinemann.

GRAY, B. (1985) 'Helping Children Become Language Learners in the Classroom', in CHRISTIE, M. (Ed.) *Aboriginal Perspectives on Experience and Learning: The Role of Language in Aboriginal Education*, Geelong, Deakin University Press; Paper originally presented at the Annual Conference of the Meanjin Reading Council, Brisbane, May 1983.

GREEN, B. (1990) 'A Dividing Practice: 'Literature', English Teaching and Cultural

Politics', in GOODSON, I. and MEDWAY, P. (Eds) *Bringing English to Order: The History and Politics of a School Subject*, London, Falmer Press, pp. 135–61.

GREGORY, M. and CARROLL, S. (1978) *Language and Situation: Language Varieties and their Social Contexts*, Language and Society Series, London, Routledge and Kegan Paul.

HALLIDAY, M.A.K. (1969) 'Relevant Models of Language', in 'The State of Language', *Educational Review*, University of Birmingham, **22**, 1, pages 26–37; Reprinted in HALLIDAY, M.A.K. (1975) *Explorations in the Functions of Language*, London, Edward Arnold.

HALLIDAY, M.A.K. (1974) *Language and Social Man*, London, Schools Council and Longmans.

HALLIDAY, M.A.K. (1978) *Language as Social Semiotic: The Social Interpretation of Language and Meaning*, London, Edward Arnold.

HALLIDAY, M.A.K. (1985a) *Spoken and Written Language*, Geelong, Deakin University Press; republished in the Language Education Series, 1989, London, Oxford University Press.

HALLIDAY, M.A.K. (1985b) *An Introduction to Functional Grammar*, London, Edward Arnold.

HALLIDAY, M.A.K. and HASAN, R. (1985) *Language, Context and Text: A Social Semiotic Perspective*, Geelong, Deakin University Press; republished in the Language Education Series, 1989, London, Oxford University Press.

HALLIDAY, M.A.K., MCINTOSH, A. and STREVENS, P. (1964) *The Linguistic Sciences and Language Teaching*, London, Longmans, Green and Company.

HOLBROOK, D. (1967) *English for Maturity*, Cambridge, Cambridge University Press.

INGLIS, F. (1969) *The Englishness of English Teaching*, London, Longmans,

JOHNSON, S. (1775) *A Dictionary of the English Language in which the Words are Deduced from their Originals, and illustrated in their different Significations, by examples from the best Writers, to which are prefixed a History of the Language and an English Grammar*, London, Strahan.

KAMLER, B. (1990) 'Gender and Genre: A Case Study of a Girl and a Boy Learning to Write', unpublished PhD thesis, Deakin University.

LEAVIS, F.R. (1979a) *Education and the University*, Cambridge, University Press.

LEAVIS, F.R. (1979b) *English Literature in our Time and the University*, Cambridge, University Press.

LOWTH, R. (1762, 1969) *A Short Introduction to English Grammar*, Facsimile Reprint No. 18, Menston, Scolar Press.

MARTIN, J.R. and ROTHERY, J. (1980, 1981) *Writing Project Reports Numbers 1 and 2*, Department of Linguistics, University of Sydney.

MATHIESON, M. (1975) *The Preachers of Culture*, London, Unwin Education Books.

MCKNIGHT, G.H. (1928) *Modern English in the Making*, New York, Appleton-Century-Crofts.

MORELL, J.D. (n.d.) *A Biographical History of English Literature. Being an Elementary Introduction to the Greater English Writers with Three Hundred Exercises*, revised ed., London, W. and R. Chambers.

MORELL, J.D. (1872) *The First Steps in English Composition on a New Plan with One Hundred and Eight Exercises*, London, Longman, Green Reader and Dyer.

MORELL, J.D. (1881) *The Analysis of Sentences with an Exposition of the Fundamental Laws of Syntax*, London, Longman, Green and Co.

MURRAY, L. (1795, 1968) *English Grammar*, Facsimile Reprint No. 106, Menston, Scolar Press.

THE NEWBOLT REPORT (1921) *The Teaching of English in England*, London, HMSO.

NEW SOUTH WALES COUNCIL OF EDUCATION (1867) *Progress Report*, Appendix A.

ONG, W.J. (1982) *Orality and Literacy: The Technologizing of the Word*, New Accents Series, London, Methuen.

PARKER, I. (1914) *Dissenting Academies in England — Their Rise and Progress and their Place among the Educational Systems of the Country*, Cambridge, Cambridge University Press.

PEARCE, J., THORNTON, G. and MACKAY, D. (1989) 'The Programme in Linguistics and English Teaching, University College London, 1964–1971', in HASAN, R. and MARTIN, J.R. (Eds) *Language Development: Learning Language, Learning Culture: Meaning and Choice in Language: Studies for Michael Halliday*, Advances in Discourse Processes, **XXVII**, Norwood, NJ, Ablex.

PERRERA, K. (1990) 'Grammatical Differentiation between Speech and Writing in Children Aged 8 to 12', in CARTER, R. (Ed.) *Knowledge about Language and the Curriculum: The LINC Reader*, Suffolk, Hodder and Stoughton, pp. 216–33.

PRIESTLEY, J. (1761, 1969) *The Rudiments of English Grammar adapted to the Use of Schools with Observations on Style*, Facsimile Reprint No. 210, Menston, Scolar Press.

REDDY, M.J. (1979) 'The Conduit Metaphor — A Case of Frame Conflict in our Language about Language', in ORTONY, A. (Ed.) *Metaphor and Thought*, Philadelphia, Cambridge University Press, pp. 284–324.

ROSEN, C. and ROSEN, H. (1973) *The Language of Primary School Children*, London, Penguin Education and the Schools Council.

ROTHERY, J. (1989) 'Learning about Language', in HASAN, R. and MARTIN, J.R. (Eds) *Language Development: Learning Language, Learning Culture. Meaning and Choice in Language: Studies for Michael Halliday*, Advances in Discourse Processes, **XXVII**, Norwood, NJ, Ablex, pp. 199–256.

ROTHERY, J. and MACKEN, M. (1991) *Developing Critical Literacy: An Analysis of the Writing Task in a Year 10 Reference Class*, Monograph No. 1, Sydney, The Metropolitan East Disadvantaged Schools Program.

SAMPSON, G. (1921) *English for the English*, Cambridge, Cambridge University Press.

SHAYER, D. (1972) *The Teaching of English in Schools 1900–1970*, London, Routledge and Kegan Paul.

TORBE, M. (1986) 'Language across the Curriculum: Policies and Practice' in BARNES, D., BRITTON, J. and TORBE, M., *Language, the Learner and the School*, 3rd edition, Middlesex, Penguin Books, pp. 131–66.

WALTON, C. (1986) 'Aboriginal Children Learning to Write: Kriol and Warlpiri Speakers in an English-Speaking Classroom', Unpublished MEd thesis, University of New England.

WHITEHEAD, F. (1966) *The Disappearing Dais: A Study of the Principles and Practices of English Teaching*, London, Chatto and Windus.

WHORF, B.J. (1956) *Benjamin Lee Whorf: Language, Thought and Reality: Selected Writings*, edited by J.B. CARROLL, Cambridge, MA, MIT Press.

WILKINS, W. (1886) *The Principles That Underly the Practice of Teaching*, Sydney, Government Printer.

Chapter 6

Returning History: Literacy, Difference, and English Teaching in the Post-War Period

Tony Burgess

Different Literacies

In my childhood, I met many good reads: annuals, funny school stories, senti-mental ones, adventures. I learned abundance in a converted barn, used as a play-room by my brother and myself, where books from my parents' childhood were stored. At school, there were English classics, one or two a year. My classmates and I read these with a steady attention, brought from the study of Latin and Greek, our main business until after 'O' levels. Our skills were easily transferred. We rendered into English. We wrote essays.

My family favoured and afforded a British public school. Neither early schooling nor early literacy seem to have mattered greatly as it was war-time and family life was disrupted. It was necessary to learn to read but not special. Then childhood took another turn. I recall the train ride to a country town, the laden walk back from the station along returning streets. Arcane, bizarre, ill-adjusted as well as privileged, at Winchester College, literacy began to matter.

I moved easily enough between home and school literacies. Those who went to school with me and I might dislike school or find reasons to deplore it. But we did not doubt the literacy on offer. The texts we read and the activities which accompanied them were received by us as part of a larger journey, one secured by the past and surely destined towards adult life. School and curriculum coincided. Universities did not mistrust this, their principal constituency. They were implicated too much. Nor did we dispute school's literacy, as students. We did not depend on education; we assumed it. The distinction is crucial.

In our contemporary classrooms, issues about school and other literacies, about credibility, consent, compulsion, legitimacy, ideology and power arise on a daily basis and are echoed, beyond, in the psychology, sociology and politics of literacy. Public education has both to negotiate, with different populations, from below, inherited traditions of literacy, *and* win credibility as schooling. There has been a gradual recognition in English teaching that these broader, social issues lurk within literacy. I want to explore this gathering awareness here, through referring to ways of theorizing literacy, literature and reading which have devel-oped in Britain in the post-war years. English teaching may be described as having shifted in its focus from a concentration on the processes of reading towards an understanding of wider literacy. In doing so, it has rediscovered history.

I had wanted to begin with a basic recognition. There are many literacies within British society. I have recalled my own schooling in order to suggest not just cultural diversity but what elsewhere (Burgess, 1988) I have called 'difference', a cultural history structured by relations of dominance and power. I have been pointing to power and difference *behind* texts, as well as to relations of power *within* them. Behind texts are the social relations within which literacies are framed, learned and maintained. Texts matter. Practices of reading and production matter. Society, however, matters as much as literacy.

I assume, then, that there is not room for infinite flexibility within public education or British society, or indeed elsewhere in the world. But also the forms of literacy are not fixed in ways which are implacably impervious to different use. The struggle in schools has been bounded by both considerations. Teachers have wanted to listen to new populations and to changing voices, while the onus to negotiate a certain kind of public credibility and consent remains. One interest of a historical perspective is in its capacity to provide a ground on which such issues of agency, control, power and difference may be recognized and understood.

Different Psychologies: Reading Lessons and Changing English Teaching

At about the same time that I was passing through my secondary boarding school, others were laying down a new framework for school English teaching in the 1950s (see Burgess and Martin, 1990). It must have seemed that, in reading pedagogy at any rate, there were work and organizations already in the field. The 'great debate' about reading methods, as Jeanne Chall was later to call it (Chall, 1967), was already under way. Unlike the newer themes of 'talk' and 'writing', there existed for reading a long tradition of work and a considerable research literature.

The work, however, lay to one side of the theoretical bases on which English was to draw. Research on reading was sited in older established traditions of educational psychology, rather than in the new centres of English curriculum theorizing. It reflected, therefore, the concentrations on perception and on the identification and measurement of abilities, characteristic of psychology at this point. New school English looked to a different psychology: to child development, and to the study of the role of language in thinking.

Also, many architects of the new school English were literature-trained and were, or had been, teachers in secondary rather than primary schools. Re-making literature and linking this to approaches to language may have seemed to be more pressing concerns than reading. For whatever reason, reading became for the time being a junior, taken-for-granted, partner, though later to be reinstated.

The critical study of literature had descended into school from Cambridge English and the work of F.R. Leavis. The new methods of literary study had brought with them no great attention to wider literacy nor to initial teaching of reading, or indeed to reading as such. Their intellectual elaboration had proceeded, beyond literary boundaries, towards the wider cultural criticism associated with the work of Denys Thompson and the 'Use of English' groups. What came to be challenged, in the developmental concerns of James Britton and his associates (to name the principals), was the predominantly *literary-critical* focus of such orientations, together with a specific and morally-oriented account of works of literature.

It is worth stressing that this challenge, in the new school English, was to a certain highly partisan view of literature and not to the importance of literature as such. James Britton's influence in this regard cannot be underestimated. In the debates of the 1970s, Britton's work was incorrectly supposed by some to have elevated language above literature and to have set aside questions of 'value' (Allen, 1980; Whitehead, 1978). This was not the case. What concerned him was the neglect of 'processes' and 'development' within a view of literature allied to a specific critical tradition. The new school English offered a *different* account of literature, not the supplanting of literature as the core of English studies by language.

The alternative argument was itself incomplete, still sketchy in its formulation and happier with philosophical and psychological issues than social ones. The argument looked back to Suzanne Langer and Ernst Cassirer, and to an account of the role of literature within human symbolizing. In place of 'critical definition' of works, it concentrated on psychological 'processes' in reading (Harding, 1962), but not on 'reading practices'. Instead of a 'selected tradition', it proposed a view of literature as 'elaborated form', but did not insist on the extent to which 'literatures' were socially constructed. Works were seen as on a continuum with more informal uses of language, connected by a common concern with evaluation of experience. Britton coined the term 'spectator role' to describe this ongoing evaluation of experience, distinct from active participation in events (e.g. Britton, 1982).

Britton's (1970) work sought to bring together language and literature, within a larger interest in symbolizing, human thinking and children's learning and development. In its synthesizing concern, it is to be distinguished utterly from the focus on language teaching which has become familiar through applied linguistics, an approach which has taught us much about language but very little about the role of language in development more widely. Also distinctive was its focus on the interaction between symbol and human agency. Human powers depended on internalizing the resources made available through symbol. What was increasingly a Vygotskian emphasis in Britton's work separated it from other developmental theories of the time, and from a merely generalized stress on creativity (e.g. Britton, 1985, 1987). It gave rise to a particular insistence, which remains equally relevant to all the several areas of English teaching, from language to literature and on to cultural criticism: this was on the necessity to ask *how children learn*, a commitment to explain, rather than take for granted, the course of development.

Britton returned the artist to everyday life. He severed the connection with the academy and critical study. He allowed for an account of reading as a wide human process and brought together art and human reflection. Criticism was subordinated. Literature was made a matter of heightened organization, but was seen as continuous with looser forms of the shaping of experience in informal writing, storytelling, gossip. The approach is, to this extent, secular and democratic in its challenge. It is plainly also universalist in its orientation and offers no purchase on how it is that some works or some readings come to be preferred, as a matter of cultural practice. It ties literature to reading and writing, but not to society or history.

In retrospect, it seems an odd contingency that school teaching of literature and its underlying rationales should have been locked into this particular struggle: between a post-Leavisite emphasis on literary-critical study, and a version of literature as significant form supported by accounts of psychological process. The Leavisites had behind them the achievements and prestige of Cambridge English. Britton's version articulated with ways in which language development was coming to be explained, and with shifts in linguistics and psychology. To this extent, the Leavisites were right in sensing the challenge to come from language, though wrong in failing to perceive that it was their version of literature which was in question, not literature itself. In neither account, however, was much attention paid to a wider social theory of literacy and reading.

The evidence for these remarks is to be found in texts and documents about English which were current at the time. In the line which stretches from Marjorie Hourd's *Education of the Poetic Spirit* (1949) to the Dartmouth Seminar and John Dixon's *Growth through English* (1967), writing, talking, a new sense of literature and of children's creative uses of language are what receive the principal attention. There is little notice taken of reading as such. Similarly, in the programme of research envisaged by the Schools Council English committee, a groundplan of investigations which shaped English teaching through to the report of the Bullock Committee, reading receives only a passing mention.

Then came the changes in psychology. In a recent article, Cliff Moon, an educational psychologist closely associated with these new directions, sets out the story. Moon begins at a slightly later point than I have reached by citing Margaret Donaldson's (1978) account of *Children's Minds*, referring to it as 'the most accessible account of developments over the last thirty years in our understanding of how children learn oral and written language competences'. The key moment, Moon recalls, was the revision in the early 1970s of Chomsky's geneticist account of language development.

> By 1972 the picture was clearer. Language-learning took place within interpersonal contexts and the *only* genetic predisposition seemed to be a social one: the propensity of the child to interact with significant others. Some researchers even tracked the eye, hand, arm and leg movements of new-born babies in the presence and absence of their mothers. Macnamara's (1972) seminal paper, to quote Donaldson, 'stood Chomsky's argument upon its head'. The time was right for longitudinal, naturalistic studies of oral language acquisition based on the *interactionist* position: this is precisely what Gordon Wells attempted in the '*Bristol Language Development Project*' (Wells, 1981, 1985, 1987) (Moon, 1988: 173–174).

The new reading theory derived, then, from post-Chomskyan work on language and language development. Theories of language development became interactional and naturalistic, and the teaching of reading followed. The resulting work, drawing on the accounts of Frank Smith and Ken and Yetta Goodman, is perhaps well known enough not to need elaboration. Reading was conceptualized as *process*. Attention was focused on the learner's strategies and on the apparatus brought from prior knowledge of language to the task. As Moon continues, there were two stages in this work: first, establishing that the reading process is 'common to all readers, regardless of proficiency'; second, coming to accept that 'children begin to learn how to read and write long before formal schooling commences'.

So, a new psychology of reading processes came together, in English teaching, with a 'developmental' account of language and of the role of literature. One consequence was that reading was restored to something like a central place in conceptualizing English, reordering to some extent the importance attached to talk and writing. Alongside this, as Green (1990) notes, English teaching, henceforth, refused to separate and to polarize 'literature', 'literacy' and 'reading'. Here, the work of my colleague, Margaret Meek (1977, 1983), was of especial importance in promoting and extending the transition, balancing — in English teaching — the work of the psychologists. But it followed also that reading, in this new version, was conceived primarily as process, and described in cognitive rather than in social or historical terms.

I began teaching English in secondary schools in 1964. I can illustrate these developments from my own first experiences in teaching. In the now forgotten heat of 1964's 'technological revolution', we were reading through Constance Garnett's *The Family from One End Street*, my one sure-fire text. Thirteen wasted years were coming to an end outside the window. I cracked on vigorously. Many of my little team, in this south London classroom, could have used some individual attention to their reading. I had thought about *literature*. About the teaching of *reading*, I, their teacher, knew virtually nothing.

My sense of shame in this chastening memory derives from the rethinking of English teaching among secondary and, in different ways, primary teachers from the 1970s onwards. In my preparation for teaching, I had concentrated on children's talking and writing and had spent much time collecting scripts and tracing patterns of development, a course reflected straightforwardly enough in my own contribution to Margaret Meek's (1977) *The Cool Web* (Burgess, 1977). I had gladly reconstructed Leavisite assumptions about literature, exchanging them for an emphasis on 'response'. Reading, I believed, pretty much came naturally, a part of normal development. Most learned to read early on, I supposed. What counted for this age was talk about what they had read.

Upstairs, in a colleague's classroom, it was certainly the case that there was a remedial department for some non-readers, from which as it happened many of my little group had recently descended and to which in due course some would return, but this was a different place. Those who started secondary school there, in the remedial department, would, I thought, their short stay past, simply tumble downstairs, released, like others, to acquire the skills they needed from use. Their doing so required, in turn, that teachers provide interesting and motivating enough work. On my corridor, this was my part.

I learned to rethink English teaching, backwards, from my then later vantage in teacher education and from being with my own children as they grew up. But that is not a matter of great moment. In referring to it, I only want to keep alive the sense of a particular history and of how teachers have travelled in recent years. The development of school practices can be made to seem too linear and too straightforward. Developments in the teaching of reading were not even. They reflected transitions in two enterprises which had previously been mostly separate: in the teaching of literature within English teaching, and in reading instruction as described by psychology. They were brought together by a common resistance to behavioural psychology. The union was to be cemented subsequently, in response to the discovered literacy 'crisis' of the 1970s, and in becoming the common object of attacks by Black Papers on 'progressive' methodologies.

I shall not pursue further the line of genealogy. I have tried to suggest a baseline. I want to concentrate instead on kinds of clarification and extension which have emerged since then, and argue for their compatibility. Both the extensions to which I shall refer have a common origin: the rediscovery of history. One implication of this rediscovery has been a changed, less individualized account of learning and of pedagogy. Another has been a new attention to the relations between schooling and literacy in society, and, relatedly, a deeper awareness of literacy outside school.

The Turn of History

I can best illustrate the first of these developments by commenting on a particular work. In 1982, Carolyn Steedman published *The Tidy House*, her study of the narrative constructed by three working-class girls, in a joint exploration of the mothers they expected to become. Steedman's work may be related, in retrospect, to other and parallel lines of social and feminist thought, occurring at the turn of this decade, but has its own distinctive focus.

The shared interest is in a reassessment of the individualist and universalist tendencies in interactional psychology. This was common to Valerie Walkerdine's (1984) work on psychology and discourse, to the re-presentation of Vygotskian thought by Michael Cole, James Wertsch and others (Cole *et al.*, 1978; Wertsch, 1985), and to the later work of Jerome Bruner (1987). All sought, in different ways, to reprioritize the cultural bases of learning and development. Steedman's work brought a sense of history to this undertaking. Her small-scale but powerful study, drawing on experience as a primary teacher, has held implications for the study of literacy, and indeed for literacy pedagogy, which have been insufficiently recognized.

In brief, Steedman's is rare among insider accounts of classrooms in two ways: she refuses to idealize the girls' narrative, and at the same time she denies the possibility of a transforming pedagogy. Her uncompromising stand contains in it the seeds of a critique, implicit if not wholly explicit, of a false optimism in many educational and purely process-oriented accounts of literacy and learning.

The impetus of Steedman's work is undeniably bleak. But it is arguable that some rearticulation of the earlier arguments is possible and that what is required is the *reformulation* of accounts of language and learning on more realistic and historical lines, rather than their rejection. A strengthening of quite familiar theoretical bases within English teaching, rather than total reconstruction, may be what is needed. As I have argued elsewhere, 'recovery of the full historical project in Vygotskian (and Bakhtinian) thought offers English teaching a way forward which is consistent with its own traditions' (Burgess, 1988: 165; also, Burgess, 1985).

Steedman sets out to contrast the social accounting in the girls' narrative with the selective tradition in the publication of children's writing which has been constructed over about a century and a half. She shows that most of this writing was drawn from middle-class homes and private schoolrooms. She comments that public interest was almost entirely in the writing of little girls, not boys. Steedman analyzes the content of these texts and shows how those which reached the public presses can be related to changing adult motivations. She identifies the cult of the Wordsworthian child and the later taste for evocation of a 'type of special and revelatory girlhood and a feminine poetic'. A further adult preoccupation reflected in the writing selected for publication is in the romance of bourgeois individualism, where intelligent children might 'dodge the governess and let the rest of the world go hang'.

Against this backdrop, Steedman foregrounds what is specific in a narrative arising from the social experience of the 1970s, told by three girls in a contemporary classroom on a southern British housing estate. She sets beside the nineteenth-century schoolrooms and the pencilled journals, these girls' dissection of the ambivalence of mothering and the contradictions of being children in 'the tidy house'. Movingly, she dissolves the frame of three girls constructing their story around a school tape recorder into the figure of Mayhew's 'matchseller girl', not playing at being a mother but already caring for the even younger members of her family.

Steedman terms 'interpretative devices' the constructed perspectives which are available to bring to children's writing. As well as middle-class tastes in reading about childhood and about little girls in particular, Steedman includes developments in psychoanalytic theory and in child psychology. She also illustrates the writing practices from which her nineteenth-century examples came. Contrasting these by implication with the practices of twentieth-century classrooms, she demonstrates the continuing relevance of considerations such as these to social history.

Mainstream English teaching approaches to children's reading and writing have been derived from a concentration on process, as I have indicated, and, behind this, from a psychology of a particular, interactionist kind. Steedman takes writing out of the framework of this psychology and places both writing and its analysis squarely into history. Children's uses of language — whether, as here, writing, or, by implication, reading and talking — are analyzed as occuring within lived social experience, not just as processes. Educational theories are seen as interpretative devices, as historical not timeless accounts. Both implications are important; together, they form the alternative and the corrective to earlier positions.

The girls whom Steedman has shown might be fitted into individualistic and interactionist models of development. They could be described as using language 'actively'. Their achievement could be glossed as exemplifying the acquisition of abilities in reading and writing by using language for 'real purposes'. Along these familiar lines, it would become possible to recognize here generalizable learning strategies and to propose from this example an optimistic account of development in literacy and a benevolent account of school. Steedman does not tame the force of their example in this way. She shows us not a general but a specific literacy, a difficult, awkward flowering among the stones of working-class girlhood.

Carla and Lindie and Melissa are not the universalized exemplars of the foundational accounts of English teaching. They are the spiky, interrogating carriers of the history of their gender and their class. They negotiate with accuracy and realism a working-class history and a working-class schooling. Not trapped by either class or schooling as people, they are not less creatures of their time. Steedman offers no way out from history. She will not dissolve this into a generalized, philosophical notion of freedom. Nor will she translate her perceptions into sociology, replacing empirical specificity with structured determinations.

I have been attempting a *reading* rather than a *summary* of Steedman's work because it is possible, if negligently so, to construe her argument as less searching in its implications than it actually is. The girls' story, which I cannot reproduce here, is in its way remarkable and on a cursory reading could look as if it were being claimed within another kind of teacherly discourse: one which begins in appreciation of what children are able to do, and which then opens up into an argument about educational possibilities and the value of an understanding of process. To labour the point, it is just this form of interpretation and argument which Steedman seeks to counter, in privileging the historical and the social in her account.

I wanted to interpret this as an extension, rather than a rejection, of the previous perspectives in language, learning and literacy. I should give my reasons, since they involve some qualification of Steedman's position, on my part. Steedman adds *difference* and *particularity*, a step forward from general and universal perspectives. Carla and Melissa and Lindie do not illustrate a general thesis. Their particularity extends our awareness of the complexity of young people's engagements with literacy and schooling. This relocates insights into language and learning within the framework of a social history, and is one aspect of the extension which Steedman makes. Another, I want to argue, is in the challenge which she makes to pedagogy, and to the claims to be entered for its possible achievements.

I take Steedman to be more pessimistic than I am about schooling and about its possibilities. It is a pessimism which leads her to resist child-centred claims to supportive nurturing of inner abilities and the political mandate for a pedagogy which is culturally transformative, critical or liberatory. Her concern is to force a crucial recognition: a recognition, that is, of the *limits* of pedagogy and its necessary *incompleteness*.

An acknowledgment of the incompleteness of pedagogy was, in my view, always characteristic of the earlier tradition of attention to language and learning, derived from the work of James Britton. This tradition recognized a balance between the teacher and the learner. The implications were neither for an inflation nor for a denial of pedagogy's place. There was, in addition, a particular stress: teaching needed to recognize the otherness, the separateness, of the learner. The Bullock Inquiry argued for this recognition as a way of transcending the false polarity between 'traditional' and 'child-centred education': 'In order to accept something when we are told something we have to have somewhere to put it' (HMSO, 1975: 55). The point is important.

The difficulty for my argument is that a recognition of this kind, one made on interactionist rather than historical grounds, has sometimes been lost in subsequent, more stirring formulations of reading theory of a developmental kind. It would be a mistake to be too solemn about this. At times, though, Bullock's exact emphasis has been pushed aside. A claim to special powers for pedagogy, in releasing children from the constraints of class and schooling, has appeared to emerge from the grounds of an understanding of the reading process. Or there has been too easy an adoption of a Freirean vocabulary of 'liberation' or 'empowerment'. Paradoxically, such inflated claims for pedagogy are often to be found counterpointed by a tendency apparently in the opposite direction: by an emphasis on the experience and autonomy of the learner, which appears to deny the teacher's role. Critics have rightly seen in this denial a certain duplicity, and the danger of leaving teaching intentions mysterious and implicit (Bernstein, 1975).

Steedman's reservations are apposite in the context of such claims. I want to argue for them, though, as an extension rather than as a denial of an emphasis on children's learning, properly conceived, and as implying realism about schooling rather than pessimism. If the implications of recognizing process are for a balance kept between teacher and learner, one which neither inflates nor denies pedagogy's place, Steedman's argument can be interpreted as similarly realistic. She insists on the irreducible separateness of history and the social world.

I may go less far than Steedman's argument in saying so, for here as elsewhere in her writing she makes a further criticism of primary schooling which extends to the places assigned to women as teachers and to the roles which they come to occupy. The storm in waiting here has barely begun to blow. But I believe it is reasonable to interpret acceptance of the historicity of learning and of the limits of pedagogy in this way, as mutually supportive emphases, as two sides of the same concern to counter, alike, over-optimistic claims for reading pedagogy and too strong a corresponding pessimism. The perception is a simple one, which I find arising memorably in Steedman's work and echoed in other and associated undertakings: neither learner nor teacher can cancel out each other, nor cancel out the social context. Teaching and learning happen in history.

Literacy Outside Schooling

Steedman showed us a literacy awkwardly flowering in a working-class school. Others turned to the study of literacy outside schooling. In the last decade, the road travelled by literacy researchers such as the North American historian and educator, Harvey Graff, has added time as a dimension of literacy debates and pictures of literacy and schooling. Through the study of particular cases and periods, Graff (1979, 1987) has dismantled the 'myth' that literacy precedes industrial and economic progress, and that the course of development of literate societies is uniform, linear or invariably connected with schooling. He demonstrates that there has been no single route to the development of literate societies. Religion has been more significant an influence than schooling, in some societies, at least. But means and arrangements have varied, bringing a different social experience to different social groups. Such insights counter-balance the largely in-school study of reading processes and the concentration on methods of teaching and development which have tended to dominate educational research in written language until now. What has emerged from Graff's work, and that of historians and anthropologists more widely, is a more variegated view of different literacies coexisting in society (Street, 1984, Heath, 1983). With this goes a qualified importance to be attached to schooling and an awareness of more complex relations between written and spoken language, between oral and literate tradition, than those of polarized contrast.

In English teaching, a proper respect for the learner has always implied respect for literacy achieved outside school and awareness of different cultural traditions. Also, children's reading outside school has long been explored in English teaching research. An interest in relating school practices to children's wider development as readers can be traced back at least to A.J. Jenkinson's *What Do Boys and Girls Read?* (Jenkinson, 1940). But the recent investigations of wider social literacy go further.

Jenkinson's question, heir to the advances in understanding child development in the 1920s and 1930s, began a tradition of work in English teaching. Sometimes shocking but more usually familiar, quantitative surveys of children's reading continue to fascinate English teachers and to serve a useful wider purpose. Such work seems limited, however, when set against the enquiries of the historians and anthropologists, and may even disguise some issues in working from too undifferentiated a theory of literacy and offering too ready-made a set of explanations.

The qualitative analysis of literacy events outside school and of traditions of reading and writing in different communities poses questions of a new and more fundamental kind. They allow for a complex perception of school and schooling. Shirley Brice Heath's anthropological investigations of literacy in three communities has invited teachers to look out from school and to identify the resources and particular experiences which children bring. She also makes it possible to look back at schooling with different eyes. It has become possible to see schooling's assumptions about literacy and its promotion of some literacy practices, rather than others, as also matters of cultural construction (Heath, 1983).

I have called such work a second extension to earlier work on language and learning. It is, perhaps, an extension on a different level. Whole societies and even epochs are held in view, in the historians' perspective, and, typically, the anthropologists have used ethnographies to picture cultures rather than to map the lines between society, literacy and identity. There is a difference of scale between work of this kind and that of Steedman, considered in the previous section. In Graff's work, the reader stands, vertiginously, at the door of the laboratory of history. In Heath's powerful and detailed study, moments resonate with the recognition of whole ways of life.

The focus also differs. Steedman's is history from below, and is motivated specially by an interest in identity. It is perhaps reasonable to read back from her later autobiographical work (Steedman, 1986), to the children of *The Tidy House*, a consistent concern 'to particularize this profoundly a-historical landscape', the landscape of much writing about the working class. Her point is

> to find a way of theorizing the result of such difference and particularity, not in order to find a description that can be universally applied ... but so that the people in exile, the inhabitants of the long streets may start to use the autobiographical 'I', and tell the stories of their life (Steedman, 1986: 16).

In Graff's work, and less explicitly but similarly in Heath's, the writers stand, as it has been aptly put, 'at the elbow of the policy maker' (CCCS, 1981).

Both claim, and deserve, the authority of social science. Their eye is on the legislators, administrators and funders of programmes. They have policies to propose. In drawing out this difference of perspective, I am not suggesting conflict between the two undertakings and the intentions and scope to which each hold. But there is, perhaps, a special kind of case to be made for work of Steedman's kind, in which the relation between the personal and the historical is made the subject of investigation. As Steedman comments of familial relations, in a manner which has broader application: 'We need historical accounts of such relationships, not just a longing that they might be different. Above all, perhaps, we need a sense of people's complexity of relationship to the historical situations they inherit' (Steedman, 1986: 19).

Conclusion: Classroom Learning and Other Literacies

There have been, then, two transitions. One has been from an English teaching where reading was considered a junior and taken-for-granted partner to being accorded something like equality in the development of language processes, guided by new accounts of learning to read and reading development. A second has been from an approach focused by process to one which recognizes historical perspective, and is informed by the wider study of literacy in society. The prospect has opened up for a commentary on literacy and schooling which is aware of difference and of different literacies, and which is rooted also in a sense of past and present.

In a growing body of work along these lines, a number of us have tried to develop accounts of reading and writing and classrooms in ways which have their sources in Steedman's sense of history, coupled with a Gramscian version of hegemony. We have wanted also to articulate with this the full, social dimensions of Vygotskian and Bakhtinian thought about language, learning and development. We have come to approach classrooms as cultural and historical sites (Burgess, 1984, 1985), as 'sites of cultural making', in Hardcastle's (1985) phrase. Our focus has been on ways in which classrooms come to hear and allow for the different elements in the social experience of young people, all of whom are complexly related to the historical situations in which they find themselves and all of whom are, in a sense, migratory, across boundaries, and in time. In studies influenced by Jane Miller's (1986, 1990) work on women reading and writing, there have been investigations of young women reading and writing fiction (Moss, 1989) and of teaching black literature (Scafe, 1989). For younger children, Hilary Minns (1990) has recently studied literacies inside and outside school from a similar perspective.

What has been at issue is achieving, first, a view of literacy which is released from the misleading assumption that schooled literacy is the only literacy, or that only one relation to schooled literacy is possible. Released, it becomes possible not only to attend to the problem of practice differently but to face towards the future. Once literacy is seen historically and as a matter of tradition and different use, questions can be posed about who wants what from literacy and about how the power and social relations within and behind literacy operate and are negotiated.

Meanwhile, encouragement is needed for further study of literacies both outside and inside schooling, of an historical kind. There is the potential in these for a new, more complex description of schooling itself and for a vision of a social future which would allow for difference and point towards flexibility and change. There are already signs that in Britain a national and centralized curriculum could come to divert attention from wider and changing literacies and end by narrowing debate and encouraging too concentrated a focus. It is important, too, that the issues of class, inequality and conflict which underlie present literacies remain open to discussion, and further, that the scope of exploration should not be restricted by too insistent a concern for ideological consensus, whether this derives, politically, from Left or Right.

References

ALLEN, D. (1980) *English Teaching Since 1965: How Much Growth?* London, Heinemann.

BERNSTEIN, B. (1975) 'Class and Pedagogies: Visible and Invisible' in *Class, Codes and Control Volume 3*, London, Routledge and Kegan Paul, pp. 116–51.

BRITTON, J. (1970) *Language and Learning*, London, Allen Lane, The Penguin Press.

BRITTON, J. (1982) 'Spectator Role and the Beginnings of Writing', in PRADL, G.M. (Ed.) *Prospect and Retrospect: Selected Essays of James Britton*, Montclair, NJ, Boynton/Cook, pp. 46–67.

BRITTON, J. (1985) 'Research Currents: Second Thoughts on Learning', *Language Arts*, **62**, 1, pp. 72–77.

BRITTON, J. (1987) 'Vygotsky's Contribution to Pedagogical Theory', *English in Education*, **21**, 3, pp. 22–26.

BRUNER, J. (1987) *Actual Minds, Possible Worlds*, Cambridge, MA, Harvard University Press.

BURGESS, T. (1977) 'Telling Stories: What the Young Writer Does', in MEEK, M., WARLOW, A. and BARTON, G. (Eds) *The Cool Web: The Pattern of Children's Reading*, London, The Bodley Head, pp. 363–75.

BURGESS, T. (1984) 'Diverse Melodies', in MILLER, J. (Ed.) *Eccentric Propositions*, London, Routledge and Kegan Paul, pp. 56–69.

BURGESS, T. (1985) 'The Question of English' in MILLER, J. and MEEK, M. (Eds) *Changing English: Essays for Harold Rosen*, London, Heinemann, pp. 1–26.

BURGESS, T. (1988) 'On Difference: Cultural and Linguistic Diversity and English Teaching' in LIGHTFOOT, M. and MARTIN, N. (Eds) *The Word for Teaching is Learning: Essays for James Britton*, London, Heinemann Educational Books and Boynton/Cook, pp. 155–68.

BURGESS, T. and MARTIN, N. (1990) 'Teaching English in England, 1945–86: Politics and Practice' in BRITTON, J., SHAFER, R.E. and WATSON, K. (Eds) *Teaching and Learning English Worldwide*, Philadelphia, Clevedon, Multilingual Matters, pp. 7–38.

CCCS (1981) *Unpopular Education: Schooling and Social Democracy in England since 1944*, Education Group, Centre for Contemporary Cultural Studies, London, Hutchinson.

CHALL, J. (1967) *Learning to Read: The Great Debate*, New York, McGraw Hill.

COLE, M., JOHN-STEINER, V., SCRIBNER, S. and SOUBERMANN, E. (Eds) (1978) *L.S. Vygotsky: Mind in Society*, Cambridge, MA, Harvard University Press.

DIXON, J. (1967, 1975) *Growth through English*, revised ed., Oxford, Oxford University Press.

DONALDSON, M. (1978) *Children's Minds*, London, Fontana.

GRAFF, H.J. (1979) *The Literacy Myth: Literacy and Social Structure in the Nineteenth-Century City*, New York, Academic Press.

GRAFF, H.J. (1987) *The Labyrinths of Literacy*, London, Falmer Press.

GREEN, B. (1990) 'A Dividing Practice: "Literature", English Teaching and Cultural Politics', in GOODSON, I. and MEDWAY, P. (Eds) *Bringing English to Order: The History and Politics of a School Subject*, London, Falmer Press, pp. 135–61.

HARDCASTLE, J. (1985) 'Classrooms as Sites for Cultural Making', *English in Education*, **19**, 3, pp. 8–22.

HARDING, D. (1962) 'Psychological Processes in the Reading of Fiction', in *British Journal of Aesthetics*, London, Thames and Hudson, **II**, 2, pp. 133–47.

HEATH, S.B. (1983) *Ways with Words*, London, Cambridge University Press.

HMSO (1975) *A Language for Life* (The Bullock Report), London, Her Majesty's Stationery Office.

HOURD, M. (1949) *The Education of the Poetic Spirit*, London, Heinemann.

JENKINSON, A.J. (1940) *What Do Boys and Girls Read?* London, Methuen.

MACNAMARA, J. (1972) 'Cognitive Basis of Language Learning in Infants', *Child Development*, **44**, pp. 1–13.

MEEK, M. (1983) *Achieving Literacy*, London, Routledge and Kegan Paul.

MEEK, M., WARLOW, A. and BARTON, G. (Eds) (1977) *The Cool Web*, London, The Bodley Head.

MILLER, J. (1986) *Women Writing about Men*, London, Virago Press.

MILLER, J. (1990) *Seductions: Studies in Reading and Culture*, London, Virago Press.

MINNS, H. (1990) *Read It to Me Now*, London, Virago Press.

MOON, C. (1988) 'Reading: Where Are We Now?', in MEEK, M. and MILLS, C. (Eds) *Language and Literacy in the Primary School*, London, Falmer Press, pp. 171–87.

MOSS, G. (1989) *Unpopular Fictions*, London, Virago Press.

SCAFE, S. (1989) *Teaching Black Literature*, London, Virago Press.

STEEDMAN, C. (1982) *The Tidy House*, London, Virago Press.

STEEDMAN, C. (1986) *Landscape for a Good Woman*, London, Virago Press.

STREET, B. (1984) *Literacy in Theory and Practice*, Cambridge, Cambridge University Press.

WALKERDINE, V. (1984) 'Developmental Psychology and the Child-Centred Pedagogy: The Insertion of Piaget into Early Education' in HENRIQUES, J., HOLLWAY, W., URWIN, C., VENN, C. and WALKERDINE, V. *Changing the Subject: Psychology, Social Regulation and Subjectivity*, London, Methuen, pp. 153–202.

WELLS, G. (1981) 'Describing Children's Linguistic Development at Home and School', in ADELMAN, L. (Ed.) *Uttering, Muttering*, London, Grant McIntyre, pp. 134–62.

WELLS, G. (1985) *Language Development in the Pre-School Years: Language at Home and School*, London, Cambridge University Press.

WELLS, G. (1987) *The Meaning Makers*, London, Hodder and Stoughton.

WERTSCH, J. (Ed.) (1985) *Culture, Communication, and Cognition: Vygotskyan Perspectives*, Cambridge, Cambridge University Press.

WHITEHEAD, F. (1978) 'What's the Use, Indeed?', *Use of English*, **29**, 2, pp. 15–22.

Chapter 7

Literacy and the Limits of Democracy[1]

James Donald

But the work of education is constructive, not critical.

John Dewey

In a lecture on 'The Idea of an Educated Public', the moral philosopher Alisdair MacIntyre describes teachers as 'the forlorn hope of Western modernity' (MacIntyre, 1987). Why forlorn? Because they are charged with a mission that is both essential and impossible. Any rationale for education, argues MacIntyre, invariably boils down to the demand that young people be taught, first, to fit into some social role and function that requires recruits, and, second, to think for themselves. The particular nature of post-Enlightenment societies means that these imperatives of socialization and individuation are mutually incompatible. Only when critical discussion on shared terms is a *feature* of the roles for which students are socialized can the two go together, and this, according to MacIntyre, entails the existence of an educated public. His paradigm of such a public is the Scottish Enlightenment. This was by no means universal. Here there was a 'tolerably large' but self-consciously limited public sphere held together by mutually accepted standards of authority, canonical cultural references, and shared modes of argumentation and justification. Informal debates about what constitutes the good life became institutionalized as 'both an extension of and an interchange with the discussions within its universities'. This was the consequence not simply of their curriculum or their agreement on issues of philosophical debate, but also of 'an understanding of their social roles by ministers, lawyers, merchants, schoolmasters and others which enabled them in such local forums as town councils, presbyteries, boards of bank directors and law courts to look beyond immediate questions to issues of first principles' (MacIntyre, 1987: 24–25). Without this sort of understanding and that sort, and scale, of social organization, an educated public is not possible and the two purposes of education — socialization and individuation — become irreconcilably divorced.

In tracing the emergence of this familiar opposition between domestication and emancipation, MacIntyre identifies a fault line in the tradition of progressive educational thinking that runs from Rousseau to Piaget and beyond.[2] This produces its disabling oscillation between utopianism and despair, as education repeatedly promises to liberate the creative human talents of all people and then fails to do so. Once it is recognized that education is an apparatus for instituting the social, not dismantling or escaping it in order to emancipate human nature, then what matters are clearly the principles that should guide its organization and conduct. In thinking how these might be negotiated democratically, the ideal of a universal educated public should not be set up as an achievable objective, but rather as an imaginative horizon, a regulating limit case.

This means going one step further than MacIntyre, and questioning his own opposition between socialization and individuation. Do the governmental strategies of post-Enlightenment liberal democracies really work by constraining or 'socializing' the liberty and aspirations of individuals? Don't they rather work *through* them, attempting to attune their desires and self-governing capacities to political objectives?[3] If individuation is the subtlest form of socialization, however, so by the same token learning to 'think for yourself' is far from thinking *by* yourself. In practice, it refers to identification with particular symbolic rules and grammars, and thus socialization into particular intellectual and academic subcultures. It is not just that language and discursive genres necessarily pre-exist and constrain thought. There is also a paradox in teaching independence of mind. If I as your teacher tell you to think for yourself, you are caught in an impossible position. Think for yourself, and you are still thinking as I tell you, in my terms. Think not as I tell you, and you must decide *not* to think for yourself. 'Thinking for yourself' is a state that is essentially a by-product, an indirect (though not undesired) consequence of some other social and intellectual activity: the learning of skills, techniques and information, participation in debate and decision-making, and so forth.[4] What is at issue in the idea of democratic education is therefore less emancipation or liberation than styles of participation, styles in which subjection and autonomy inevitably coexist.

How might this ambivalence of education, which reflects an ambivalence inherent to the exercise of liberty, be regulated so that the different ways in which people experience it would be just and reasonable? This is the type of question that Michael Walzer has addressed in his attempt to formulate a theory of distributive justice compatible with a society both heterogeneous and egalitarian. In complex modern societies, asserts Walzer (1983), the idea of 'simple equality' — everyone getting the same amount of the same thing in the same form — is neither achievable nor desirable. In principle, it is inadequate to their heterogeneity, to the real differences of power and aspiration that divide social groups. In practice, it could only be achieved by unacceptable constraints on individual liberty by the state. Instead Walzer argues for a 'complex equality': the distribution of different social goods according to different criteria reflecting the specificity of these goods, their social significance, and the variety of their recipients. Rather than deriving normative principles that would apply in all cases from either the rights of individuals or the promise of universal emancipation, Walzer insists on a respect for the boundaries between social spheres and the negotiation of meanings and criteria appropriate to that particular sphere. In his discussion of education, for example, he suggests that complex criteria are needed to balance the requirements of a democratic polity with the different interests and capacities of individual students. 'Equal citizenship requires a common schooling', he argues, 'but it does not require a uniform educational career.' So what institutional principles of association and differentiation, and what patterns of access to different forms and traditions of knowledge, would be compatible with the requirements of complex equality, social justice, and individual liberty? (Walzer, 1983: 208).

Amy Gutmann (1987) asserts as fundamental to her liberal case the premise that democratic education should provide 'the ability to participate effectively in the democratic process.' Because this ability needs to be universal, it has two negative corollaries which should constrain the exercise of educational authority. One is the principle of non-repression: unpopular (but rational) conceptions of the good life and the good society must not be excluded. The other is the principle of non-discrimination: 'no educable child may be excluded from an education adequate to participating in the political processes that structure choice among good lives' (Gutmann, 1987: 71, 74).

A critical perspective on education can usefully learn from Gutmann and Walzer not only their emphasis on the evaluative criteria of *participation* and *accountability*, but also the principle that justice involves a sensitivity and a responsibility to otherness. What might this mean in terms of the relationship of democratic education to democratic citizenship? Translated into a British context, it seems close to Raymond Williams's social democratic vision in *The Long Revolution* (1965). When Gutmann asserts that its priorities should be teaching the *essential democratic values* and cultivating a *common culture*, she is echoing (consciously or not) his argument that Britain's old hierarchical and divisive forms of schooling should be replaced by 'a public education designed to express and create the values of an educated democracy and a common culture' (Williams, 1965: 173–76).

Bearing in mind the problems in Williams's formulation — the dangers of assuming education can engineer the full expression of either society or individual and the exclusive limits of the community embraced by a common culture[5] — what new possibilities and problems are opened up by this approach? How might an emphasis on the construction of the social (the institution of authority) and the terms of participation (the authorization of agency) help us to think about the democratization of education? It is in this context that I want to consider aspects of the politics of literacy today.

Managing the Symbolic

'An illiterate person stands outside,' Lenin once remarked. 'He must first be taught the ABC. Without this, there can be no politics; without this, there are only rumours, gossip, tales, prejudices, but not politics.' This can be read as saying that literacy is a minimal requirement for participation in the political negotiations of civil society. Equally, it implies that mass literacy is a prerequisite for effective government by a state apparatus. 'Illiteracy is incompatible with the tasks of construction,' Lenin observed on another occasion.[6]

Literacy thus denotes both autonomous membership of an educated public, and yet also a technique of socialization. This ambivalence of literacy was evident in the different dispositions towards the standard language and the curriculum produced by popular education in the nineteenth century (Donald, 1982, 1983; Crowley, 1989). It remains central to the cultural strategy of the National Curriculum (Donald, 1990). Rather than opting for a view of literacy as *either* empowering *or* oppressing, therefore, my argument is once again that literacy entails both the institution of structures of cultural authority, and their negotiation. This suggests a new set of questions. What sort of social good and/or social practice is literacy? What problems is it supposed to solve, and how? What desirable outcomes is it supposed to achieve? On whom is it targeted? What knowledges are invoked in defining these problems, outcomes and targets? What are the ethics of different styles of teaching literacy?

I have structured my discussion around two symptomatic contemporary texts. In conventional educational terms, E.D. Hirsch's *Cultural Literacy: What Every American Needs to Know* (1987) has been denounced as part of the same educational backlash as Allan Bloom's (1988) bilious jeremiad, *The Closing of the American Mind*; this is Henry Giroux's reading in *Schooling for Democracy* (Giroux, 1989), for example. The *Handbook for Teachers* produced by the Inner London Education Authority's Centre for Language in Primary Education to accompany their *Primary Language Record* (ILEA, 1989), hereafter *PLR*, on the other hand, has been received as a thoughtful reaffirmation of the progressive tradition at a time when this has been under sustained, and often mischievous, political attack.[7] Part of my aim is to challenge the comforting stability of those categories of 'traditionalist' and 'progressive', and to decouple arguments about the role of literacy in democracy from any a priori commitment to particular styles of teaching.

E.D. Hirsch's polemic against progressivism has certainly been taken up and endorsed by conservative politicians in the United States, where it has spawned a generously funded Foundation running extensive research projects. Although not widely discussed in Britain, its influence may well have filtered through into the then Secretary of State Kenneth Baker's initial conception of the National Curriculum as a catalogue of 'what every British child needs to know'. (It seems to have had a similar impact in Australia.) Nevertheless, to read Hirsch as just another sign of the New Right times is a mistake. Although I certainly would not go as far as Richard Rorty (1989) and claim that Hirsch represents a Deweyan approach for our times — nor, I suspect, would Hirsch — his arguments do seem to represent, almost seventy years on, a throwback to the 'new humanism' of the Newbolt Report on *The Teaching of English in England* (1921).[8] Not only does he define problems in a similar way, he also invests the same desperate hope as Newbolt in literacy and literary education as paths to consensual citizenship.

It would equally wrong to lampoon the *PLR* authors as naive Rousseauians standing back and letting children's natural aptitudes develop — a stereotype Hirsch continues to peddle. They are self-reflexive about their commitment to progressivism: the document can be read as a practical yet implicitly polemical alternative to Piagetian notions of individual development and maturation, one that draws instead on a Vygotskian notion of the social formation of cognitive abilities. But they remain very much *within* the tradition. They do not address the growing body of critical work that places their 'technologies of the self' in the mainstream of what Foucault calls pastoral power, and so questions whether, or in what sense, their approach should be regarded as 'liberatory'. In this regard, I am thinking especially of the work of Valerie Walkerdine (1983, 1984) and Ian Hunter (1988), as noted previously.

Both Hirsch and the *PLR* authors share the aim of 'empowering' children, and both believe that literacy has something important to contribute to that end. They certainly disagree about the mechanisms of empowerment, not least because of their different understandings of what constitutes literacy. Here I am less concerned with their avowed political or theoretical positions than the pragmatics of their arguments: that is, the techniques they recommend, the knowledges and definitions these embody, and their implication in the government of publics and individuals.

E.D. Hirsch: 'Cultural Literacy' and Curriculum Politics

Hirsch's approach to literacy has both technical and political aspects. His technical argument is that reading is a process of decoding words, phrases, and clauses so as to recover the meaning a text contains, and that 'world knowledge' is a prerequisite for this process to be carried out successfully; if, that is, it is to go beyond a purely mechanical decoding. 'Although disadvantaged children often show an acceptable ability to decode and pronounce individual words, they are frequently unable to gain an integrated sense of the whole' (Hirsch, 1987: 27). A full understanding is only possible when meanings are matched to broader cultural templates: 'the reader constantly connects a few words into clauses that have meaning and the clauses to appropriate schemata based on past experience' (Hirsch, 1987: 53).

This account of reading is linked to Hirsch's political concern to break the cultural and educational cycle which condemns disadvantaged children to remain poor and illiterate. His premise is that 'all human communities are founded upon specific shared information', and that therefore '[o]nly by piling up specific, communally shared information can children learn to participate in complex cooperative activities with other members of their community'. The problem is that schools 'teach a fragmented curriculum based on faulty educational theories' — specifically, Rousseau's 'content-neutral conception of educational development' and John Dewey's excessive 'faith in children's ability to learn general skills from a few typical experiences' and his over-hasty rejection of ' "the piling up of information" '. Instead, they should teach everyone, and *especially* disadvantaged children, the communally shared information that Hirsch catalogues in a List (his capital) of names, dates, events, and concepts. In short, 'to be culturally literate is to posses the basic information needed to thrive in the modern world.' This need not mean mastering it in every detail, but having at least the passing acquaintance necessary to grasp the references and allusions in non-specialist texts (Hirsch, 1987: xiii–xv).

For Hirsch, cultural literacy is a social good because it allows the continuation and reproduction of society — which he interprets as a national sign community — and because it offers individuals the opportunity for mobility within it. In order 'to achieve not only greater economic prosperity but also greater social justice and more effective democracy', Hirsch argues in effect that the Enlightenment ideal of the educated public needs to become a universal reality:

> [L]iterate culture has become the common currency for social and economic exchange in our democracy, and the only available ticket to full citizenship. Getting one's membership card is not tied to class or race. Membership is automatic if one learns the background information and the linguistic conventions that are needed to read, write, and speak effectively. Although everyone is literate in some local, regional, or ethnic culture, the connection between mainstream culture and the national

written language justifies calling mainstream culture *the* basic culture
of the nation (Hirsch, 1987: 22).

Here Hirsch shows that he is no conservative elitist and certainly no neo-liberal.
He does not argue, as T.S. Eliot (1948) did, that the health of a culture depends
not only on shared membership of a single national community *but also* on the
differentiation of classes within that community. Eliot's premise was that 'it is
an essential condition of the preservation of the quality of the culture of the
minority, that it should continue to be a minority culture'; his conclusion, that 'a
high average of general education is perhaps less necessary for a civil society than
is a respect for learning' (Eliot, 1948: 100). Nor would Hirsch go along with
G.H. Bantock's (1971) educational programme, based on this style of thought,
in which the 'bottom fifty per cent of pupils' would be excluded from an
irrelevantly academic culture and offered instead a 'popular education' consisting
of Leavisite inoculation against the mass media, physical and emotional discipline
and expression, and gender-specific vocationalism. In contrast to Eliot and
Bantock, Hirsch is wholeheartedly a democrat. He wants social mobility, and he
accepts that educational and cultural differentiation inhibit it by sustaining hierarchy and disadvantage. He wants *everyone* to be literate on the same terms, to
have access to the power embodied in the national culture.[9]

Again in contrast to the conservative logic, he argues that the national
culture is not simply the culture or language of one class, but to some extent an
artificial construct which operates as a universal 'second culture'. Here Hirsch's
argument breaks down. The national culture and the standard language do not
need to be restricted in that way for literacy to work as a mechanism of
exclusion. Their divisiveness works not through ownership, but through the
different *dispositions* towards that shared set of signs and narratives. That is
evident in Hirsch's subtitle. By defining 'what every American needs to know',
he implies that those who do not know all this are in some sense *not* American.
(The implicit racialization of his categories is especially clear at this point.)
Although Hirsch might like to issue everyone with the 'membership card' of
literate culture, the image of citizenship as a 'club' only underlines MacIntyre's
insistence on the *limits* and *rules* of an educated public. Even if as a liberal-minded
democrat Hirsch does not share Eliot's reactionary politics, he does share his
vision and evaluation of what constitutes culture, and this pulls against his desire
for democratization. Although he wants to expand the educated public to
encompass the whole nation, Hirsch actually shrinks the nation to the size of an
educated public.

In that light, his argument can be seen to run something like this. First, he
defines the problem as how to break the cycle of poverty and illiteracy. Next, he
observes that the poor and oppressed do not generally read Shakespeare. Then
he makes the startling claim that they are poor and oppressed *because* they don't
read Shakespeare. Finally, from this unwarranted assumption he deduces that, if
they can be taught to read Shakespeare, they will no longer be poor and oppressed.
Of course, I am caricaturing. Hirsch does not only mean Shakespeare, nor even
high culture as traditionally conceived. But whether the content of the List is right
or wrong is largely beside the point. My objection is that the structure of his argument — his syllogistic formulation of the problem and its possible solutions — is
fundamentally flawed. Although it is true that education and the accumulation of

cultural capital can provide a route for individual social mobility, this knowledge is perfectly compatible with the production and maintenance of unequal social relations.

The delusions and disavowals of Hirsch's faith in the integrative power of literacy and education are particularly evident in his account of how the bonds of national community are established through a shared language. He remains blind to the *differences* produced through the 'imagined community' of the national culture and the imposition of a standard language. For me, however, these are absolutely central (Donald, 1982, 1983; Crowley, 1989). The classic presentation of an anti-Hirschian alternative is Renée Balibar's (1974) account of the imposition of a standard French as the national language in the post-Revolutionary period. This strategy allowed a *formal* equality at the same time as giving a new significance and value to the different dispositions towards the language. What had previously been simply regional and dialectal differences were now incorporated into new patterns of discrimination (between 'correct' and 'incorrect' usages, between 'polite' and 'vulgar' forms). Although we can accept Hirsch's insistence that the standard language is not simply the language of any one class faction or region, nevertheless it is clear from Balibar's research that children of the bourgeoisie in their secondary schools were offered some understanding of how language works and so in some sense experienced it as their own. They learned that they had been speaking prose all their lives. In contrast to this, working-class pupils in the elementary schools established in the nineteenth century were instructed in the mechanical rules of 'grammar'. This school language, argues Balibar, was experienced as an external imposition, and also as an exclusion from a superior language and culture. These children learned that they didn't talk 'proper'.

More recently, Gauri Viswanathan (1987) has provided another compelling contradiction of Hirsch's faith through her history of the origins of English literary studies as a technique of government in colonial India. As one administrator put in 1838: 'The Natives must either be kept down by a sense of our power, or they must willingly submit from a conviction that we are more wise, more just, more humane, and more anxious to improve their condition than any other rulers they could have'. This is the context in which supposedly moralizing English texts became the objects of study for a class of translators, civil servants, and so forth. Even here, though, the power of literacy retained its ambivalence. C.E. Trevelyan, an influential member of the Council of Education, noted in 1853 that this strategy could not avoid the idea that the power and authority embodied in the provided texts might become accessible to those supposedly subordinated to them. Some of the educated natives, he observed, had an idea that 'we have gained everything by our superior knowledge; that it is this superiority which has enabled us to conquer India, and to keep it; and they want to put themselves as much as they can upon an equality with us' (Viswanathan, 1987: 22). *As much as they can* — the consequence of those limits was the formation of what Homi Bhabha (1984), adapting V.S. Naipaul, has called 'mimic men'. This subaltern class takes on the values and mannerisms of the provided culture, but without them ever quite fitting: 'almost the same, but not white', says Bhabha (1984: 130).[10]

The moral of these other histories of language, power and exclusion is that Hirsch misrecognizes national language and cultural literacy. They are never *only* means of healing social divisions and so of achieving economic efficiency and social justice: they always also produce cultural differences and evaluative hierarchies. Nevertheless, it is important not to underestimate or trivialize his desire for universality and community. Literacy is not just an individual capacity. It does play an important role in organizing law, citizenship and public life. So yes, Hirsch's account of reading remains too mechanical; yes, his List of information is a grotesque simplification of a culture's operative symbolic codes; yes, he disavows the patterns of difference and discrimination contained by the precarious 'identity' of a national community. But the problem of how to democratize literacy and culture remains.

Renewing Progressivism: Literacy Pedagogy and the National Curriculum

The authors of the *The Primary Language Record* differ markedly from Hirsch in their conception of literacy and its democratic potential. They see it less in terms of securing access to a body of valued information than as the cultivation of an innate capacity. They therefore promote the 'language-experience approach' to literacy, which 'stressed the importance of using children's first-hand experiences and natural interests in helping them to acquire and develop reading and writing skills'. What this means in practice is an emphasis on monitoring and recording 'significant aspects of language growth' in each child, in exhaustive detail. The teacher's authority thus derives less from her or his role as representative of the literate culture than from her or his performance as interlocutor, scribe, confidant(e) and guide. The pedagogic art lies in managing both the 'social and curriculum dimensions' of 'the learning environment', creating the contexts which will elicit the various linguistic performances for which the teacher is looking. Drama is especially important as it allows children 'to use what they already know about the world (their understanding and experience of it) in an imagined context, and through it to explore issues and concepts important for them and the communities they live in'. Because she or he is 'working alongside children in creating imagined realities', drama also means that 'a teacher can change her [or his] status in the classroom, enabling children to talk with each other and with her [or him] in a way which is often difficult in the real life of the classroom, where the power relationships between adults and children are usually fixed (ILEA, 1989; 24, 38, 22).

If this account of the formation of the child, the exemplary role of the teacher, and the special claims of English and drama to be true to children's experience sounds familiar, that may be because here the *PLR* recalls an influential approach from the 1960s. This was lucidly expressed in John Dixon's (1967) *Growth Through English*:

> The taking on of dramatic roles, the dramatic encounter with new situations and with new possibilities of the self, is not something we *teach* children but something they bring to school for us to help them develop ... How can a teacher help pupils engaged in so personal a task to weigh up what has been achieved? All of us test the validity of what we have said by sensing how far others that we trust have shared our

response. An English teacher tries to be a person to whom pupils turn with that sense of trust. The sensitivity, honesty and tact of his [or her] response to what pupils say will confirm their half-formed certainties and doubts in what they have said (cited in Hunter, 1988: 16–17).[11]

In *Culture and Government*, his book on the emergence of English, Ian Hunter (1988) juxtaposes this against another text that shares its view of the special role of the teacher as moral exemplar and the recognizable embodiment of the child's conscience, and its emphasis on the management of 'the learning environment' in order to reveal the 'true character and dispositions' of the children:

> A play-ground is in fact the principal scene of the real life of children, both in the juvenile and initiatory departments — the arena on which their true character and dispositions are exhibited; and where, free and unconstrained, they can hop and jump about, swing, or play at tag, ball, or marbles ...
>
> Whilst the pupils sympathize with each other, it is important that the children sympathize with their master. For this purpose, it is necessary that he place himself on such terms with his pupils as that they can, without fear, make him their confidant, unburden their minds, and tell him any little story, or mischievous occurence. Teachers and parents, desirous of gaining the confidence of their children, must in fact, themselves as it were, become children, by bending to, and occasionally engaging in, their plays and amusements. Without such condescension, a perfect knowledge of real character and dispositions cannot be gained (cited in Hunter, 1988: 17).

This is from David Stow's *The Training System, the Moral Training School, and the Normal Seminary*, published in 1850 and one of the manuals that had most impact on the design and operation of the nineteenth-century popular school. The point of the comparison is not to suggest that there is nothing new under the educational sun, but simply to underline that the *PLR*'s presuppositions and strategies only make sense within the long pastoral tradition in the history of popular education. This has never been concerned only with the *discipline* of individuals, but also with their physical and moral *welfare*, their aptitudes and competences, their tastes and recreations. Hence the *PLR*'s demand on children to narrate and acknowledge their own experience, its appeal to norms and principles defined by educational psychology, and its proposals for structured interviews about language and literacy with parents and pupils.

The interviews with pupils, for example, are supposed to be 'a continuation of an already existing dialogue between child and teacher' in which it can 'be made clear to children that interests that exist beyond the confines of the school are not only relevant and valid in themselves, but also of great interest in discussions about their language/literacy development'. The summary of the conference becomes part of the archive of information about the individual pupil, and the flip side of indicating to children 'that what they say is being taken seriously' is that they take on a key role in their own supervision. They are required to take responsibility for their own formation and development (ILEA,

1989: 14, 15). Here, then, we are dealing with what Hunter takes to be central to the apparatus of popular education: that is, techniques for the inculcation of self-monitoring capacities.

This is not to imply that the *PLR* approach has no educational value. It has clearly galvanized many primary teachers and provided a structure that children can often negotiate with considerable benefit. Its authors' commitment to the notion of English as emancipation, however, does tend to disavow the ambivalence of literacy. It is therefore legitimate to ask in what sense their methods prove more 'emancipatory' or 'empowering' than other pedagogic styles. If advocates of this approach were to criticize Hirsch on the grounds that his endorsement of 'literate culture' disdains the experiences, languages and cultures of 'disadvantaged' children as deficient or inadequate, for example, the Hirschian might riposte that the misrecognition of social norms as innate capacities establishes a pathological model of those who do not conform to that pattern. If the progressive objects that Hirsch's strategy will not work because he misconceives unequal relations of power as a body of socially neutral information, the Hirschian could point out that the *PLR Handbook* consistently reduces 'the social' to questions of interpersonal relations. And this critic might go on to argue that whereas Hirsch's insistence on socialization into the literate national culture as a necessary 'second culture' at least opens up the possibility for a critical distance on experience, and so of individual mobility and cultural change, the progressive insistence that schools should 'value children's cultures, lives and experiences' entails a moral relativism that could be culturally quite conservative. There is often a tension between the progressives' desire for mobility and change, on the one hand, and their scruples about disturbing the claims and comforts of community, on the other. Theirs is not the Lyotardian idea of community as an always-to-be-achieved aspiration, but the familiar notion of community as cultural baggage.

A left-wing Hirschian (if such a hybrid creature is imaginable) might therefore invoke Gramsci's injunction that the teacher 'must be aware of the contrast between the type of culture and society which he [sic] represents and the type of culture and society represented by his pupils, and conscious of his obligation to accelerate and regulate the child's formation in conformity with the former and in conflict with the latter' (Gramsci, 1971: 35–36). This underlines an important lesson of which Hirsch's crusade is a flawed and inadvertent reminder: that culture is never something we own, it remains always elusively other. This shifts the criteria for what constitutes a democratic education away from an emphasis on the *expression* of community or experience or identity, and towards the terms on which students *participate* in social and cultural transactions. From this perspective, the important difference between Hirsch and the *PLR* authors is that, whereas he sees submission to established cultural norms as a precondition for autonomous participation later, they concentrate instead on involving children in the educational possibilities of self-formation here and now.

If Hirsch thus overemphasizes universalizing modes of power and the *PLR* individuating modes, they both share an overinflated notion of what literacy can deliver. If only we could get literacy right, they imply, that will produce (for Hirsch) or reveal (for *PLR*) citizens who would exercise their talents and innate creative abilities to the full. It would also ensure the full flowering of a democratic culture. And at that point, the debate usually congeals into stale oppositions between 'individuation' and 'socialization', 'progressivism' and 'traditionalism', 'liberal education' and 'vocationalism', 'emancipation' and 'social control'.

Refunctioning Literacy

How might the question of literacy be rephrased so as to avoid that sclerosis? Neither human nature nor an idealized national community offers a plausible starting point. It may be more productive to begin by acknowledging both the impossibility of a universal educated public and yet also the tragi-comic inescapability of participating in collective relations of power. That recognition at least gets rid of images of the full development and expression of individual talents being thwarted and deformed by the dull compulsion of wage labour and the oppressions of everyday life. Accept the ambivalence of participation and agency — we are always both *subjects of* and *subject to* — and it is impossible to imagine the exercise of liberty as a psychotic escape from relations of power. Instead, it becomes an invitation or an obligation to act on the basis that the rules of the game can be changed *while it is being played*, however rigged the game may be in favour of some players and against others.

From this point of view, education is revealed both as an instance of participation in the social and the symbolic, and also as a threshold to further participation in the labour market and civil society. The next task, then, is to identify those authoritative discourses and practices that define the terms of this participation, and to consider how they might be organized so as to enhance their democratic or improvisatory aspects. This is what I would understand by cultural and social literacy.

How would my version of it differ from Hirsch's? Whereas he presents community as the solution, I see it as the question. Rather than prescribe what every American (or Briton, or Australian) needs to know, I would focus on the educational conditions necessary for the possibility of a radical democracy. What knowledges, skills and resources would citizens need in order to be able to participate effectively in its dialogue and negotiations? To answer that, I would look again at the conditions of existence of an Enlightenment educated public that Alisdair MacIntyre identified, and seek to recast them for our post-Enlightenment times.

His principal condition was that critical discussion on shared terms should be a feature of the roles and functions into which students are socialized. This finds an almost uncanny echo in the powerful case that has been made in recent years for what I call a *critical vocationalism*. This apparently oxymoronic concept points to the need to dismantle the existing opposition between 'academic' and 'vocational' education. Its premise is that a general education should teach some understanding of the complex technological, economic and industrial systems that structure the organization of production and the exercise of power in modern Western societies. Otherwise it produces students who are, in a partial but practical way, *illiterate*. Equally, any vocationalism that is not critical — that teaches only mechanical skills and deference, that ignores the determinants and consequences of decisions and practices, and that does not require students to think about them — is irrelevant to the creation of the skilled, informed and participatory workforce implicit in the idea of industrial democracy.[12]

MacIntyre's second condition for an educated public was the existence of canonical cultural references. Defining the political community in terms of a nationalist assimilationism was, of course, central to the initial strategy of the National Curriculum. Here the literate or educated public was to be identified in terms of the cultural *content* of the curriculum. To qualify for membership is to be at home with *this* form of language, *this* selection of books, *this* Christianity, *this* heritage — Kenneth Baker's List, as tempered (or subverted, some would claim) by the working parties of the National Curriculum Council, in this case, rather than E.D. Hirsch's. However offensive or dotty such inventories may be, the idea of an educated public does presuppose some shared points of reference. To deny certain groups access to valued cultural forms is one way in which cultural inequalities are reproduced. That is why the demand for such access has often been a characteristic of working-class and feminist educational movements. They have realized that what is at stake in debates about content and access is the authority embodied in and instituted by cultural traditions. The problem is that in a multicultural society, there can be no one centre of authority, although that is precisely the premise of most official educational multiculturalism, which incorporates other cultures and traditions only as long as they do not trouble established norms and categories. To define literacy as one, and only one, set of cultural luggage is to set in place effective mechanisms of differentiation and discrimination rather than of universal inclusiveness.

The challenge is therefore to decouple the identification of shared cultural referents — the terms in which community is imagined — from the retroactive legitimacy bestowed on them by traditions of nationality or ethnicity. However much we are taught that they are handed down from past generations, such canons are present inventions that identify 'us' and differentiate 'us' from 'them'. What multiculturalism requires, if taken seriously, is to displace this version of community as always already fixed in favour of the idea of community as unknown, uncentred, always to be constructed in the process of dialogue and self-naming. That aspiration, I think, lies behind this description of the range of activities that might now make up English teaching in a London secondary school:

> A first year class might be discussing cultural assumptions and narrative forms through the reading of folk-tales and fairy stories, using simple deconstruction strategies. A second year class might be considering the publicity and marketing of a class reader or its adaptation for television while a third year group plan and draft pieces for a poetry anthology to be used in primary schools. In the fourth year, language itself might be under discussion with pupils exploring regional and historical shifts in dialect. Fifth years might be involved in Literature Open Studies; exploring the genre of crime fiction or comparing a Hardy novel to a work of contemporary popular fiction. In the sixth form GCSE mature students might be analysing the representation of children in television advertisements. CPVE (Certificate of Pre-Vocational Education) students might be writing an account of their work experience. An A-level class might be reading a Hemingway short story from the perspective of a number of critical stances; Leavisite, post-structuralist, feminist, psychoanalytical (Broadbent and Moger, 1990: 47).

Here it is recognized that the content of the syllabus is provisional and always subject to change and negotiation. What matters is the strategy governing its selection: not just the question of who gets access to what, but above all the emphasis on concepts, perspectives, and semiotic skills. Literary language is treated as one discursive genre amongst others. Texts are set in their historical and institutional contexts to show how the production of meaning is linked to the exercise of power. Students are familiarized with the techniques of different media, and are confronted with a variety of frameworks for making sense of themselves and the social world.

This version of literacy is restricted neither to a familiarity with the best that has supposedly been thought and written, nor to the exercise of an innate aesthetic capacity, nor to the acknowledgment of an essential experience. Nevertheless, recalling MacIntyre's category of mutually accepted standards of authority, it does still refer at least implicitly to a kernel of shared values and beliefs: empathy, sensitivity to difference, tolerance and mutual respect. From this point of view, it does not matter whether or not you have read the same books as your fellow citizens, whether you share their religious or political convictions, or even speak the same language. But you do have to accept the same rules of the game for political negotiation. The minimal requirement for membership of an educated public would then be a shared definition of what is at issue, and agreement about how to disagree.

This anyway is the premise of Amy Gutmann's liberal argument. She makes the assertion, for example, that '[c]hildren must learn not just to *behave* in accordance with authority but to *think* critically about authority if they are to live up to the democratic ideal of sharing political sovereignty as citizens' (Gutmann, 1987: 51). Although that encapsulates forcefully the version of liberty I have been arguing for, Gutmann's formulation also indicates some of its limits. Her commitment to critical thought is predicated on the acceptance of the 'democratic ideal' as the only conceivable outcome of the interrogation. Gutmann does not seem to allow for the possibility of critical perspectives incommensurable with this axiom and so, in effect, pre-empts the outcome of the dialogue. She may substitute the democratic ideal for the enlightened monarch, but in effect she reasserts Kant's (1986: 269) paradoxical principle of *intellectual* autonomy within strict *political* limits: 'Argue as much as you will, and about what you will, only obey!' Where, in 'our' post-colonial democracy, does that leave those who — whether by alternative affiliation or by exclusion — do not share Gutmann's ideal and so experience that 'obey' as pure coercion? To seek universally shared values or dispositions is once again to highlight the experience of division.

This aporia suggests that the literacy adequate to a radical, heterogeneous democracy might need to be driven neither by a normative identity nor a performative political ideal, but by the principle and skills of cultural translation, the ability to negotiate across incommensurable traditions. Alisdair MacIntyre has suggested what might be involved:

> [T]he only rational way for the adherents of any tradition to approach intellectually, culturally, and linguistically alien rivals is one that allows for the possibility that in one or more areas the other may be rationally superior to it in respect precisely of that in the alien tradition which it cannot comprehend. The claim made within each tradition that the

presently established beliefs shared by the adherents of that tradition are true entails a denial that this is in fact going to happen in respect of those beliefs, but it is the possibility of this nonetheless happening which ... gives point to the assertion of truth and provides assertions of truth and falsity with a content which makes them other than even idealized versions of assertions of warranted assertability. The existence of large possibilities of untranslatability and therefore of potential threats to the cultural, linguistic, social, and rational hegemony of one's own tradition, either in some particular area or overall, is therefore more and other than a threat. Only those whose tradition allows for the possibility of its hegemony being put in question can have rational warrant for asserting such a hegemony. And only those traditions whose adherents recognize the possibility of untranslatability into their own language-in-use are able to reckon adequately with that possibility (MacIntyre, 1988: 388).

Although this does presuppose an effective political pluralism, it entails neither a corporatism that takes interest groups and cultural identities at face value, nor an 'anything-goes' relativism. Instead, it sees the institution of authority — or hegemony — as definitive of a tradition, while acknowledging that such authority is always limited by the terms of that tradition and so is provisional and open to question. This is therefore the exact opposite of that version of tradition as absolute and unquestionable imposed through the National Curriculum. In its insistence on the recursiveness of reason and its scepticism towards foundationalism, MacIntyre's account of tradition and translation suggests an approach to literacy in tune with Lyotard's (1984: 67) call at the end of *The Postmodern Condition* for 'a politics that would respect both the desire for justice and the desire for the unknown'.

Does this indicate that, given that there are no modes of argumentation and justification that are universally shared, we should try to desacralize literacy, to rid it of encrusted cultural accretions? Could it then be interpreted purely as those skills and competences necessary for interpreting differences, for analyzing information, for reaching decisions, and for acting on them? This is an attractive option in that it implies a practical orientation for teaching, and opens up the possibility of negotiating criteria of accountability; that is, establishing 'performance indicators' for institutions and teachers which would at the same time be 'entitlements' for students.[13] This could respect the various interests in the process of schooling without falling back into the lazy imagery of consumerism. In the end, however, it only partly sidesteps the problem. Techniques and skills — the *processes* of literacy — are as embedded in intellectual and cultural traditions as values and artefacts — literacy as *product*. Society cannot be rendered transparent. Our fantasmatic investment in identities and communities ensures the continuation of a social imaginary bounded by the sacred and the abject. That aspect of schooling and literacy cannot be so hygienically packaged as rights and entitlements.

A Concluding Note: Authority and Agency

There are no universally agreed criteria for what constitutes a social and cultural literacy. It follows that the type of educated public required by an Enlightenment theory of participatory democracy cannot exist. Today, that idea of a public lingers on as part of a republican myth of the Ideal City. To counter its seductive but dangerous appeal, I have been attempting a critical rearticulation of its constituent themes. I have tried to show, first, *how* authoritative concepts, categories and values are embodied in the discourses and representations of education, and, second, the *terms* on which students might engage with them. That is why I have emphasized the ambivalence of participation. My sketch of an expansive social and cultural literacy is not so much a prescription for a different curriculum or a new pedagogy, as a practical critique of existing principles of syllabus construction and a provocation to debate what is really at issue in notions like 'quality' and 'relevance'. It sees literacy in terms of the negotiation of authority, the formation of tradition, and the authorization of agency. It sees democracy not as the aspiration to total social transformation, but like Dewey's pragmatic progressivism, as a restless and recursive experimentalism.

Notes

1 This article is based on a chapter of my book *Sentimental Education: Schooling, Popular Culture and the Regulation of Liberty* (London: Verso, 1992/in press). The reading of Hirsch and the *Primary Literacy Record* formed part of a talk delivered at the conference *Literacy for the Twenty-First Century*, The Literacy Centre, Brighton Polytechnic, Falmer, 16–18 July 1990.
2 For the critique of 'child-centred' pedagogies based on psychological expertise, see Walkerdine (1983, 1984). On 'progressivism' as an instance of pastoral power, see Hunter (1988).
3 On this matter, see Rose (1989); see, further, Rose (1990).
4 On states that are essentially a by-product, see Salecl (1988: 89ff.); she adapts the concept from Elster (1983).
5 For critiques of Williams along these lines, see Hunter (1988) and Gilroy (1987: 49ff.).
6 Lenin cited in Grant (1964: 29–30), and also in Hoyles (1977: 20).
7 I am grateful to Jay Snow for introducing me to this document, and for his helpful reading of it.
8 On Newbolt, see Ball (1985), Hunter (1988), and Doyle (1989).
9 On the tensions between neo-liberalism and neo-conservatism in Thatcherite Conservatism, see my *Sentimental Education*, (1992/in press) chapter 6.
10 Such an approach suggests a more nuanced map of class differentiation than Balibar's rather schematic version, with a special emphasis on the formation of a petty bourgeoisie in the metropolitan societies.
11 See also Ball (1985, 1987).
12 For a more extensive account of 'critical vocationalism', see my *Sentimental Education*, (1992, in press) chapter 7. See also Spours and Young (1988), Ahier (1989), and Esland (1990).
13 For a political programme along such lines, see Plant (1988).

References

AHIER, J. (1989) 'Explaining Economic Decline and Teaching Children about Industry: Some Unintended Continuities?', unpublished manuscript, August.
BALIBAR, R. (1974) *Les Francais Fictifs*, Paris, Hatchette.

BALL, S.J. (1985) 'English for the English since 1906', in GOODSON, I. (Ed.) *Social Histories of the Secondary Curriculum*, London, Falmer Press, pp. 53–88.

BALL, S.J. (1987) 'English Teaching, the State, and Forms of Literacy', in KROON, S. and STURM, J. (Eds) *Research on Mother Tongue Teaching in an International Perspective*, Enschede, Netherlands, International Mother Tongue Education Network, pp. 19–35.

BANTOCK, G.H. (1971) 'Towards a Theory of Popular Education', in HOOPER, R. (Ed.) *The Curriculum: Context, Design and Development*, London, Oliver Boyd, pp. 251–64.

BHABHA, H.K. (1984) 'Of Mimicry and Man: The Ambivalence of Colonial Discourse', *October*, 28, pp. 125–33.

BLOOM, A. (1988) *The Closing of the American Mind*, Harmondsworth, Penguin.

BROADBENT, S. and MOGER, R. (1990) 'But Is It English ...? The National Curriculum and Progressive English Teaching', in BROOKER, P. and HUMM, P. (Eds) *Dialogue and Difference: English into the Nineties*, London, Routledge, pp. 43–54.

CROWLEY, T. (1989) *The Politics of Discourse: The Standard Language Question in British Cultural Debates*, London, Macmillan.

DONALD, J. (1982) 'Language, Literacy and Schooling', Unit 2 of *U203 Popular Culture*, Milton Keynes, Open University Press, pp. 42–74.

DONALD, J. (1983) 'How Illiteracy Became a Problem (and Literacy Stopped Being One)', *Journal Of Education* (Boston) 165, 1, Winter, pp, 12–34.

DONALD, J. (1990) 'Beyond Our Ken: English, Englishness, and the National Curriculum', in BROOKER, P. and HUMM, P. (Eds) *Dialogue and Difference: English into the Nineties*, London, Routledge, pp. 13–30.

DOYLE, B. (1989) *English and Englishness*, London, Routledge.

ELIOT, T.S. (1948, 1962) *Notes Towards the Definition of Culture*, London, Faber and Faber.

ELSTER, J. (1983) *Sour Grapes: Studies in the Subversion of Rationality*, Cambridge, Cambridge University Press.

ESLAND, G. (Ed.) (1990) *Education, Training and Employment*, 2 vols, Wokingham, Addison Wesley.

GILROY, P. (1987) *There Ain't No Black in the Union Jack*, London, Hutchinson.

GIROUX, H. (1989) *Schooling for Democracy*, London, Routledge.

GRAMSCI, A. (1971) *Selections from the Prison Notebooks*, London, Lawrence and Wishart.

GRANT, N. (1964) *Soviet Education*, Harmondsworth, Penguin.

GUTMANN, A. (1987) *Democratic Education*, Princeton, Princeton University Press.

HIRSCH, E.D. JR (1987) *Cultural Literacy: What Every American Needs to Know*, Boston, Houghton Mifflin.

HOYLES, M. (1977) *The Politics of Literacy*, London, Writers and Readers Cooperative.

HUNTER, I. (1988) *Culture and Government: The Emergence of Literary Education*, London, Macmillan.

ILEA (1989) *The Primary Language Record: A Handbook for Teachers*, London, Inner London Education Authority (ILEA), Centre for Language in Primary Education.

KANT, I. (1986) 'What is Enlightenment?', *Philosophical Writings*, New York, Continuum, pp. 236–69.

LYOTARD, J-F. (1984) *The Postmodern Condition: A Report on Knowledge*, Manchester, Manchester University Press.

MACINTYRE, A. (1987) 'The Idea of an Educated Public', in HAYDON, G. (Ed.) *Education and Values*, London, University of London Institute of Education, pp. 15–36.

MACINTYRE, A. (1988) *Whose Justice? Which Rationality?* London, Duckworth.

PLANT, R. (1988) *Citizenship, Rights, and Socialism*, London, Fabian Society.

RORTY, R. (1989) 'Education without Dogma: Truth, Freedom, and Our Universities', *Dissent*, Spring, pp. 198–204.

ROSE, N. (1989) 'Governing the Enterprising Self', paper presented at the conference *The Values of the Enterprise Culture*, University of Lancaster, September.

ROSE, N. (1990) *Governing the Soul: The Shaping of the Private Self*, London, Routledge.

SALECL, R. (1988) 'Homage to the Great Other', *Prose Studies*, **11**, 3, December, pp. 84–93.

SPOURS, K. and YOUNG, M. (1988) *Beyond Vocationalism: A New Perspective on the Relationship Between Work and Education*, Working Paper No. 4, London, Institute of Education Post-16 Education Centre.

VISWANATHAN, G. (1987) 'The Beginnings of English Literary Study in British India', *Oxford Literary Review*, **9**, pp. 2–26.

WALKERDINE, V. (1983) 'It's Only Natural: Re-Thinking Child-Centred Pedagogy', in WOLPE, A. and DONALD, J. (Eds) *Is There Anyone Here from Education?* London, Pluto Press, pp. 79–87.

WALKERDINE, V. (1984) 'Developmental Psychology and the Child-Centred Pedagogy: The Insertion of Piaget into Early Education', in HENRIQUES, J., HOLLWAY, W., URWIN, C., VENN, C. and WALKERDINE, V., *Changing the Subject: Psychology, Social Regulation and Subjectivity*, London, Methuen, pp. 153–202.

WALZER, M. (1983) *Spheres of Justice*, New York, Basic Books.

WILLIAMS, R. (1965) *The Long Revolution*, Harmondsworth, Penguin.

Chapter 8

Stories of Social Regulation: The Micropolitics of Classroom Narrative

Allan Luke

There is ample advocacy of the centrality of narrative to the educational enterprise. This ranges from claims about the centrality of 'story-form' as a developmentally appropriate and ontologically significant genre for classroom talk, reading and writing, to the romanticist belief in the universal power of literature to enhance 'personal growth' at all stages of literacy learning. How such positions are realized in classrooms is straightforward. Across English-speaking nations, literacy training is premised on the unproblematic value of the reading, writing and speaking of fictional narratives. The early 'immersion' in stories is viewed by many as a 'natural' developmental prelude to the analytic, expository texts of the human and natural sciences.

The resultant neglect of non-fiction writing in elementary literacy training may lead to a mystification of disciplinary registers and genres, with the political consequence of the exclusion of working-class and non-mainstream children from academically significant, scientific discourses (Martin, 1985). Yet this critique, and the various curricular interventions designed to teach what has been called 'content-area' reading and writing, is based on a binary distinction of the linguistic characteristics and epistemological consequences of 'non-literary' (e.g. expository) and 'literary' (e.g. narrative) prose. Indeed such dualism is rife in traditional curriculum organization, the former seen as the rightful domain of disciplinary study and the latter of those curriculum fields traditionally affiliated with literacy: language arts, reading, and English education. It also figures prominently in assignments of rational effects to literacy, which tend to rank scientific knowledge as a specialized, higher-order competence following on from narrative competence.

Examination of the epistemological and sociocultural consequences of narrative in education is well underway, in recent years encouraged by post-structuralist scepticism towards the transparency of writing, and feminist and postmodernist critiques of the political function of master narratives. In academic work, these range from methodological reappraisals of the centrality of narrative in curriculum theory (e.g. Inglis, 1986), to refigurings of ethnography and academic writing as narrative form (e.g. Brodkey, 1987), and whole-scale critiques of the patriarchal character of modern scientific discourse (e.g. Harding, 1986). In curriculum analysis, studies of narrative have included neo-Marxist analyses of narrative structure as a means for enculturation (e.g. Rose, 1985; Luke, 1988), ethnographic and sociological analyses of 'what counts' as appropriate school narratives (Heath, 1983; Michaels and Collins, 1984; Baker and Freebody, 1989), and feminist descriptions of the differential distribution of 'gendered genres' of narrative (e.g. Gilbert and Taylor, 1991; Christian-Smith, 1990). All of the foregoing is closely tied to the emergence of cross-disciplinary discourse analytic strategies for the study of narrative structure (Toolan, 1986).

This work notwithstanding, at the heart of educational common sense and classroom practice are modernist descriptions of what counts as narrative and its significance, whether these definitions are lodged in romantic notions of the storying individual, or in structuralist parsings of narrative descended from Aristotle via Propp. But what kinds of gendered cultural logic, common sense and rationality are produced by the early childhood emphasis on narrative? Is rationality, with all of its manifest symptoms, indigenous to the social technology of literacy *per se*? Or is it, and the 'shadowy epistemic subject' (Walkerdine, 1982) associated with it, an effect of how literacy is institutionally constructed?

This chapter traces the discursive construction of the consequences of literacy, specifically of the cultural logic prefigured in 'doing' narrative in an early childhood writing lesson. To show how stories are a key moment in gendered social regulation, my focus here is on discursive displays and procedures for doing and showing 'narrative rationality' in this particular classroom (Baker and Freebody, 1989; Walkerdine, 1987, 1988; Luke, 1991/in press). Using Lyotard's (1984) account of the functions of narrative and scientific discourse in postmodern conditions, I turn this analysis to a reconsideration of the social and political consequences of early literacy training in postmodern conditions. My aim is to reassess the question of the cognitive and social effects of literacy, and to offer an alternative explanation of how the formal introduction to the technology of writing is a moment in the articulation of cultural metanarratives of science, progress and patriarchy.

Theory and Description of Literacies

The question of the consequences of literacy remains central to schooling, particularly given current demands for technical skills by human capital advocates, and the press for explicit teaching of the codes of scientific texts both as economic and political strategies. Whether the effects typically assigned to writing — the expression and development of personal identity, logical and abstract thinking, decontextualization and metalinguistic awareness — are intrinsic characteristics of the technology of writing or innate developmental sequences is, of course, problematic. Cross-cultural studies suggest that those cognitive consequences which have become affiliated with writing may be the effects of formal, Western-style schooling (e.g. Scribner and Cole, 1981).

While such studies tend to relocate the constitutive power of literacy in schooling, they stop short of detailing how spoken and written discourses in the site of the classroom construct literacy and its alleged effects. I begin from the position that the consequences of literacy — both socio/cultural and individual/cognate — are discursive constructions, enacted and confirmed in institutional sites such as the school. Such a perspective on literacy as a social construction

(Cook-Gumperz, 1986) forces a rethinking of the possibilities of theorizing universal effects of literacy from description of face-to-face literacy events.

While Scribner and Cole (1981) critiqued the cognitive effects hypothesis, they did so by readjusting but not querying the efficacy of psychological measurement. Specifically their analyses are based on the development and use of culturally appropriate measures of cognitive effects. That is, while acutely sensitive to the embeddedness of mental phenomena in cultural contexts, neither they nor Luria and Vygotsky disputed the notion that literacy, developed in relation to an array of cultural practices for acquisition and use, had transferable, verifiable 'higher' cognitive effects. As Walkerdine (1982, 1988), Green (1991) and others indicate, such a move retains a subject/context dualism, the supposition that particular competences developed in local cultural ecologies can be analytically and practically separated from those milieux. This dualism, ever more common in the rush to account for social context and culture as methodological and pedagogic variables,[1] has several limits. It embeds practice in culture, but it fails to see how when culture and subjectivity are redefined in terms of discourses in local sites the competence/context distinction becomes, at least, problematic and, at best, reflexive. In curricular practice and policy, it remains nonetheless the basis for arguments that competence can somehow be empirically observed in contexts, scientifically parsed and deconstructed, and transferred or reconstructed as semi-autonomous entities in new or different sites.

Literacy is something which is done in everyday sites, and cross-cultural research underlines the variability of possible literacies which can be achieved in institutions with the artifacts of texts. Cross-cultural studies point to the range of textual practices which cultures deem functional and valuable, as well as noting that many of those practices valorized in Western schooling play little part in community life (e.g. Heath, 1983; Schieffelin and Gilmore, 1986). Describable are families of textual practices (McHoul, 1991) that recur with some degree of regularity and variability in particular institutional sites. As moments in discourse, the procedures of literacy events configure reading and writing practices, positions and subjectivities. Yet in classrooms, the construction of literacy is far from arbitrary or idiosyncratic. It is a key normalizing and reproductive strategy of schooling. The status and power of texts and textual practices, particular readers/writers and speakers/hearers is constructed and parcelled out differentially (Freebody, Luke and Gilbert, 1991). The political point is this: groups of aspiring readers and writers are marked for entry into stratified interpretive communities, which in modernist educational culture continue to fall along the historical grids of gender, class and colour.

Given the significant variability with which cultures and subcultures shape literate practices and literate subjectivities, we can query the possibility of universal, non-normative educational theories and approaches. Based as they are on observable social and discursive practices, theories of reading and writing are always theories of 'having read' or 'having written'.[2] Such theories themselves are institutionally sited practices, shaped by and shaping of discourses, as Heap (1991) suggests, and they can only be verified or falsified in terms of how adequately they describe and predict further practices. Hence theories of reading and writing are reliant upon particular extra-discursive and discursive institutional conditions being in play, and insofar as they are used to build pedagogy in schools, quite readily become discourses for the political legitimation of those same practices. A tautology, suggests Freebody (1991), is built between description and prescription, between experimental setting and classroom, between psycho-educational theory and discourse practice.

The Classroom Construction of Literate Logic

Families of textual practices are built in classroom language games played by teachers and students. There what counts as reading and writing is procedurally constructed for students (Baker and Freebody, 1989). As part of their ritual introduction to school literacy in early elementary education, children practice the genres and ideologies of narrative, *and* of events for the construction of narrative. Michaels and Collins (1984) show how classroom talk entails the systematic selection of those children's narratives which are characterized by 'literate discourse style', while those texts of children who reproduce, for instance, oral discourse styles (e.g. prosodic cues to highlight shift, referential relations) are in effect ruled out as non-stories. Hence, an invisible logic of narrative texts and of story events is built in mainstream classrooms. There children's narratives which do not have the surface features of Anglo-European literary narrative simply do not count as stories (Heath, 1983). In effect, the local procedures of classroom talk and bodily arrangement rule in and out of the game particular discourse procedures and displays of how to do narrative, of narrative rationality. In this way, the classroom articulation of a logic of narrative relies on the identification and marking of formal propositional links in a text and of formal turns in talk around text.

To examine these procedures, I turn to a sequence of classroom literacy events. It is typical of the daily featured lesson in grade one classrooms taken from a total corpus of twenty-six days, approximately 120 hours of classroom interaction.[3] The class consists of twenty-one students, aged 5 to 6, who live in a working-class suburb of a Northern Australian city. Six of the children are of Aboriginal and Torres Strait Islander descent. These latter children are part of the largest 'at risk' group in early literacy training among the Australian populace (Walton, 1992/in press), although the teachers and administrators in the school maintain that the high rate of 'reading failure' is shared equally by mainstream working-class children.

The interconnection of reading and writing activities is a central feature of the child-centred, progressivist pedagogy aimed for in many Australian schools. This particular event focuses on group composition of a story, constructed through teacher question/student answer sequences. At each stage in the following sequence, the teacher records with a felt pen the words of the story on a large sheet visible to the children gathered at her feet. The twenty-minute lesson leads on to the children's individual writing session, when they head off into their clustered desks to attempt to replicate the procedures they have rehearsed through talk with the teacher. Here I develop a 'reading' of the event with excerpts from the lesson ordered as they occurred.

Teacher: Now ... We're going to do something now, you're gonna have to help me because, I'm going to write a story, and you're gonna help me write the story, and afterwards, you might go and write yourselves a story. But help me first.

> OK, and now, seeing we've been doing lots of stories about princesses and things like that.
>
> Student 1: What we're gonna do?
> T: What we're gonna do today is a story about a princess.
> S 2: Princess
> S 3: and a prince.
> T: Come in a bit, boys over here.
> S 2: and a prince.
> T: You reckon we should have a prince in it?
> Ss: [unison] Yes.
> T: Aw, I was thinking of a dragon.
> Ss: NO ... [unison, laughter]
> T: And a prince too?
> Ss: [inaudible commentary]
> T: Lauren.
> S 1: A big fairy tale?
> T: A fairy tale yet.

The teacher's introduction cues up what for the children is apparently a familiar language game: how to 'do' and 'make' a story through talk. The teacher states at the onset a framework for proceeding: she is the author, and the students are apprentices. However, the author function extends beyond the power to construct on paper the story in question. It includes the capacity to stage-manage the literacy event, to structure how 'we' talk (and, however inaccessible to the observer, 'think') about stories. Within this script, the borders between author and apprentice are subject to subtle shifts. As in most primary school lessons, there is a continual slippage back and forth in pronominalization from the teacher's persona ('I') to the collective 'we' (Luke, 1991/in press).

Ostensibly this talk is an introduction to the procedures of composing the genre of the story, specifically the sub-genre of 'fairy tale' as named by Lauren. Yet interwoven in the introduction of the literary paradigm (the generic structure) is the specification of discourse syntagm (the ideological 'contents'). From the onset, the latter becomes the ground for a classroom contest, won by the teacher as she asserts her prerogative to nominate and adjudicate character, setting, topic and so forth. So part and parcel of apprenticing in the craft-like procedure of text conception and production is the selection and articulation of discourses. The initial topic selection is followed by the naming and elaboration of generic parts (i.e. the text macropropositions):

> Teacher: What's the first part of the story?
> Students: [various comments, inaudible]
> T: A story starter? Not quite, there's something before a story starter? What's the first part of the story? Put your hand up.
> S 1: [raises hand]
> S: [shouted answers]
> S 1: ... Once upon a time ...
> T: No, that's the story starter ... what comes before the story starter?
> S 2: I ...

T:	No, oh come on, whaddaya read first when you read a story?
S 3:	A long time ago.
S 4:	Today ...
S 2:	[inaudible]
T:	No, that's the story starter.
S 5:	The date.
S 4:	the day.
T:	No, that's in journals. Come on, you still haven't told me what comes first in the story? Nadia.
S 6:	A name of the story.
T:	You clever girl. That's right, the name comes first. So we'll have to choose a name for our story. Now ...

Here the language game requires six initiations and re-initiations by the teacher to name a part. Overlapping Initiation-Response-Evaluation (IRE)[4] sequences are undertaken, often with the teacher filling in and inferring 'incorrect' responses. This kind of teacher guessing is common across our early primary classroom corpus. When children make inaudible or partial responses, the teacher in effect 'fills in' the response turn with what s/he assumed was said (e.g. 'No, that's the story starter'). Here the wrong naming has to do with a confusion of genres: 'the date' refers to the genre of 'journals'. Finally, Nadia, a 'clever girl', labels the opening item: 'A name of the story'. Once that naming of the generic component is in place, the next move is to instantiate it, to slot in the requisite ideological content:

Teacher:	I thought ... what'll I call my story?
Student 1:	Princess of the world.
T:	[gesturing to Aboriginal girl] just sit down anywhere there, Kay.
S 2:	Ninja Turtles.
T:	No, no Ninja turtles in my story. This is called ...
S 3:	Princess of the world.
T:	The princess
S 3:	Aw
T:	And the dragon.
S 3:	Aww
S 2:	Swwssh ...
T:	Now, Jake, This is my story and I can write what I like in my story, when you write your story, you can put a Ninja Turtle in it if you want to because that's your very own story. You're going to help me with my story, but you're not going to write it ...

The naming of the story component is done by statements of prior knowledge, consensus, guessing 'what's in the teacher's head', usually a single term or clause in the response turn in the IRE sequence (Baker and Freebody, 1989). Yet while the naming of parts is non-negotiable, the selection of content is contingent on who 'owns' the story: 'helping' an author is different than 'being' an author.

Embedded as it is in this strict IRE sequence, the naming of generic parts becomes a matter of indisputable 'fact', verified by the teacher's evaluation turn. By contrast, the actual syntagmatic content is based on the authority of authorship, in this case also that of the teacher. Despite its appearance to Jake and other students, this is no collective story construction. Instead the conception and production of narrative entails, in its very doing in classroom talk, the privileging of the individual author function (Foucault, 1977; Gilbert, 1989). Jake, whose enthusiasm forgets and violates the author's privilege, is reminded just whose story this is ('this is my story').

In this way, the privileged yet invisible agency of a 'romantic' author, one with freedom of semantic choice, is established in classroom talk. Yet the grounds for authorial choice are not explicated in that talk by the teacher. In other words, how one goes about deciding on an ideational instantiation of a story proposition (e.g. by experience, by cultural background knowledge, by intertextual reference) is not discussed or foregrounded. Instead, the criteria for such choices are here sutured over by invisible pedagogic codes (Bernstein, 1986): they remain silent, internal meaning options.

Teacher:	... OK, there's a name, what comes next.
Student 1:	...
T:	Yes Nadia.
S 2:	A story starter.
T:	A story starter, what do you figure will be the best story starter for a story about a princess and a dragon? Kim?
S 3:	Once upon a time.
T:	Once upon a time is a pretty good one, yes?
S 4:	A long time ago?
T:	I like that one. Yes, Daniel.
S 5:	A long long time ago?
T:	Oh, That's very good. Know your story starters, don't you? That was lovely. What about, last night.
S 3:	Yesss ... Noo ...
S 5:	Yea, Last night there was a dragon comin' to get me.
T:	I like stories about dragons and princesses a long time ago. So I'm gonna have Daniel's story starter, with ... what do I have to start with ...
S:	'A' ... [confusion]
T:	What do I have to start with.
S:	[Unison] ... Big A.
T:	Good, 'a long, long time a
S:	a
T:	ago, there lived a princess'....

Here the second macroproposition is being filled in, again cued by the IRE structure, notoriously functional for eliciting short informational statements from students (Mehan, 1979). Each ideational instantiation, each 'slotting' of story content into the generic frame, is set up in talk procedurally in the same way as the naming of the generic parts. This has the effect of marking out an equivalence in logical types between the two kinds of knowledge, between the paradigmatic and the syntagmatic, between the formal structure of the story and its ideological content. In both cases, many options are mooted, but the choice is the ultimate decision of the teacher/author: the criterial grounds for selection of one 'story starter' rather than another are located in the 'taste' exercised by individual authority, but not otherwise explicated. Quite simply, it's a matter of what the sovereign author/teacher 'likes', of an implicit but authoritative desire and will.

In the following sequence, however, the teacher ventures further into making visible what it is that an author does:

> Teacher: ... Now, when you write a story, Alison, there's something very important you gotta do. You gotta keep reading your story as you write it because you might miss out a really important word. So I'm gonna read mine again [points to story script on paper]: 'A long, long time ago there lived a princess'. I think I can make it a bit better than that.
>
> Student 1: A dragon too.
>
> T: No, no. No. What. How about: when you think about a princess, what'do you think about?
>
> S 2: A prince ...
>
> T: No.
>
> S 2: A prince ...
>
> T: No, what do you think she'd look like?
>
> S 3: A ...
>
> T: With long hair? What colour?
>
> S 3: Yellow, black ... [chorus laughter]
>
> T: What about long, long golden hair.

Specifically, to 'make it a bit better', the grounds and criteria for quality, requires that one reread a story 'as you write' and attend to words. However, this technical activity does little to explicate the logical and analogical, normative or descriptive operations for choosing and transforming words and sentences in the first place.

In the absence of criteria, such choices appear to reside in teacher/author authority. The teacher asks for an analogy, a free association: 'When you think about a princess, what do you think about?' The child's response, 'a prince', is discounted (as *not* what he was thinking about?). The resultant logic which is authorized in this passage of classroom talk reads: princess → distinctive feature (e.g. hair, colour, 'nice') → golden — *not* princess → prince. A set of associations between propositions, between ideational components is being established procedurally. What an author is to 'think about' — and desire — in relation to the female character is a (characteristically Anglo-European) physical attribute.

At this point in the lesson, the text on the easel paper is read aloud by the teacher, who proceeds to extend attributes and plot propositions.

> Teacher: 'A long long time ago there lived a princess with long long golden hair.' Now if she had long hair, what sort of princess do you think she'd be? What would she look like?
>
> Student 1: Nice.
>
> T: Nice, Oh yes, wonderful, that's very good. I might put

down some of these words ... [reads aloud] 'The princess and the dragon. A long long time ago there lived a beautiful princess with long golden hair. She lived in a big castle with a pink tower. One day the princess was playing outside when she heard a loud growl and out of the bushes rushed a big dragon'.

S 2:   dragon.

T: Now I think we could find a better word than big.

S 2:   Long.

T: A long dragon, yes. Nadia.

S 3:   huge ... and sharp teeth.

T: No, we're talking about size, Jake. Another word for big, we're talking about huge, giant.

S 4:   Enormous.

T: Enormous, what a beauty.

In this case, the category of 'size' is used to correct a lexical assignment to a character. Most curiously, the distinctive features schema established for the princess has shifted from 'hair colour' to 'size'. What is notable here is that even the category of distinctive features is subdivided into (gendered) assignments: to complete the analogic of distinctive features, in this case, princess → physical adornment, monsters → size. Here the very binary classification schemes of a gendered universe are being produced and reproduced in the earliest stages of literacy training (Pateman, 1988; Cocks, 1989).

Turning from the selection of words, the lesson now is used to cue up the fifteen-minute event to follow, in which the children will undertake their own 'private' story as authors. Varying procedures for topic selection are framed:

Teacher: Let's talk about some of the things that we could do ... shall, you could write a story about a princess, all right? Or what did you say, Greg?

Student 1:   Dinosaur. Or what did you say, Jake, Ninja turtles out there.

S 2:   nin ... ja ... turtles.

S 3:   Queen

T: Queen? What about those little ... in the Snow White movies, what were they called?

S 3:   Dwarves

T: You could write about a dwarf. What about those things in the movie. You can write a story about anything you like, really. Machines ...

S 2:   Jack in the beanstock? [sic]

T: Jack and the beanstalk, decide what you would like to write [a] story on, talk about it with someone, now back to your places, and get your pencils.

How does one decide on the topic for her or his story? While topic choice here is set out as 'what[ever] you would like to write ... on', the gendered selection of contents for narrative for these grade one students is already well practiced

(Davies, 1989): the white Australian boys voiced topics about 'machines', 'Ninja Turtles', 'dinosaurs' and traditional tales with male protagonists ('Jack and the beanstalk'); many of the girls opted for the 'princess' scenario. Intertextual resources flagged by the teacher for the students include movies, TV shows and other popular culture texts, and talk with other children.

For these grade one students, this lesson signals how one 'does' the story. One names the part, and then one fills it with an apparently arbitrary personal choice. The naming and sequencing of the generic structure is non-negotiable; the individual filling of the parts, however, is driven by 'what sounds good', 'what I like', and other apparently self-evident criteria, sourced in the privileged author/teacher. Finding the 'right word', getting it to 'sound right', is by all appearances an activity of connoisseurship, an 'embodied competence' (Bourdieu, 1977; Luke, 1991/in press) possessed by and constructing the rights of the author to speak.

This teaching and learning of narrative thus consists of alternating talk that shifts back and forth from paradigm to syntagm, from story component to propositional instantiation, from generic form to ideological content. This alternation, however, is staged but invisible, done but not spoken about in classroom talk: the IRE pattern equates the two into similar logical types. As a result, knowledge and practice of 'storying' entails the articulation and naturalization of a cultural logic; learning the story syntax entails buying into conventional cultural ideologies and power relations (Threadgold, 1989). That logic, in turn, operates at two levels: first, a logic of practice of talk about stories, 'what *no* ... story means', in Heath's (1982) words. In this case, talk about stories entails nominated turns at second-guessing an authoritative writer/teacher's namings of parts. Second, an invisible ideo*logic* is at work. The same turn structure is used to elicit and classify appropriate contents, analogies, distinctive features and metaphors. The correct namings and instantiations are those taken up in the collective literary product, the teacher's actual physical 'writing' with the felt pen on the enlarged sheet of paper.

For this group of children — naming and placing the 'story starter', associating character and setting with distinctive features, forming up the 'problem' and 'try' elements of the story grammar — these and other procedures for making stories are interwoven with the semantic choices of white, blonde princesses, pink castles and enormous dragons. Patriarchal discourses of sequestered aristocratic females, males rescuing females from a threatening nature become a regulative cultural logic. This, I would add, is hardly a 'natural', experiential or common-sense archetype for Aboriginal, Islander and working-class Northern Australian children more familiar with the *Simpsons* and Madonna than with Grimm. At least two of the Islander girls observed faithfully reproduced 'story starters' featuring princesses with blonde hair in the writing activity which followed.

Beyond this observable ideological function, classroom discourse shapes the very subjectivity of the child as literate/writer/author. In this instance at least, classroom discourse constructs

> the conditions under which the individual who writes [and reads] may
> come to possess particular kinds of authorial personality ... governed not
> by the logic of subject formation but by the historical emergence of

particular cultural techniques and social institutions (Saunders and Hunter, 1991: 483).

Contrary to the belief driving many child-centred and natural language learning pedagogies, there is no transparent or authentic 'author's' role to be elicited and neutrally facilitated (Gilbert, 1989). Nor does the 'embodied competence' of literary taste arise spontaneously or organically (Bourdieu, 1986). Rather, the historic and culture-specific techniques and texts of the social institution of the school constitute the act and practice of narrating. The 'running metatextual commentary' (Luke, DeCastell and Luke, 1983) of classroom talk constructs 'authorship', and constructs the 'story' as a language game with definitive and appropriate cultural logic.

My aim here has been to move from 'the shadowy and always disembodied figure' of the 'abstract epistemic subject' towards an analysis which shows 'human subjects as created through the incorporation, through the medium of signs, of children into the social practices which make up our everyday life' (Walkerdine, 1982: 129). Yet the tracking of the effects of that incorporation turns on a reconsideration of the status and legitimacy of narrative discourse in postmodern conditions.

Postmodern Reappraisals of Narrative

All cultures have their means for rehearsing entry into discourses on 'how things are'. In historical and contemporary settings, stories have been and remain discourses of legitimation. As textual codings of knowledges, they stand as central means for incorporation into institutional relations of power, not the least of which is the construction and assignment of authorship. As epistemic tools, they naturalize — sometimes overtly, sometimes invisibly — the place of knowledges and practices, not the least of which is the site and significance of stories.

In *The Postmodern Condition: A Report on Knowledge* (1984), Lyotard's analysis centres on a reconsideration of the relationships between 'narrative' and 'scientific' knowledge. He begins from the claim that language games are the necessary constitutive condition for society, and that they can be analyzed in terms of their performativity and consequent claims to legitimation and power. Narrative enables a 'variety of language games', among which he includes: denotative statements about the natural world; deontic statements regarding social relations; interrogatives, evaluatives and so forth. As these occur in the foregoing lesson, we are able to see exactly how narrative is able to 'bestow legitimacy upon social institutions', to provide social models and thus designate social (and, as we will see, scientific) 'criteria of competence' (Lyotard, 1984: 20).

According to Lyotard, narrative gains legitimacy through its performativity: in effect, because it is done appropriately according to convention in a particular setting such as, in the case above, that of the classroom. Here Lyotard underplays the status of the author/teller as a significant element of narrative legitimacy. The 'death of the author' notwithstanding, in oral narrative, the credentials of the speaker often precede and foreground the telling of the tale; in contemporary written narrative, with increasingly pervasive mass marketing, the reputation of an author precedes and positions the reading and reader.

Nonetheless, Lyotard's stress on performativity has important implications. Despite its representation of social relations, narrative is not premised on free-standing criterial benchmarks in the 'real', and hence it is not subject to falsification, as scientific discourse is. Whether those criteria are criteria of hearing in the case of oral stories, viewing in the case of movies and mini-series, or stylistic criteria of literariness in the case of novels, what counts as a valued narrative in both oral and modernist traditions tends to pivot away from a direct mimetic relation to the signified. Even in verisimilitudinous work like documentary and cinema-vérité, or variations on literary realism, performative criteria enter into normative judgments.

It is this very criterion of performativity which is used to discredit narrative as leisure dalliance, as an activity of women and children, or as elite aesthetic activity, a literary activity capable of yielding 'truths' only about mentalistic domains of affect, metaphysical domains of the 'human spirit' and so forth. In both human and natural sciences, and in their applied domains (e.g. econometrics, legal discourse, computer 'sciences'), the ostensive pursuit of the 'facts' and 'truths' — objective and falsifiable — has the effect of cancelling the value of narrative, of rendering it Other.[5] Hence, technocratic culture is premised on a hierarchy of the scientific over the literary, of expository over fictional text — the very binarism of curricular knowledge noted at the onset of this chapter.

The irony is that scientific endeavour looks at least in part to performativity ('face validity' that scientific procedures had been followed, documented and reported conventionally) for its legitimacy. More importantly, for Lyotard, *scientific discourse ultimately gains its legitimacy not through traditional grounds of falsification, but by placing itself within modernist grand narratives of emancipation and/or technological development.* Harding (1986: 199) makes similar claims about the history of science as patriarchal text: that it relies for its legitimacy as 'story' on internal and external histories characterized by masculinist agency.

Lyotard's deliberately polemical and strategic position has been the subject of various commentaries and critiques.[6] Many of his claims about social organization and history are sweeping, lacking detailed evidence. Further, feminist critiques of totalization and domination in the metanarratives of patriarchal science are not addressed by Lyotard, a worrying tendency shared by many of the now canonical Fathers of postmodernism. As Nicholson (1990) and others have recently observed, the dangers of patriarchy reproduced in these postmodern narratives is great. There is also ample ground for querying the status of Lyotard's very discourse of explanation. For insofar as Lyotard elides the very possibility of a social 'scientific' theoretic critique, he relegates his own description and philosophy to the slippery procedures of 'panopoly'. His is just another story (Lyotard, 1990). Yet the postmodern scepticism towards grand narratives does not preclude its application as a political reading position from which critique and analysis can be generated, as many feminists and poststructuralists have found. That is my strategy here: to use Lyotard's critique of the binary opposition of scientific and narrative knowledge as a way of revisiting the consequences of early introduction into narrative.

Early childhood literacy training fixes criteria for narrative performativity. The institutional site of the school sets out what will count as interactional procedures for the construction of narrative, and the selection of appropriate semantic/ideological contents. Here, then, criteria for 'doing the story' run side by side with criteria for describing the natural and social world. If indeed narrative proceeds as a chaining together of propositions into nature-like sequences of setting, agency, relation, cause, determination and outcome, then indeed students are learning that the genre of the story consists of typical sequences of agency and action, stitched together according to internal codes of authorial logic and analogy, and conventionalized in the precious worlds of the school story.

Yet, like much other school knowledge in postmodern conditions, the resultant narratives are simulations, with few freestanding referents in children's everyday lives, and only occasional intertextual references to 'Snow White', 'Ninja Turtles' and other figments of popular culture (Luke and Luke, 1990). Further, the representation here is not a mimetic one to experience or to background knowledge, but rather to labels and namings in the teacher's head. Particularly when constructed through the classroom talk, the relationships between signifier and signified have quite readily become blurred and muffled (Lash, 1988).

Conclusion: Reworking the Consequences of Literacy

In modernist educational culture, literacy is seen as a marker of the Apollonian and Dionysian alike. Writing is considered by many educators as the key technological means for the development of the rational, scientifically competent, and predominantly male, subject. Alternatively, humanist and progressive educators view children's literature as the surface of emergence for the romantic, sentient individual.

In the narrative of the Enlightenment, the technology of print holds a special metaphoric place. Far beyond its status as technology of inscription, it is portrayed as the very phylogenic engine of science and civilization, and *the* central marker of ontogenic entry and participation in this *grand recit*.[7] The place of the school in the construction of the rational subject has a closely interleaved folklore. In modernist explanations of the consequences of literacy, the development of the individual is explained by the way in which that development dovetails with a particular Western vision of progress. We find inflections of this theme in Kohlberg's and Piaget's, Vygotsky's and Habermas's contending accounts of the development of consciousness, wherein the (male) child is busy teleologically 'catching up' to the moral/political consciousness of the *geist*.

A question to be asked on behalf of the children I have described here is: Whose footsteps are being retraced here and where will they lead? What part does school narrative play in this? Is it a simple developmental testing ground for movement into analytical knowledge? Is it a crucial moment for 'personal growth', 'self-esteem' and self-identification? If Lyotard, Harding, Walkerdine and others are correct, literacy training enables social regulation and explanation. But as importantly, it clears a space for a patriarchal, technocratic 'science', both as a different, allegedly 'higher' form of thought, and as a gendered protagonist in a narrative to be concluded in a later episode. Articulated in later classes, lessons, events and texts, propositions about the authority and place of science, capital and progress, of patriarchy, of age-authority relations, will be silently fit into what begins as, for most educators, a seemingly innocent narrative schema. Read science (whether 'emancipatory' and/or positivist) for princes, read dragons for physical obstacles and natural anomalies, and read 'winning the princess' for progress.

I have here offered a 'story' of one classroom. This description opens for inspection the discursive machinery of literacy training and it reframes how the classroom operates as a site of regulation. In this light, consider the classroom described here: it is a child-centred environment, where children receive a great deal of personal and, at times, physical attention and there is little overt punitive action. Further, in lessons like those above, children are eager participants — little of the teachers' time and talk are spent dealing with signs of active or passive resistance.

But what discourse practices and positions are yielded in this kind of training? And how available are they and their logics for discussion and contestation? A key problem in the foregoing lesson and others like it is that the rules of the language game in question, the criteria, rationale and site for building a text, are both invisible and non-negotiable. It is indeed difficult, if not impossible, for children in this classroom and for 'mature' literates alike to contest, rewrite, transform or even reproduce, with some degree of innovation, texts whose rules and parts appear 'natural', inevitable and sourced in a slippery institutional authority.

What is necessary, particularly for the Aboriginal, Torres Strait Islander and working-class children here described as 'at risk', is a systematic and explicit introduction to: (1) the dominant texts, genres and discourses which retain cultural capital in a patriarchal social system, *and* (2) a learned 'scepticism' towards these same texts and the metanarratives in which they are embedded. Without the former, the play of difference and identity valorized in a postmodern critical pedagogy may fail to link up with mainstream school and occupational cultures, entry into which periodically demands the innovative reproduction of convention. Without the latter, the risk is of a simple uncritical reproduction, and with it a perpetuation of the procedures of incorporation into those same cultures (Threadgold, 1989). As it stands, with a steady diet of the kinds of literacy events described here, these children are getting neither.

Revision of the canon in itself will not suffice (Luke and Gore, 1991/in press). While it is a necessary move in a long-term educational strategy, substitution of heretofore marginal faces, 'voices', 'images' and values may leave the very narrative structures of dominant cultures intact and beyond criticism. To achieve social power *and* scepticism, the logic of conventional texts needs to be demonstrated and deconstructed from the onset of literacy instruction. In practice, this requires a reworking of: (1) the very games of talk around text, with an eye to making explicit the possibilities of what can be done, said and meant with texts; and, (2) a critical exploration of elasticity and difference of texts, genres and discourses at the earliest stages of literacy training. In classrooms, this entails nothing less than a naming and renaming, ordering and reordering, using and discarding of the parts. As Wilden (1986) reminds us, you can't play the game unless you know the rules. But to change the game, you gotta know that the rules are neither static nor non-negotiable.

Acknowledgments

The author wishes to thank Carmen Luke, Pam Gilbert, Bill Green and Bronwyn Davies for their advice on drafts, the Australian Research Council, and Favardin Deliri for support in data collection.

Notes

1 The emergence of Vygotskian psychology in the West can be viewed as another historical moment in the deployment of psychology as a discourse of legitimation, rather than as a cancelling of now disputed theories (e.g. behaviourism, cognitivism) by 'true' ones. To accept the latter explanation is to buy into the essential validity of psychology as a positivist enterprise. Just as behaviourism can be viewed as a discourse strategy which served a particular industrial capitalist agenda, the rise of 'culture' and 'context'-sensitive psychologies (and linguistic 'sciences') can be read as responses to state crises in the management of increasingly culturally and linguistically diverse populaces.

2 This is Peter Freebody's observation. The problems of a unified cognitive theorization of reading are discussed in Freebody (1991), Baker and Freebody (1989) and Freebody's monograph in progress on reading and social class.

3 This data was collected in 1991 as part of an Australian Research Council study of literacy and numeracy among urban Aborigine and Torres Strait Islander children, undertaken by Favardin Deliri, Joan Kale, Michael Singh, Tracey Hill, Richard Smith and myself. The lesson transcript is here reproduced in full, except for the omission of an intrusion by a teacher's aid on school business. Ellipses mark two-second or longer pauses and hesitations. Students' contributions are numbered by speaker in each excerpt.

4 'IRE' pattern of classroom discourse, first formally discussed as such in Sinclair and Coulthard (1975).

5 This fiction/non-fiction, literary/scientific dualism is mirrored across popular media. In the TV series *Dragnet*, a modernist TV narrative if there ever was one, Detective Joe Friday would usually interrogate female witnesses with the enjoinder 'just the facts, ma'am': in effect, drawing *her* from the fictional genre of the story to the non-fiction genre of the recount. Masculinist discourse — of detectives, princes, scientists and the lot — has little time for anything other than 'facts' which push along the narrative of progress. Problem-solving behaviour waits for nobody.

6 There is some documentary corroboration for Lyotard's notion of science as 'panopoly' and narrative in post-war developments in physics, medical science and related fields. Alternative narrative accounts of scientific procedure and discovery are now available, some of which highlight counter-positivist methods of inquiry, others of which focus on the political economy of scientific discovery (Schaffer, 1991). Yet there is ample evidence that mass public loyalty to science as a social (and military, as the Gulf War attests) protagonist in multinational capitalist culture is unwavering, in spite of signs of ecological and geopoliticial ramifications of unbridled growth and development.

7 The aims of scientific literacy were epitomized in Spratt's Royal Society prose, which aimed at a one-to-one denotation between word and object, signifier and signified. Ironically, within the total science of the Enlightenment, inquiry entailed the objective 'naming' of the world, a mastery of nature not dissimilar from Edenic language or the task of 'renaming' the social which many poststructuralist feminists have set as a goal.

References

BAKER, C.D. and FREEBODY, P. (1989) *Children's First Schoolbooks: Introductions to the Culture of Literacy*, Oxford, Blackwell.

BERNSTEIN, B. (1986) 'On Pedagogic Discourse', in RICHARDSON, J.G. (Ed.) *Handbook of Theory and Research for the Sociology of Education*, London, Greenwood, pp. 205–40.

BOURDIEU, P. (1977) 'The Economics of Linguistic Exchange', *Social Science Information*, **6**, pp. 645–88.

BOURDIEU, P. (1986) *Distinction*, translated R. Nice, London, Routledge.

BRODKEY, L. (1987) *Academic Writing as Social Practice*, Philadelphia, Temple University Press.

CHRISTIAN-SMITH, L.C. (1990) *Becoming a Woman through Romance*, London, Routledge and Kegan Paul.

COCKS, J. (1989) *The Oppositional Imagination*, London, Routledge and Kegan Paul.

COOK-GUMPERZ, J. (Ed.) (1986) *The Social Construction of Literacy*, Cambridge, Cambridge University Press.

DAVIES, B. (1989) *Frogs and Snails and Feminist Tales*, Sydney, Allen and Unwin.

FOUCAULT, M. (1977) 'What is an Author?', in BOUCHARD, D.F. (Ed.) *Language, Counter-Memory, Practice: Selected Essays and Interviews by Michel Foucault*, Ithaca, NY, Cornell University Press, pp. 113–38.

FREEBODY, P. (1991) 'Remarks on Cognitive-Psychological and Critical-Sociological Accounts of Reading', in BAKER, C.D. and LUKE, A. (Eds) *Towards a Critical Sociology of Reading Pedagogy*, Amsterdam, John Benjamins, pp. 239–56.

FREEBODY, P., LUKE, A. and GILBERT, P. (1991) 'Reading Positions and Practices in the Classroom', *Curriculum Inquiry*, **21**, 4, pp. 435–57.

GILBERT, P. (1989) *Writing, Schooling and Deconstruction*, London, Routledge and Kegan Paul.

GILBERT, P. and TAYLOR, S. (1991) *Fashioning the Feminine*, Sydney, Allen and Unwin.

GREEN, B. (1991) 'Reading "readingS"', in BAKER, C.D. and LUKE, A. (Eds) *Towards a Critical Sociology of Reading Pedagogy*, Amsterdam, John Benjamins, pp. 211–38.

HARDING, S. (1986) *The Science Question in Feminism*, Milton Keynes, Open University Press.

HEAP, J.L. (1991) 'A Situated Perspective on What Counts as Reading', in BAKER, C.D. and LUKE, A. (Eds) *Towards a Critical Sociology of Reading Pedagogy*, Amsterdam, John Benjamins, pp. 103–40.

HEATH, S.B. (1982) 'What No Bedtime Story Means: Narrative Skills at Home and School', *Language in Society*, **11**, pp. 49–76.

HEATH, S.B. (1983) *Ways with Words*, Cambridge, Cambridge University Press.

INGLIS, F. (1986) *The Management of Ignorance*, Oxford, Blackwell.

LASH, S. (1988) 'Discourse or Figure: Postmodernism as a "Regime of Signification"', *Theory, Culture and Society*, **5**, pp. 311–36.

LUKE, A. (1988) *Literacy, Textbooks and Ideology*, London, Falmer Press.

LUKE, A. (1991/in press) 'The Body Literate: Discursive Inscription in Early Literacy Training', *Linguistics in Education*.

LUKE, A. and LUKE, C. (1990) 'School Knowledge as Simulation: Curriculum in Postmodern Conditions', *Discourse*, **10**, 2, pp. 75–91.

LUKE, C., DeCASTELL, S.C. and LUKE, A. (1983) 'Beyond Criticism: The Authority of the School Textbook', *Curriculum Inquiry*, **13**, pp. 111–27.

LUKE, C. and GORE, J. (Eds) (1991/in press) *Feminisms and Critical Pedagogy*, New York, Routledge.

LYOTARD, J.C. (1984) *The Postmodern Condition: A Report on Knowledge*, translated by G. Bennington and B. Massumi, Manchester, Manchester University Press.

LYOTARD, J.C. (1990) 'The Gulf, the War, the Sun: A Fable', Seminar paper presented at the Critical Theory Institute, University of California, Irvine.

MARTIN, J.R. (1985) *Factual Writing*, Geelong, Deakin University Press.

McHOUL, A. (1991) 'readingS', in BAKER, C.D. and LUKE, A. (Eds) *Towards a Critical Sociology of Reading Pedagogy*, Amsterdam, John Benjamins, pp. 191–210.

MEHAN, H. (1979) *Learning Lessons*, Cambridge, MA, Harvard University Press.

MICHAELS, S. and COLLINS, J. (1984) 'Oral Discourse Styles: Classroom Interaction and the Acquisition of Literacy', in TANNEN, D. (Ed.) *Coherence in Spoken and Written Discourse*, Norwood, NJ, Ablex, pp. 219–24.

NICHOLSON, L. (Ed.) (1990) *Feminism/Postmodernism*, London, Routledge and Kegan Paul.

PATEMAN, C. (1988) *The Sexual Contract*, Cambridge, Polity.

ROSE, J. (1985) 'State and Language: *Peter Pan* as Written for the Child', in STEEDMAN, C., URWIN, C. and WALKERDINE, V. (Eds) *Language, Gender and Childhood*, London, Routledge and Kegan Paul, pp. 88–112.

SAUNDERS, D. and HUNTER, I. (1991) 'Lessons from the "Literatory": How to Historicize Authorship', *Critical Inquiry*, **17**, pp. 479–509.

SCHAFFER, S. (1991) 'Utopia Unlimited: On the End of Science', *Strategies*, **4/5**, pp. 151–81.

SCHIEFFELIN, B.B. and GILMORE, P. (Eds) (1986) *Ethnographic Perspectives on Literacy*, Norwood, NJ, Ablex.

SCRIBNER, S. and COLE, M. (1981) *The Psychology of Literacy*, Cambridge, Cambridge University Press.

SINCLAIR, J. and COULTHARD, R.M. (1975) *Towards an Analysis of Discourse*, London, Oxford University Press.

THREADGOLD, T. (1989) 'Talking about Genre: Ideologies and Incompatible Discourses', *Cultural Studies*, **3**, 1, pp. 101–27.

TOOLAN, M.J. (1988) *Narrative: A Critical Linguistic Introduction*, London, Routledge.

WALKERDINE, V. (1982) 'From Context to Text: A Psychosemiotic Approach to Abstract Thought', in BEVERIDGE, M. (Ed.) *Children Thinking through Language*, London, Edward Arnold, pp. 129–55.

WALKERDINE, V. (1987) *Surveillance, Subjectivity and Struggle: Lessons from Pedagogic and Domestic Practices*, Center for Humanities Studies Occasional Paper No. 11, Stonybrook, NY, State University of New York.

WALKERDINE, V. (1988) *The Mastery of Reason*, London, Routledge.

WALTON, C. (1992/in press) 'Aboriginal Education in Northern Australia: A Case Study of Policies and Practices', in WELCH, T. and FREEBODY, P. (Eds) *Knowledge, Culture and Power: Perspectives on Literacy Policies and Practices*, London, Falmer Press.

WILDEN, A. (1986) *The Rules Are No Game*, London, Routledge and Kegan Paul.

Chapter 9

Curriculum as Literacy: Reading and Writing in 'New Times'

Colin Lankshear

Introduction: Curriculum as Literacy

During recent years, numerous discussion and policy documents addressing curriculum have emanated from ministries of education, curriculum review teams, and consultant task forces in Britain, Australasia and North America.[1] Invariably these have incorporated statements concerning literacy and the need to enhance literacy attainment among students.

Considerable work undertaken from a range of disciplinary perspectives during the past two decades has exposed common misunderstandings of the nature and significance of literacy (Street, 1984; Graff, 1987; Lankshear and Lawler, 1987: Ch. 2). Despite this, current curriculum documents are replete with mistaken assumptions and views concerning the nature and significance of literacy and, especially, its relationship to curriculum. In particular, official curriculum documents persist in the view that literacy consists in some kind of unitary 'essence', typically a *skill* or *technology*. Even where literacy is not reduced to a single skill — such as decoding print — curriculum talk remains skill-bound and technicist. Students must be taught the 'skills' of literacy and oracy; curriculum must ensure that all achieve high levels of communications and information skills, and master problem solving and work-related skills. Literacy is perceived as 'the most important of vocational skills' (NSW Ministry, 1990: 33); 'the ability to ... read, write, and express oneself with confidence and skill is fundamental to learning and to participating effectively in society and in the world of work' (Ministry of Education, 1991: 11). Such talk implies that literacy is somehow *prior* to curriculum, being a necessary vehicle or medium for curricular study. Thus we teach pupils to read and write, *after* which they can engage in serious subject study. Insofar as literacy is identified with curriculum subject study at all, it is with English or Language. Other curriculum subjects are not seen as contributions to becoming literate as such. The relationship between literacy and curriculum, seemingly, is one-way. Literacy is seen as a prerequisite for intellectual growth through curricular study, but not the other way round.

The work of theorists like Brian Street (1984) and Harvey Graff (1979, 1981, 1987) dispels such literacy myths. Street's 'ideological model of literacy' provides a cogent base from which to reject the relationship between literacy and curriculum implied overwhelmingly in curriculum documents. Street rejects talk of literacy in terms of some 'essence', whether skill(s) or technique(s). Rather, the nature and meaning of literacy consists in the myriad *forms* reading and writing practice actually takes, within various social settings. To understand literacy, we need to 'concentrate on the specific social practices of reading and writing' (Street, 1984: 2), observing the forms reading and writing actually take, or *what they are made into* within particular social settings. To focus on technique and to regard literacy as prior to curriculum is to miss the important points.

Conceptions and practices — or what elsewhere I call *forms*[2] — of reading and writing evolve and serve within ideological settings. The views people actually have of what literacy comprises, of what counts as being literate; what they see as 'real' or appropriate 'uses' of reading and writing; the ways people actually read and write in the course of their daily lives — these all reflect and promote values, beliefs, assumptions and practices, which shape the way life is lived within a given social milieu and, in turn, influence which interests are promoted or undermined as a consequence of how life is lived there. Consequently, literacy is best understood as 'a shorthand for the social practices and conceptions of reading and writing' (Street, 1984: 1). For many social contexts, therefore, we do better to think more in terms of *literacies* than literacy; that is, of quantitatively and qualitatively different literacies which have different consequences for the lives of groups and individuals, rather than a unitary 'literacy' which is indirectly linked to personal and collective outcomes via the applications people happen, contingently, to make of it or encounter. This undercuts the presumption either that literacy is *prior* to curriculum, or that insofar as literacy is situated *within* curriculum its 'home' is in English or Language. Once we recognize that the ways in which people come to understand and practise reading and writing are strongly shaped by the exemplars, values, processes, and requirements operating in the social contexts within which they engage print, it becomes clear that curriculum is a most important site of literacy formation; and further, that as a site of literacy formation, curriculum includes all areas and subjects of formal school learning and the connections (or lack of connection) between them.

For example, whether or not students become capable of using print in ways that enable them to adopt a critical-transformative approach to social reality may depend significantly on how learning and knowledge is 'modelled' to them via curriculum. Within curriculum, knowledge is often boxed into so many discrete, autonomous subjects, encouraging fragmentation of inquiry and awareness. The study of discrete school-subjects quickly becomes an exercise of reading and writing to produce 'parts', with little or no opportunity to integrate them seriously into 'wholes'. Such a fragmented, partial approach to understanding the world presents a poor basis from which to frame courses of transforming social action that stand a reasonable chance of being effective. Similarly, if curriculum, as a context in which our conceptions and practices of print are formed and informed, is reduced to so many exercises in discovering *what is*, as opposed to *what might be* or *what ought to be*, we are unlikely to encourage the harnessing of print to transformative social ends. Clearly, then, a wish to develop critically literate persons has implications for the organization and practice of curriculum as a whole.

The same is true for whatever form(s) of literacy we seek. Once we see literacy in terms of actual and possible *forms* of reading and writing, rather than as a tool, a skill (or so many skills), or a technique/technology, we can ask serious questions about what curriculum should be aiming *to make literacy into*. We have reached an historical juncture where such insights from recent literacy studies assume great importance — ethically and educationally. To sum up, then: the principal thesis of this chapter is that curricula effectively help to induct students into literacies of one form or another, and that we need to understand curriculum as very much an initiation into literacy (or rather, literacies). Thus, if we want to foster a certain type of literacy, we can begin to ask what this implies for curriculum. Conversely we can ask of a given curriculum what its literacy outcomes are likely to be. Further, there is clearly a need to take into account here matters such as 'curriculum *against* critical literacy'[3] and the complex and changing character of literacy itself, including the intriguing notion of 'literacies in a post-industrial scene'.

To carry such arguments forward, then, let us consider some key features of the world today's students will enter, upon leaving attendance at school curriculum. These, in conjunction with the broad perspective on literacy and curriculum gleaned from the ideological model of literacy, provide a basis for recommending curriculum innovations in respect of literacy.

New Times: The Emerging Post-Industrial Order

The so-called developed countries, including Australia and New Zealand, are entering a new economic era. Industrial capitalism is seemingly being superseded by a 'post-industrial' economy characterized by a more flexible regime of capital accumulation. Individual countries see themselves as having to renegotiate their places within a new world economic order. Schools and other educational agencies are being called upon to play a more active and appropriate role in preparing young people for entering the post-industrial work world and to help strengthen the hand of 'their' national economy in the current process of jockeying for position within the world economy. A strong functional literacy and human capital rationale for education has emerged in this context, with profound implications for curriculum, literacy, and the relationship between them.

While intellectuals of varying stripes continue to argue matters of detail and interpretation relating to 'the new times',[4] there is now considerable broad agreement across a spectrum of theoretical and (other) ideological positions that industrial capitalism is giving way to post-industrial economic activity based on services rather than manufacturing and primary production, information rather than goods, and a displacement of borders by the triumph of multinational-corporate organization of production, marketing and trade (Harvey, 1989; Gee, 1992/in press). The shift from the Fordist mode of production to the current 'regime of flexible accumulation'

> involves [several] obvious developments: the internationalization of production through the compression of space and time made possible by rapid travel and communication; small batch production techniques, quicker responses to market conditions, and quick turnover time; the decentering and diffusion of money and markets across national borders;

and the reorganization of cities to respond to these conditions (Berlin, 1992: 225).[5]

Harvey (1989: 147) adds that the new accumulative regime 'rests on flexibility with respect to labour processes, labour markets, products, and patterns of consumption'.

Three key facets of recent economic change have special significance here:

1   'Developed' economies have changed from a manufacturing and goods-producing base to a situation where service industries provide most jobs. In many countries white-collar workers now outnumber blue-collar workers. There is less purely manual work and more jobs requiring people to read and count, even if only to be able to understand safety instructions on equipment, or prices at a check-out counter. Most people will now have several jobs during their working lives (questions of unemployment aside). Often these will cover quite different areas and levels of skill and knowledge. A person made redundant from a low-skilled job in a factory might turn a hobby into a service. Such shifts are increasingly common and can go in both directions.

2   Information technology is the key tool of post-industrial society, in the way that machine technology was basic to industrial capitalism. Information technology enters most areas of contemporary life.

3   High impact innovation and the social rewards — in money, prestige, esteem, mobility, etc. — flowing from it now come from applied theoretical knowledge. The big impact inventions of this century (e.g. the computer, jet aircraft, laser surgery, the contraceptive pill, and the social survey — together with their many derivations and applications) have come from theory-driven scientific laboratories (Levett and Lankshear, 1990: 4–5).

As understood here, post-industrialism and the growth of knowledge and technology supporting it have produced new kinds of inequality.[6] Technological changes and the control of work within late capitalism have polarized economic activity between forms of work which demand high levels of knowledge and skill and which are well rewarded by money and job satisfaction, and jobs which have low skill demands and are poorly rewarded. (In the UK, for example, over 50 per cent of new jobs are said to require no formal qualification). Moreover, there have been considerable increases in part-time and part-year work, and drastic increases in temporary and long-term unemployment during the transition from an industrial to a post-industrial economy (Apple, 1986). Outside of sheer unemployment, then, work and workers increasingly fall into two categories. Berlin identifies the first group as comprising higher-level managerial positions enjoying large salaries, benefits, and job security. To these may be added such groups as those working in theoretical and applied theoretical areas, and the dwindling executive positions that remain in the public sector. The second group comprises

poorly paid, expendable slots that bear the brunt of the rapid shifts corporations make in quickly responding to market conditions. The isolation of workers in smaller and less stable units, in addition, results in a significant reduction in the ability of workers to organize for better wages, benefits, and conditions (Berlin, 1992/in press: 225).

Of course, the problem of structural unemployment cannot be overlooked. Current rates of around 15 per cent of real unemployment appear likely to remain, and may well increase, in the foreseeable future.

Against this background we must also note the direction and impact of recent state policies in the economic and social spheres. The trend has been toward a much leaner state bureaucracy and a drastically reduced social and welfare role for the state. In part this reflects the impact of technology and the hegemonic influence of revamped models of management and private corporate enterprise on the state/public sector. Also, of course, it reflects the role of the state in the service of capital — implementing policies which redirect wealth to capital accumulation by limiting revenue requirements through reducing the scope of state enterprise in the social and welfare sphere, privatizing a range of services, and so on. The net effect of such policies is to intensify the vulnerability of those on the wrong end of the new inequality inherent in the post-industrial economic and social order.

Some Implications for Literacy and Curriculum

The changing social order which simultaneously reflects and engenders the policies and practices sketched here has important implications for literacy and curriculum. Let me identify what I see as three broad imperatives. Ideally these would be argued at length, but the present context allows only that they be asserted. Briefly, our present situation demands a curriculum which promotes universal literacy equal to three needs.

The first is to ensure that all students acquire at the very least the high and escalating minimum competencies necessary for survival (or 'functionality'). Second, a curriculum is needed which ensures the possibility for personal advancement in accordance with the principle of equity, conceived as equal opportunity. Finally, because of the serious threat to social justice inherent in the polarized economy and free market ethos which currently besets us, it is essential that schools promote literacy conducive to keeping the ideal of social justice alive and equipping citizens with the capacity and commitment to pursue it. Some elaboration is in order.

The high-tech information society imposes increasingly high minimum levels of literacy and numeracy on all members of modern populations. These are not necessarily linked to individuals' actual employment needs. For many people, ordinary living will demand more in the way of literacy than the jobs they will be doing. In short, fluency with written language and good arithmetical skills have become essential for living healthy and independent lives — particularly in times of decreasing social and welfare provision by the state for poorly defended groups.

Kozol (1985) used actual performance at a grade nine reading level as the criterion for qualifying as literate in terms of US print communication in 1985. He cites one expert who claimed that 'anyone who doesn't have at least a twelfth grade reading, writing, and calculating level will be absolutely lost' by the 1990s

(Kozol, 1985: 58). This is the context of concern which has recently seen the threat of a burgeoning 'underclass', touted as either a pressing current social problem — as in the US (e.g. Garland, Therrien and Hammonds, 1988) — or an imminent one — as in Australia and, more recently, in New Zealand. Schools are promulgated as a first line of defence against this threat. It is feared that confinement to an urban underclass will become the only 'option' available to (especially black and migrant) children caught in the poverty cycle and who leave school illiterate and otherwise 'uneducated', disaffected and vulnerable.[7]

While nobody questions the importance of ensuring 'functional literacy' for all, critics from quite different normative positions are adamant that this is not enough; we should be aiming for considerably more. An interesting argument is provided by the Carnegie Foundation for the Advancement of Teaching, in a critique of the basic curriculum for urban schools that burgeoned in the US during the 1980s. While this critique addresses basic work-related literacy rather than 'functional literacy' *per se*, it applies *a fortiori* to the functionalist ethic. Dennis Carlson (1992/in press) presents a telling backdrop to this critique, describing how an insidious logic of social reproduction reflecting the polarization evident in the post-industrial workforce unfolded in the US along a urban-suburban school divide. He argues that in the attempt to use schools to compensate for economic and educational disadvantage, and to align school programs more closely with changes in the economy, school reform effectively assumed that the literacy needs of urban students are those appropriate for the new post-industrial semi-skilled worker.

In practice, the literacy curriculum for US urban students became increasingly a curriculum for generalizable basic print skills, accompanied by a heavy emphasis on compensatory and remedial learning for 'disadvantaged' students. The competencies in question amount to generalizable open-ended skills grouping around the ability to follow written instructions and operating procedures which would be transferable to a range of work sites and tasks, being able to decode and recode data for management information systems and computer programmes, and knowing how to produce data on outputs, job performance, etc. It is very much a 'following' or 'response-to-instructions' form of literacy, with no serious demand for interpretation, evaluation, or other such 'higher-order' processes involving print.

This reform agenda lent itself to highly standardized, technocratic approaches to instruction. Programmed materials, drillsheets, and workbooks prevailed:

> Technical advances in curriculum design and organization of instruction consistent with new 'systems theory' models of production, allowed state officials and local bureaucratic elites to come much closer than ever before to 'targeting' instruction to the functional literacy skill 'deficits' of urban students (Carlson, 1992/in press: 202).

This 'basic literacy' offensive approached its logical conclusion in the late 1980s, with many states adopting minimum-competency tests for high school graduation. Disadvantaged students would commonly be assigned three or four 'basic skills' or 'communication skills' classes a day. Teachers were obliged to teach to the test, using materials designed to prepare students for the tests, and 'to keep students "on task" using skill-based curricular materials' (Carlson, 1992/in press:

203). However, while urban students in public schools were tracked increasingly down a 'basics' path, students in better suburban public schools (and private schools) were exposed to college-preparatory curricula housing a higher-order literacy. This split, which occurred very much along class and racial-ethnic lines, became a focus for liberal critique of the emphasis on 'basics' in urban schools, and the 'two nations' logic it observed.[8]

Against this background, the Carnegie Foundation moved to protect the possibility of personal advancement in accordance with equity. *In A Nation Prepared: Teachers for the 21st Century* (1986), the Foundation criticized the narrow 'skill and drill' basics curriculum of urban schools, buttressed with 'teaching to the test' methods, and lamented the 'over-enrolment of urban students in [such] basic remedial courses that effectively locked them into semi-skilled jobs' (Carlson, 1992/in press: 213). Clearly, ethics are at stake in an arrangement that can only consolidate socio-economic disadvantage and inferiority. The principle of equal opportunity seems, at the very least, to entail linking 'equity' to 'excellence'; that is to say, exposing urban/disadvantaged students to the same higher-order literacy curriculum facing more 'advantaged' students attending 'better' schools.

This theme was pursued vigorously in the Foundation's 1988 report *An Imperiled Generation: Saving Urban Schools*. As Carlson indicates, its authors warned that

> the division of America into 'the two separate societies envisioned by the Kerner Commission two decades ago' was 'a very real possibility' in the coming decade, and that the 'public schools were contributing to such a division'. Too many urban students were 'academically restricted by the curriculum itself' which presumed that 'students were divided between those who think and those who work', with most urban students relegated to the latter category. The real 'unfinished agenda for the nation's schools' [was] 'equality of opportunity, along with the support to make it real and not merely rhetorical ... Clearly, equity and excellence cannot be divided' (Carlson, 1992/in press).

The Report called for ensuring a higher-order core curriculum for all students. It rejected accountability based on state-mandated competency testing, advocating its replacement with a wider range of qualitative and quantitative evaluation measures. The Foundation had already described the higher-order abilities it favoured in its 1986 Report. To be in the running for the kind of work that brings advancement, reward, and economic prosperity for the individual and the nation alike, students

> must possess ... an ability to see patterns where others see only confusion: a cultivated creativity that leads them to new problems, new products, and new services ... and in many cases, the ability to work with other people in complex organizational environments where groups must decide for themselves how to get the job done (cited in Carlson, 1992/in press: 212–213).

This is a call to a form of literacy which informs and sustains creative, innovative, independent, active, and entrepreneurial dispositions and abilities. It is informed by a clear awareness of the economic and administrative/managerial ethos of the new times. If adults are to 'make it' in the current climate, they must have the qualities required for the 'better jobs' that are available; or else must be able actually to *create* satisfying well-paid work. The qualities are more or less the same in either case. The normative demand seems to be that equity calls, at the very least, for all students to be exposed to curricula that model and embody the requisite dispositions and abilities.

There is, however, a further and deeper concern which impacts on normative considerations of curriculum and literacy. This turns on recognition that the unfolding economic and social order harbours large and intensifying injustices. I have already described the polarized labour market and the new inequality inherent in the information and services economy, together with the high current levels of structural unemployment and the drastic reduction in the social wage that has come with the severe erosion of state social and welfare provisions. It is, perhaps, also worth mentioning the quality of work at the bottom. In addition to being poorly paid, uncertain and often temporary, and increasingly poorly protected in terms of organized labour and arbitration laws, much of this work is frankly unsatisfying. It is boring, dead-end, bereft of any need for imagination or initiative, stultifying of spirit and intellect. Not surprisingly, such work as is available in bottom-level job slots is often spurned. Garland *et al.* (1988) note this in relation to what they describe as the emergence and escalation of an urban underclass in the US:

> Even when jobs are available, few are perceived as true opportunities because pay is low and prospects for promotion are virtually nil ... In some tight labor markets, fast-food restaurants pay nearly twice the minimum wage, but local youth unemployment rates remain high. 'Fast-food places aren't paying enough, not for what they want you to do', [as one interviewee said] (Garland, Therrien and Hammonds, 1988: 61).

Unfortunately, the 'attractive' alternatives available, and modelled to many youth caught in the poverty trap, are illegal and/or involve personal risk; for example, theft, drug dealing, pimping, prostitution, and extortion.

The structural problem facing unemployed youth and displaced older workers is that, under prevailing economic conditions, opportunity for one person typically means a loss of opportunity for another. The pressing need is to create an expanded pool of genuine opportunities. Here, however, we run into difficulties. In the first place, to expand opportunities within a national or local economy it will be necessary to transform existing economic structures and practices. To date, the policy favoured by governments presiding over 'developed' economies has been to work towards creating 'a competitive edge', and 'becoming clever countries', in conjunction with economic and social policies favouring free and open markets.

There are deep problems in the strategies currently being employed, however. In Australia and New Zealand, for instance, the alleged benefits of economic restructuring, state asset sales and privatization, which open the way for greater multinational involvement in local economies, have so far delivered little or nothing to local people. This is not to say that they won't in time —

although we do well here to bear in mind the wretched experience of so many Third World countries, for whom economic 'revitalization' and 'development' through multinational 'investment' in their well-being has not, typically, produced even significant 'trickle down' effects. Moreover, even if countries like Australia and New Zealand do succeed in becoming 'clever' and in establishing competitive advantage, the strategies most favoured at present will simply shift problems increasingly to other, and generally poorer, countries. That is, the logic of a 'clever country' currently presupposes 'unclever countries'. From an ethical point of view, the gains to be derived from enhancing local advantage at the cost of intensified immiseration elsewhere are dubious — albeit real to local populations.

The challenge, as I see it, is to seek change which is compatible with economic and social justice, both locally and globally. This is only the ethically acceptable goal. The educational challenge, and the challenge for literacy pedagogy specifically, is to educate our students in a way that equips them to live through the current moment with optimally equal and expanding opportunities for dignity and satisfaction, while striving to build a world which maximizes justice for all. The suggestion I wish to advance in support of this quest centres on curriculum activity to foster literacy consonant with an enlightened form of 'entrepreneurship'.

Entrepreneurship: A Focus for Educational Action

David Harvey (1989) provides a fascinating analysis of the shift from Fordism to the regime of flexible accumulation, highlighting major changes in both the production and consumption sides of the accumulation equation and the accompanying 'remarkable proportionate surge in service employment'. In an economic climate 'of heightened competition and greater risk', flexibility is of the essence. Economies of scope have superseded Fordist economies of scale. Enterprises must be able to make fast shifts, produce cheaply in small batches, and cater to 'a greater range of market needs, including quick changing ones' (Harvey, 1989: 156). Turnover time in production has been greatly accelerated. This, necessarily, has been matched by a dramatically reduced turnover time in consumption, involving 'much greater attention to quick changing fashions and the mobilisation of all the artifices of need inducement and cultural transformation that this implies'. Harvey suggests that much of the upsurge in service employment might be a function of the need to accelerate turnover time in consumption inherent in flexible accumulation. This produces a shift in emphasis 'from production of goods (most of which, like knives and forks, have a substantial lifetime) to the production of events (such as spectacles which have an almost instantaneous turnover time)' (Harvey, 1989: 157).

Harvey's analysis goes a long way toward explaining the premium currently placed on 'entrepreneurship'. In an Inaugural Lecture to Durham University, Alan Gibb (1985) claims that the entrepreneur 'has become the god (or goddess) of current political ideology and the leading actor in the theatre of the "new economics"'. In a period of shrunken 'Situations Vacant' columns, the individual who can create paid work opportunities becomes something of a hero. Those who can create opportunities which both pay well *and* bring work enjoyment or satisfaction by putting together smart ideas and marketing talent are among the new breed of economic 'winners'. The same broad qualities that make for the independent 'entrepreneur-hero' are increasingly prized by corporations and sub-corporate enterprises as well. Even at the 'bottom line' level of economic survival, it is clear that individuals who develop attributes associated with 'being enterprising' and 'showing initiative' will stand better chances in the immediate future than those who lack them.

While they don't typically offer any rationale, official curriculum documents are clearly endorsing the value and urgency currently ascribed to entrepreneurial attributes. The National Curriculum of New Zealand, for example, identifies several such attributes in the guise of problem-solving, self-management, and work and study 'skills'. These include the ability to exercise imagination and initiative in solving problems; developing adaptability and initiative; becoming capable of making constructive responses to challenging situations (involving stress and conflict, success and failure, etc.); assuming responsibility in matters of personal well-being; acquiring the qualities of enterprise and initiative (Gibb, 1985: 2–3). The fact that initiative is identified as an intended curriculum outcome under no less than three categories of 'essential skills' indicates much about the tone and normative investment of New Zealand's National Curriculum direction.

The increasing emphasis placed on entrepreneurship within daily life in general and educational life specifically has met with considerable opposition among educationists, however, many of whom see the current mood as turning education away from its 'true' goals and reducing it to a reflex of corporate-commercial-managerial interests and concerns. For many, the term 'entrepreneur' has strongly pejorative connotations, smacking of opportunism, self-serving tendencies, narrow instrumentality, profit or sales maximization, etc. — all of which seemingly negate the *educational* enterprise, with its emphasis on intrinsic values, ethical high-mindedness, attitudes of impartiality and critical rigour, and visions of a collective good. Even though mass schooling hitherto has manifestly failed to realize its self-professed goals and values on behalf of any more than a tiny minority of students, the goals and values themselves remain non-negotiable. Education is a noble calling; its integrity is compromised by the taint of the entrepreneurial.[9]

I want to challenge this pervasive prejudice against entrepreneurial attributes and seek a way of drawing them into the educational heartland such that they are writ large in classroom literacy endeavours. At the same time, I want to pre-serve what is legitimate in the critical and ethical highground of education. This can be done, I believe, by taking a fresh look at entrepreneurial values in relation to the task of developing a sense and practice of historical agency among our young, and a commitment to building a more just and democratic world.

Gibb (1985: 1) claims that 'entrepreneurship' has diverse meanings which are coloured by context, culture and values. The entrepreneur, he says, is not really understood, particularly within the social sciences.[10] Since Gibb is similarly interested in reconciling educational endeavour with the promotion of entre-preneurial attributes among learners, his ideas are particularly germane here. In seeking a clearer understanding of the entrepreneur, he suggests a range of attributes — amalgams of values, abilities, and motivations or dispositions — which may be regarded as entrepreneurial. Behaviour is properly described as 'entrepreneurial' (or 'enterprising') the more it partakes of the attributes in question. They include initiative, persuasive powers, willingness to entertain a degree of risk, flexibility, creativity, independence/autonomy, problem-solving strengths, imagination, innovativeness, a need for achievement, belief in control of one's own destiny, and leadership qualities. Entrepreneurship consists in 'the marked use of [such] attributes in pursuit of a particular task' (Gibb, 1985: 9). Within productive activity, for example, the entrepreneur brings together the various factors of production, managing and employing these in an innovative way. The innovative outcomes can range from mere incremental change to major step change (Gibb, 1985: 10). In all cases, the entrepreneur draws on the sorts of attributes listed here to generate opportunities or outcomes which would otherwise have lapsed.

It is, perhaps, worth noting that considerable entrepreneurial activity, as defined here, can often be observed among educationists who otherwise disparage the idea of entrepreneurship as a way of life. High achievement-oriented academics who move outside conventional paradigms, developing new theoretical positions which they write up as papers or books and seek, by creative means, to flog off to publishers, are operating on the basis of the very attributes Gibb identifies as entrepreneurial. Indeed, many academic educationists choose to work in universities and research institutions *precisely* because they require the degree of autonomy, independence, and control over their productive activity that allows scope for innovation and creative expression. It is less common, however, for them to see this will to shape one's destiny and identity in terms of 'entrepreneurship'. Yet it can accurately be described as such. The practice of double standards and withholding from others what one claims for oneself are, all too often, conveniently masked by ideologies of academic integrity, disinterested scholarly pursuit, a sense of contributing to the greater good through educational advance, etc. The satisfactions of expressing enterprise are welcomed and enjoyed, guilt-free, since entrepreneurship only goes on 'out there', in the market place. So far as the market comes to the university, it is confined to the philistinic centres of Commerce, Business Studies, Management, and the more crass enclaves of applied theory. Such is the view through the eyes of the 'politically correct'.

This point therefore applies as much to the academic Left as to others in the academic-intellectual community, if not more so. Indeed it is perhaps especially pertinent, given the *effective* marginalization of the Left's political and critical-pedagogic projects in recent times, notwithstanding its undeniable commitment and efforts across various educational forums. Hence what might well be taken very seriously, especially on the Left, is the idea that in a seemingly entrepreneurial age we might have to consider developing curricula for entrepreneurial forms of literacy and pedagogy. In doing this, I want to argue that entrepreneurial literacy need not be construed as necessarily a competitive, aggressive, 'capitalistic' matter, and that, in fact, in many ways the politics of the Left needs to become more actively 'entrepreneurial' — creating and selling ideas and agendas, in the service of a critical-democratic culture. The qualities that make for an entrepreneur include creative attitudes and abilities, eyes for 'gaps' that can be exploited, means of communicating ideas and ideals effectively, being persuasive, knowing how to broke power, knowing the social forces of the time — in short, potentially at least, possessing both rhetorical skills and the very kinds of sociological and historical imagination that I have argued elsewhere to be crucial features of critical literacy and critical-transformative pedagogy (Lankshear with Lawler, 1987, Lankshear, 1989, 1991).

Hence such delusion and self-righteousness as characterizes many educationists' response to the notion of 'entrepreneurialism' seems unnecessary. Gibb notes that when education is linked with desirable behavioural outcomes, 'some very close parallels can be drawn between education and entrepreneurship'. There is considerable agreement in the educational rhetoric of liberals and the Left alike that education should foster 'innovation; creativity; flexibility; capability to respond to widely different situations; autonomy; self direction; and self expression' (Gibb, 1985: 13). Thus encouraged let us consider two simple examples I witnessed casually during a week in September, 1991. Both were born of the drive to economic survival, and reflect an interesting transcendence of the current economic 'moment'.

Exemplifying Entrepreneurship

In the first, a man living in a rural village produces imitation shipping chests using native timber recycled from house demolition. He dresses the timber, builds a range of chests varying in size and design, and sells them to 'thirtysomething' types to adorn the lounges of their refurbished 'character homes'. He has set up his business in what looks like a long-deserted former retail store, presumably on low rent. The front of the shop serves as the showroom. His workshop is out back, where he designs and produces to the accompaniment of classical orchestral music and operas. He offers potential buyers excellent coffee.

The second case involves a woman supplementing her primary income by offering training courses for nannies. She designs a course, advertises and markets it, takes the fees, and arranges for acquaintances with appropriate knowledge and experience (in early childhood education, health and first aid, etc.) to take some of the sessions. She runs the other sessions herself. Graduates of the course are provided with references and appropriate endorsements. Her service is recognized internationally, and she frequently fields requests for nannies from abroad. For the amount of work involved, her operation pays well.

While we must be wary of generalizing too much from such limited cases, it is clear that such examples are far from uncommon, and further, that they present considerable opportunities for personal satisfaction and growth, variety, personal expression, and other desirable outcomes commonly associated with mental health, personal agency, and independence. Envisaging such opportunities and carrying them through to a degree of success presupposes a range of entrepreneurial attributes. At the same time, the very process of expressing these attributes by establishing an enterprise creates a context wherein to develop new skills, master new challenges, blend conception and execution into a praxis of work, encounter new ideas, and entertain new possibilities.

In particular, it is interesting to contrast such enterprises with work available in the semi-skilled post-industrial workforce and in many job slots within government bureaucracies. It is also interesting to consider them in relation to much of the current rhetoric of 'skill' and 'skilling' that pervades curriculum policy documents. Without wishing to underestimate the skills involved in these instances, it seems fair to say that neither enterprise scales lofty heights of *skill per se*. The formal woodworking techniques required to produce the imitation chests, for instance, would easily be covered by the first two years of secondary school woodwork, under any curriculum of recent decades. Accurate measuring and cutting, and ability to use clamps to join the tongue and groove timber for gluing and nailing, comprise the extent of technique required. Design-wise, the only variations on a standard pattern obtainable from photos, sketches, or direct copying from an original, are in size. In the second example, the woman organizing the training courses for nannies had been trained as a kindergarten teacher and taught there for five years. The skills employed in establishing a viable course were largely administrative and clerical. Of course, rather more is required for preparing and delivering the course content, although much of this could be contracted out without diminishing the entrepreneurial character of this initiative.

To a large extent, then, these enterprises are not about 'skill' in the technocratic sense that pervades curriculum documents. They draw much more on attitudes, values, a distinctive orientation toward the world, and an ability to spot 'gaps' to be filled, than on abstracted techniques. In short, they are about entrepreneurial attributes of the type identified by Gibb. The skills deployed are 'housed' within a mode of personal being which affords them possibilities for expression, refinement and extension, not available to those who have, as it were, 'the skills without the clothes of enterprise'.

Of course, the quality of productive life experienced within the sorts of activities described here is vastly superior to that of many employees in the semi-skilled reaches of the post-industrial workforce, even though the gross level of actual skill demands — so far as these can be quantified — may not differ markedly. Gibb finds themes in Marx's account of small scale industrial enterprise that seem pertinent here. Where the worker controls the means of production, in ways similar to those described here, a necessary condition for realizing 'the free individuality of the worker' is met (Gibbs, 1985: 11; Marx, 1976: 927). Work is elevated above the mere repetition or conduct of tasks heteronomously determined and allocated, and assumes a range of activities which transcends the divide between conception and execution. Home and work may be drawn closer together. The need to administer the operation (tax, invoicing, etc.), to research markets, locate materials and resources, and coordinate activity with other agents and agencies, generates possibilities for further growth, interpersonal contact, expanded experience and responsibility, and exposure to new challenges and unexpected opportunities, all of which create conditions for a fuller and richer expression of human potential.

Given an economic setting where ready-made jobs are in scarce supply, and where many of those which *do* exist are demeaning and poorly paid, the possible advantages of educating students for more entrepreneurial approaches to working life should be considered closely. It is, surely, the first calling of educators to enable our young to become *more* rather than less, and given the centrality of productive life in influencing what people become more generally, the education-economy nexus must be taken seriously. If the various 'essential skills' beloved of curriculum policymakers can be dressed up in suitable 'entrepreneurial' garb, and transmitted in the context of socialization into an enterprising mode of social being, the outcome must represent a quantum advance over churning out bearers of decontextualized skills for the semi-skilled job market.

Entrepreneurship and Agency

The attributes of the entrepreneur identified here have significance beyond the economic sphere alone. The entrepreneur models personal *agency*. S/he has an active stance toward the world and a commitment to making things happen. Whether or not these attributes are expressed primarily or solely within economic activity is a contingent matter. Indeed, Gibb (1985: 9) claims it is perfectly possible for entrepreneurial behaviour to be displayed by individuals or groups, for example, fighting to save jobs, to conserve the local environment or 'prevent a motorway being driven through their garden'. In trying to sharpen our understanding of entrepreneurship, Gibb (1985: 28) alerts us to the distinction between 'those who sell out to the world, those who run out of it, and those who are actively interested in shaping it'.

The link between entrepreneurial activity and having an active interest in shaping the world is important. For historical agency is precisely about shaping the world. There is much that can fairly be described as entrepreneurial in the activities of individuals and organizations as diverse as Martin Luther King Jr., the ANC, Greenpeace, Boris Yeltsin, Oxfam, and UNESCO — not to mention V.I. Lenin and Fidel Castro. In devising curricula to enhance an entrepreneurial spirit among our young, we may well, given appropriate content and pedagogy, make an investment in democratic historical agency. In other words, properly conceived, entrepreneurship represents a mode of orientation toward the world which has the potential to enable individuals and groups to survive an uncertain, shifting, testing present, and to transcend that present through informed action aimed at shaping the world along more just and emancipatory lines.

Clearly, there is much more that could and should said by way of description and justification of entrepreneurship as an appropriate educational goal. At this point, it is necessary, however, to address more specifically the practice of curriculum as entrepreneurial literacy, and to show how reading and writing in the classroom — specifically understood within a 'critical literacy' frame — can be made into a form which stimulates and deploys entrepreneurial attributes with the potential for expression in transformative social action for collective benefit.

Curriculum as Entrepreneurial Literacy

The early arguments in this chapter establish the basis for approaching activity across the curriculum in terms of an attempt to create and transmit a *form* of literate practice which may appropriately be called 'entrepreneurial'. Curriculum, in other words, becomes a site of educational engagement aimed at actualizing certain values, purposes, procedures, and ways of being, within print-mediated activity. This, of course, is about much more than merely shaping up reading and writing practices in some self-contained kind of way. Rather, it is to recognize the centrality of language — in this case, literate language — within modes of social being, or forms of life. What we *are*, what we could *be*, is to an important extent a function of linguistic practice: how we talk, listen, read and write; what we say, hear, read and write; why we talk, listen, read, and write as we do. To engage human beings in particular forms of literate practice (rather than others) is to affirm some mode(s) of being and disaffirm others.

This is a major implication of the ideological model of literacy; a key insight to be derived from going beyond perceiving literacy in terms of skill or technique. Interestingly, however, this same insight underlies E.D. Hirsch's (1987) advocacy of what he calls 'cultural literacy'. Hirsch sees very clearly that the creation and maintenance of a national culture is intimately bound up with 'appropriate' conceptions and practices of reading and writing. In other words, if you want bearers of Hirsch's vision of American culture, you practise curriculum as cultural literacy along Hirsch's lines. A similar point can be made about entrepreneurial literacy, which itself may be approached as a cultural mode and phenomenon in its own right. To envisage, design, and practise curriculum as literacy around the values and *modus operandi* of entrepreneurship *is* to engage in the social-cultural creation of entrepreneurial being. What might this involve in practice, and how might it also accommodate the emergence of a critical, historically-informed, moral sense conducive to transformative action for collective good?

To address curriculum as entrepreneurial literacy is to consider how learning can be constituted as a set of activities, grounded in print, which *commit students affectively* to such values and attitudes as initiative, creativity, willingness to take risks, autonomy, imagination, leadership, and so on, while simultaneously *engaging them in the lived practice* of these same values and attitudes. It involves generating literacy/knowledge as 'content' and literacy/knowledge as 'skill', in tandem.

Elsewhere I have dealt at length with a celebrated case of approaching curriculum as literacy in the pursuit of a new mode of social being — namely, the 1980 Nicaraguan Literacy Crusade (Lankshear with Lawler, 1987: Ch. 5). The key point is simple. The Nicaraguan literacy officials conceived the crusade in terms of promoting historical agency on the part of previously marginalized people. Among peasants and the urban poor, illiteracy was precisely an index of marginality. The practical question was how to make 'literacy work' a medium for cultivating historical agents. In part the challenge was *ideological*. Via texts and discussion, learners would come to understand what is meant by (assuming) historical agency; how it had previously been denied them; and why they needed to embrace it. Beyond this, however, the challenge was *practical*. People become historical agents only by *practising* agency; not merely by encountering new words, ideas, or slogans. The genius of the crusade was that it involved literacy learners (and teachers) in simple but appropriate acts of historical agency — building hospitals, improving sanitation, participating in health campaigns, creating community organizations and political structures (like trade unions, women's groups), constructing dams, roads and schools, participating in forums and debates about political and economic priorities, and so on — at the same time as they were being exposed ideologically to ideas and values of historical agency.

This is the broad logic to be observed in constituting curriculum as entrepreneurial literacy. In other words, reading and writing must be made into activities for understanding entrepreneurship and accessing appropriate values, examples and ideas, *at the same time* as they are employed in acts of practising entrepreneurial behaviour. Within the curriculum, and across learning areas, reading and writing will be directed in part to uncovering and generating relevant *content*. Alongside this, reading and writing will be practised as appropriate *acts* within the conduct of projects or enterprises which encapsulate the required personal attributes.

How? A useful starting place is with two related points made by Gibb. He argues that while there clearly is a distinction to be drawn between entre-preneurship and small business, small businesses or organizations with high degrees of independence offer 'a means of stimulating and allowing full use of entrepreneurial abilities ... Owning your own business is likely to force develop-ment of a number of the [entrepreneurial] attributes by the nature of the task structure' (Gibb, 1985: 9). His second point concerns the possible role business schools within universities might play in fostering entrepreneurship. This poses a challenge to business schools, 'namely, to alter the balance in what they teach — away from subjects, knowledge and techniques towards greater concern for developing ... entrepreneurial attributes ... around the solution of "issues" regarded as important by industry' (Gibb, 1985: 24).

The implication is clear. The focus of curriculum activity across subjects or learning areas must be on some actual project or enterprise. Students must, so far as possible, *own* the enterprise that focuses their print-mediated activity; an enterprise that generates issues or problems/challenges of serious, 'real life' type, calling for the practice of agency in resolving them, and where practising agency involves initiative, imagination, divergent thinking, adopting innovative approaches, entertaining risk, and experiencing autonomy, independence, and responsibility. Print becomes a medium for investigating possible solutions to challenges or for finding new ways of framing problems, for exploring a range of actual cases, eliciting information or support, organizing meetings with 'experts', writing up results, researching markets, applying for grants, presenting cred-entials, drawing up inventories, invoicing, accounting, reporting, and so on.

Examples of potential enterprises are endless. Some schools already involve students in income or resource-generating ventures which require them to envis-age a product or service, research market demand, produce and market their product/service, sell it, do the necessary administration and accounting, explore time or cost-cutting variations, or variations in design, locate raw materials at the best price, and so on. In such ventures, curriculum activity can be integrated across several subjects: craft, design, maths and computer studies, commercial practice, technology, economics, language and art, for example. In well con-ceived and executed cases, the outcome is a characteristic form of personal and collective agency, articulated to identifiable conceptions and practices of reading and writing consonant with the overall enterprise, and having undoubted value in the 'adult' world.

Conclusion: A Way Forward?

By way of conclusion, let me suggest how an escalating problem within some urban New Zealand schools might, imaginatively, be made into an opportunity to conceive curriculum as entrepreneurial literacy for a group of learners. The particular problem is hunger or malnutrition. During the past year, principals have reported increasing cases of students suffering hunger/malnutrition, as domestic economies break. Schools face a dilemma here. To ignore the problem is to compromise educational endeavour: clearly, children cannot learn effectively if they are malnourished. To assume responsibility for feeding students, as some schools have, however, is to risk taking on a task that might not be sustainable, and that does not rightfully belong to the school. Moreover, it absolves some other agent or agency from their proper obligation.

Without pronouncing on the ethics of school involvement here, let us approach the problem as one which potentially creates an opportunity for politically and ethically informed entrepreneurial activity. The challenge is to find ways of meeting a material need without imposing a further burden on the school or in any way detracting from its *educational* calling.[11]

A likely strategy might be to involve a collective of students across a range of learning areas. It is important that the collective be finite and formal, so that roles and responsibilities can be allocated and accountability ensured. Ideally, the project should be integrated across several learning areas to bring a broad range of knowledge perspectives to bear on the problem, as well as to enhance learners' awareness of the particular contributions that various disciplines can make to addressing human issues. Within cooking, home economics, and health, students could research ways of maximizing nutrition and variety at minimal expense. Reading and writing may be deployed in a range of activities, from seeking 'expert' advice to researching facts about nutrition and relative prices of different types of foods, and producing recipes and menus for cafeteria meals. Furthermore, 'hunger' could be developed as a theme for critical investigation within, say, social studies/history and geography, as well as English. By means of studies across different countries and periods of time, students could investigate causes of hunger and try to understand and explain why some people experience hunger while others do not. With appropriate guidance from teachers, students could draw on these theoretical inquiries to identify specific factors contributing to hunger in their own neighbourhood. Such work would certainly enhance understanding of important dimensions of the politics and ethics of daily life — offering the chance to explore writings which suggest possible connections (for students themselves to put together, as they see appropriate) between ownership of productive resources, patterns of employment and unemployment, determinants of wage levels, the link between profit, capital flight and local hardship, the politics of welfare and the erosion of the welfare state, etc.

For the school actually to provide for its hungry, however, it will be necessary to generate a supply of food. This is where initiative, creativity, and innovation is most obviously called for. One possibility is to procure donations of food — for example, surplus bread and vegetables from supermarkets. While this may have a place as a short-term measure, a more durable arrangement will be required. Possibilities range from generating income out of productive activity in craft, technology, home economics, say, or by organizing work-experience courses which barter student labour for food or vouchers — for example, in arrangements with orchardists, market gardeners, supermarkets, wholesalers, and so on. Students might lobby Social Welfare, or the Ministry of Health, for funds to subsidize running a bona fide meal service. English classes might provide a venue for writing articles for magazines or newspapers, petitions to MPs, letters to editors, and the like, to politicize the issue of local hunger and to demand appropriate welfare support. Organizational strategies could be developed in English, Social Studies, or Liberal Studies classes to create networks of people and organizations to come up with solutions and contingency measures, and to frame policy initiatives. This would link the school to community and service institutions, local and central government, relief agencies, local business and industry. The potential here for countering the effects of 'school bashing' and generating positive perceptions of school 'relevance' and 'effectiveness' is considerable.

The *educational* potential is almost unlimited, in short. Clearly, a wide range of print activities will be involved in any such project — ranging from reading theoretical studies related to employment, economics and hunger, to drafting letters and petitions requesting support; from engaging the science of nutrition to designing menus and recipes, researching food prices, striking a balance in bartering, exchanging, or tendering; tracking down the cheapest sources of good food, communicating with other schools and agencies facing the hunger problem, swapping ideas, brainstorming, and so on. It could also provide a strong basis for rethinking curriculum and literacy alike along critical-pedagogic lines, yet in ways which 'impact more directly and tellingly on the world of the classroom' (Lankshear, 1991: 224). Further what could be particularly useful about a critically entrepreneurial literacy is that it might well effectively transcend the borders between what currently are the dominant discourses of 'functional', 'cultural' and 'critical literacy', all of which seem to have positive virtues going for them — *despite* their respective problems and failings, and their current polarization — which might therefore be usefully drawn into a new formulation, linking literacy and curriculum in politically progressive ways.[12]

The point here is not to provide any kind of blueprint for entrepreneurial activity, but merely to suggest that it *can* wear a human face, and be politically and ethically informed; that initiative, independence, responsibility, risk taking, creativity, leadership, and innovativeness *can* be practised within socially-critical forms of curriculum, given suitable incentives; that solidarity and efficiency *can* be generated out of adversity, drawing on no more than the normal stock of human sympathies and 'talents' (actual and latent) available within a group; that practical projects *can* be problematized within curriculum in ways that yield critical understanding and sociological imagination;[13] and that highly relevant, well-honed, active conceptions and practices of reading and writing *can* be developed and transmitted within the quest to foster entrepreneurial attributes. Following a period in which schools have been roundly accused of failing in their duty to promote appropriate forms of literacy at high levels, I submit that conceiving and practising curriculum — at least in part — as entrepreneurial literacy can only carry us forward. This requires, however, first that we bear in mind always that, as I have written elsewhere (Lankshear, 1989: 181), '[p]romoting critical literacy is the educator's first calling', and second, that we seek continually to understand what this involves in ways consistent with the 'new times' in which we now find ourselves living.

Notes

1 For example, *National Curriculum of England and Wales* (1989), *The National Curriculum of New Zealand* (1991), and *Excellence and Equity: New South Wales Curriculum Reform* (1990).
2 'By a *form* of literacy I mean an identifiable enduring set of reading and writing practices governed by a conception of what to read and write, when, and why' (Lankshear, 1989: 181). See also Lankshear with Lawler (1987: 44–47).

3   As I have written elsewhere: 'School is a major — some say *the* major — shaper of consciousness.... Whether or not people win through to a sociological imagination depends heavily on their formal educational experience. Print is the fundamental medium by which consciousness is shaped within the transmission and production of school knowledge. Reading and writing are acquired, practised and consolidated within a context of assimilating and generating school knowledge. How people read and write, what they read and write, why they read and write — in short, how they conceive and practise literacy — is vitally dependent on what literacy is "made into" within formal education. And what literacy is "made into" within schools, universities, teachers' colleges and other formal institutions of learning, is almost entirely naive' (Lankshear, 1989: 176–177).

4   For typical although different dimensions of the debate, see Baudrillard (1988), Habermas (1987), Jameson (1984), Lyotard (1984), and Williams (1977).

5   In Lankshear and McLaren (1992/in press); all page references to articles in this collection refer to the manuscript copy.

6   As I have stressed elsewhere (Lankshear, 1991: 218): 'It is ... important to be wary of generalized talk about a post-industrial economy if it involves focusing on detailed differences between industrial manufacture and post-industrial services and information technology *at the expense of recalling the crucial similarities between the two as moments of capital accumulation*' — and hence of exploitation and the reproduction of inequalities.

7   It should be noted that elsewhere I discuss more fully the article by Garland, Therrien and Hammonds that is referred to here, as exemplifying *and contributing to* what I describe as a 'naive literacy' position — an 'improper literacy', in short — specifically in relation to contemporary formulations of literacy, education and the 'underclass' (Lankshear, 1989).

8   For a more extensive analysis of this, and related issues, see Lankshear (1991), and also Lankshear and McLaren (1992/in press).

9   For a good example of this tone, see *Access: Picot and Beyond*, **7**, 1988, University of Auckland: Education Department.

10 For typical treatments of entrepreneurship and the entrepreneur, see Gough (1969), Hébert and Link (1988), Wyckham, Meredith and Bushe (1987) and Ronen (1983).

11 For a somewhat similar example of a literacy pedagogy conceived along these lines, although without direct reference to the entrepreneurial framework introduced in this chapter, see my account of Chris Searle's work in a London East End school (Lankshear, 1989: 179–81).

12 For an elaboration of these 'discourses' and their respective strengths and weaknesses, see Lankshear (1991).

13 For an account of what I define as 'critical understanding', see the 'Introduction' to Lankshear and McLaren (1992/in press). For the original formulation of the notion of 'sociological imagination', see Mills (1959). It is elaborated on with specific reference to literacy studies and literacy pedagogy in Lankshear with Lawler (1987); see also Lankshear (1989).

References

APPLE, M. (1986) *Teachers and Texts*, London, Routledge and Kegan Paul.

BAUDRILLARD, J. (1988) *Selected Writings*, edited by M. POSTER, Stanford, Stanford University Press.

BERLIN, J. (1992/in press) 'Literacy, Pedagogy, and English Studies: Postmodern Connections', in LANKSHEAR, C. and MCLAREN, P. (Eds) *Critical Literacy: Politics, Praxis and the Postmodern*, Albany, NY, State University of New York Press.

CARLSON, D. (1992/in press) 'Literacy and Urban School Reform: Beyond Vulgar Pragmatism', in LANKSHEAR, C. and MCLAREN, P. (Eds) *Critical Literacy: Politics, Praxis and the Postmodern*, Albany, NY, State University of New York Press.

CARNEGIE FOUNDATION (1986) *A Nation Prepared: Teachers for the 21st Century*, New York, Carnegie Foundation for the Advancement of Teaching.

CARNEGIE FOUNDATION (1988) *An Imperiled Generation: Saving Urban Schools*, Lawrenceville, NJ, Princeton University Press.

GARLAND, S., THERRIEN, L. and HAMMONDS, K. (1988) 'Why The Underclass Can't Get Out From Under', *Business Week* (International edition), September 19, New York, McGraw Hill, pp. 60–63.

GEE, J. (1992/in press) 'Postmodernism and Literacies', in LANKSHEAR, C. and MCLAREN, P. (Eds) *Critical Literacy: Politics, Praxis and the Postmodern*, Albany, NY, State University of New York Press.

GIBB, A. (1985) *Has Entrepreneurship a Place in the University?* Durham, University of Durham.

GOUGH, J.W. (1969) *The Rise of the Entrepreneur*, London, Batsford.

GRAFF, H. (1979) *The Literacy Myth*, New York, Academic Press.

GRAFF, H. (1981) *Literacy and Social Development in the West*, Cambridge, Cambridge University Press.

GRAFF, H. (1987) *The Labyrinths of Literacy*, London, Falmer Press.

HABERMAS, J. (1987) *The Philosophical Discourse of Modernity*, Cambridge, Polity Press.

HARVEY, D. (1989) *The Condition of Postmodernity*, Oxford, Basil Blackwell.

HÉBERT, R. and LINK, A. (1988) *The Entrepreneur: Mainstream Views and Radical Critiques*, New York, Praeger.

HIRSCH, E.D. JR. (1987) *Cultural Literacy: What Every American Needs to Know*, Boston, Houghton Mifflin.

HMSO (1989) *National Curriculum of England and Wales*, London, HMSO.

JAMESON, F. (1984) 'Postmodernism, or the Cultural Logic of Late Capitalism', *New Left Review*, 146, pp. 53–93.

KOZOL, J. (1985) *Illiterate America*, New York, Anchor and Doubleday.

LANKSHEAR, C. (1989) 'Reading and Righting Wrongs: Literacy and the Underclass', *Language and Education*, **3**, 3, pp. 167–82.

LANKSHEAR, C. (1991) 'Getting It Right is Hard: Redressing the Politics of Literacy in the 1990s', in CORMACK, P. (Ed.) *Literacy: Making It Explicit, Making It Possible — Selected Papers from the 16th Australian Reading Association Conference, Adelaide, South Australia, 7–11 July, 1991*, Carlton South, Victoria, Australian Reading Association, pp. 209–28.

LANKSHEAR, C. with LAWLER, M. (1987) *Literacy, Schooling and Revolution*, London, Falmer Press.

LANKSHEAR, C. and MCLAREN, P. (Eds) (1992/in press) *Critical Literacy: Politics, Praxis and the Postmodern*, Albany, NY, State University of New York Press.

LEVETT, A. and LANKSHEAR, C. (1990) *Going for Gold: Priorities for Schooling in the Nineties*, Wellington, Daphne Brasell Press.

LYOTARD, J-F. (1984) *The Postmodern Condition: A Report On Knowledge*, Minneapolis, University of Minnesota Press.

MARX, K. (1976) *Capital*, Vol. **1**, Harmondsworth, Penguin.

MILLS, C.W. (1959) *The Sociological Imagination*, New York, Oxford University Press.

MINISTRY OF EDUCATION (1991) *The National Curriculum for New Zealand*, Wellington, Ministry of Education.

NSW MINISTRY OF EDUCATION AND YOUTH AFFAIRS (1990) *Excellence and Equity: New South Wales Curriculum Reform*, Sydney, NSW Ministry of Education and Youth Affairs.

RONEN, J. (Ed.) (1983) *Entrepreneurship*, Lexington, D.C. Heath and Co.

STREET, B. (1984) *Literacy in Theory and Practice*, Cambridge, Cambridge University Press.

WILLIAMS, R. (1977) *Marxism and Literature*, Oxford, Oxford University Press.

WYCKHAM, R., MEREDITH, L. and BUSHE, G. (Eds) (1987) *The Spirit of Entre-preneurship*, Burnaby, British Columbia, Simon Fraser University.

Chapter 10

Television Curriculum and Popular Literacy: Feminine Identity Politics and Family Discourse

Carmen Luke

This chapter takes a different approach to curriculum and literacy. Historically, curriculum and literacy have been thought of, and theorized, only in the context of institutional pedagogical contexts. But we know from two decades of cultural studies and many more decades of empiricist research that an equally if not more powerful curriculum for children and adults is that of television texts. In this chapter, accordingly, I want to focus on the informal curriculum of TV textuality and the self/other productions that emerge out of the relationship between TV and viewers.

The hundreds of thousands of hours people spend during a lifetime in front of the screen far exceed the time they spend as children in classrooms with teachers and texts. Children begin their schooling with a substantial stock of TV knowledge. Most, if not all, 6-year-olds are not print-literate but they are media-'literate'. They are familiar with TV's semiotic and narrative conventions, they have learned what counts as feminine and masculine, and they can recite commercial jingles better than teachers' lessons. Children grow up in various family configurations and TV is the one universal discourse that cuts across all variations of family forms, class, culture, and location. And since children watch TV at home (however that home is defined and lived), TV is the obvious conduit into children's 'lived experience'.

Traditionally, however, teachers have tended to have notoriously elitist attitudes towards TV and few spend the time to watch children's and adolescents' favorite fare. Moreover, the fixation on print in schools and teacher education programs contributes to teachers' visual illiteracy, their denigration of popular cultural texts, and their reluctance to use media texts in the classroom. There is a certain irony in this attitude. In particular, progressive pedagogies have long insisted on the need to 'start with the child', but TV knowledge — children's favorite and most elaborate frame of reference — is not considered as valid knowledge, as a legitimate curricular field or form of literacy. I have argued elsewhere of the need to challenge the school's resistance to teaching critical literacies of the popular (Luke, 1987, 1989, 1990). Based on the work I present in this chapter, I suggest that a curriculum that aims to deconstruct TV must abandon traditional notions of teaching manageable and assessable 'text units' as these are constructed in print-based curricula. What this suggests is a radical reconceptual-ization of educational content and pedagogy, one that enables entry into cultural studies of gender, the family, community, popular literacy and culture, of ident-ity and location, and of knowledge production. In other words, a study of televisual texts and audiences enables a study of how TV structures family social patterns and hierarchies of control, how subjects construct themselves in relation to TV content and schedules, how discourses of the popular become discourses of ourselves. Conversely, 'social' studies — whether in specialist areas such as English, geography, history, or social education — can be accessed through TV texts because it is from these that children acquire so much of their knowledge about the world. A cultural studies approach to curriculum means therefore that teachers can access students' knowledge through the use of TV which simultaneously opens up the possibility for critical analyses of how these texts construct our understandings and desires: from the construction of consumption as a means for identity (re)formation, to constructs of science, society, class, race, gender, and so forth.

To reframe curriculum and literacy into a cultural studies approach to knowledge and learning, then, requires that we uncouple 'curriculum' and 'liter-acy' from strictly school-based knowledges and forms of pedagogy. It implies that we incorporate TV as a source of learning since arguably it teaches children and adults much more, and perhaps even more effectively, than the school ever did. Such a pedagogy does not raise the question of where one can find an educational video to kick off a lesson on, say, 'bushrangers' or 'outlaws'. It raises the question of how can we take a broadly-defined cultural studies approach to teaching with and about TV and its intertextual connection to other popular cultural texts. This kind of cultural study does not venerate culture as 'canon' but, rather, views culture as site and lived experience of relations of domination and reproduction, of cultural representations and productions, of identity and social formation. Moreover, it takes an 'anti-disciplinary' position in its interdis-ciplinary commitment and conceptualizes knowledge as cultural and historical artifacts. I return to this point briefly at the end of the chapter. Suffice it for now to propose that such a re-vision requires that we challenge contemporary pedago-gical and curricular models that guide school practice, as well as the theories which guide our own teaching and research.

More is at issue here than presenting an account of television and popular culture, however. Perhaps the divisive and hegemonic powers we have long ascribed to schooling's text-based curriculum are less powerful and 'real' than the more universal curriculum of TV (Luke and Luke, 1990). Children and adults don't, as a matter of course, make reference to school texts in everyday encounters — TV talk, however, *is* part of the verbal and semiotic network that structures everyday talk. We hear it in the office, the shopping mall and res-taurants, in the schoolyard, the school and university classroom. TV is central to the culture of everyday life. It cuts across national and political boundaries, and few communities in the world today remain disconnected to McLuhan's global village. Yet, how subjects in different locations are inscribed by, and inscribe themselves, within local and global TV texts is the task of a cultural studies that is sensitive to differences of location and identity. And this is a further point from which I begin in this chapter: I question the universality espoused in much of current cultural studies literature of the so-called 'postmodernist subject' in 'postmodernist conditions'. Most communities around the world may well be wired into the global network of re-presentation and hyper-real signification. There is also sufficient evidence now to suggest that modernist capitalism, culture, and technology have undergone significant changes which have transformed the West and its satellite clients into postmodern conditions (Harvey, 1989). In intellectual work, current rejections of modernist epistemologies claim an academic, philosophical postmodernism. These various, at times uneasy, moves towards the 'post' (from 'post-Marxism', 'post-feminism', to 'post-critical') do not, however, logically justify the conceptual naming of a universalized postmodernist subject. Part of my argument, then, is to question the totalizability of the postmodernist subject.

Guiding my argument is my belief that we must apply the self-reflexivity we advocate for teacher education students to our own theoretical, pedagogical, and research practice. In that regard, we should heed poststructuralism's lesson and challenge our own complicity in the theoretical totalization of postmodernist subjectivities, popular culture, genres, or even postmodernist society itself. If we want to contest the insistence of the letter in print-based school knowledge and pedagogy, then we must begin with ourselves. Through a reconceptualized understanding of curriculum and literacy that is cultural, critical and contextual, one that can theorize identity and difference within the texts of wall-to-wall *CNN* or *Sesame Street*, we can begin to dislodge the modernist epistemology which remains foundational to most educational theory and practice. We need to proceed, however, rather more cautiously than tends to be the case in much contemporary avant-garde intellectual discussion, not just in cultural studies more generally but also, increasingly, in educational theory.

I begin, then, with questioning the construct of the postmodernist subject in current cultural studies. I then present parts of my own recent research on rural TV viewers which support my claims of the impossibility of the universal postmodernist subject. My analysis centers on the gendered practice of televiewing, and on the specificity of identity and location. Of particular relevance here is the role and significance of women — more specifically, of mothers — in early literacy education and the development of popular literacies. I conclude with a discussion of televiewing as social practice, and outline implications for a re-vision of curriculum and literacy.

Postmodernist Spaces, Postmodernist Subjects

There is in pop and academic cultural studies a general assumption that we are economically in a 'post-industrial' era, and culturally in a 'postmodernist' era. The postmodernist premise, among cultural theorists at least, is that women and men in the West are not hegemonically duped masses, but active agents with fractured subjectivities who occupy multiple subject reading positions, some resistant, even as they 'make do' (Fiske, 1990) with available cultural resources. This construct of the postmodernist subject has reached the stage of theoretical orthodoxy which Foucault (1972) calls 'epistemologization'. In short, the postmodernist subject is currently the subject of choice in cultural studies. Countless studies on media texts and female and male viewer reading positions have naturalized and universalized this subject, perceived as adept at reading the ironic in media texts and her/his own ironically resistant yet complicitous relation to the text. This is part of what I understand Meaghan Morris (1990) to mean in her charges of banality levelled at 'mainstream' cultural studies. Now that we have discarded the homogeneous duped mass audience and have centered the gendered, resistant, and multi-positioned media text reading subject, what next?

I want here not so much to go forward theoretically to forge the 'what next' but, rather, to present evidence which suggests that we should exercise caution in making universalist claims about the subject in the allegedly 'postmodernist' and 'post-feminist' 1990s. In line with feminism's firm theoretical commitment to the historical and cultural specificities of difference, this chapter reaffirms the importance of paying theoretical and research attention to particularities of location and identity in relation to subjects' access to and readings of popular culture. My focus here is on rural Australian women in nuclear family contexts. The aim of the research from which this data is derived was to examine how the family structures women's relationships to TV texts: how women discuss TV as it relates to themselves and their families, and what aspects of everyday rural life impinge on their relationship to and readings of TV texts. In other words, I look at how the cultural curriculum of TV discourse is interpreted by rural women and how their televiewing practices can be read as gendered social practice. The women's testimony presented here suggest two things: first, in discussions about TV, children, and (nuclear) family life, women tend to bring certain dimensions to their explanations and justifications which are not evident in male discourse (see Morley, 1986). Second, postmodernist theoretical assumptions about subjectivity or cultural experience do not adequately apply to the families in this study and, I suspect, do not hold for vast populations of rural people in other (Western and non-Western) countries.

In a recent *Screen* article, Elspeth Probyn (1990) discusses the incorporation of a new radical traditionalism in 'post-feminist' TV programs. Probyn argues that the recent surge of women-centered prime-time programs (from the over-analyzed *Cagney and Lacey* to *Murphy Brown*, *Golden Girls*, *China Beach* or *Designing Women*) and new post-feminist TV family arrangements (e.g. *Whose the Boss?*, *thirtysomething*, *Golden Girls* and *Living Dolls*) is nothing short of a repackaged *status quo*: a replay of the same 1950s gender ideology tapes. What is different about the TV family in the post-feminist, new-traditionalist era of the 1990s is that it is meant to represent women's 'choice' (that is, to return to the family fold). Probyn (1990: 152) comments: 'If new traditionalism naturalizes the home into a fundamental and unchanging site of love and fulfilment, the discourse of post-feminism turns on a re-articulation of the choice. Post-feminism then returns a sense of difference to the rather flat landscape of new traditionalism'. The point Probyn makes is important to analyses of the politics of TV texts. Yet the flipside of TV texts — the locale of the viewer and the politics of viewing — suggests scenarios of the local in which, for countless women, post-feminism and new traditionalism are *non sequiturs* even as these women 'live' the experience of watching such programs. In communities where the 'old' traditionalism has never seriously been under threat and where, by association, post-feminist spaces and choices are untenable given the absence of any visible signs of (first-wave) feminist discourses, one can hardly speak of a post-feminist or post-modernist subject. In these spaces, millions of women of all ages and colours remain mapped on the rather flat landscape of old traditionalism. The communities I refer to are the innumerable rural and semi-rural townships across America, Canada and Australia. In rural America, as in Canada and Australia, women don't appear to live at all like their urban counterparts in New York, Toronto, or Sydney. Baudrillard's (1988) hyper-reality peopled by human mirror refractions is wholly contingent upon multi-mediated environments. It is my contention, however, that massive populations in the West (and certainly most in non-Western countries) are not positioned in multi-mediated electronic environments in which they are the screen on which TV projects choice, identity, culture and desire (Grossberg, 1984). The 'lived experience' of postmodern positionality and subjectivity, one which is said to float and refract in the boundary-less fluidity of the urban mirror-and-glass landscape, one that conflates inside/outside, nature/culture, is clearly absent from the rural landscape. Not everyone is media-wired into fifty channels, operating several remote controls simultaneously while the fax, answering machine, and printer are pumping out information in the background. It is precisely this group — decidedly non-postmodernist, rural Australian working-class families — that I set out to study. Because my research was motivated by the kinds of questions already asked by 'critical cultural studies' researchers of urban and suburban viewers, I had initially not looked for much else than the anticipated differences in gendered reading positions and the anticipated discrepancies between what kinds of control parents claim to have over their children's viewing and the children's accounts. Throughout the project I certainly found what I had anticipated, but I also began to develop a deeper sense of how rural women's lives differ profoundly from the 'post-modernist', 'post-feminist' woman-subject constructed in much of contemporary cultural, literary, and feminist discourse.

TV and Rural Families: A Cultural Studies Framework

I began this study following David Morley's (1986) case study of nineteen working-class families in England on the gender dynamics of family viewing. We interviewed twenty-seven families in five rural Australian communities. I focus in this chapter only on the aspect of women's articulations of their positioning in relation to TV texts, and women's TV watching as experience and activity, as these are coloured by the dynamics of family relations. My conception of what it means to re-write the interview transcript does not assume that speech or speech written down is a mirror reflection of truth, the real, or of experience. Mindful that my own theoretical position produces a specific reading of the women interviewed, of their interview speech and that speech recreated in the transcript, I acknowledge my own discursively mediated political investments in this project and this writing. I believe, however, that interview talk gets as close to people's justifications for viewing, their interpretations, rationalizations and positions in discourse, as any informal chat in office staffrooms or the factory floor about what was watched on TV the night before, about a new Pepsi or Apple ad, or speculations about next week's episodes of a current mini-series (Game, 1989; Hobson, 1990).

Talk about TV is where meanings and understandings of TV text are made and remade, negotiated and contested. Hegemonic, resistant or combined consensual-oppositional readings among viewers are neither stable across TV texts nor across time. Even within what appear to be homogeneous viewing audiences and viewing patterns, viewers develop shifting positions and interpretive schema within the nexus of historically fluid subject positions and socio-situational, communicational circumstances. Thus, for instance, Cassandra Amesley (1989), in her study of *Star Trek* viewers, found that at the periphery of self-possessed *Star Trek* fans (i.e. convention-goers, club members, fanzine writers and subscribers), a 'proprietary audience' of Trekkies exist who develop their own 'interpretive relationship' to the program which is separate from yet overlaps the dominant reading of and relationship to *Star Trek* among its frontline fans. The polysemous character of the visual, oral and print sign taken up by socio-historical, gendered and class-positioned subjects suggests that the meanings people assign to texts and the ways in which those meanings are carried over into worldviews, social encounters, and moral and ethical templates, are infinitely complex and multiplicitous — even if only by degree, within broad patterns of sameness.

Family life-cycle and mobility are important contextual aspects to understanding why TV and specific program genres are important or unimportant to family members at particular moments in time in particular geographic locales. Rather than dehistoricizing and universalizing gender-specific 'TV use' or 'program preferences', it is important to acknowledge the historical (and geographic) specificity of viewing subjects, particularly also because any interview event occurs at a particular moment in what are fluid familial and socioeconomic conditions and geographic contingencies. In one family, for instance, an older son had recently moved to the city, yet his mother still incorporated into her account how her viewing had been influenced by his preferences. In other families, those in communities located in regions that are annually battered by tropical cyclones, women repeatedly stressed the importance of TV news and weather reports in keeping them informed of impending weather events, evacuation procedures, whether school buses would run, whether their husbands would go to work, and so forth. A woman in another family, recently moved from England, explained that she watched 'anything British' to retain a sense of 'home', including programs such as *Fawlty Towers* which she labelled as patently sexist, a program she never chose to watch while living in the UK, but one which she now looked forward to because it provided a sense of cultural identification and familiarity. It seems from this research, therefore, that people's stated reasons for viewing are never simple enough to be attributable to one or two variables that can then be situated on the master social science grid under 'gender differences'. It is the subtle complexities within that gendered difference that I attempt to represent here.

Women's Viewing, Women's Lives: Decentered Subjectivities

Since Morley's (1986) study was the springboard from which the research in question here was conceptualized, I will outline in brief some of his findings against which we read our own data. Morley found that viewing preferences tended to fall along predictable gender patterns. Men in Morley's sample stated preferences for factual content (news, documentaries, sports) whereas women stated preferences for fictional content (soaps, serials). Men's viewing styles

Morley found to be more focused than women's. Family members tended to agree with fathers' claims that they view TV in a highly focused manner, generally intolerant of interruptions and commonly not engaging in other activities. Women, by contrast, tend to accept interrupted viewing and most reported that they engage in other domestic and childcare duties during viewing. In Morley's sample, men tended to control family viewing. In TV remote-control households, male control over viewing was most apparent. Women and daughters, on the other hand, claimed to have far less control over TV program choice, over the remote control, or over the operation of VCRs. Men also tended to select programs for the evening or week more consistently and systematically than women. Women, Morley found, tended to take a more 'take-it-or-leave-it' attitude to viewing: they did not plan their viewing by checking TV guides, nor did they plan time-shifting logistics. For the most part, women in VCR households reported giving up 'their' video tapes for other family members to tape over; furthermore, they rarely operated the VCR, and rarely planned to tape a favorite program. Viewers generally talk about TV both within family contexts and in the workplace. The women in Morley's sample, however, seemed far less reluctant than the men to admit to 'TV talk' with friends and colleagues at work. Morley interprets this pattern to mean that the men in his sample either were reluctant to admit to another male (interviewer) that TV is important enough to them that they should talk about it at work, or that men in fact do not talk about TV as women do. If the latter is the case, then, as Morley suggests, men's viewing experience, their 'consumption of television material is of a quite different kind from that of their wives' (Morley, 1986: 158). In view of these findings, one of our aims was to see if these gendered patterns of reported TV use and TV talk would be similar among our sample of rural Australian viewers who, unlike Morley's group, were interviewed by a woman.

Drawing on the notion of subjectivity as constructed through the social relations embedded in and deployed by language (always already given in discourses, the social, and consciousness), Fiske (1987: 48–61) applies what some would call a 'poststructuralist' and others a 'postmodernist' concept of the subject to the study of TV texts and TV-viewer relationships. Starting with a concept of the subject as fragmented and variously constituted by and in multiple discourses and sites, and a concept of identity as fluid and not fixed, in contrast to the ontologically stable and unified rationalist individual, Fiske and others (e.g. Brown, 1990) read women's (TV) texts and women's position in patriarchy as characterized by deferment, disruption and decenteredness. Women's domestic work, for instance, their viewing styles, and feminine TV texts (soap opera, family drama serials) are repetitive, simultaneous, and open-ended. Fiske (1987) explains:

> The multiplicity of [soap] characters and plots is equivalent to the multiplicity of simultaneous tasks that make up housework. The frequent interruptions of the television text ... are the textual equivalent of the constant interruptions of housework, and the lack of narrative closure parallels the unending nature of housework.... Feminine work, feminine viewing practices, and feminine texts combine to produce decentered, flexible, multifocused feminine subjectivities. All of these elements are contrasted with male work, masculine texts, and a masculine subjectivity.

I take Fiske's position here to mean not so much that feminine TV texts produce the postmodernist subject but, rather, that a postmodernist construct of subjectivity enables a reading and theoretical explanation of women's relationships within patriarchy (including the relationship to popular culture) as characterized by deferment, interruption, and repetition. After all, women's soap texts and repetitive and unending housework characterized women's lives long before TV and before the theoretical advent of the postmodernist subject.

That is, it is not women's *viewing* that is decentered and open to constant interruptions but, more significantly, women's *lives* are more prone to interruption. Women restructure their lives more frequently around and adapt to the age-specific needs of children, a family move to the male's employment relocation, or altogether new family arrangements as husbands embark on new career ventures. Women's waged and domestic work adapts to the life-cycle of the family — the family does not adapt to her. Most of the women in our sample claimed to have watched more TV while raising young children. Once children had reached school age, many women resumed part- and full-time work which, although it did not alter their domestic and childcare responsibilities, altered their viewing patterns and program preferences. Women's reading/watching and consumption of cultural artefacts (TV, magazines, toys, children's books and homework) follows a different trajectory from that of men. One woman in her forties, recently returned to full-time work as a clerk, reminisced about watching *Sesame Street* with her young children: 'We all watched and enjoyed *Sesame Street*. I wasn't working at that time. We'd all sit up and we'd all watch it and laugh'. Now her sons are 15 and 16, and she has learned to enjoy a three-hour music video program broadcast on Saturday mornings:

> They [i.e. her sons] finally got me around. I've got that way now that we sit, the boys and I and we say, 'What's going to be number one this week?' I watch from about 7 a.m. till 9 a.m. That's my time on Saturday morning to have a couple of cups of coffee and sit and know that I don't have to go to work.

Another woman recalled that, when her son was a baby, she used to watch *Days of Our Lives*, 'not because I wanted to watch it', but it came right after her favorite midday talk show, and coincided with her son's naptime. She too spent three years watching *Playschool* and *Sesame Street* with her son and recalls one year looking desperately for daytime educational programs while she was teaching her son through correspondence.

In rural communities, employment by the railway, telephone company, or self-employment were common among the men in our sample. Working for the railway or telephone company means that men are absent from the household on weekends and in the evenings, due to shiftwork, or they are often away for several days at a time. Self-employed men reportedly spend twelve- to sixteen-hour days in their business premises, which for many includes weekends as well. Women organize their lives and leisure around men's work: men control the TV when they are at home, while women forego their own pleasures. However, when the men are away, women get free reign on their TV pleasures. As the wife of a country veterinarian commented: 'Sometimes he's off and away, so I'll sit down and watch things which I know he wouldn't really bother to watch ... if he's away for two days or something, I'll definitely watch more TV'. In this family, because both wife and husband work at the veterinary clinic, 'we're not normally sitting down and eating until about 8 p.m., which is a bit of a problem because it clashes with TV programs that you want to watch'. Yet the husband gets a headstart on watching TV at 8 p.m., whereas she is busy with 'meal preparations'. This pattern was evident in all the families.

Whereas women tend to organize their lives around their families, husbands and children, by contrast, do not organize their lives around wife/mother. Women's waged work is structured around childbearing and rearing, and the organization of women's leisure, their pursuit of personal interests, their viewing patterns and preferences all stand in secondary relation to husband and children. This positioning of the self extends to self-ascriptions of ignorance about events in the world, indeed events outside the local community, as well as ignorance about use of VCRs or the remote control. Grown women defer to their 4-year-old sons on VCR technical expertise.

Feminine Identity in Family Discourse: Deferment, Exscription, Denial

Gendered power dynamics between husbands and wives were consistently evident in the way men and sons would answer for women, and in women's repeated testimony to their ignorance *in relation* to their husbands. When asked what else she usually does while watching TV, one woman's husband answered for her: 'If you're breastfeeding you'll turn it on'. She claims not to watch news because she's always busy with dinner preparation during the news hour, but her husband keeps her informed of what transpires on the screen: 'He knows what's going on more than me. He gets annoyed with me because I keep asking questions.... I hear nothing and know nothing'. In another family, an 8-year-old son answered for his mother when she was asked what else she does while viewing; he cuts her off with: 'She usually does reading, she sews, goes outside and tends the garden. She watches movies'. Following this, the woman launched into a lengthy explanation defending her viewing. Another man discussed his wife's favourite program this way: 'The old girl likes *Days of Or Lives*, all that bloody crap, which I don't like. If there's nothing good on the commercial station, the old girl puts the tape on to catch up on *Days of Our Lives*'. A man in another family similarly discussed his wife's viewing in her absence: 'she will sit here and do the ironing. Like you can miss two dozen episodes of *Days of Our Lives* and still catch up and I say "Turn that shit off"'. This man also readily admitted that he more or less controls the TV 'a fair percentage of the time. Sound like a real male chauvinist, don't I?' As he sees it, 'when I'm home I want to watch what I want to watch because I'm only home a couple of nights a week sometimes'. When the kids watch programs he doesn't like, 'there again I'm a real stick in the mud, like, "Turn that shit off"'. In other families, too, fathers' control of TV and their 'religious obsession' with news and current affairs programs was explained by reference to 'his big brains' (a comment by an 8-year-old son), a woman confirming that 'at least he knows what's going on in the world', another woman explaining in front of her children why the father wins when conflict arises over program choice: 'well, he wins because he's bigger than us'. In several families, women and children move into other rooms to watch what they want to see on the 'spare' TV because 'his programs' are on the main TV. In another family, the mother commented on her husband's evening monopoly over the family TV, which relocates her children in front of the second set 'where they fight over the TV'.

Womens' explanations of their aversion to news most commonly generated negative comments about themselves. One women explained her dislike of news this way: 'No, I don't watch news or current affairs. Not a newsy type of person. I'd make a boring person, I never know the answers'. Her husband likes *Sale of the Century*, she does crosswords, 'but I don't do it often enough to get anywhere with them.... Don't mind me. My brain doesn't function very well when it's busy'. When asked what else she does while viewing, such as reading, she responds: 'No I do not dare read. I get so busy that if I read I won't put a book down, and then I get behind [with housework], or I don't do what I'm supposed to do. So I have to control myself'. Fear of losing control of domestic routines through reading, because she presumes she might not be able to put the book down, is sad testimony to the kind of internal self-disciplining gaze which keeps her on task with what she's 'supposed' to do: 'I have to control myself'.

News and Weather in the Rural Tropics: Gendered Readings

Women's relationships to and interpretations of TV differ significantly among women, even within what appear as uniform gendered patterns. Among rural women those differences intersect further with specific regional contexts which cannot analytically be subsumed under a general 'rural' variable. All the communities in our study were rural, yet the regional differences among rural towns generate different program preferences and interpretations that are not a function of channel or program availability. The following community is a case in point.

One of the smallest and most isolated communities we visited was a town of a thousand people located on the Coral Sea on the north-eastern Cape York Peninsula. The Cape is Australia's largest rainforest region. It was at the time, and still is, under considerable political conflict between conservationists and developers who propose to establish a space-shuttle port. The town is accessible via air and sea, and the nearest town is a two-hour drive south by four-wheel drive on a ninety-mile gravel road which is impassable during the summer rains. This is cyclone country and people's lives and labour are very dependent upon the weather and accurate weather information. The annual cyclone season brings with it not just storms and rains, but extended rain depressions that wash out roads and landing strips, and that feed the accelerated growth of rainforest reclamations of dirt roads and tracks. The state of the roads, as some men commented, and the ravages of the rains support a relatively large male labour force working on road repair. In this community, weather news rated highly in importance among all respondents: women and men repeatedly linked discussion of various topics to the weather. Unlike other women in our sample, the women in this town all made substantial contributions to discussions about the TV news and weather service, a genre in which few women commonly expressed interest.

For the women in this community, the weather reports often give advance information as to whether school buses will operate or not. As one woman explained: 'We've had our school buses haven't been able to get out for the last three mornings because of that slippery bit of road ... we've only got about ninety miles now that's not asphalt'. For husbands' work, TV weather reports are also important: 'See, it affects his work. He's a plant operator. He's got machinery and sells sand and gravel and stuff and so that has affected him greatly this year. Ever since about January we haven't been able to do much at all because it's too wet'. Like other women we interviewed in this community, she likes watching the 'satellite photo', but 'that probably gives you as much as what you may see'.

In another family, as the discussion turned to favorite programs, the couple launched into a lengthy explanation of how the weather service had improved since the introduction of commercial TV, and how important that information is to them. The husband's explanations are technical: 'we like watching the weather map itself, where the isobars are and plus the satellite photography, where all the cloud is ... the channel has the proper satellite thing and it's in color and you can see the red, and the yellow and the intensity of it'. The woman is more sceptical of the new TV weather service, and takes a less technical approach to her explanations:

> Like, they had us getting 7mm when that cyclone was on, and people in town were getting 50mm, so there's a big difference. The cyclone updates are good, I mean the fact that they put them on often enough, but they're never accurate. We can get a better idea of what's going on by watching that ourselves, and just listening to what they say and thinking 'Oh well, we'll half listen'.

Other women too had much to say about the TV weather service; some commented that they liked the inclusion of the name of their town on the new (commercial station) weather map, and all linked the importance of weather news to family concerns: from school buses and mail delivery, to husbands' work and delivery of supplies. Men, by contrast, discussed the weather news only in terms of their jobs, and tended to discuss weather information in more technical terms. Unlike their husbands, all the women intimated that their own common-sense knowledge and intuition gave them more reliable weather information. As one woman put it, 'You just have to stick your head out the window'.

Mapping the Rural: Differences of Location

Most women in our sample consistently affirmed their dislike of news and current affairs programs. That news programs are 'depressing' was a recurring description. However, most of the women were in fact TV news listeners since their husbands, when they are at home, insist on watching the evening news several times over on different channels. During the news hours, almost all the women are busy with meal preparation in kitchen areas that most commonly adjoin the family eating and TV watching area. Only one family out of twenty-seven had located the TV out of visual range of the kitchen table. News, then, is not a genre that women purposely watch or list as a favorite program.

They do, however, stay tuned into what they find so 'depressing' via husbands' reports, by listening and partial watching.

Given the vagaries of a tropical climate, men's steady employment is not always guaranteed. When men do spend significant periods of time out of work and at home, women's viewing is reorganized around their husbands' presence. In railway towns, similarly, men's long absences seem to increase women's viewing of programs their husbands won't watch, or won't let them watch. Yet, when husbands are home in the evenings and weekends after spending days and weeks on the railroad, women's viewing takes a back seat to men's TV priorities. Yet, in communities such as the one discussed above, where work, transportation, availability of consumer goods, and school for the children is dependent on the weather, women do take an interest in TV news.

Although many women in our sample dismissed the TV weather news as less accurate than their own intuitive assessment gleaned by 'sticking your head out the window', all the women seemed to enjoy watching the weather news, all had much to say about it, and all spoke at length about how the weather affects their lives. In drier inland communities, by contrast, concern about the weather and its effects on everyday life were not raised by any respondents. Much as TV users or viewer interpretations of TV texts vary among subjects of the same age, race, socioeconomic status or educational level, among rural viewers such differences intersect further with specific regional contexts. As our data demonstrated, 'rural' is itself a highly contingent category which subsumes a complexity of geographic and climatic differences which do impinge differently on the lives people lead, and on their relationship to TV.

Feminine Interpretive Communities: TV Talk and Social Networks

Clearly, there are significant variations among the women reported on here, within overall identifiably gendered viewing patterns and preferences, domestic leisure, and relations to childcare and home. The women we interviewed appeared to watch a fair amount of TV that was not of their choosing: from children's programs to husbands' evening program choices. Such TV viewing/listening by default was also evident for the women in our sample whom I did not report on here. In some families, but certainly not in all, women watched more TV and more of the programs they liked in their husbands' absence. When men are present in the evenings and on weekends, working and non-working women give men first priority over program and channel choice.

Most women acknowledged talking about soap operas with their friends. Women tape soaps for their friends, and some call friends long distance: 'if you want to know what's going on ahead of time, ring up people and find out'. Women tend to explain their soap habits in terms other than their own pleasures. One woman projected her pleasure onto her 5-year-old son: 'he sits there and watches it and tells me what happened.... You like Beau and Hope, don't you? He likes Beau. Good bloke, isn't he? I think it's more for the kids'. Another woman tried to disclaim her allegiance to *Days of Our Lives* by directing us to her friend, a 'real' fan: 'I only get to see that once a week.... But my friend Mary said to tell you that she watches it every day ... and *General Hospital*. They're the ones you should have sent your paper [questionnaire] to. She really gets excited about them and she fills me in'. One woman was 'forced' into the soaps because her aunt asked her to tape them, others began watching because it fit in with their daily domestic routines.

Two factors in relation to 'TV talk' are worth noting here. First, Morley found that, unlike the women he interviewed, the men in his sample were reluctant to admit that they talk about TV with friends and workmates. In our sample, this was not the case. Although far more women than men acknowledged TV-related talk at work and with friends, a surprising number of men did in fact acknowledge talking about TV with their 'mates'. Men's reported 'TV talk' ranged from discussion about factual TV (sports, 'interesting' documentaries, news), to fictional TV. As one man commented: 'we've talked at work, because I think we all relate to it, to Bill Cosby. I think he relates to most family situations. There's a couple of them down at work that watch it and they have kids that do exactly the same type of thing'. One man, a grocer, claimed to talk about TV with his customers, most of whom are women. According to several women, men directly and vicariously follow the soaps much like women indirectly stay in touch with the news and current affairs. As one woman put it: 'It's funny you know, all the blokes at work chuck off about the women staying home and watching *Days*, but they all know what's happening, because a couple of weeks ago they were talking about it and they all knew what was happening on *Days*'. She explained that they follow the program by catching up on events on days off, and by asking their wives. Others, like her aunt, tape it and 'watch it at night' when her husband watches with her.

Unlike Morley's study, our interviewer was a woman. I suspect that this generated a radically different gender dynamic in the interview situation which undoubtedly accounts for a number of different features in the interview text, one of which may be men's greater ease of slipping into a feminine discourse. It is possible that men might not readily admit to another male (interviewer) that they talk at work about something as 'trivial' as TV, much less that they follow the soaps. It may be that in the context of a female respondent and female interviewer discussing explicit or assumed shared knowledges (about feminine texts and talk about those texts, about children's viewing, or housework), the male makes the discursive move from outsider to insider by positioning himself as participant in that discourse.

Second, the women in our sample frequently related their viewing of 'women's programs' (e.g. *Days*) to other women's viewing of this and other soaps. Men, by contrast, did not position themselves as part of a viewer community. It seems that because soaps, soap viewing and 'soap talk' are seen as devalued texts and activities by both women and men, women may be aligning themselves with other women in a viewer collective, and thereby 'normalize' what for them clearly are guilty and denigrated pleasures. Aunts, mothers, daughters, friends, all were harnessed into women's explanations of their viewing of soaps. Women volunteered information about swapping soap tapes, taping for others, and 'getting on the phone' (often long-distance). Such an information and friendship network centered on a program or genre was not evident with men, or at least men made no mention of it.

Women's reasons of watching soaps were less concerned with 'social learning' (Brundson, 1982; Modleski, 1983, 1984) and had more to do with escape from boredom and loneliness, and lack of program alternatives given limited channel choice. Clearly, justifying soap watching as a means to learn about how others deal with family and gender relationships and crises does not apply to the rural women we interviewed since their lives, their communities and community cultures are radically different from those portrayed on US soaps. Family life and labor in rural railway towns or the cyclone-prone tropics generate different crises, different social networks and relationships than those encountered by US urban soap opera families. Most of the *Days* viewers in our sample watched it because it was something to do while doing housework or as a break from housework, or because it coincided with children's naptime. Some stated they 'simply love the soaps', they are fun because they are 'not real', or because their friends got them started. The one exception was a woman who displaced her interest in the program to her 5-year-old son by explaining how much he likes the program, and by claiming that 'I think it's more for the kids'. The empty spaces of boredom and loneliness, and the lack of cultural activities afforded sub/urban women, may very well generate a more specific space for fantasy among rural women viewers. Watching US soaps in the Australian rural hinterland can thus be read as generating pleasure through fantasy: 'the imaginary occupation of other subject positions which are outside the scope of ... everyday social and cultural identities' (Ang, 1990: 84).

A View of One's Own: The Gendered Division of Labour and Leisure

Most of the women in our sample discussed their current viewing patterns and preferences in relation to their personal histories. Some spoke of the family's social life and activities in terms of time 'before TV', others recalled different viewing patterns during the years of raising young children. By contrast, none of the men in our sample linked their present TV habits to earlier viewing patterns. Women's confinement to the domestic sphere as a consequence of their role as primary childrearers positions them in historically different relations to TV (if and where it is available) from men. Undoubtedly, wage-earning males retain a similar relation to TV throughout the family's history: that is, their viewing is more consistently regular and regulated by work obligations than that of women. Women, however, move in and out of home and the workforce as a consequence of their childbearing and rearing responsibilities. Thus, in contrast to men, women generally are repositioned between the public and private spheres more frequently in the life-cycle of the family. Women's relation to the objects and patterns of domestic life, of which TV is for many both a domestic appliance and a time-patterning device, are experienced for sustained periods of time which seem to leave a significant impact on women, significant enough that it becomes a recurring theme in discussions about the present. For some, that confinement to the private sphere, to housework, childrearing and daytime TV was a pleasurable experience, while for others it left unpleasant memories.

Women's position in the sexual division of labour — their role in the production and socialization of children — suggests that their relation to time, to their own and their children's history, is markedly different from that of their husbands. In other words, the social relations of women who become mothers are significantly more closely tied to the life-cycle of the family than that of men who become fathers. Among the women in our sample, the non-historicization of their viewing is one facet of feminine identity and re-presentation of the self which mirrors and is formed by the arrival and caretaking period of children. These events position women, unlike men, in the home, often for many years with only TV (or radio) and small children for company. And, as many women recalled, watching preschoolers' TV becomes part of their daily routines for several years. As children grow older, their mothers' viewing changes in tandem; socially 'relevant' programs for family discussion or music video programs displace children's programs. Women's viewing adapts not only to the maturing cognitive and social needs of their children, particularly since it is mothers and not fathers who watch TV with the children for educational purposes and for 'family discussion', but adapts as well to their husband's work patterns and program choices. For instance, several women whose husbands are shiftworkers, reported that they get to watch what they want because husbands are asleep in the evenings: 'then when I'm alone with the TV on I'm doing things like folding ... I turn the TV down very low so as not to disturb him'. One woman had recently surrendered her sewing table to her boys to use as a graphics bench and she had moved her sewing to the kitchen table. This move put her in the crossfire of family activity, noise, as well as TV. Her favorite past-time, sewing ('which takes up a lot of my time'), was repositioned in a traditional move of motherly-feminine selflessness. Because men's relationships to family and family leisure are more consistently structured by the demands and patterns of wage labour, they do not experience the same historically shifting relations to TV as women do.

As Fiske and Morley have pointed out, women's conflated labour-leisure relation to the domestic suggests that 'home' is always 'work' for women, whereas it is a place of domestic refuge and leisure for husband and children. Women's TV viewing, as all the women in our sample confirmed, is something to be done concurrently with other housework (ironing, folding, meal pre-paration) or constructive leisure activities (crocheting, knitting, sewing). Through-out the life-cycle of the family and on a daily basis, women's viewing styles and preferences are decentered, interrupted, and discontinuous. Women's viewing in the context of family life is, therefore, clearly of a quite different kind from that of their husbands. Furthermore, in communities such as the ones we visited, there are no cinemas, no shopping malls, no fitness centres, no public transport, no free-ways or high-rise buildings. All five communities receive only one government and one commercial channel. These communities offer none of the amenities available to urban and suburban middle-class mothers who can divest them-selves of children in fitness and shopping mall childcare centres and then engage in public and collective activities of women's culture such as shopping, aerobics, or social volunteer work. Women in isolated communities have far fewer mass cultural and consumer options available to them. In short, these communities are not high-tech post-modernist spaces. By extension, none of the women held what could be construed as politically feminist, let alone post-feminist, positions. None spoke critically of their gendered position in the context of family life. Although several women seemed to take pleasure in subverting their husbands by watching what they liked when the men are absent, this hardly counts as feminist resistance to or contestation of patriarchal hegemony. TV offers these women a 'window' to a world far removed from their own daily experiences, and also serves as a source of companionship during what for many women were years of childrearing, and evenings and weekends alone with children while husbands were working.

Lessons in Isolation: Schooling without Schools

It seemed commonplace for many rural women that their children leave the household early to go to high school in the nearest center. Unlike the men in our sample, all the women spoke about either their own or their children's schooling. Several spoke of their experience of schooling by correspondence or through School of the Air, and it is possible that many more in our sample received their early schooling without going to school: another early experience in isolation, in learning alone, and learning to be alone. Repeatedly, it seemed that women spend much time alone or with only preschool children and TV for company. Work keeps husbands away evenings and on weekends. Telephone linesmen and railway workers are often away for weeks at a time, as we have seen, and when the men are at home, they take control of 'family viewing'.

One woman recalled the days when she had time to read, when her children were infants: 'It was when you were home all day, and it was such a long time. You know, your jobs are caught up on, your house is clean, and you're sort of just sitting there reading a magazine ... nobody was home to go and visit'. This same woman reminisced about having taught her son through correspondence which, in her estimation, didn't keep him busy enough: 'that was a stage when he sat and watched TV till he was blank'. When he did have access to regular schooling again, 'all he did was rush home to sit in front of the TV and was having trouble getting his homework done'. Several women with older children spoke about losing their children early to schooling in other towns with high schools. One woman compensated for the loss of her children to the nearest high school by taking in a 10-year-old girl boarder during weekdays. This girl had also been schooled through correspondence until her move to this small town to attend elementary school. The woman explained the girl's 'TV addiction' because living in the bush means that children are cut off from the social life of schooling and from TV. This woman too 'did correspondence when I was a child. It's not hard too ... I can remember we had miles of time'. She, like many other women, spoke about the times 'before TV', the times when the family would 'get out the cards or get out the Scrabble or Monopoly or whatever and have a game'. None of the men, but almost all the women in our sample spoke of time before TV.

Rearing and schooling young children is clearly women's work. Rural women's relationship to TV is therefore closely tied to the gendered division of labour which positions women in the home as primary caretakers and teachers of children. The structural position offered women in the Western family extends beyond their gendered relationship to TV and to children. Their active involvement in children's learning (Walkerdine and Lucey, 1989) suggests that women play a far more significant role in children's literacy training than has been acknowledged. Based on what the women in this sample spoke about, and on my own experience with parents in other contexts, it is women who shop for books for their children, women who comprise the majority in parent-teacher organizations (particularly at pre-school and primary levels), and women who engage tirelessly with children's homework (Miller, Nenoianu and DeJong, 1986). The extension of pedagogic discourse to the home includes women's efforts to make televiewing an educational experience for their children. This suggests that research into the home-school connection which bridges school and family literacy needs to take account of women's work in children's education, and also the notion of women as mediators between children and the texts of popular culture.

TV Viewing as Social Practice: Some Implications for Curriculum and Literacy

Reading TV, like reading print, is a socially mediated practice. Ways of reading are always historically and culturally variable, and reading positions are always constructed and socially assigned. There is no 'natural' text or natural way to read or write a text. For many (but admittedly not all) adults and children, the televiewing event occurs in a social grouping, most often a family context. For women in nuclear family formations, their relationship to TV texts and their televiewing practices clearly are circumscribed by the gendered position the patriarchal family structure affords them. The women in this study engaged in televiewing practices with the face-to-face complicity of social subjects: husbands disallow certain programs, programs are watched for the benefit of children, and girlfriends and female relatives make up a viewer community, a social network. The institutional structure of the family locates women in charge of domestic and childcare labour in the home. The organization of family life thus generates gendered domestic labour and leisure practices, including gendered TV practices. Such demarcated gendered televiewing practices, then, position women (TV) readers to construct pleasure out of what is available to them. They watch programs they like when husbands are absent, tape soaps for friends, or call long distance to catch up on the latest soap events, and take charge of their children's 'educational' viewing. Some women look back fondly on years of watching preschool TV or take pleasure in watching rock video programs when they become their children's favorite fare.

Watching TV, like reading print, historically has been conceptualized as a psychological skill, and internal function of mind (Luke, 1990). Even more recent conceptualizations which foreground the resistant viewer, one who 'makes do' with available cultural resources (Fiske, 1990), still locate televiewing as an internal act. It seems to me, however, that there is nothing essential, or cognitively a priori in women's shifting relationships to TV texts. Women, particularly rural women with children in traditional family contexts, are afforded a limited range of popular cultural choices and TV reading positions which are structured through the social relations of domesticity within patriarchy. The women in our sample certainly 'read as women' (Showalter, 1987). That is, they interpreted TV texts, their relation to those texts, and their own identity and everyday experiences as (predictably) women — as the identity of women inserted into the structure and discourse of the family. Their readings as women, it seems to me, thus reflect the power of patriarchal social formations in shaping, if not muting, identity. The women's consistent testimony to their 'ignorance' in contrast to their husbands, and their consistent deferral to husband and children, suggest an identity politics located squarely in the organization of power within family discourse and structure. What, if not self-effacement, exscription, and muted identity, do the following statements suggest: 'He knows what's going on more than me'; 'He gets annoyed with me because I keep asking questions'; 'I hear nothing and know nothing'; 'My brain doesn't function very well when it's busy'; 'No I don't dare read ... I have to control myself'; 'At least he knows what's going on in the world'. We encountered no comparable identity statements from the men in our sample, men whom the family constructs as husbands and fathers in a radically different power and identity discourse.

It is to that powerful discursive formation of 'family', within which motherhood still figures as privileged center, that any critical inquiry into TV gendered audiences must look to map how one dimension of the female viewer — the woman-mother — is constituted, and how she constitutes herself within that discursive network. The socialization of children, particularly daughters, into family discourse and the gendered patterns of popular culture consumption has important implications for theorizing a gender-responsive pedagogy, as well as critical media curriculum. Critical inquiry into educational theory or cultural studies requires accordingly a re-vision of the social, and of the taken-for-granted organizing principles entrenched in theory, conceptual templates and methodologies (Acker, 1989; Smith, 1989, 1990). By a re-vision of the social, I mean that in the current rush to universalize the socio-cultural space of identity formation as a 'postmodernist' site, we must not lose sight of the vast social and geographic terrain which cannot rightfully be labelled as either culturally modernist or postmodernist. These are the spaces of vast rural sectors in the West, and of the millions of Third World villages and inner-city ghettos, none of which can claim identity with the postmodernist moment.

By a re-vision beyond current theory, I mean that we should exercise caution in granting theoretical privilege to the cultural postmodernist subject. We teach the children from these rural sites and theorize pedagogies for them. Although in this study we did not formally set out to study children or schooling, the familial discourses and community spaces we encountered gave us oblique insights into a very different childhood from that conceptualized in traditional and emergent 'postmodernist' educational theorizing (e.g. Giroux and Simon, 1989; Wexler, 1987). Cultural studies run the risk, in my estimation, of subsuming difference once again, of writing over 'others' who are not at the center of our field of vision. I would argue that in the ecstasy of liberation from the tyranny of totalizing metanarratives — in the turn to philosophical postmodernism — we have unwittingly made a wholesale turn to cultural postmodernism as well. The task of re-vision, and the task of a feminist cultural studies based on a philosophical postmodernist standpoint, requires an ongoing commitment to struggle against theoretical incorporation and universalisms (Nicholson, 1990). It requires that we theorize and write identity and location not as a signifier of the same but of *difference*.

If we begin with an epistemology based on difference and theorize difference as foundational to an 'anti-disciplinary' cultural studies, then we can begin to think about school knowledge and literacy pedagogy in a radically different way (Luke, 1991). Such a position acknowledges its position: it does not float uncommitted in a sea of postmodernist theoretical indeterminacy. In line with the feminist project of 'standpoint' — of standing firm on a politics of location —

feminist cultural studies does not disclaim 'foundation'. Instead, it grounds its epistemology on the foundation of *difference*. A construct of difference that extends beyond the monolithic sociological triumvirate of class, race, gender and makes conceptual space for cultural difference in subject location and knowledges renders such a foundation anti-essentialist and indeterminate. The indeterminacy lies in the rejection of unified self-contained knowledges and single-strategy pedagogies. Knowledge and knowing are always provisional, open-ended and relational, which suggests that there are many different access points (and media) for teaching and learning, including that associated with literacy.

In conclusion, what I have been concerned to present in this chapter is a somewhat different view of curriculum and literacy, one which takes more explicitly into account two distinct but related matters: the role and significance of *women* — more specifically, of mothers — and that of *television*, with regard to changing forms of, as well as perspectives on, curriculum and literacy. This involves developing a better understanding of feminine identity politics and family discourse as a significant and even crucial context for literacy pedagogy, as well as for curriculum more generally. As Green (1987: 84) has noted, among others, literacy education proceeds 'overwhelmingly in the company of women', especially in the contexts of early childhood education and primary schooling. Moreover, as Walkerdine (1982, 1986) has argued, there is a striking convergence of domestic and pedagogic discourses in the primary classroom. These arguments need to be supplemented by further investigation of children's cultural contexts and experiences before they come to school, as well as outside school. The environments children grow up in need to be understood therefore as gendered in particular ways, and as characterized by media other than those typically focused on in classrooms, a point which has important implications for their subject-formation as well as for their school learning. A further, final consideration here is that proper account needs to be taken of the difference *within* the category 'women', depending on such considerations as class and geography. As we have seen, the rural women discussed in this chapter were caught up in particular regimes of gender and genre which have a significant impact on their lives, their learning, and their children. Therefore, such matters are of considerable importance for literacy studies and curriculum theorizing.

References

ACKER, J. (1989) 'Making Gender Visible', in WALLACE, R. (Ed.) *Feminism and Social Theory*, London, Sage, pp. 65–81.

AMESLEY, C. (1989) 'How to Watch "Star Trek"', *Cultural Studies*, **3**, 3, pp. 323–39.

ANG, I. (1990) 'Melodramatic Identifications: Television Fiction and Women's Fantasy', in BROWN, M.E. (Ed.) *Television and Women's Culture: The Politics of the Popular*, Beverly Hills, CA, Sage, pp. 75–88.

BAUDRILLARD, J. (1988) *Selected Writings*, edited by POSTER, M., Cambridge, Polity, Press.

BROWN, M.E. (Ed.) (1990) *Television and Women's Culture: The Politics of the Popular*, Beverly Hills, CA, Sage.

BRUNDSON, C. (1981) '"Crossroads": Notes on Soap Opera', *Screen*, **22**, 4, pp. 32–37.

FISKE, J. (1987) *Television Culture*, London, Methuen.

FISKE, J. (1990) *Understanding Popular Culture*, Winchester, MA, Unwin Hyman.

FOUCAULT, M. (1972) *The Archeology of Knowledge*, New York, NY, Harper and Row.

GAME, A. (1989) 'Research and Writing: Secretaries and Bosses', *Journal of Pragmatics*, **13**, 3, pp. 343–62.

GIROUX, H. and SIMON, R. (Eds) (1989) *Popular Culture, Schooling and Everyday Life.* Granby, MA, Bergin and Garvey.

GREEN, B. (1987) 'Gender, Genre and Writing Pedagogy', in REID, I. (Ed.) *The Place of Genre in Learning: Current Debates* (Centre for Studies in Literary Education: Typereader Publications No. 1) Geelong, Deakin University Press, pp. 83–90.

GROSSBERG, L. (1984) 'I'd Rather Feel Bad Than Not Feel Anything at All: Rock and Roll, Pleasure and Power', *Enclitic*, **8**, pp. 94–111.

HARVEY, D. (1989) *The Condition of Postmodernity*, Oxford, Blackwell.

HOBSON, D. (1990) 'Women Audiences and the Workplace', in BROWN, M.E. (Ed.) *Television and Women's Culture: The Politics of the Popular*, Beverly Hills, CA, Sage, pp. 61–71.

LUKE, C. (1987) 'Television, Children, and Socialization: Demystifying the Relationship', *Educational Research and Perpectives*, **14**, 2, pp. 85–99.

LUKE, C. (1989) *Television and Your Child*, Sydney, Angus and Robertson.

LUKE, C. (1990) *Constructing the Child Viewer*, New York, NY, Praeger Press.

LUKE, C. (1991) 'On Reading the Child: A Feminist Poststructuralist Perspective', *Australian Journal of Reading*, **14**, **2**, pp. 109–16.

LUKE, A. and LUKE, C. (1990) 'School Knowledge as Simulation: Curriculum in Postmodern Conditions', *Discourse*, **10**, 2, pp. 75–91.

MILLER, P., NENOIANU, A. and DEJONG, J. (1986) 'Early Reading at Home: Its Practice and Meaning in a Working Class Community', in GILMORE, P. and SCHEFFELIN, B. (Eds) *The Acquisition of Literacy: Ethnographic Perspectives*, Norwood, NJ, Ablex, pp. 3–15.

MODLESKI, T. (1983) 'The Rhythms of Reception: Daytime Television and Women's Work', in E.A. KAPLAN, (Ed.) *Regarding Television*, Los Angeles, CA, American Film Institute, University Publications of America, pp. 67–75.

MODLESKI, T. (1984) *Loving with a Vengeance: Mass Produced Fantasies for Women*, London, Methuen.

MORLEY, D. (1986) *Family Television: Cultural Power and Domestic Leisure*, London, Comedia.

MORRIS, M. (1990) 'Banality in Cultural Studies', in MELLENCAMP, P. (Ed.) *Logics of Television: Essays in Cultural Criticism*, Bloomington, IN, Indiana University Press, pp. 14–43.

NICHOLSON, L. (Ed.) (1990) *Feminism/Postmodernism*. New York, NY, Routledge.

PROBYN, E. (1990) 'New Traditionalism and Post-Feminism: TV Does the Home', *Screen*, **31**, 2, pp. 147–59.

SHOWALTER, E. (1987) 'Critical Cross-Dressing: Male Feminists and the Woman of the Year', in JARDINE, A. and SMITH, P. (Eds) *Men in Feminism*, New York, NY, Methuen, pp. 116–32.

SMITH, D. (1989) 'Sociology Theory: Methods of Writing Patriarchy', in WALLACE, R. (Ed.) *Feminism and Sociological Theory*, London, Sage, pp. 34–64.

SMITH, D. (1990) *The Conceptual Practices of Power: A Feminist Sociology of Knowledge*, Boston, MA, Northeastern University Press.

WALKERDINE, V. (1982) 'Sex, Power and Pedagogy', *Screen Education*, 38, pp. 14–25.

WALKERDINE, V. (1986) 'Progressive Pedagogy and Political Struggle', *Screen*, **27**, 5, pp. 54–60.

WALKERDINE, V. and LUCEY, H. (1989) *Democracy in the Kitchen: Regulating Mothers and Socialising Daughters*, London, Virago.

WEXLER, P. (1987) *Social Analysis of Education: After the New Sociology*, London, Routledge and Kegan Paul.

Chapter 11

Literacy Studies and Curriculum Theorizing; or, The Insistence of the Letter

Bill Green

Strings of language extend in every direction to bind the world into a rushing, ribald whole.

Donald Barthelme

Introduction: Reading Writing Lessons

Consider the following: two accounts of literacy lessons, brief images, snapshots taken from the curriculum history of primary schooling in Australia, in this last decade of the twentieth century. The first is taken from a student-teacher's report on his School-Experience placement in a combined year one/two class, in the first half of 1990:

> [I]n a normal lesson Judith [the teacher] will firstly have the children offering to her the appropriate letter of the day. The children are then given the opportunity to read this letter and then express a number of sentence options highlighting the letter. Judith draws on these to derive the sentence of the day. Next the sentence is gone through as a class orally, and an opportunity for queries on related questions is given. Finally the children are set to task with a concentration placed upon taking the necessary time for completion and pride in neatness and appearance of work.

Another student-teacher, from the same Language Education course and similarly in the second year of her primary teacher education programme, wrote the following:

> In the 'Language' classes, I found the teacher would draw a lot of the information for the work from the children. For example I remember a lesson which focused on the capital letter M being correctly written. The teacher opened the lesson by having the children tell her how to draw the letter. She began with the very basic steps, asking where to start,

where to put the first line. When the letter was completed, the class was asked as a whole if they thought it was right. Most said yes, but there were a few who were unsure. One of the children who had doubt came out and wrote what they thought was correct on the board. It was wrong, but the action of trying was reinforced by the teacher: 'Thank you, for having a go'. After the correct form was established (this turned out to be a mixture of what was on the board), the teacher went onto ask for words beginning with the letter, drawing on the children's knowledge of its use. They were then given the task of practising the letter by writing down the words they came up with. In writing the words on the board that the children gave, the teacher gave them a say in that they were doing, allowed them to create, to be involved, instead of just being the observers.

She was referring to a class combining grades five and six — that is, 10 and 11 year-olds in the Australian education system, for some of whom this was their last year before making the transition to high school. Two scenarios, then, at the beginning and end of primary schooling, in an age of educational Enlightenment.

It would be far too easy to simply dismiss these accounts, drawn from different primary schools, as indicating either an anomaly or an anachronism — not to mention the uninformed reportage of novices. Certainly such 'snapshots' do less than justice to what is always a much more complex and dynamic classroom reality. However, they are powerfully illustrative, all the same, of what I believe to be a common enough experience in many contemporary classrooms. There is much that might be considered in these accounts; for instance, their contradictory eclecticism with regard to behaviourist and constructivist epistemologies, and the curious intermixing of child-centredness and a traditionalist transmission pedagogy — not that this is unexpected or all that unusual (e.g. Boomer [in press]). Here, however, what I want to focus on is the *image* that animates them, and hence their evocativeness with regard to the concept-metaphor that informs and organizes this book: the insistence of the letter.

Both involve teaching to the letter, literally; or rather, an insistence *on* the letter. Teaching and learning here are presented as organized around a particular version of alphabetic literacy, and already the seeds are sown for the discursive construction of a distinctive school subjectivity. What, we may well ask, are the *untaught* lessons in curricular experiences such as these, those lessons that inscribe themselves all the more forcefully on the learning body because they constitute the 'normal' course of schooling, and thus become second nature, writing and rewriting the school-subject, the body-subject: the Subject of culture and schooling? Here, curriculum and literacy are so intertwined, each so intimately entering into and informing the other, that in effect they are inextricable. Indeed they always are, even though this is all too often obscured in our institutionalized habits of thinking about things, our disciplinary practices and the forms of our enquiry and our praxis, in classrooms and in the academy.

In mainstream literacy studies and curriculum research alike, an assumption all too often made is that history may be read relatively unproblematically, in terms of the inexorable march of progress and the rational movement towards 'truth'. Recently, critical-revisionist historical work has forcefully challenged this view, however, understanding it as symptomatic of what Luke (1989: 2) describes as 'the modernist discourse of educational reform'. What is striking in these emblematic accounts, then, from a curriculum-historical and critical-reconcept-ualist point of view, are the traces of pedagogies and educational ideologies long held to have been well and truly superseded, in accordance with the evolu-tion of educational science, and hence the persistence of the past in the practices of the present. For instance, as Monaghan and Saul (1987: 99) indicate, in colonial New England '[t]he basic unit of instruction was the letter'; 'literacy learning was held to proceed incrementally, from small units (the letters of the alphabet) to large ones (sentences)'. Further: 'Successful reading was the faithful reproduction, orally, of what the writer had written' (Monaghan and Saul, 1987: 95), within a largely Calvinist educational-ideological framework, based on repetition and discipline; 'writing, at least in the sense of penmanship, was similarly hard work in colonial America. Mastery of the pen was to be achieved by constant repetition — namely, copying' (Monaghan and Saul, 1987: 96). Later, under the influence of the education progressivism movement largely associated with John Dewey, emphasis was placed increasingly on matters of experience and meaning, and '[t]he basic unit of instruction' became 'the whole word'. Even so, what emerged as the dominant *procedural* discourse in American literacy education was the psycho-scientific perspective which Monaghan and Saul (1987: 96) describe as 'the "scientific" approach to education with its attendant measurement move-ment'.[1] What counted, in the final analysis, was what could be quantified and measured, in accordance with the principle of 'prescriptive technology' (Franklin, 1990: 18) and its congruence with 'industrial' models of literacy education. As noted elsewhere (Bigum and Green, 1992/in press): Central defining features in such technologies are 'what they [mean] in terms of discipline and planning, of organization and command', and their congruence with new social and industrial 'need[s] for precision, prescription and control' (Franklin, 1990: 23).

Significantly, Monaghan and Saul note that this increasingly dominant perspective faced particular difficulties with regard to writing pedagogy princi-pally because 'composition' was not easily amenable to a behaviouristic account. Given this, '[i]t is hardly surprising that the measurers turned their attention towards those aspects of writing that were more amenable to objective measure-ment', and hence '[h]andwriting, historically one of the earliest of the ways in which writing had been viewed, was also the earliest aspect of writing to be measured' (Monaghan and Saul, 1987: 99). This has continued to the present day, of course, with the focus in 'Back to Basics' campaigns, emphasizing testing as they invariably do, being overwhemingly on matters of so-called 'visible inadequacy' in literacy competence, namely spelling, punctutation, presentation skills and the like.

With reference to literacy education in Australia from the colonial period on, Christie (1990: 4) observes that typically 'the teaching of literacy had sought to do no more than develop very basic capacities indeed' (see also Christie, this volume). As she indicates, referring more specifically to the first half of this century:

> The first years of a primary education were devoted to copying first letters, then words, then simple phrases and sentences. Once children had learned these, they graduated to learning the parts of speech and to parsing, while sentence analysis, considered an advanced activity

appropriate to the later stages of cognition, belonged to the upper
primary school and the secondary school (Christie, 1990: 6)

Here we can see very clearly the configurations of what Hoskin (1979, 1990) has
described as the structure of 'rational schooling', quintessentially 'a hierarchical
system', in Goodson's (1988: 35) terms. As Christie goes on to write:

> Overall, literacy was developed through a series of measured stages in
> school learning, so that the learner could move from the smaller to the
> larger units of language. Learning to read involved learning to recognize
> the alphabet and exercising the letters firstly in monosyllabic, later poly-
> syllabic, words before graduating to reading phrases and/or sentences
> more remarkable for their lack of sense than otherwise. The class readers
> consitututed the major reading material even for those students who
> stayed at primary school for the full period, enjoying the relative advan-
> tages in control of literacy that this conferred. For most of the primary
> school years, writing consisted of copying improving expressions,
> chosen both for their moral uplift and for the opportunity they afforded
> to perfect handwriting skills. Composition, to the extent that children
> practised it at all, involved writing formal letters or short improving
> features on moral themes (Christie, 1990: 6–7).

Sometimes it is difficult not to feel that little has really changed in the ensuing
period, despite the enormous research and administrative efforts that have
characterized the twentieth century, perhaps most particularly in the area of literacy pedagogy and policy. In fact, of course much *has* changed, and it would be
quite erroneous simply to dismiss the subsequent work of literacy researchers and
educators, or to view it as essentially misguided, given the supposedly overween-
ing constraints of power and ideology conceived as *necessarily* prior considerations
in the critical sociology of schooling. Much has been achieved in recent times,
often within so-called 'progressivist' frames, in terms of what has been described
as a practice-based politics of possibility, based on the notions of curriculum
power, critical pedagogy and classroom production (Burgess, 1984; Hardcastle,
1985; see also Lankshear, 1989). It is also undeniable, however, that there are
certainly powerful regularities in the historical discourse of curriculum and
schooling, and these must be accounted for. One such persistent motif is the
image of the 'letter', related to which is the way in which literacy pedagogy and
school learning more generally are fundamentally organized around and by the
'text', operating as both the object of attention and the principal means of
educational discipline.

Derrida (1976) has written eloquently of what he calls 'The Violence of the
Letter', arguing that violence is not to be conceived as something that is imposed
upon language, in all its essential innocence; rather, that what must be
acknowledged is 'the originary violence of a language which is always a writing'
(Derrida, 1976: 106). His concern here, as elsewhere, is with the problematical
relationship between the double binaries of speech/writing and nature/culture —
arguably central not just to Western culture, as in his analysis, but to the project
of modern(ist) schooling as well. He focuses his concerns on Levi-Strauss and

Rousseau, the latter figure of course being one much discussed in the discourse on education, and often evoked in direct relation to literacy education (e.g. Willinsky, 1990). As he writes:

> Rousseau and Levi-Strauss are not for a moment to be challenged when they relate the power of writing to the exercise of violence. But radicalizing this theme, no longer considering this violence as *derivative* with respect to a naturally innocent speech, one reverses the entire sense of a proposition — the unity of violence and writing — which one must therefore be careful not to abstract and isolate (Derrida, 1976: 106).

What interests me here is his account of Levi-Strauss' anthropological work among the Nambikwara, and hence the introduction of another side to the 'colonialism' to which I have already referred. He focuses his discussion on Levi-Strauss' text 'A Writing Lesson', an account of the introduction of writing into a previously 'illiterate' tribe, noting how this represented a fundamental, exemplary act of violence not only on the part of Levi-Strauss himself, but also, paradoxically, inscribed in the very nature of representation and human existence. Describing the 'Writing Lesson' as 'an episode in what may be called the anthropological war, the essential confrontation that opens communication between people and culture, even when that communication is not practised under the banner of colonial or missionary oppression', he observes that [t]he entire "Writing Lesson" is recounted in the tones of violence repressed or deferred, a violence sometimes veiled, but always oppressed and heavy' (Derrida, 1976: 107). He reflects on Levi-Strauss' account of the violence enacted by the West, by anthropology and by writing on 'the "lost world" of the Nambikwara'. His reading, therefore, of 'The Writing Lesson' is a parable of the nexus between literacy and violence, symbolic and otherwise, and of the nature of writing itself as the very condition of meaning and value:

> writing as the possibility of the road and of difference, the history of writing and the history of the road, of the rupture, of the *via rupta*, of the path that is broken, beaten, *fracta*, of the space of reversibility and of repetition traced by the opening, the divergence from, and the violent spacing, of nature, the natural, savage, salvage, forest (Derrida, 1976: 107–108).

Writing, that is, as an act of 'penetration', a violation of what Levi-Strauss presents in the Nambikwara as an image of natural goodness and harmony, of nature (Nature?) itself. Crucially, what characterizes these people, in Levi-Strauss' account, is that they are presented as a people 'without writing' (Derrida 1976: 110), and thus representative in a certain, somewhat qualified sense of 'the childhood of our race' (Derrida, 1976: 108).

This brings us to two symptomatic scenes, in the tableaux I am presenting here. In the first, the anthropologist is watching children playing when something happens which throws the culture into an entirely new light:

> One day, when I was playing with a group of children, a little girl was struck by one of her comrades. She ran to me for protection and began to whisper something, a 'great secret', in my ear. As I did not understand

I had to ask her to repeat it over and over again. Eventually her adversary found out what was going on, came up to me in a rage, and tried in her turn to tell me what seemed to be another secret. After a while I was able to get to the bottom of the secret. The first girl was trying to tell me her enemy's name, and when the enemy found out what was going on she decided to tell me the other girl's name, by way of reprisal. Thenceforth it was easy enough, though not very scrupulous, to egg the children on, one against the other, till in time I knew all their names (Levi-Strauss, cited in Derrida, 1976: 111).

As Levi-Strauss further indicates, he then went on to get 'the adult's names too', since 'we were all, in a sense, one another's accomplices'. The significance of this is two-fold: first, not only is there a specific relationship to be observed between writing and the proper name, but also a politics in writing and naming; and second, this can be seen as an exemplary image of primary schooling and of schooling more generally, both historically (e.g. Hunter, 1987) and contemporaneously, as indicated in the scenes of pedagogy with which I opened this chapter.

The second scene — also powerfully evocative of the primary classroom — involves the leader of the tribe in question, a man who 'saw further into the problem' when, as Levi-Strauss notes, the villagers began imitating his acts of writing:

Then, one day, I saw that they were all busy drawing wavy horizontal lines. What were they trying to do? I could only conclude that they were writing — or, more exactly, they were trying to do as I did with my pencils. As I had never tried to amuse them with drawings, they could not conceive of any other use for this implement. With most of them, that was as far as they got: but their leader saw further into the problem. *Doubtless he was the only one among them to have understood what writing was for* (cited in Derrida, 1976: 122, my emphasis).

What this is, how it is understood by the chief, is later revealed as intimately associated with power and status, and the secret scarcity of knowledge; as a matter of difference and distinction, and a way of maintaining sovereignty.[2]

Admittedly, the chief cannot 'write', in the conventional sense at least; yet what he does do, in mimicking the actions of writing, in going through the motions as he sees them — as he *reads* them — in the writing activity of the anthropologist, is emblematic of the power of writing and the writing of power. In effect, he *is* writing. Derrida's summary statement of what is to be read in the 'Writing Lesson' — at least as it understands itself — is appropriately cited here:

Lesson in a double sense. The title effectively preserves both senses. Writing lesson because it is a question of the learning of writing. The Nambikwara chief learns writing from the anthropologist, at first without comprehension, he mimics writing before he understands its functions as language; or rather he understands its profoundly enslaving function before understanding its function, here accessory, of communication, signification, of the tradition of a signified. But the writing lesson is also a lesson learned from writing; instruction that the anthropologist believes he can induce from the incident in the course of a long meditation, when, fighting against insomnia, he reflects on the origins, function, and meaning of writing. Having taught the gesture of writing to a Nambikwara chief who learned without comprehension, the anthropologist understands what he had taught and induces the lesson of writing (Derrida, 1976: 122).

What might be the lessons to be noted here? First, Levi-Strauss radically misrepresents the situation, investing it with a pervasive nostalgia that stems basically from a metaphysics of speech and presence, and in effect a refusal of 'writing' as such. This is a matter to be understood within the terms of Derrida's critique of Western logocentric culture and epistemology. Second, and importantly, there is much to be read into this text as an allegory of the relations between curriculum and literacy, and of primary schooling and literacy pedagogy in particular. There are not only teasing echoes of a whole range of ideologies and practices — including, for instance, 'invented spelling', or the initiation rites of various introductions into the culture of literacy, from 'rote learning' and 'modelling' to the apprenticeship and training regimes associated with genre pedagogy, as well as the 'reflective practitioner'. Also foregrounded here is the very significance of writing and the letter, in terms of the general metaphysics and the disciplinary economy of schooling, in a culture of logocentric rationality. These broad issues raise a number of implications and consequences for literacy studies and curriculum theorizing, and this is what I shall now turn to, in elaborating on various themes in these adjacent and intersecting fields of research and praxis. In the next section, I shall consider various versions of the letter in curriculum and schooling, on the way to an educationalist assessment of recent 'postmodernist' initiatives in cultural studies and critical theory.

The Linguistic Turn: Schooling (and) the Letter

The cultural role and significance of language — and more generally, following Donald (1985), the symbolic order — needs to be better understood, expressly in educational terms. This can be usefully described as marking a distinctive 'linguistic turn' in curriculum theorizing and literacy studies, paralleling developments and initiatives of a similar kind in the wider sphere of social and cultural theory. The most important register of this has been an increased awareness of the relation between language and education, both pedagogically and institutionally. This has manifested itself, on the one hand, in the 'language-across-the-curriculum' movement — a matter worthy of curriculum research in its own right, but which has surprisingly received little formal attention to date — and on the other, in heightened sociological interest in questions of social structuration and cultural transmission, specifically in relation to education.

A crucial consideration here is the significance of 'reproduction' as a distinctive concept in recent curriculum and social theory. 'Reproduction' clearly has been a matter of considerable concern in curriculum studies since the early 1970s, particularly among neo-Marxist and socially-critical educational researchers, following the English publication of Althusser's 'Ideology and Ideological State Apparatuses' essay in 1971, but arguably increasingly a central concept in the

201

sociology of education more generally, bearing as it does significantly on the crucial cultural and educational problem of intergenerational continuity and change. In the debates around the concept of 'reproduction', including its critique and transformation, what has tended to receive much less explicit attention than it warrants is the role and significance of literacy, and the relationship between literacy and schooling. A notable exception to this is the work of Giroux (1983, 1989) and Luke (1988), although it is also notable that the overwhelming orientation in much of this work to date has been on what Giroux originally termed 'reproductive literacy' and what for Luke and others has been a primary focus on 'ideological critique'. Importantly, the 'reproductionist' thesis in its various formulations cannot be dissociated from considerations of language and ideology; and, further, it has been largely based on a extremely problematical understanding of each of these. Donald (1985: 241) suggests something of what is involved here when he notes a 'tension between the two strands' in Althusser's essay, one focused on 'the axiomatic link between ideology and the reproduction of the relations of production' and the other notions of 'interpellation' and 'subjectivity', with reference made here in particular to the work of the French psychoanalyst Jacques Lacan. As he observes:

> It is the first strand of Althusser's work which has generally been taken up in sociological studies of education. The result has been a step back from the unstable, fragmentary subject of interpellation to the coherent, self-conscious subject of an unruffled socialization functioning to reproduce the social order (Donald, 1985: 242).

Although it is a matter which cannot be elaborated on here, I suggest that the 'break' in question can be usefully discussed in terms of the different perspectives of 'modernism' and 'post-modernism' respectively, related to which is a shift from 'reproduction' to 'representation' as an organizing principle for curriculum research and critical pedagogy. Nonetheless, the significance of the 'reproduction' thesis with regard to understanding the relationship between curriculum and literacy should be neither underestimated nor overlooked.

Given the premises and problems of the 'reproduction' thesis, then, what can be said about literacy pedagogy? One is the well-documented priority of reading over writing, in terms of both research and pedagogy (Resnick and Resnick, 1988; Monaghan and Saul, 1987; Lankshear with Lawler, 1987). As Monaghan and Saul (1987: 91) write:

> [H]owever variously reading and writing has been defined, it still remains the case that reading, even when oral, is the receptive skill (for reading aloud is only pronouncing what someone else has written), while writing is the productive skill. This distinction is relevant when the question of control is considered. The curriculum is, at least in part, the formal statement of what society believes is important for students to know. Society has focused on children as readers because, historically, it has been much more interested in children as receptors rather than producers of the written word.

Levine (1986: 41–42) similarly notes 'the omission of writing in all but its most rudimentary forms' in most literacy programmes, describing it as 'a powerful and distinctive medium of self-expression and self-reflection' and as possessing 'great potential for recording *and conveying* innovation, dissent and criticism' (my emphasis). Even more trenchantly, Emig (1983: 174) observes the following: 'One possibility is that being asked to stay within the constraints of another's text, or at least a single interpretation of the text, can perhaps be a training in docility that can well serve any religious, political or aesthetic majority'. The political implication of what is, unquestionably, a devaluing of active writing pedagogy in the history of schooling should therefore be patently clear. This is further highlighted when school writing in what might be called its normative form is considered: a regime of copying and regurgitation, within a closed, highly regulated curriculum economy, one which is in essence the embodiment of 'reproduction' pedagogy. Furthermore, what is at issue here is not just the daily repetition of regularized activities, legislated fields and modes of writing, and hence the (re)production of school subjectivities in accordance with the 'lines marked out by social distances, oppositions and struggles' (Foucault, 1981: 64), but also, importantly, the production of disciplined bodies. We need only recall here the strenuous physical efforts involved in the early acquisition of writing on the part of young children, or the choregraphic pedagogies traditionally associated with the development of handwriting abilities.[3]

Such considerations are further strengthened as matters of concern in terms of the interface between literacy studies and curriculum theorizing when the focus shifts to the concept of curriculum itself, and relatedly, to recent developments and initiatives in the field of curriculum studies. Although it has rarely been remarked upon in these terms, there is good reason, I suggest, for viewing these within the framework of 'the linguistic turn', or at least a particular version of it. It is important to see the concept of curriculum expressly in critical-reconceptualist terms, so as to draw in a range of new perspectives and developments in recent social, cultural and educational theory, and in particular to enable contemporary post-structuralist research to inform curriculum research and enquiry (Weedon, 1987; Cherryholmes, 1988: Lather, 1991). Curriculum must be understood specifically as a *social practice*, and hence notions of discourse, subjectivity, power and ideology become of particular relevance in and for appropriate and congruent forms of curriculum theorizing. Curriculum also needs to be conceived within the terms of cultural transmission and ideological communication, and as comprising three intricated message-systems: *school knowledge* (including school-subjects and related issues of disciplinarity, as well as the notions of 'syllabus' and the textbook), *pedagogy*, and *assessment* (Bernstein, 1975). Each involves a specific discourse, and each contributes, sometimes conflictually, to the (re)production of school subjectivities and the construction of distinctive regimes of subject-positionings, as well as the organization of social relations more generally. What needs to be recognized, however, is that such a view of curriculum locates it firmly within the frameworks of semiotics and discourse theory, within a new social-theoretical paradigm.

Here, Bernstein's somewhat ambivalent affinities with the (post-)structuralist tradition become pertinent, not just with regard to the relationship of his work to neo-Althusserianism and the problems and perspectives of the reproductionist thesis, but also, perhaps even more pertinently, the links to be observed between Bernstein and Foucault (Atkinson, 1985).[4] This is indicated, for instance, in formulations such as the following from Foucault (1981: 64): 'What,

after all, is an education system, other then a ritualization of speech, a qualification and a fixing of the roles for speaking subjects, the constitution of a
doctrinal group, however diffuse, a distribution and an appropriation of discourse
with its powers and knowledges?' This expanded sense of curriculum obviously
also expands the possibilities for curriculum theorizing; however, it will be
important not to lose sight of the *specificity* of curriculum and the curriculum
concept, as a unique site for the play of cultural politics and ideological struggle,
in and through specific teaching practices and forms of student learning, as well as
a distinctive theoretical object in and for educational and social theory.

What needs to be further noted, however, is that each of Bernstein's 'message-systems' involves specific forms of realization of language and semiosis, and
in particular, each needs to be recognized in its relation to *written* language. This
is perhaps most readily apparent in the case of school knowledge, as recent
research by Goodson (1988) and others makes abundantly clear. Of particular
relevance here is the conceptualization of the school-subject. As Goodson (1988:
7) writes: 'The written curriculum is part of the complex nature of institutionalized state schooling'. Further, writing understood in these terms is closely
linked to considerations of prescription and control:

> The state, when playing a part in developing schooling, was perhaps
> unlikely to initiate classrooms as sites of uncontrolled action; this was
> particularly the case as schooling moved from being an elite enterprise to
> a mass educational endeavour. State schooling and mass clienteles
> presaged detailed attempts to control the content and form of classroom
> life; initially through attempts ... at the definition of pedagogy and the
> subjectivity of teachers, but soon by prescribing written curriculum.
> Curriculum [i.e. school knowledge] developed in this way, is institu-
> tionalized and, subsequently, allied to an examination system.

As he concludes: 'The definition of written curriculum for subsequent classroom
realization developed in a manner which provided elements and mechanisms for
directing and controlling the activity of schooling' (Goodson, 1988: 7). Crucial to
this argument is the emergence of the school-subject and the disciplinary
organization of school knowledges: 'In the modern era we are essentially dealing
with the *curriculum as subject*' (Goodson, 1988: 29).

Equally tied to written language, however, is the system of assessment. This
needs to be understood in terms both of the institutionalization of a system of
examinations, especially those associated with formal credentialling and 'rites of
passage' between different levels of schooling and between schooling and society,
and of what might be described as technologies of testing and measurement more
generally. As Hoskin (1979) has argued, the role of the 'examination' in what he
calls 'rational schooling' is inseparable from Foucault's concept of *discipline*, and
constitutes and contributes to one form of what Foucault (1977: 191) describes
as 'a network of [disciplinary] writing', whereby populations and cohorts are
created, organized and controlled, and relatedly, individuals are brought within
the ambit of the Law. A more recent observation by Hoskin (1990) is particularly
apposite here, given the identification of mass compulsory state-subsidized
schooling with a particular emphasis on, and realization of, written language.
Noting that the convention of the examination was in evidence prior to its

incorporation into the modern schooling system, he distinguishes between the previous formalized examination and its modern counterpart in the following terms:

> The difference between them is that the former was an oral form of examination, primarily, and the assessment made was on a qualitative as opposed to a quantitative basis. Written examination and arithmetical marks appear to develop, and then to predominate, from around 1800. The change in format and technology is decisive. Only the modern modes of testing activate the full power of writing (where everyone is required to write in order to demonstrate the inner truth about themselves) while putting an objective numerical value upon and inside you (Hoskin, 1990: 46).

The links between writing and assessment, including testing, formal and otherwise, have been well documented. This then is one form of the insistence of the letter, deeply inscribed in curriculum and schooling in the modern(ist) era.

'Disciplinary writing' is manifestly pertinent to school knowledge and assessment as discursive-regulative regimes. The system of pedagogy, on the other hand, would certainly appear less oriented to writing and to written language, and more emphatically oriented to the realm of speech, especially given the nature of 'the modern classroom system', in Hamilton's (1980) terms, and the primary interactive character of pedagogic relations and of teaching-learning conceived as quintessentially a 'face-to-face encounter'. It is true that a different relation between speech and writing may be observed in pedagogy, and that there tend to be 'speech-like' forms of interactivity and dialogue in classroom practice in the ordinary course of daily lessons. However, the degree of 'freedom' in the speech-events of the classroom should not be overestimated, since not only do the other interlocking systems of knowledge and assessment act as significant constraints on pedagogy, but normative classroom exchange itself is highly influenced by the features of written language. This pertains not only to the persistence of the 'recitation' and the overwhelming predominance of teacher talk and whole-class 'simultaneous instruction' (Hamilton, 1989), but also the characteristic structure of classroom discourse (Sinclair and Coulthard, 1975), echoing as it does the tripartite structure of schooling as a semiotic system and hence the discursive-regulative practice of curriculum itself. Burgess (1988: 133) notes, in this regard, 'the rock-like stability of classroom exchange (teacher initiates, pupil responds, teacher gives feedback), whatever may be the implications of curriculum innovation or of new accounts of language development'. He later suggests that, notwithstanding the much-welcomed and renewed emphasis in recent times on 'the importance of talk to learning' — an emphasis directly associated with the 'language and learning' movement — attention needs to be given to the relationship between talk and writing as regards to both student learning and cultural transmission, and to the question 'whether or not presuppositions about literacy and about the forms of written language are not central determinants in the systems of classroom communication which have typically been developed' (Burgess, 1988: 135).

This point is similarly emphasized by Halliday (1990) who suggests that popular misconceptions about the nature of speech and writing, particularly as they manifest themselves in educational settings and forums, rest to a significant degree on the more or less uninformed privileging of written grammaticality over that associated with speech genres: among other things,

> if you ... analyze both varieties [i.e. speech and writing] in terms of a logic and grammar that were constructed out of, and for the purposes of, written language in the first place — you will have guaranteed in advance that written language will appear more orderly and more elaborately structured than spoken (Halliday, 1990: 8)

— and by implication, more 'rational' as well. He also emphasizes the distinctions which must be made between what he calls, here and elsewhere, 'educational knowledge' and 'common-sense knowledge':

> Common-sense knowledge is typically transmitted in the home; it tends to be spoken, non-technical, informal, without boundaries, and with some room for discretion on the part of the child learner, who can take it or leave it. Educational knowledge usually comes packaged by the school; and it differs in these five ways: it is written, technical, formal, with strong boundaries and with much less discretion on the part of the learner (Halliday, 1988: 11).

The crucial point to draw from this is that school knowledge is characteristically associated with the written mode, with *writing*, and this pertains not just to school-subjects, syllabus statements and textbooks but also to student learning itself, conceived as becoming 'disciplined' and hence socialized into the cultural and semiotic fields of formal school knowledges and subject-specific literacies. That is, in accordance with the design of institutionalized education, the subject of schooling is also the subject of writing; schooling 'writes' the subject — or rather, schooling involves the production, in and through writing, of what Lather (1989: 17) describes as 'the subject-ed subject'. This is, of course, far too pessimistic and deterministic a view of pedagogy, as I shall indicate at a later point in this discussion; for the moment, however, it is consistent with my concern here to stress the insistence of written textuality and its associated epistemologies and effects in curriculum, and its significance in schooling more generally.

Approaching (Post-)Modernism

Developments such as these, which involve a reassessment of the significance of written language and the forms of symbolic power associated with normative schooling, may be usefully further conceived in terms of a rather different understanding of the 'linguistic turn' in curriculum theorizing, linked to and paralleling a similar movement in recent developments in philosophy, social theory and cultural scholarship. Lather (1989) refers to this, following Ihab Hassan, as the 'postmodern turn', while for Giroux (1990: 23), arguing for a reconceptualized understanding of curriculum discourse as 'postmodernist critical practice', '[p]erhaps the most important feature of postmodernism is its stress on the centrality of language and subjectivity as new fronts from which to rethink the issues of meaning, identity and politics.' Derrida's (1978: 280) observation of 'the moment when language invaded the universal problematic' may serve, therefore, as a particularly expressive linking formulation between these various and some-times quite conflicting developments in what is presented here as 'the linguistic turn' in cultural and curriculum theorizing. Similarly, Lacan (1977: 149) argues that language has come to occupy 'the key position' in the domain of the human sciences, and suggests further that 'the reclassification of the sciences and a regrouping of them around it signals, as is usually the case, a revolution in knowledge'. Halliday (1987: 152) is equally emphatic in this regard, albeit from a different theoretical perspective: '[A]mong the human sciences, it is linguistics that finds itself inescapably in the front line'.[5]

Considerations of these kinds recall some of the preoccupations and concerns of the Reconceptualist movement in curriculum theorizing (Pinar, 1975), and subsequent developments which might well be associated with that movement; for instance, work in 'curriculum criticism' (Barone, 1989) and 'educational con-noisseurship' (Eisner, 1979), in narrative inquiry and educational autobiography (Grumet, 1988; Bowers and Flinders, 1990), and in a heightened awareness of the poetic and expressive dimensions of curriculum practice conceived holistically, within an ecologically and culturally sensitive framework of understanding and action and in accordance with a renewed (eco-)political mandate, increasingly identified with the notion of 'postmodernism' (Griffin, 1988). Lather (1989: 21) captures something of what is involved here in her observation that '[i]n ways we are only beginning to understand, perhaps "the postmodern turn" is about more freely admitting politics, desires, belief into our discourse as we attempt to resolve the contradictions of theory and practice ... ' — not simply in education, it should be stressed, but in society and culture more generally. Central to such work is a heightened sensitivity to matters of discourse, textuality, literacy and interpretation, and more generally the politics of subjectivity and representation.[6]

At issue here, then, is a growing recognition of the significance of a heightened focus in social theory — and hence, in curriculum theory — on questions and problems of language and meaning. Such developments are usefully described within the terms of debate on *postmodernism*, understood as a specific cultural-intellectual formation arising out of the convergence of insights and interests associated with poststructuralism, neo-Marxism and feminism. A further consideration here is recent work in what has been called 'postmodern science', including research in artificial intelligence and information technology (Lyotard, 1984; Toulmin, 1982; Best, 1991). Such developments and initiatives are not to be seen exclusively in cultural or scientific terms, however, rather, they are linked decisively, albeit non-deterministically, to profound shifts in political economy (Lash and Urry, 1987), and the emergence of what might be called post-industrial problematics in advanced capitalist societies.

To date, there is little fully developed work available on the educational, and specifically the curriculum, implications of these particular arguments and perspectives. Some recent notable exceptions to this are Lather (1991), Giroux (1990) and Hinkson (1991), as well as Doll (1989) and Wexler (1989). Of con-siderable interest here is the hypothesis that both curriculum and curriculum theorizing, in their current-traditional formulations, are to be understood within the terms of *modernity*, predicated as they are on particular forms of literacy, rationality and scientificity (Olson, 1988b). This raises the possibility that there

Figure 1:   The relationship between curriculum and literacy (with reference to modernism and postmodernism)

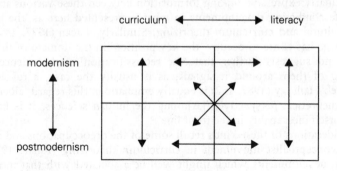

are intriguing issues to explore in the shift to *postmodernity* in terms of social organization and cultural formation (Hinkson, 1991; Giroux, 1990), with specific regard to curriculum, literacy and the relationships between them. For the moment, it must suffice merely to represent the relationship between curriculum and literacy with reference to the modernism/postmodernism debate in Figure 1. The total field of the relations to be observed between curriculum and literacy, within this framework, is indicated by the arrows, which might well provide a guide for further research and enquiry along these lines, both of a conceptual and an empirical nature. For instance, if we can observe in modern(ist) schooling particular forms of curriculum and literacy predicated on what Reiss (1982) has described as the 'analytico-referential' paradigm and the discourse of modernism, forms which are essentially complementary and congruent with each other, we can also speculate on what forms might emerge out of the shift to postmodernity and the cultural discourses associated with it, and whether these are likely to be equally congruent with each other or else less integrated, at least in the ways that have characterized schooling to date. What is more likely, however, is that there may well be significant disjunctions between, for instance, persistently modernist forms of curriculum — perhaps even 'hyper-modernist' — and increasingly postmodernist forms of textual practice and student subjectivity.[7]

This is all the more likely to happen if schooling remains locked into its present formulations; if, that is, the very concept of 'schooling' in postmodern conditions isn't reconceptualized. This task of reconceptualizing curriculum and schooling is particularly important, given the increasing significance of information and media culture in contemporary social life, and the prospect of a widening gulf between the generations as a consequence of children's immersion in a qualitatively different cultural field increasingly dominated by electronic textuality and secondary orality, and characterized by what Ulmer (1989: vii) describes as '... the new discursive and conceptual ecology interrelating orality, literacy, and videocy'. For one thing, it makes for increasing difficulties, disciplinary, communicative and otherwise, in the complex, contested cultural site of the conventional classroom, as students and teachers increasingly inhabit different conceptual worlds and participate in different information and social networks. Furthermore, something which must be noted here is the possibility of a *decoupling* of curriculum and schooling, and the emergence of television and other media-based technologies as new sources of information and learning, as well as social integration and identity-formation. This would not necessarily mean the end of schooling but, rather, its transmutation, with a new emphasis on notions such as 'on-line education' and the 'virtual classroom'; what might be described, in effect, as a new era of 'disorganized schooling', with all that is implied in such a description, in both its negative and its positive aspects.[8]

What such a representation enables, then, is a sense of the *different* and *changing* relations between curriculum and literacy — curriculum as literacy, literacy as curriculum — in the context of the complex historical and conceptual relations between the respective cultures of modernity and postmodernity. This is, importantly, a matter of different and changing forms of textual practice and knowledge, and different relations to culture and technology, which in turn raises critical questions about subjectivity and identity politics in the context of what clearly are radically socio-economic conditions.

An important qualification must be added at this point. I am not suggesting here a simple shift from 'modernism' to 'postmodernism' as the changing context for literacy studies and curriculum theorizing, nor do I want to present one as necessarily preferable in this regard, or more generative and appropriate than the other. Rather, what must be taken into account here is that elements of both modernism and postmodernism necessarily coexist, sometimes contradictorily and even conflictually, in contemporary forms of curriculum and cultural analysis, and that in neither instance is a politics to be either assumed or assigned in advance. Rather, what needs to be worked with here is what is, on the one hand, a *contradictory* politics, and on the other, a politics of *undecidability* — a politics, in short, which must be constructed, in what can only be ongoing forms of struggle and contestation. What is indisputable, however, it seems to me, is that the introduction of what has been described as 'postmodernist problematics' (Linda Hutcheon, cited in Giroux, 1990: 16) into the discourse of educational research, with regard to both curriculum and literacy, as well as the relationship between them, changes the game quite dramatically, challenging as it does some of its most fundamental presuppositions and assumptions. In what follows, consequently, I want to outline some of the implications of these arguments, and suggest some further lines of enquiry.

One potentially very fruitful line of future development lies in thinking through the curriculum and literacy implications of the work associated with Jacques Derrida (1976, 1978) and the concepts of *deconstruction* and *grammatology* — in this context, to be defined simply as particular understandings of 'reading' and 'writing' respectively, as conceived within Derrida's distinctive project.[9] Central to this is a recognition of the relevance to curriculum theorizing of an expanded sense of 'Writing', a complex concept which is neither exhausted by linguistic description nor to be reduced to the more common-sense, specific understanding of 'writing'. Leitch (1986) has suggested that drawing these notions into account has major implications for pedagogy, involving decisive forms of 'attitude adjustment' and 'epistemological transformations'. Part of what is entailed here is the relationship between literacy and *logocentricism* — that is, the articulation of reason and the Logos, conceived as a metaphysical foundation for Western culture. With specific regard to curriculum and literacy, schools can be seen as (verbal) language-bound institutions, certainly in their official order, with certain consequences in terms of rationality and meaning, which opens up the possibility of asking about those forms of human semiosis which are currently slighted, if not suppressed, in the official discourse on curriculum and schooling. Work such as that of Gardner (1983) on what he terms 'multiple intelligences' raises provocative questions about the different 'literacies' that might well be associated with such a view, and their occlusion within the increasingly hyper-rationalized, linear practices of normative forms of curriculum and schooling.

It may be inappropriate, of course, to employ the concept 'literacy' at all with regard to this definition, unless it be expressly understood in a metaphorical sense, since many would want to argue that, strictly speaking, the notion of 'literacy' is specific to written language, taking this as encompassing matters of the written medium itself, writing systems, grammars of writing, literacy technologies, and ideological, socio-cultural and epistemological dimensions of what Halliday (1990) calls 'the written world'. Certainly there are other extremely significant forms of human 'meaning-making' which involve semiotic systems other than spoken and written language (although they might be articulated with these, in particular textual practices), and which have been little attended to in traditional and mainstream schooling; indeed, these have tended to be seen, by and large, as lying outside the province of the dominant-hegemonic curriculum (the 'competitive academic curriculum', as it has been described) and marginalized accordingly — outside, that is, the proper realm of the intellect, as classically understood, and hence of school knowledge more generally.

A particularly important consideration has to do with the question of new and emergent literacies (Spencer, 1986; Bazalgette, 1988) and their implications for curriculum and schooling. While it is clear that to some extent there will be similar problems of *inscription* and *representation* to those associated with print literacies, it is also more than likely that the development of new information and communication technologies, including but not limited to computing, will have particular and decisive impact on pedagogy and literacy (Ulmer, 1985, 1989). At the same time, it is equally clear that such 'emergent literacies' are not necessarily linked to, or conducive of, socially-critical curriculum developments, and hence are centrally implicated in new forms of curriculum and cultural politics (Apple, 1986; Robins and Webster, 1989; Bigum and Green, [1992/in press]).

One issue of particular interest here is what various commentators are describing as the shift from a predominantly book-oriented, print culture to one which is image-oriented or 'filmic', in Ulmer's (1985) sense, and dominated by electronic forms of textuality. This has been described as a general shift in emphasis from print literacies to electronic literacies, as the principal mode of meaning-making in advanced techno-capitalist societies. Of especial significance here is television and related forms of video-based technology, something which is increasingly articulated with computing and other information technologies.[10] Ulmer has suggested, among others, that what is at issue in the rise into prominence of television and video is the emergence of new and alternative forms of cognition and learning. Within what is an extremely wide-ranging argument, he considers this in terms of recent theories of the hemispherical specialization of the human brain, whereby a distinction is posited between 'left brain cognition', associated with analytical thinking, artificial intelligence and computer programming, and print literacy, and 'right-brain cognition', which he associates primarily with television and other image-technologies as well as what he calls 'electronic thinking' (Ulmer, 1989: 66). As he argues, our culture and schooling has focused its energies and attention on 'the dominant analytico-referential style of thought' which is to be linked to the literacies associated with print and the alphabet, at the expense of more holistic modes of perception and understanding. Noting the medical and psychological implications for a person 'in whom the right and left brains are disconnected', he writes:

> A culture that has split the two sides of its intelligence the way ours has is seriously disabled. The analogy suggests several lessons: that life, or rather, survival itself, depends upon the communication of these two parts; that one aspect of this intercommunication concerns the technical invention of computer-video interface; that another aspect concerns the invention of a cognitive style integrating right and left modes (Ulmer, 1989: 66).

As he stresses: 'electronic thinking does not abandon, exclude, or replace analytical thinking; it puts it in its place in a larger system of reasoning' (Ulmer, 1989: 66). There are, in fact, intriguing parallels to be drawn here with certain arguments put forward some years earlier by Moffett (1981), specifically in relation to television and language learning.[11] Arguing for a new emphasis in schooling on pluralism and holism, among other things he referred to the need for 'balancing the brain', given research indicating that 'the human brain cognizes in two main modes. One is analytical, intellectual, verbal, and literal and processes data serially. The other is synthesizing or holistic, intuitive, nonverbal, and metaphorical and processes data simultaneously' (Moffett, 1981: 101). He goes on to write:

> Until around [the age of] eight years or so, people cognize both ways in both hemispheres of the brain, but then, perhaps because socialization and acculturation begin to threaten with extinction the holistic mode, the hemispheres specialize so that, in most right-handed people, the left takes charge of the analytical and linear associated with the 'academic curriculum', while the right takes charges of the mode associated with metaphor, arts, crafts and sports (Moffett, 1981: 102).

The result he postulates is a serious imbalance both in our culture and in human cognition and the formation of subjectivities. This imbalance may be linked, he suggests, to the effects of 'stereotyping and premature stress on verbal/conceptual learning during primary school'. Central in this formulation is the role of literacy learning, conceived in the current-traditional manner. Although the combination of cognitivism and biologism in such argument might be seen as somewhat problematical, nonetheless they are extremely suggestive, at least metaphorically,[12] with regard to considering the effects of print culture and the significance of 'essayistic literacy' in the formation of human attributes, within the culture of modernity.

Olson has argued forcefully, in fact, for a fundamental association to be observed between literacy and modernity, proposing that particular forms of rationality and subjectivity are attendant on alphabetic and print literacy, based on 'the clear distinction between the "given" and the "interpreted"' (Olson, 1988b: 428–9). As he writes, literacy understood in this way 'is tied to the development of Cartesian mental states' (Olson, 1988b: 431); in short, to the notion of analytical rationality that has been the hallmark of modernist culture and school-ing. As might be expected, television and associated shifts in communication, culture and technology are viewed negatively: 'Because it makes criticism difficult, television is a threat to literacy and rationality' (Olson, 1988b: 437).[13] Yet, as Ulmer and others suggest, this is not only falsely to equate literacy and rationality but also it essentializes them; moreover, it limits both 'literacy' and 'rationality' to their hegemonic Western, masculinist forms and to the ideological and metaphysical parameters of modernism, which might be usefully identified with the legacies of the Cartesian-Newtonian complex, something realized more recently in the paradigmatic figure of Piaget's abstract epistemic subject (Walker-dine, 1982) — the subject of knowledge *par excellence*. This matter cannot be pursued further here; it is, however, of obvious importance in the project of reassessing curriculum and literacy, in the light of the modernism/post-modernism debate, providing as it does powerful new insight into the historical relationship between schooling and subjectivity, and the emergent significance of televisual textuality and information culture in this regard.

To return to the implications of Derrida's work for literacy pedagogy and curriculum more generally: as Leitch (1986: 53) observes: 'In deconstructive terms, everything we know is written or, more dramatically, *writing* produces all our knowledge'. Given this, Leitch indicates how a deconstructionist perspective radically destabilizes our deepseated and longstanding commitment to *realism* in curriculum and pedagogy: 'in the realm of knowledge, everything is constituted by one or more people. Some "things" are included, some are excluded, some are marginalized. Boundaries are set up. The "made up" quality of knowledge, its fictitious character, evidences itself as inscription' (Leitch, 1986: 53). Noting that this 'adjustment' involves, on the one hand, accepting the transference of 'traditional epistemological matters' to 'the ground of philosophy of language or linguistics', and on the other, an expanded understanding of 'writing' (that is, expressly in Derrida's grammatological sense, as 'Writing' or 'writing-in-general'), based in the ubiquity of 'difference' and the logic of non-identity. As he writes: 'The effect in this whole operation, which traces a key paradigm shift of our time from world as orderly array of substances and things to world as differential text, is to defamiliarize or denaturalize our knowledge. Knowledge is constituted as *historical* writing' (Leitch, 1986: 53). That such a view offers a major challenge to the educational institution as it is presently constituted is made very clear: 'Our knowledge, in its present and past formations and branches, could have been, and may yet be, constituted in other ways. Our relation to "facts", disciplines, departments, and hierarchies of knowledge is less "natural" or "normal" than concocted *and thus alterable*' (Leitch, 1986: 53; my emphasis).

The educational order of things is therefore more fragile and at risk than commonly realized; as artifice, as construction, as selection and combination within available codes of intelligibility which are themselves historical config-urations of knowledge/power/desire, curriculum is always already susceptible to *counter*-construction and *re*-writing. Such a discourse-theoretical or semiotic view, with its attendant politics, has already been adumbrated in work such as that of Wexler (1982) and Alvarado and Ferguson (1983), and more recently in Whitson (1988). However, while noted in Whitty (1985: 45–46) as a potentially new and important initiative in curriculum studies, there has to date been little in the way of a full and rigorous realization of its possibilities and implications in

terms of curriculum politics and critical pedagogy, and the radical reconceptualization of curriculum studies itself. Curriculum praxis in such a view
becomes inextricable from postmodern(ist) literacy, and a heightened concern for
matters of rhetoric and textuality becomes fundamental to literacy pedagogy
at every level, in every subject-area and across the school curriculum more
generally.

On the Insistence of the Letter

One of the most important features of mass compulsory state-sponsored schooling has been the manner in which it has brought together what, in Foucault's
terms, are disciplinary and pastoral forms of power. This has meant combining
control and welfare concerns, on the one hand, and on the other, text-based
forms of social management, on the level specifically of classrooms. It is something which has not been limited to the English subjects, either, although it
might well be the case that pastoral power arrangements and technologies have
been especially significant in the areas of literary education and English teaching.
However, as Hamilton suggests in this volume, the textbook has long been a
central organizing principle in general educational practice, and this is a matter
which has become increasingly important over the course of the twentieth
century, given the nexus between a multinational educational publishing industry
and the professionalization of schooling (Apple, 1986; Luke, 1989). A related
matter has been the general shift from 'speech' to 'writing' as the basis of formal
education, which needs to be seen as crucial to the emergence and consolidation
of modern schooling. This shift went together historically with a new valuation
of silence in education and, increasingly, an official emphasis on reading and
writing, rather than speaking and listening: 'reading and writing, rather than the
more "natural" means of learning such as oral discussion and practical engagement, are the established modality of schooling' (Goodson and Medway, 1990:
vii). Stressing the decline of interest in oral language, linked to the decline of
traditional forms of education based on classical rhetoric, Christie (1990: 12)
points to 'the related pedagogical requirement that children be educated in large
numbers and disciplined to work in silence, a requirement which became
commonplace in the nineteenth century, the period of mass education'. As she
further writes, following Shirley Brice Heath: 'children were encouraged to talk
less and less, while their progress was measured more and more through the written mode, a practice which survives today' (Christie, 1990: 15; see also Christie,
this volume).

This 'silence' is certainly one aspect of the insistence of the letter in curriculum and schooling: that is, a programmatic emphasis on 'text' as the organizing
and authorizing centre of one's attention and the source of one's educational
identity, as it is and as it is becoming, and what it must eventually be — in short,
an insistence *on* the letter. One way of grasping the significance of post-1960s
efforts to restore the significance of speech in the practice of education, which
Medway (1984) describes as analogous to the revolution associated with the translation of the Bible into the vernacular, was that it represented a major challenge
to the normative ordering of modern schooling, emphasizing as this had long

done the principles of hierarchy, linearity and what Hoskin (1979: 146) calls 'rational authority', together with the 'closed system' forms of thinking which Ong (1977) associates with the literacies and cultural technologies of writing and print. In a similar way, the shift from reading to writing, especially when associated with and linked to the new emphasis on speech, needs to be similarly reassessed, and viewed as constituting at least a *contradictory* politics.[14] This is certainly the case politically, in my view, and historical accounts of educational initiatives on the part of working-class and other subaltern groups prior to the invention of state-subsidized schooling, as an apparatus of social discipline and moral regulation via management of the symbolic order, are particularly salutory in this regard, as Willinsky suggests in this volume.

In this regard, Goodson's (1988: 32) account of 'the progressive refinement of an epistemology suited to state schooling' is pertinent, and particularly his observation that '[a]t root such a hierarchical system [can] be seen as denying the dialectic of education, the notion of dialogue and flexibility which some viewed (and view) as central to the way we learn' (Goodson, 1988: 35–36). He specifically links this with adult education and working-class schools prior to what can be seen here as the assertion of the Law, in association with the insistence on the letter. Yet post-1960s initiatives in curriculum and pedagogy might well also be noted here, as evincing a similar resurgence of 'dialogue and flexibility' and as renewing the democratic and expressive possibilities in educational practice, long suppressed in the social-disciplinary complex of mandatory schooling, hegemonic rationality and current-traditional forms of 'universal' literacy. Ong's early explorations of the technologies, cultural and otherwise, of what he calls 'secondary orality' are important matters to take into account here, linked as they are to 'open-systems thinking' which he describes as 'interactional, transactional, developmental [and] process-oriented' (Ong, 1977: 329). Ong's argument is taken up and elaborated by Ulmer (1985, 1989) in terms of a new 'open pedagogy', fostering what he calls 'the writerly student', a pedagogy and a perspective deeply influenced by the new technologies of communication and culture, including video and computing, and one which 'promotes a heuristic, inventive mode, in which the aesthetic dimension replaces the referential as a guide for the productive participation of the addressee' (Ulmer, 1985: 307). What is worth stressing, then, is that the emergence of what can be recognized as a distinctively new sensibility in the post-1960s period is not something restricted to education, or even more specifically to literacy pedagogy and English teaching, nor to a renewed emphasis on spoken language *per se*; rather, it has a much wider compass and implication, involving decisive shifts in culture and economy and new relations between technology and textuality, something which, as I have suggested, has become increasingly and usefully discussed in terms of the post-modern turn.

Something which must be addressed here, then, is the question of *form* — that is, the form that both curriculum and literacy takes, or has taken, in the period corresponding to the social history of modern(ist) schooling; how the forms of curriculum and of literacy are constituted, and relatedly, their conditions of possibility and intelligibility. As Derrida has suggested, it is not so much what is said in academic-institutional sites, such as schools or universities, as how it is said — that is, not so much the *logic* of curriculum and literacy events as their forms of presentation and address: their *rhetoric*. He puts it thus:

The reproductive forces of authority can get along more comfortably with declarations or theses whose content presents itself as revolutionary, provided that they respect the rites of legitimation, the rhetoric and the institutional symbolism which defuses and neutralizes whatever comes from outside the system. What is unacceptable is what, underlying positions or theses, upsets this deeply entrenched contract, the order of these norms, and which does so in the very *form* of works, of teaching or of writing (Derrida, 1983: 44).[15]

What then can be said about 'school literacy', specifically as conceived in accordance with the normative-symbolic order of curriculum, literacy and schooling?

As various commentators have noted, the literacy commonly and characteristically associated with schooling — 'literacy' itself, as it is commonly understood — must be recognized as both specific and restricted, rather than being a general and all-inclusive category. That is to say, what has been named here as 'school literacy' has a certain, clearly defined formal-ideological identity, and further, this identity has been naturalized and normalized to the point where it becomes coextensive with the notion of literacy itself. Hence, it involves as much as anything else a radical *exclusion*, an exclusionary act of symbolic appropriation which is specific both to the interests of certain social groups rather than others and to the expression of certain 'worldviews' rather than others. This normative understanding of literacy has been identified with 'the essayistic tradition', and called accordingly 'essayistic literacy', as originally expounded by David Olson (1988a), who has already been discussed in this chapter in terms of the relationship between literacy and modernity.

What Street describes as 'the "autonomous" model of literacy' and associates with those '"academic" literacy practices which are often treated in schools as if they are "universal" and vital' (Street, 1984: 224) — that is, necessary — 'tends ... to be based on the "essay-text" form of literacy and to generalize broadly from what is in fact a narrow, culture-specific literacy practice' (Street, 1984: 1). The influence of this formulation has been considerable and far-reaching, and appropriately so; however, it is now urgently in need of deconstruction and radical critique, because it has been so central to the ideological project of social modernity, and to the distinctive nexus between language and rationality in modernist schooling. This can be readily seen in positions such as the following, made with direct reference to Olson's work: 'Under this view literacy [the awareness of the power of letters] can be seen as an extension of the logical process of controlled cognition' (Herriman, 1986: 170). For Street (1984) and other commentators, however, such positions and formulations involve fetishizations of both 'text' and 'rationality' and the assertion of a fundamental autonomy which realizes itself in a certain mythic or ideological understanding of 'objectivity', linked to the hypostatization of written language; further, importantly, in a refusal of the principles of difference and undecidability. The emphasis in 'essayistic literacy', in sharp contrast, is on closure and control, and on being 'disciplined', features which as we have seen are specific to the alphabetic-print apparatus — something Ong (1967: 92) suggestively associates with anality in psychosexual development and techno-cultural analysis.[16]

Street makes brief reference to Derrida's work and that of others in the (post)structuralist tradition, as supporting what he describes as 'an alternative "ideological" model of literacy' (Street, 1984: 104), something which Lankshear refers to in this volume. However, Street does not draw on this work in any extended sense, and hence his critique cannot take into account the potential such work offers for the formulation of a critical literacy pedagogy appropriate in and for postmodern conditions. What I want to propose, however, is that in fact a radically different literacy praxis is possible on the basis of such work, a different way of understanding textuality and rhetoric, based on and informed by developments in poststructuralism and psychoanalysis, which has truly radicalizing political and institutional implications.

A new understanding of language and knowledge is crucial, that is, and entirely possible, as well as a new relation to them on the part of human beings, and more specifically, a re-evaluation and reconceptualization of 'the status and function of language in the educational institution' (Ulmer, 1985: 170). Here attention is directed to the significant materiality of language, the priority of signifiers over signifieds in textual practice and knowledge-production, and the relationship between language and the unconscious. The role of psychoanalysis is of particular relevance in this context. For Kristeva (1989), it is a matter of reassessing the relationship between language and subjectivity and hence the question of Reason and rationality in terms of (differential) access to the symbolic order, a position explored recently with more specific reference to educational practice and gender in Walkerdine's (1988) work (see also Donald, 1985). As Kristeva (1989: 274) writes:

> Psychoanalysis renders impossible the habit commonly accepted by current linguistics of considering language outside its *realization* in *discourse*, that is, by forgetting that language does not exist outside the discourse of a subject, or by considering the subject as *implicit*, as equal to himself [sic], as a fixed unit coinciding with his discourse.[17]

For Ulmer, similarly, psychoanalysis is important because it has opened up new possibilities for conceiving the nature of and the relations among language, subjectivity, representation and the unconscious, in 'focusing its attention on the *parletrê*, the speaking being' — a particularly fortunate formulation here because, as he notes, it 'equate[s] *l'être* with the letter, *la lettre*' (Ulmer, 1988: 175). Lacan is obviously an important figure in this regard, and it is also not coincidental to this present project that he has written specifically of what has been variously translated as 'the insistence of the letter' and 'the agency of the letter'. His concern is with 'how the signifier enters the signified, namely, in a form which, not being immaterial, raises the question of its place in reality' (Lacan, 1977: 151).

A further theme then is not just the priority of the signifer over the signified but also, importantly, the materiality of the signifier itself: 'by "letter" I designate that material support that concrete discourse borrows from language' (Lacan, 1977: 147). Kristeva elaborates on this by referring to 'the doubly discernible materiality' of language, that is, both 'the phonic, gestural, or graphic aspects that *la langue* assumes (there is no language without sounds, gestures or writing)' and the social determinations of language, including its 'rules' and 'conventions', its laws and regularities (Kristeva, 1989: 18). The point is to insist on the necessary connection between these two dimensions of language's significant materiality, as well as its productivity. This is also what is at issue, then, in the notion of 'the insistence of the letter': the press and urgency of its sensuous materiality, its nature as signifying *practice* — which necessitates a different kind of engagement with language, namely, as textuality and as rhetoric, within a certain understanding of the practice of power and the power of practice.

Such a view also goes hand-in-hand with a proper regard for the repressions and violence built into the ordinary use of language, and hence opens up the question of what has been repressed in the practices of modern(ist) schooling. What has been repressed and denied in this manner is, in fact, language itself. This is notwithstanding the insistent — and as I have suggested, ever-increasing — emphasis on *abstraction* in schooling, of a specifically linguistic nature, and moreover, one intimately associated with a certain understanding of *written* language ('a certain metaphysics': Derrida, 1983: 43). The emphasis is increasingly on conceptuality, 'thinking', cognition, rationality, logic, that is, 'mind' at the expense of the 'body', feeling, affect, emotionality, desire, the irrational; and therefore constitutes in effect the refusal of language as such, *despite* schooling being extraordinarily (verbal) language-bound, as noted previously. Ulmer describes this situation in terms of a paradigm shift in education, 'a shift away from the exclusive domination of mind (intellect as verbal discourse ...) to a mode which includes the body (desire, and the will to knowledge), a shift with important implications for instructional method' (Ulmer, 1985: 168), and hence for curriculum and literacy more generally. He further relates this to the need for a critical reassessment of what he describes as 'the privileging of a literate and verbalizing relationship to language in the schools as a feature of bourgeois hegemony' (Ulmer, 1985: 170), and from within his distinctive rendering of the poststructuralist project refers to the way that 'the culture is shifting away from a paradigm based on language towards one based on writing.... The resurgence of the graphic element, escaping from the domination of the spoken word, is a symptom of the end of the metaphysical era' (Ulmer, 1985: 5). This concern is clearly Derrida's (1983: 46) when he writes of his own project in terms of 'the deconstruction of a certain hermeneutics as well as of a certain theorizing about the signifier and the letter with its authority and institutional power ...', including 'the analysis of logocentrism *as* phallogocentrism, the essential indissociability of logocentrism and phallogocentrism ...'

This latter point is particularly important. If 'the insistence of the letter' involves an assertion of the signifier over the signified (crudely, of 'form' over 'meaning' or 'content') and also refers to the 'significant materiality' of language and textuality, then there is also a need to recognize and stress the *gender* dimensions and implications of this position. The 'return of the repressed' in culture and schooling is to be conceived, as much as anything else, as a reference to the fluid and the 'irrational' the so-called 'promiscuous', the dynamics associated with the priority of becoming over being, and the assertion of the interpersonal over the ideational aspects of schooling, which can be mapped readily onto the ideological category 'woman' — thus evoking the general binary [man: woman] which has figured so prominently in Western thought as well as modern(ist) schooling. The first term is always effectively privileged over the second, in a similar fashion to the relations between signifiers and signifieds in hegemonic regimes of knowledge and signification. In this regard it is important to note that Lacan (1977) explicitly associates his formulation of the insistence and agency of the letter with 'Reason since Freud', thus evoking the crisis of those forms of Cartesian rationality and subjectivity that have for so long been foundational to the phallogocentric culture of modernism. This highlights the gender politics deeply inscribed in the current-traditional forms of curriculum and literacy, and the need accordingly to call into question the hegemonic regimes of gender and genre in the project of rational schooling, as well as those current research practices which effectively sustain them (Lee and Green, 1990).

Conclusion: Reassessing the Letter

What does all of the above mean, then, for (re)thinking curriculum and literacy? First, it means that more regard must be given to what Lather (1992: 1) eloquently describes as 'the textual staging of knowledge, the constitutive effects of our use of language', in curriculum and classrooms all throughout the educational site. This in turn means encouraging and developing a new understanding of language and learning in terms of textuality and rhetoric, and relatedly, a critique of the pervasive realism in curriculum discourse, to be understood as a general metaphysics of correspondence and reference which has become increasingly problematical in the context of new and emergent forms of electronic culture and technocapitalist society. More specifically, it means reassessing the significance of matters of language and genre in and for (post)modern education, with the rider that matters such as these — already very usefully put on the agenda in contemporary educational linguistics — need to be reconceptualized within postmodernist frames and in accordance with poststructuralist and psychoanalytic understandings of textuality and the symbolic order. This also means supplementing the formal-linguistic conception of these matters, in terms not so much of considering what Halliday (1990) calls 'the frontiers of literacy' — taking into account 'the creation of new systems of visual semiotic that are not themselves forms of writing ... yet are used in conjunction with written text' — as of engaging altogether new imaginings of textuality, 'writing' and literacy. In this respect, Ulmer's work is of extraordinary interest, I suggest, providing an exciting basis for developing a postmodern pedagogy able to address what he calls 'the needs of multichannelled performance' (Ulmer, 1985: vii) in contemporary cultural practice, mixing spoken, written and audio-visual languages, as well as new information, communications and image technologies.

With regard to language, this entails developing specific kinds of 'meta-linguistic' and 'meta-textual' awarenesses, and new forms of attention to the signifying elements and processes associated with 'language-in-use', in all its heterogeneity. What this involves is the kind of 'alert attention' to textual practice, operating at its different levels, 'which allows language to say what it knows, or allows the unconscious to show itself in the play of language' (Ulmer, 1988: 175). On this basis, then, a Derridaen perspective on curriculum and literacy, together with the 'supplement' that psychoanalysis extends to 'conventional pedagogy, which tends to forget language or assume its transparency and secondarity, by asking *what language itself knows*' (Ulmer, 1988: 177; my emphasis), opens up new pedagogical possibilities based on the strategic interplay between '*discovery*' and '*recovery*' and the shift from '(re)production' to 'invention' as a organizing principle for curriculum research and praxis.

Similarly, with regard to the question of genre, it needs to be understood within what I would describe as an emergent postmodern view of curriculum and textual dynamics, emphasizing 'becoming' over 'being' and new formulations of 'process' pedagogy in accordance with insights drawn from postmodern science and social theory (Best, 1991; Hayles, 1990). Ulmer's calls for a re-evaluation of current-traditional regimes of production and reception and of the 'essayistic', expository, analytical genres associated with modernist culture and epistemology warrant careful consideration here.[18] Importantly, however, he does not conceive this solely within the terms of critique; rather, he seeks to intervene at the level of material-institutional practices, thereby transforming our understandings of what is appropriate in and for changing socio-cultural conditions by introducing new educational reforms based on what he presents as a two-fold project: 'firstly, to translate into the "vulgate" (audio-visual writing in the formats of film and video, rather than the national languages) the principal works of the disciplines of knowledge' — a matter of 'popularization' — 'and second to develop new genres that will serve educators in the electronic era as well as did the literary essay in the Gutenberg era' (Ulmer, 1989: viii–ix). This does not mean abandoning the criti-cal-analytical resources of modernist culture and schooling so much as *supplementing* them, so as to enable us to 'participate in the invention of a style of thought as powerful and productive as was the invention of conceptual thinking that grew out of the alphabetic apparatus'; that is, 'to learn how to write and think electronically — in a way that supplements without replacing analytical reason' (Ulmer, 1989: ix–x). Such a position is consistent with Giroux's (1990: 9) concern to bring together the 'positivities' in both modernism and post-modernism, since — notwithstanding their respective flaws — '[t]hey each contain elements of strength, and educators have an opportunity to fashion a critical pedagogy that draws on the best insights of each'.

In conclusion, as Derrida has shown us, any act of 'supplementarity', how-ever simple and straightforward it might at first appear, enters into that which is being 'added to' and 'extended' or 'enhanced', and thus inevitably changes it. It is in this sense, then, that we might well take very seriously indeed the radical possibilities of (r)evolution and the production of difference, in engaging what would appear distinctively new and emergent cultures of curriculum and literacy.[19]

Notes

1 Arguing that 'Progressivism', broadly conceived, needs to be understood in terms of 'the discursive relationship of humanism and psychologism', Luke (1989: 7) suggests that 'humanist psychology provided a discourse of *ends*, while behaviourist psychology provided a discourse of *means*' (my emphases).

2 As Levi-Strauss puts it: 'His attitude to writing is revealing. He immediately understood its role as sign, and the social superiority that it confers' (cited Derrida, 1976: 125).

3 Referring more specifically to the eighteenth century, but arguably with reson-ance also for much pedagogy right up to the present, Foucault (1977: 152) writes: 'Good handwriting ... presupposes a gymnastics — a whole routine whose rigor-ous code invests the body in its entirety, from the points of the feet to the tip of the index finger'.

4 As Atkinson (1985: 11) writes: 'language, though perhaps not linguistics, is a key component of Bernstein's sociology and is central to the structuralist tradition

in which he is located'. See also, in particular, Atkinson (1985: 177–81) for comments on the relationship between Bernstein and Foucault.

5   Significantly, he also stresses the increasing significance of the category 'information' in the natural sciences, linking language and what he calls 'the order of nature' — a phrase employed somewhat differently by David Hamilton in this volume.

6   A matter well worth further investigation, in fact, is work on the links to be made between the Reconceptualist tradition — among other things, to be understood as an exemplary 'counter-cultural' initiative — and the emergence of 'postmodernism' as an increasingly important theme in curriculum theorizing.

7   Note, however, Carmen Luke's cautionary comments in this volume on the problems of over-generalizing the notion of the 'postmodernist subject'.

8   Carmen Luke's chapter in this volume is indicative of this 'decoupling' effect, specifically raising as it does the curriculum implications of television and popular culture.

9   Ulmer (1985) provides a useful account of these concepts, as well as of Derrida's project more generally, albeit within his own rendering of that project. Essentially he links what he calls 'applied grammatology' to the notion of 'Writing', and contrasts this with those understandings of 'deconstruction' currently in circulation: 'Writing, as Derrida practices it, is something other than deconstruction, the latter being a mode of analysis, while the former is a mode of composition' (Ulmer, 1985: xi).

10 Reid's chapter in this volume concludes with a brief commentary on the curriculum implications of developments of this kind, and might be usefully extended by drawing in some of the speculations and arguments outlined here.

11 Indeed, there are more important links to be made, I suggest, between certain aspects of post-1960s developments in English teaching and literacy pedagogy more generally and recent work in educational postmodernism and cultural studies, an argument that I am currently developing elsewhere (Green, 1991).

12 It is worth recording here Ulmer's (1989: 66) acknowledgment of some of these difficulties, and his observation that nonetheless '[w]hat matters is that the *descriptions* of the unconscious, the right brain, inner speech, the mind of the savage, child, or even "feminine style", all share common features, which we recognize to have been generated for the most part in opposition to analytic-referential reason'.

13 It is worth noting here that Olson perceives a direct link between literacy, understood in his curiously constricted terms, and computing; 'Computing ... is a direct extension of literacy. *Computers insist on unambiguous messages; there is no scope for interpretation*' (Olson, 1988b: 437; my emphasis).

14 Especially when reconsidered with reference to new communications technology, notions of 'secondary orality', and what Culler (1987: 175) describes as 'a certain textuality of voice', as well as the relationship posited by various commentators between post-modernism and popular culture (Giroux, 1990).

15 Interestingly, he explicitly relates this formulation to the significance of 'that event which one still does not know how to name other than by its date, 1968, without ever having any very clear idea of just what it is one is naming in this way' (Derrida, 1983: 44). '1968' remains an important icon in contemporary theory.

16 An image from Donald Barthelme's short story 'The Indian Uprising' (originally published in 1968) is usefully drawn in here, to evoke something of what is involved in this normative understanding of literacy. One of the characters is a teacher, Miss R, who is presented as the guardian of protective speech and the official order, and the relationship between language and authority: '"Young people", Miss R said, "run to more and more unpleasant combinations as they

sense the nature of our society. Some people", Miss R said, "run to conceits or wisdom but I hold to the hard, brown, nutlike word"' (Barthelme, 1981: 112).

17 An exception must be noted here with regard to the neo-Firthian tradition in linguistics, principally associated with the work of Michael Halliday; even so, it is not clear that work in this tradition entirely escapes Kristeva's criticism, particularly with respect to poststructuralist-psychoanalytical understandings of subjectivity (Walkerdine, 1988; Lee and Green, 1990).

18 In this regard, note Allan Luke's account in this volume of what he calls 'post-modern appraisals of narrative', and the problem of 'binarism' in 'curricular knowledge'.

19 I wish to thank Marie Brennan, Fazal Rizvi and Allan Luke for their help and advice in the drafting of this chapter. They are absolved, of course, of any responsibility for its idiosyncracies.

References

ALTHUSSER, L. (1971) 'Ideology and Ideological State Apparatuses', *Lenin and Philosophy, and Other Essays*, New Left Books, pp. 123–73.

ALVARADO, M. and FERGUSON, B. (1983) 'The Curriculum, Media Studies and Discursivity', *Screen*, **24**, 3.

APPLE, M. (1986) *Teachers and Texts: A Political Economy of Class and Gender Relations in Education*, New York, Routledge and Kegan Paul.

ATKINSON, P. (1985) *Language, Structure and Reproduction: An Introduction to the Sociology of Basil Bernstein*, London, Methuen.

BARONE, T.E. (1988) 'Curriculum Platforms and Literature', in BEYER, L.E. and APPLE, M.W. (Eds) *The Curriculum: Problems, Politics, and Possibilities*, Albany, State University of New York Press, pp. 140–65.

BARTHELME, D. (1981) 'The Indian Uprising', *Sixty Stories*, London, Secker and Warburg, pp. 108–14.

BAZALGETTE, C. (1988) '"They changed the picture in the middle of the fight": New Kinds of Literacy?' in MEEK, M. and MILLS, C. (Eds) *Language and Literacy in the Primary School*, London, Falmer Press, pp. 221–22.

BERNSTEIN, B. (1975) 'On the Classification and Framing of Educational Knowledge', in *Class, Codes and Control Vol. 3*, London, Routledge and Kegan Paul, pp. 85–115.

BEST, S. (1991) 'Chaos and Entropy: Metaphors in Postmodern Science and Social Theory', *Science as Culture*, **2**, Part 2 (1), pp. 188–226.

BIGUM, C. and GREEN, B. (1992/in press) 'Technologizing Literacy: The Dark Side of the Dream', *Discourse: Australian Journal of Educational Studies*, **12**, 2.

BOOMER, G. (in press) 'Curriculum and Teaching in Australian Schools 1960–1990: A Tale of Two Epistemologies', in LINKE, R. (Ed.) *Australian Education and Training in Perspective*, Oxford, Pergamon.

BOWERS, C.A. and FLINDERS, D.R. (1990) *Responsive Teaching: An Ecological Approach to Classroom Patterns of Language, Culture and Thought*, New York, Teachers College Press.

BURGESS, T. (1984) 'Diverse Melodies: A First-Year Class n a Secondary School', in MILLER, J. (Ed.) *Eccentric Propositions: Essays on Literature and the Curriculum*, London, Routledge and Kegan Paul, pp. 56–69.

BURGESS, T. (1988) 'Review: *Investigating Classroom Talk*', *Language and Education*, **2**, 2, pp. 133–6.

CHERRYHOLMES, C. (1988) *Power and Criticism: Poststructural Investigations in Education*, New York, Teachers College Press.

CHRISTIE, F. (1990) 'The Changing Face of Literacy', in CHRISTIE, F. (Ed.) *Literacy for a Changing World*, Hawthorn, Victoria, The Australian Council for Educational Research Ltd, pp. 1–25.

CULLER, J. (1987) 'Towards a Linguistics of Writing', in FABB, N., ATTRIDGE, D., DURANT, A. and MACCABE, C. (Eds) *The Linguistics of Writing: Arguments between Language and Literature*, Manchester, Manchester University Press, pp. 173–85.

DERRIDA, J. (1976) *Of Grammatology* translated by G.C. SPIVAK, Baltimore, Johns Hopkins University Press.

DERRIDA, J. (1978) 'Structure, Sign and Play in the Discourse of the Human Sciences', *Writing and Differences*, translated by A. BASS, London, Routledge and Kegan Paul, pp. 278–93.

DERRIDA, J. (1983) 'The Time of a Thesis: Punctuations', in MONTEFIORE, A. (Ed.) *Philosophy in France Today*, Cambridge, Cambridge University Press, pp. 34–50.

DOLL, W.E. JR (1989) 'Foundations for a Post-Modern Curriculum', *Journal Of Curriculum Studies*, **21**, 3, pp. 243–53.

DONALD, J. (1985) 'Beacons of the Future: Schooling, Subjection and Subjectification', in BEECHEY, V. and DONALD, J. (Eds) *Subjectivity and Social Relations*, Milton Keynes, Open University Press, pp. 214–49.

EISNER, E.W. (1979) *The Educational Imagination: On the Design and Evaluation of School Programs*, New York, Macmillan.

EMIG, J. (1983) 'Literacy and Freedom', in *The Web of Meaning*, Montclair, NJ, Boynton/Cook.

FOUCAULT, M. (1977) *Discipline and Punish*, Harmondsworth, Penguin.

FOUCAULT, M. (1981) 'The Order of Discourse', in R. YOUNG (Ed.) *Untying the Text: A Post-Structuralist Reader*, London, Routledge and Kegan Paul, pp. 48–78.

FRANKLIN, U. (1990) *The Real World of Technology*, Montreal, CBC Enterprises.

GARDNER, H. (1983) *Frames of Mind: The Theory Of Multiple Intelligences*, New York, Basic Books.

GIROUX, H. (1983) *Theory and Resistance in Education: A Pedagogy for the Opposition*, Cambridge, MA, Bergin and Garvey.

GIROUX, H.A. (1989) 'Schooling as a Form of Cultural Politics: Towards a Pedagogy of and for Difference', in GIROUX, H.A. and MCLAREN, P.L. (Eds) *Critical Pedagogy, The State, and Cultural Struggle*, Albany, NY, State University of New York, pp. 125–51.

GIROUX, H.A. (1990) *Curriculum Discourse as Postmodernist Critical Practice,* Geelong, Victoria, Deakin University Press.

GOODSON, I.F. (1988) *The Making of Curriculum: Collected Essays*, London, Falmer Press.

GOODSON, I. and MEDWAY, P. (1990), 'Bringing English to Order: Introduction', in GOODSON, I. and MEDWAY, P. (Eds) *Bringing English to Order: The History and Politics of a School Subject*, London, Falmer Press, pp. vii–xv.

GREEN, B. (1991) 'After the New English: On English Teaching, Cultural Studies, and Postmodernism', unpublished manuscript, Faculty of Education, Deakin University, Geelong, Victoria.

GRIFFIN, D.R. (Ed.) (1988) *The Reenchantment of Science: Postmodern Proposals*, Albany, NY, State University of New York Press.

GRUMET, M.R. (1988) *Bitter Milk: Women and Teaching*, Amherst, MA, The University of Massachusetts Press.

HALLIDAY, M.A.K. (1987) 'Language and the Order of Nature', in FABB, N., ATTRIDGE, D., DURANT A. and MACCABE, C. (Eds) *The Linguistics of Writing: Arguments between Language and Literature*, Manchester, Manchester University Press, pp. 135–54.

HALLIDAY, M.A.K. (1988) 'Language and Socialization: Home and School', in GEROT, L., OLDENBURY, J. and VAN LEEUWEN, T. (Eds) *Language and Socialization: Home and School*, Proceedings from the Working Conference on Language in Education, Macquarie University, 17–21 November, 1986, School of English and Linguistics, Macquarie University, pp. 1–12.

HALLIDAY, M.A.K. (1990) 'Linguistic Perspectives on Literacy: A Systemic-Functional Approach', paper presented at the Inaugural Australian Systemics Network Conference, 'Literacy in Social Processes', Deakin University, Geelong, Victoria, January 18–21.

HAMILTON, D. (1980) 'Adam Smith and the Moral Economy of the Classroom System', *Journal of Curriculum Studies*, **12**, 4, pp. 281–98.

HAMILTON, D. (1989) *Towards a Theory of Schooling*, London, Falmer Press.

HARDCASTLE, J. (1985) 'Classrooms as Sites of Cultural Making', *English in Education*, **19**, 3, pp. 8–22.

HAYLES, K.N. (1990) *Chaos Bound: Orderly Disorder in Contemporary Literature and Science*, Ithaca, NY, Cornell University Press.

HERRIMAN, M.L. (1986) 'Metalinguistic Awareness and the Growth of Literacy', in DE CASTELL, S., LUKE, A. and EGAN, K. (Eds) *Literacy, Society and Schooling: A Reader*, Cambridge, Cambridge University Press, pp. 159–74.

HINKSON, J. (1991) *Postmodernity: State and Education*, Geelong, Victoria, Deakin University Press.

HOSKIN, K. (1979) 'The Examination, Disciplinary Power and Rational Schooling', *History of Education*, **8**, 2, pp. 135–46.

HOSKIN, K. (1990) 'Foucault under Examination: The Crypto-Educationalist Unmasked', in BALL, S.J. (Ed.) *Foucault and Education: Disciplines and Knowledge*, London, Routledge, pp. 29–53.

HUNTER, I. (1987) 'Culture, Education, and English: Building "the Principal Scene of the Real Life of Children"', *Economy and Society*, **16**, 4, pp. 568–88.

KRISTEVA, J. (1989) *Language: The Unknown*, London, Harvester Wheatsheaf.

LACAN, J. (1977) *Ecrits: A Selection*, London, Tavistock.

LANKSHEAR, C. (1989) 'Reading and Righting Wrongs: Literacy and the Underclass', *Language and Education*, **3**, 3, pp. 167–82.

LANKSHEAR, C. with LAWLER, M. (1987) *Literacy, Schooling and Revolution*, London, Falmer Press.

LASH, S. and URRY, J. (1987) *The End of Organized Capitalism*, Cambridge, Polity Press.

LATHER, P. (1989) 'Postmodernism and the Politics of Enlightenment', *Educational Foundations*, **3**, 3, pp. 7–28.

LATHER, P. (1991) *Getting Smart: Feminist Research and Pedagogy with/in the Postmodern*, London, Routledge.

LATHER, P. (1992/in press) 'Post-Critical Pedagogies: A Feminist Reading', in LUKE, C. and GORE, J. (Eds) *Feminisms and Critical Pedagogy*, New York, Routledge.

LEE, A. and GREEN, B. (1990) 'Staging the Differences: On School Literacy and the Socially-Critical Curriculum', in GIBLETT, R. and O'CARROLL, J. (Eds) *Discipline/Dialogue/Difference*, Proceedings of the Language in Education Conference Murdoch University, December, 1989, Murdoch University, Perth: 4D Publications, pp. 225–61.

LEITCH, V. (1986) 'Deconstruction and Pedagogy', in NELSON, C. (Ed.) *Theory in the Classroom*, Urbana, University of Chicago Press, pp. 45–56.

LEVINE, K. (1986) *The Social Context of Literacy*, London, Routledge and Kegan Paul.

LUKE, A. (1988) *Literacy, Ideology and Textbooks: Postwar Literacy Instruction and the Mythology of Dick and Jane*, London, Falmer Press.

LUKE, A. (1989) 'Literacy as Curriculum: Historical and Sociological Perspectives', *Language, Learning and Literacy*, **1**, 2, pp. 1–16.

LYOTARD, J-F. (1984) *The Postmodern Condition: A Report on Knowledge*, Minneapolis, University of Minnesota Press.

MEDWAY, P. (1984) 'The Bible and the Vernacular: The Significance of Language Across the Curriculum', in BRITTON, J. (Ed.) *English Teaching: An International Exchange*, London, Heinemann, pp. 153–7.

MOFFETT, J. (1981) 'Instructional Television for Language Learning in the '80s', *Coming on Center: English Education in Evolution*, Montclair, NJ, Boynton/Cook, pp. 94–118.

MONAGHAN, J.E. and SAUL, E.W. (1987) 'The Reader, The Scribe, The Thinker: A Critical Look at the History of American Reading and Writing Instruction', in POPKEWITZ, T.S. (Ed.) *The Formation of the School Subjects: The Struggle for Creating an American Institution*, New York, Falmer Press, pp. 85–122.

OLSON, D.R. (1977, 1988a) 'From Utterance to Text: The Bias of Language in Speech and Writing', in KINTGEN, E.R., KROLL, B.M. and ROSE, M. (Eds) *Perspectives on Literacy*, Carbondale, Southern Illinois University Press, pp. 175–89.

OLSON, D.R. (1988b) 'Mind, Media, and Memory: The Archival and Epistemic Functions of Written Text', in DE KERCKHOVE, D. and LUMSDEN, C.J. (Eds) *The Alphabet and the Brain: The Lateralization of Writing*, Berlin, Springer-Verlag, pp. 422–41.

ONG, W.J. (1967) *The Presence of the Word: Some Prolegomena for Cultural and Religious History*, New Haven, CT, Yale University Press.

ONG, W. (1977) *Interfaces of the World: Studies in the Evolution of Consciousness and Culture*, Ithaca, NY, Cornell University Press.

PINAR, W. (Ed.) (1975) *Curriculum Theorizing: The Reconceptualists*, Berkeley, CA, McCutchan Publishing Corporation.

REISS, T.J. (1982) *The Discourse of Modernism*, Ithaca, NY, Cornell University Press.

RESNICK, D.P. and RESNICK, L.B. (1988) 'The Nature of Literacy: A Historical Perspective', in KINTGEN, E.R., KROLL, B.M. and ROSE, M. (Eds) *Perspectives on Literacy*, Carbondale, Southern Illinois University Press, pp. 190–202.

ROBINS, K. and WEBSTER, F. (1989) *The Technical Fix: Education, Computers and Industry*, New York, St Martin's Press.

SINCLAIR, C. McH. and COULTHARD, M. (1975) *Towards an Analysis of Discourse*, London, Oxford University Press.

SPENCER, M. (1986) 'Emergent Literacies: A Site for Analysis', *Language Arts*, **63**, 5, September, pp. 442–53.

STREET, B.V. (1984) *Literacy in Theory and Practice*, Cambridge, Cambridge University Press.

TOULMIN, S. (1982) 'The Construal of Reality: Criticism in Modern and Postmodern Science', in MITCHELL, W.T.J. (Ed.) *The Politics of Interpretation*, Chicago, University of Chicago Press, pp. 99–117.

ULMER, G. (1985) *Applied Grammatology: Post(e)-Pedagogy from Jacques Derrida to Joseph Beuys*, Baltimore, Johns Hopkins University Press.

ULMER, G. (1988) 'The Puncept in Grammatology', in CULLER, J. (Ed.) *On Puns: The Foundations of Letters*, Oxford, Basil Blackwell, pp. 164–89.

ULMER, G. (1989) *Teletheory: Grammatology in the Age of Video*, New York, Routledge.

WALKERDINE, V. (1982) 'From Context to Text: A Psychosemiotic Approach to Abstract Thought', in BEVERIDGE, M. (Ed.) *Children Thinking through Language*, London, Edward Arnold, pp. 129–55.

WALKERDINE, V. (1988) *The Mastery of Reason: Cognitive Development and the Production of Rationality*, London, Routledge.

WEEDON, C. (1987) *Feminist Practice and Poststructuralist Theory*, Oxford, Basil Blackwell.

WEXLER, P. (1982) 'Structure, Text, and Subject: A Critical Sociology of School Knowledge', in APPLE, M.W. (Ed.) *Cultural and Economic Reproduction in*

Education: Essays on Class, Ideology and the State, London, Routledge and Kegan Paul, pp. 275–303.

WEXLER, P. (1989) 'Curriculum in the Closed Society', in GIROUX, H.A. and MCLAREN, P.L. (Eds) *Critical Pedagogy, The State, and Cultural Struggle*, Albany, NY State University of New York, pp. 92–104.

WHITSON, T. (1988) 'The Politics of "Non-Political" Curriculum: Heteroglossia and the Discourse of "Choice" and "Effectiveness"', in PINAR, W.F. (Ed.) *Contemporary Curriculum Discourses*, Scottsdale, AZ, Gorsuch Scarisbrick, pp. 279–330.

WHITTY, G. (1985) *Sociology and School Knowledge: Curriculum Theory, Research and Politics*, London, Methuen.

WILLINSKY, J. (Ed.) (1990) *The Educational Legacy of Romanticism*, Waterloo, Ontario, Wilfrid Laurier University Press.

Notes on Contributors

Tony Burgess is a Senior Lecturer at the Institute of Education, London University. He has researched in writing and in language diversity. His most recent work has been in developing a cultural approach to classroom discourse and in historical and philosophical issues in English teaching.

Frances Christie is Foundation Professor of Education at the Northern Territory University, Darwin, Australia. She has research interests in the study of language in learning generally, and also the history of patterns of English teaching, especially over the last 200–300 years. She is the editor of the *Language Education Series*, published by Oxford University Press, and in 1990 edited the volume *Literacy for a Changing World*, published by the Australian Council for Educational Research, Melbourne.

James Donald was a Lecturer in the School of Education at the Open University from 1980 to 1991. He is now Senior Lecturer in Media Studies at the University of Sussex. His most recent books are *Sentimental Education: Schooling, Popular Culture and the Regulation of Liberty* (1992), *'Race', Culture and Difference* (1992 [Ed. with Ali Rattansi]), and *Psychoanalysis and Cultural Theory* (1990).

Bill Green is a Lecturer in Curriculum, Media and Cultural Studies in the Faculty of Education at Deakin University, Geelong, Victoria. His research interests include English curriculum studies, critical-postmodernist pedagogy, and the relationship between technology and cultural practice, with specific reference to the educational implications of the new information and image technologies.

David Hamilton is Professor of Education and Head of the Department of Education at the University of Liverpool, England. His research interests relate to the social institution of schooling and its past, present and future relationships to the wider processes of education, cultural transmission and economic transformation.

Keith Hoskin is currently Lecturer in Accounting and Finance in the Business School at the University of Warwick, having formerly been Lecturer in Educational History there. His research interests continue to span the fields of both business and education and he has written widely in these areas, with specific reference to the relationship between history and theory. He is currently engaged in a historical study of the modern business enterprise in the USA.

Allan Luke is Reader in Education at James Cook University of North Queensland, where he teaches educational sociology, language in education, and discourse analysis. His latest book, with Carolyn Baker, is *Towards a Critical Sociology of Reading Pedagogy* (1991), published by John Benjamins.

Carmen Luke is Senior Lecturer in the Department of Social and Cultural Studies at James Cook University of North Queensland, where she teaches sociology and feminisms, and media studies. She is author and editor of several books, the most recent of which is *Feminisms and Critical Pedagogy*, with Jennifer Gore.

Colin Lankshear was formerly a Senior Lecturer in the Faculty of Education at the University of Auckland, New Zealand, and is now increasingly involved in freelance forms of writing and educational consultancy, as well as part-time tertiary teaching. Trained as an educational philosopher, his main interests are in curriculum, critical theory, and the politics of literacy.

William A. Reid is Visiting Scholar at the University of California, Riverside. He was previously Reader in Curriculum Studies in the University of Birmingham, England. His work has centred on studies of deliberative curriculum theory and on research into curriculum history, which were the focus of *Thinking about the Curriculum* (1978) and *The Sixth: An Essay in Education and Democracy* (1982). The relationship between literacy and curriculum is a theme further developed in his forthcoming book *The Pursuit of Curriculum*, to be published by Ablex in 1993.

John Willinsky is Director of the Centre for the Study of Curriculum and Instruction at the University of British Columbia, and is the author of *The Well-Tempered Tongue* (1984), *The New Literacy* (1992), and *The Triumph of Literature* (1991).

Index

access, to knowledge 121, 126–7, 131–2, 168, 193
accountability 20, 122, 133, 160, 170
accounting 29, 33–6
achievement 15, 20–1, 88, 154, 164
activity, learning 20, 86, 88, 107, 131, 140, 146, 166, 168–9, 203
agency 163, 167–70
Ahlbrand, W.P. 15, 19
aim
  curriculum 156
  literacy 61
  modernity 15
alphabetic culture and learning technology 27–42, 196–8, 211
Altick, R.D. 59, 64, 66, 67, 70
analysis 16, 17–18, 20, 22–3, 80, 113, 133, 176, 178, 210–11, 219
  sentence 76–7, 81, 85–8, 93–4, 97, 101–2
Apple, M. 157, 210, 213
Arnold, Matthew 71, 72, 90–1, 94, 98
assessment 49, 82, 88, 197, 203
  examination 2, 28–9, 38, 42–3, 204–5
Atkinson, P. 203, 219–20
authority 8, 22, 121–2, 126–7, 131–4, 144, 146, 149, 213
autonomy 115, 121–2, 129, 132, 164–5, 168–9

Bacon, Francis 46, 47
Bain, A. 82, 84, 86, 89
Baker, C.D. 138, 139, 140, 142, 151
Balibar, Renee 126, 134
Ball, S.J. 2–3, 134
Barnes, D. 97, 98
Barone, T.E. 207
Barthelme, Donald 195, 220–1
Bateson, G. 28, 42
Baudrillard, J. 172, 179

Beauchamp, Guy de 22
Berlin, J. 157–8
Bernstein, B. 20, 90, 100, 115, 143, 203–4, 219–20
Best, S. 207, 219
Bigum, C. 197, 210
Blair, Hugh 79, 82, 83, 89
Bloom, Allan 4, 22, 123
Bourdieu, P. 146, 147
Bowers, C.A. 4, 207
Brice Heath, Shirley 86, 115–16, 138, 139, 140, 146, 213
Britton, James 97, 98, 99, 109–10, 114
Burgess, Tony 107–18, 198, 205

Campbell, George 79, 82, 83, 89
Carlson, Dennis 159–60
Carnegie Foundation for the Advancement of Teaching 159–60
Chartism 61–2, 66–8
child-centred education 99, 112, 114, 140, 147, 150, 196
Christie, Frances 7, 9, 75–102, 197, 213
church and education 51, 68, 71, 73, 87, 115
Clanchy, Michael T. 17–18, 22, 42
class, socio-economic 15, 20, 118, 125, 139, 159–61, 175–6, 180, 186, 193
  middle 81, 84, 87, 101, 113, 189
  working 58–9, 61–5, 68–73, 114, 126, 131, 137, 140, 146, 150, 214
Cole, Michael 41, 112, 138, 139
Collins, J. 138, 140
Comenius, Jan Amos 50, 55
commentaries 51–2
communication, literacy and 27, 34, 76, 80, 90, 100, 154, 164, 199, 203, 212, 214
competence 16, 110, 128, 133, 137, 139, 146–7, 149, 158–60, 197

composition (meaning of text) 76–7, 82, 84, 88–9, 93–4, 101, 197–8
control hierarchy 176, 181–4, 186, 188, 191
Cooper, Thomas 64, 72
copying 77, 86, 88, 197–8, 203
Coulthard, R.M. 151, 205
creativity 164–5, 168, 170–1
Crowley, T. 122, 126
cultural studies 6, 176–7, 179, 192, 201
culture 1, 6, 99–100, 112, 114, 164, 168, 175, 179, 182, 188, 191–3, 199, 201, 203, 207–8, 210–12, 214, 217, 219–20
  alphabetic 27–42
  heritage model of English teaching 94–6, 98, 102, 116–17
  and meaning 89–90
  oral 15–16, 18–25, 33, 36, 38, 80, 82
  proto-literate 19–20
  social 121–32, 139, 147, 150
curriculum 47, 52, 124
  completion of 16, 18
  elementary school 87–90
  literacy and new technology 23–5
  as literate concept 15–19
  modernization of 15, 20–1, 23–5
    impact of 22–3
  modular 21
  theorizing and literacy studies 195–219
Currie, J. 87–8

Dartmouth Seminor (1966) 76, 78, 94–100, 102, 110
Davidson, Cathy 72, 73
de Kerckhove, D. 33, 38, 43
democracy 9, 59, 60–1, 163, 214
  literacy and limits 120–34
Derrida, Jacques 3, 6, 7, 30–2, 35, 39, 40, 198–201, 207, 209, 212, 214–15, 217–20
Dewey, John 120, 124, 134, 197
discipline 86, 93, 125, 128, 196–7, 203–4, 213–14
discussion 16, 21, 128, 131, 213
Dixon, John 76, 94, 96, 99, 110, 127
Dobbs, A.E. 58, 60, 63, 68, 69, 70
Donald, James 2, 8, 9, 120–34, 201–2, 216

early learning 20, 111, 148, 175, 182, 189–91, 193, 203
economy, national 156–9, 161–3, 166

editing 50–1, 53
education
  literacy before (1800–1850) 58–72
  popular, and politics 63–6
  practices 4, 28–9, 35, 37–9, 42, 47, 78, 100–1, 111, 116, 138, 155, 168, 197, 213–14, 217
  without schooling 190–1
elementary education 20–1, 77, 84, 86–7, 90–3, 101, 115, 126, 140–1, 193, 195, 198, 200–1, 211
  curriculum 87–90
enfranchisement 58–9, 61–2, 65, 68, 71, 72, 87, 92
entrepreneurial literacy 167–71
entrepreneurship 162–7
equality 8, 65–6, 71, 90–1, 100–2, 118, 121–2, 126, 131, 157–62, 172
Erasmus, Desiderius 49–50
experience and learning 15, 17, 78, 94–5, 97, 100, 109, 115–17, 121, 124, 126–7, 129, 175, 178–9, 190–1, 193, 196–7

facilitator, teacher as 78, 97, 98–9
failure 4, 16, 18, 20, 25, 90, 140, 163
family 10, 175–6, 178, 180, 182–4, 188–9, 191–2
fiction 59, 60, 71, 73, 148, 180, 187
film 99, 148, 210, 219
Fiske, J. 177, 181–2, 189, 191
Foucault, Michel 3, 6, 28, 42, 123, 143, 177, 203, 204, 213, 219–20
Franklin, U. 197
Freebody, Peter 138, 139, 140, 142, 151
freedom, literacy and 46, 60, 120–2, 129–30, 132, 167
Freire, P. 6, 115
function of curriculum 13–26

Garland, S. 159, 161, 172
gender 5, 62, 65, 113–15, 131, 139, 145–6, 149, 176, 217–18
Gibb, Alan 162–7, 169
Gilbert, P. 138, 139, 143, 147
Giroux, Henry A. 1, 123, 192, 202, 206, 207–8, 209, 219, 220
Goodson, I.F. 198, 204, 213, 214
Goody, Jack 25, 30, 33–4
government and education of working class 60–1, 63–6, 68–9, 80
Graff, Harvey J. 58, 115–16, 154
Grafton, Anthony 48, 52–5
Graham, R.J. 72

grammar 126, 206, 210
  corruption of 75–102
grammatocentrism 29, 38, 43
grammatology 39–41, 209, 220
Gramsci, Antonio 6, 117, 129
Griffin, D.R. 8, 10, 207
growth model of English teaching 77–8,
  94–6, 98–9, 102, 108–11, 114,
  116–17, 137
Gutmann, Amy 122, 132

Habermas, J. 149, 172
Halliday, Michael A.K. 6–7, 78, 80–1,
  83, 89, 96, 98–100, 102, 205, 207,
  210, 218, 221
Hamilton, David 7, 9, 15, 18–19, 26,
  46–55, 205, 213, 220
Hammonds, K. 159, 161, 172
Hampton, C. 62, 70, 72
Hardcastle, J. 117, 198
Harding, S. 137, 148–9
Harvey, David 156–7, 162, 177
Hasan, R. 83, 89, 99, 100
Havelock, E.A. 16–17, 33, 36–9
Hinkson, J. 207–8
Hirsch, Jr, E.D. 4, 8, 129, 130–1, 168
  cultural literacy and curriculum politics
  124–7
history
  literacy in 9–10, 108, 110, 112–17,
  128, 196
  of writing 27–42
Hoetker, J. 15, 19
Hoskin, Keith 9, 27–42, 198, 204–5, 214
humanism 51–3, 66, 149, 219
Hunter, Ian 123, 128–9, 134, 147, 200

identity 8, 176–9, 181, 189, 191–2, 207,
  209, 213
  feminine, in family discourse 183–4
illiteracy 13, 15, 17, 73, 122, 124–5, 130,
  159, 168
impersonality 14–15, 23
individualism 14, 77, 95, 97, 99–100,
  112–13, 140, 149, 166–7
individuation 120–1, 127–8, 130
indoctrination 16, 66
industrialization 60, 63, 69, 91–2, 115
information technology 5, 157–8, 172,
  210
Inglis, F. 96, 137
Initiation-Response-Evaluation sequence
  (IRE) 142–3, 146, 205
initiative 163–4, 168–71

innovativeness 161–5, 169–71, 203
interaction 110, 112, 113–14, 205, 214
invention of writing 27, 29, 33, 35–6

James, Louis 58, 67, 69, 72–3
Jardine, Lisa 48, 52–5
Johnson, Richard 59, 61, 64
Johnson, Samuel 75–6, 77, 79, 85, 89,
  101
justice 60, 65, 102, 121–2, 124, 127, 133,
  158, 161–3, 167

knowledge 6, 16, 22–3, 52, 124, 147,
  149, 155, 157, 168, 175–6, 203–4,
  206–7, 212, 216
  access 168, 193
  power 200
Kozol, J. 158–9
Kristeva, Julia 3, 216, 221

labour division and leisure 188–90
Lacan, Jacques 1, 3, 202, 207, 216–17
language 1, 6, 32–3, 97–8, 100, 167, 181,
  198, 204, 206–7, 215–18
language games 140–5
Lankshear, Colin 4, 5, 9, 10, 58, 60,
  154–71, 198, 202, 216
Laqueuer, Thomas W. 64–5
Lash, S. 149, 207
Lather, P. 203, 206, 207, 218
Lawler, M. 154, 165, 168, 171
Leavis, F.R. 91, 92, 94, 95–6, 97, 98,
  108, 110
Lee, A. 218, 221
Leitch, V. 209, 212
Levin, D.M. 9, 10
literacy
  before education 1800–1850 58–72
  curriculum as 154–71
  and curriculum theory 1–13
  English teaching in post-war period
  107–18
  limits of democracy 120–34
  orality and the function of the
  curriculum 13–26
  outside schooling 155–17
  popular, television curriculum and
  175–93
  power 138
  studies and curriculum theorizing
  195–219
  texts and education 46–55
  theory 138–40

literature 76–9, 90–4, 96–9, 101–2, 107, 109–10, 131
  power 137, 149
location and television viewing 175–8, 180, 185–6, 192
logic, literate 140–7, 149–50, 206
logocentrism 3, 6, 29–30, 34, 36, 38–41, 201, 209, 217
Luke, Allan 10, 137–50, 176, 196, 202, 213, 219, 221
Luke, Carmen 10, 147, 149, 150, 175–93, 220
Lyotard, J.-F. 133, 139, 147–9, 151, 172, 207

MacIntyre, Alisdair 9, 120–1, 125, 130–1, 132–3
McKnight, G.H. 80, 84
McLintock, Robert 48–50, 53, 55
McLuhan, Marshall 28, 32, 176
Martin, J.R. 90, 137
mass education 2, 8, 20–1, 29, 48, 121–2, 163, 204, 213
Mathieson, M. 91, 92, 95
meaning 6, 76–8, 84, 87–90, 93–4, 98–100, 124, 132, 179–80, 197, 199, 207, 209–10
Meyer, J.W. 14, 22, 23, 24
Michaels, S. 138, 140
Mills, C. Wright 9, 172
mimesis 19, 148–9
mobility, social 124–6, 129, 157, 180
modernism 3, 5, 8–9, 138, 147–9, 177, 197–8, 202, 205, 208, 212, 214, 217–19
modernity 7–10, 14–15, 17, 19, 21, 24, 29, 120, 207, 209, 211, 215
modernization of curriculum 8, 15, 20–1, 23–5
  impact of 22–3
Monaghan, J.E. 197, 202
monitorial system of education 21, 70, 86
Moon, Cliff 110–11
morality 96, 98–9, 109, 126, 128, 214
Morell, J.D. 84, 86, 88–9, 90, 91
Morley, David 178–81, 187, 189
Murray, Lindley 85–6, 93

narrative 16, 20, 128, 175, 181, 207, 221
  social regulation
    micropolitics of classroom 137–50
National Curriculum 20, 25, 118, 122–3, 127–30, 131, 133, 163
news and weather reports 180, 183–7

newspaper 60–1, 63, 67, 69–70, 80
Nicholson, L. 148, 192

objectivity 14–15, 17–18, 20–3, 148
Olson, David R. 207, 211–12, 215, 220
Ong, Walter J. 7, 14–15, 21, 23–7, 30–3, 39, 43, 52–4, 80, 102, 214–15
opportunity, educational 59, 84, 90, 101, 158, 160–2, 164–6
oral culture 15–16, 18–25, 33, 36, 38, 80, 82
orality 7, 154, 214, 220
  literacy and the function of the curriculum 13–26
oratory 51, 79, 80, 82–4
ownership of meaning 77, 94–100, 142, 146, 169

paraphrasing 77, 91, 101
parsing sentences 76–7, 86–7, 97, 101–2, 138, 197
participation 122, 124, 129–30, 134
patriarchy 146, 148–50, 181–2, 190–1
performativity 147–8
phallagocentrism 217–18
Plato 16, 17, 30, 31, 36–40, 49
poetry 66–7, 77, 90–1, 131
post-secondary education 62, 77, 91–2, 102, 107, 164, 169
postfeminism 178–9, 189
postindustrialism 10, 156–9, 165–6, 172, 177, 207
postmodernism 3, 5, 8–10, 137–8, 148–50, 176–7, 181–2, 189, 192, 201–2, 206–13, 216, 218–21
  reappraisals of narrative 147–9
  spaces and subjects 177–9
poststructuralism 3, 137, 177, 203, 215–18, 221
power 150, 164, 183, 192, 203–4, 206, 213
  curriculum 198
  education 35, 46
  knowledge relationship 28–9, 38, 40, 66–7, 127, 130, 200
  literacy 117, 126, 132, 138
  literature 137, 149
  reading 72
  relations 146–7
  speech 82, 83
  writing 23, 27–31, 33, 36, 40–1, 59–60, 72, 82, 87, 90, 93, 101, 108, 199–200

printing 17–18, 22, 25, 47, 53, 58–61, 80, 82, 149
private education 20, 25, 113, 160
problem solving 163–4, 169
process, learning 99, 109, 111–13, 115, 117, 124, 133, 155, 219
progressivism 8, 10, 99, 112, 114, 123, 134, 140, 149, 171, 175, 197–8, 219
  literacy teaching and National Curriculum 127–30
proto-literate culture 19–20
psychoanalysis 9, 216, 218, 221
psychology, educational 107, 108–12, 113, 128

race 125, 131, 139, 150, 159–60, 176, 186, 193
radicalism 59, 60–3, 65, 67–9, 87, 130, 132
Ramus, Peter 19, 20–1, 22, 53, 54–5
rationality 2, 5–8, 14–15, 17, 21–2, 138, 140, 149, 201, 206, 209, 211–12, 214–18
reading 17–18, 20, 28–9, 35–6, 38, 40, 58–60, 63, 68, 88, 91, 124, 127, 131, 137, 139–40, 184, 191, 198, 202, 209, 214
  English teaching in post-war period 107–18
  in 'New Times' 154–71
  power 72
  teaching 30, 38, 41, 43
reality 22, 100, 115, 155, 212, 218
recitation 15–17, 19, 91, 101, 205
reconception 1, 10, 207–8, 213, 216, 220
regularization
  alphabet 38
  English lauguage 79, 81, 85, 93, 101
regulation, social, and classroom narrative 137–50
Reid, William A. 2, 4, 7, 13–26, 220
repetition 16–17, 80, 166, 181–2, 197, 203
representation 6, 207, 209–10, 216
representation of sound, writing as 32–3, 43
reproduction 201–3, 218
Resnick, D.P. and Resnick, L.B. 202
resource
  language as 100
  writing as 80
responsibility 102, 122, 128, 163, 169–71
rhetoric, decline of 75–102
rights 62–3, 68, 71, 73, 121

role
  language 78, 87, 108–9, 201
  literacy 123, 127, 202
  literature 109, 111–12
  speech 82, 98
  state 158
  women 177, 188, 190–1, 193
romanticism 9, 77–8, 90–1, 93–4, 97, 99–100, 137–8, 143, 149
Rothery, J. 90, 95, 102
Rousseau, Jean-Jacques 124, 199
rural women and television 177–9, 184–5

Schwab, J.J. 23, 24
Scribner, S. 41, 138, 139
secondary education 21, 77, 91–2, 101–2, 126, 131, 166
sequential learning 16, 18, 20, 22, 55, 140–5
Shayer, D. 92, 98
Sheridan, Thomas 79, 80
Simon, B. 4, 46, 48, 61, 65–8, 71, 73
skills, acquisition of 13, 15, 17–18, 20, 94, 111, 113, 121, 127, 130, 132, 138, 154–7, 159–60, 163, 165–6, 168, 197–8
Smith, D. 25, 192
socialization 7, 120–2, 128–30, 166, 188, 192, 202, 206, 211
society, literacy and 4–5, 16, 23, 46, 76–7, 79, 82, 92, 98–100, 108–10, 113–17, 121–2, 124, 127, 129–30, 132–3, 147, 154–5, 202, 207–8
speech 2, 13, 18, 20, 23–4, 31–4, 40, 60, 76, 86, 93, 97, 102, 108, 110–11, 113, 121, 126–7, 137–8, 140–1, 143, 146–50
  power 82, 83
  television 176, 179, 181, 186–8
  vs writing 6–8, 80–2, 89, 116
  writing as supplement to 30–3, 36, 41
state education 2, 8, 19, 25, 59, 71, 87, 204, 214
status
  alphabet 30–3
  English 91
  language 216
  narrative 147
  writing and artisan 33, 37
Steedman, Carolyn 112–17
storage of information, writing as 27, 33–4, 80, 90
Strauss, G. 52–3

Street, Brian V. 115, 154–5, 215–16
study 15, 18–19, 48–51, 67, 79, 81, 99,
    108–9, 154
Sturm, John 53–4
subjectivity 5, 177–83, 196, 203, 206–9,
    211–12, 216, 218, 221
Sunday Schools 60, 64–5
supplement to speech, writing as 30–3,
    36, 41
syllabaries 32, 34, 38
syntax 75, 80–2, 85–9, 93, 98, 101, 146

taxes on knowledge 69–70
technology 5, 197, 209, 214, 218, 220
    and alphabetic culture,
        learning 27–42
    learning 27–42
    literacy 23–5
    socio- 17, 19, 138, 154–6, 168
television 5, 10, 99, 131, 208, 211–12,
    214, 220
    curriculum and popular literacy
        175–93
text, literacy and education 46–55
textbook 2, 7, 18–19, 23, 47, 86
theory
    curriculum and literacy 1–13, 22
    curriculum and literacy studies
        195–219
    education 177, 192
    language development 78, 110
    literacy 107–9, 138–40
Therrien, L. 159, 161, 172
thinking 27, 31, 47, 108–9, 120–1, 130,
    132, 138, 141, 159–60, 169, 196,
    214, 217, 219
    electronic 210–11
    writing 27, 34, 38, 42
Thompson, E.P. 59, 60, 65
Thornton, Geoffrey 98
Threadgold, T. 146, 150
tradition
    cultural 123, 131–2, 137
    received English teaching 75–102
traditional education 15, 17, 21, 71, 107,
    114, 128, 130, 192, 213
transmission, education by 16, 23, 50

Ulmer, G.L. 8, 208, 210–12, 214,
    216–20
universalism 23, 25, 127, 129–30, 139,
    178
urban education 159–61
Urry, J. 207

values 122, 155, 163, 166–8, 187, 199
vocalic alphabet 32, 38, 43
vocationalism 125, 130–1, 154
Vygotsky 109, 112, 117, 139, 149, 151

Walkerdine, Valerie 112, 123, 134, 138,
    139, 149, 190, 193, 212, 216, 221
Walton, C. 90, 140
Walzer, Michael 121–2
Watt, Ian 25, 33
Wexler, P. 192, 207, 212
Whately 79, 82, 83, 89
Whitehead, F. 95, 109
Williams, Rayman 91, 122, 172
Willinsky, John 7, 9, 58–72, 199, 214
women
    feminine identity politics and family
        discourse 175–93
    feminine interpretive communities
        186–8
    television viewing and lives 180–3
writing 1, 5, 15, 17, 58–9, 63, 68, 79, 88,
    91, 97, 108, 110–11, 117, 127,
    137–40, 147, 149, 198–200, 202–6,
    209–10, 212–14, 217, 219–20
    communication 27, 34
    grammar 86
    history of 27–42
    in 'New Times' 154–71
    ordering 27, 34
    power 23, 27–31, 33, 36, 40–1,
        59–60, 72, 82, 87, 90, 93, 101, 108,
        199–200
    as representation of sound 32–3, 43
    signature 60–2, 71
    storage of information 27, 33–4, 80,
        90
    as supplement to speech 30–3, 36, 41
    vs speech 6–8, 80–2, 89, 116